WHITE LIES

White Lies considers African American bodies as the site of cultural debates over a contested "white religion" in the United States. Rooting his analysis in the work of W.E.B. DuBois and James Baldwin, Christopher Driscoll traces the shifting definitions of "white religion" from the nineteenth century up to the death of Michael Brown and other racial controversies of the present day. He engages both modern philosophers and popular imagery to isolate the instabilities central to a "white religion," including the inadequacy of this framing concept as a way of describing and processing death. The book will be of interest to students and scholars interested in African American Religion, philosophy and race, and Whiteness Studies.

Christopher M. Driscoll is a Visiting Assistant Professor at Lehigh University, where his teaching and research explore race, religion, philosophy and culture – with attention to whiteness, hip hop, and existentialism/humanism. He is Co-Founder/Co-Chair of an American Academy of Religion Group on Hip Hop and Religion and a contributing editor to *Marginalia (LA Review of Books).*

WHITE LIES

Race and Uncertainty in the Twilight of American Religion

Christopher M. Driscoll

NEW YORK AND LONDON

First published 2016
by Routledge
711 Third Avenue, New York, NY 10017

and by Routledge
2 Park Square, Milton Park, Abingdon, Oxon OX14 4RN

Routledge is an imprint of the Taylor & Francis Group, an informa business

Library of Congress Cataloging in Publication Data
Driscoll, Christopher M.
White lies : race and uncertainty in the twilight of American religion / Christopher M. Driscoll. -- 1st ed.
pages cm
Includes index.
1. African Americans--Religion. 2. United States--Church history.
3. Race relations--Religious aspects--Christianity. I. Title.
BR563.N4D75 2015
277.3'082089--dc23
2015018389

ISBN: 978-1-138-90903-8 (hbk)
ISBN: 978-1-138-91099-7 (pbk)
ISBN: 978-1-315-69308-8 (ebk)

Typeset in Bembo
by Taylor & Francis Books

Printed and bound in the United States of America by
Edwards Brothers Malloy on sustainably sourced paper

Dedicated to
Rev. Barbara H. Driscoll
whose love and support
made this book possible

CONTENTS

List of figures ix
Acknowledgement x

Introduction: Sighting *white* American religion in twilight times 1

PART I
Learning to die **23**

1 In the shadows of whiteness: Giving life (through death) to a *White Lie* 25

2 The white man's god complex: Most Americans, the (white) power of theism, and beginning to *believe* in twilight 65

3 Battling white lies: Exaggerated identity and the twilight of American religion 117

PART II
Learning to die *with others* **167**

4 Accepting the hell of death: Narrating sources, methods, and norms of a *limited religious outlook* 169

5 Rejecting the "gift of death": White social responsibility in twilight times 217

6 Requiem for whiteness: Mourning, freedom in uncertainty, and the final embrace of twilight 257

Postmortem: A warning 307

Index 309

FIGURES

3.1 Photo of the Gawker Privilege Tournament Bracket. Image by Jim Cooke. Available at: http://gawker.com/the-privilege-tournament-1377171054. (Reprinted here with permission from Gawker Media Group.) 158
4.1 Personal photo representing radical contingency. 195
4.2 Personal photo representing an Imago Superlata outlook on radical contingency, an exaggeration of radical contingency. 196
4.3 Personal photo representing a Limited Religious Outlook on radical contingency. 198

ACKNOWLEDGEMENT

White Lies is an effort to look squarely into the mirror of past and contemporary white American social life and recognize that the ones who teach us to love are the same ones who teach us how to hate and fear difference. Wrestling with such tragic complexities has been difficult, but enriching, and I hope my efforts will contribute to growing conversations, long overdue, that take seriously the legacy inherited by white Americans so that we aren't all suffocated by silence, indifference, or outright hostility.

My voice in these conversations has been made possible by other voices, other thinkers, whose critical insights and intellectual imaginations far outweigh my own, and who have taught me much more about love than hate. *White Lies* is a product of their efforts. Space prevents specific mention of everyone who has helped shape the ideas presented here, but the book would literally not have been possible without the support of: Past colleagues at Brite Divinity School, Vanderbilt Divinity School, and Rice University. In particular, the current students and graduates of Rice's African American Religious Studies concentration and those at the Center for Engaged Research and Collaborative Learning, specifically Mrs. Maya Reine. Thanks are also owed to Caroline Levander, Vice Provost for Interdisciplinary Initiatives, and those at Rice's Humanities Research Center. And a huge thanks to James Faubion, Elias Bongmba, and Anthony B. Pinn, whose mentoring and guidance have shaped this book and my intellectual development as a whole.

Outside of Rice, special thanks are owed to Jürgen Manemann, Eike Brock, and Dominik Hammer of the Institute for Philosophical Research, Hannover, Germany, for space and conversation to work out final aspects of the manuscript and for ongoing support. And thanks to Carol Ross for her vital feedback. I am also indebted to certain towering figures in the field of religion, whose inspiration and insights substantially shape the ideas presented here. They include Katie Geneva Cannon, James Cone, Cornel West, James Perkinson, Michael Eric Dyson, John Jackson, Jr., and Stacey Floyd-Thomas. I would also like to thank all of my colleagues at Lehigh University, specifically Michael Raposa, Chava E. Weissler, James Peterson, Kwame Essien, and Marian Gaumer. And three of my students, Eric Waxler and Jake Ingrassia, for thoughtful feedback on early drafts, and De'Anna Daniels. Lastly, I would like to thank the team at Routledge, including Eve Mayer, Margo Irvin, and Laura Briskman. Your professionalism and intellectual insights have made this volume far stronger than it would have been without you.

There are also those whose contributions to *White Lies*, or to my sanity as I wrote it, make them more co-authors than bystanders. They include David Kline, Benji Rolsky, David Atwood, Elonda Clay, Daniel White Hodge, Juan Floyd-Thomas, Stacey M. Floyd-Thomas, Biko Mandela Gray, Jason Jeffries; Frances L. Davis, Alvin and Addie Pace, Charlotte Miller, Nick Crews, Adam and Jackie Hubbard, and Isaac and Nicole Tricoche; Kelli A. Driscoll, the most brilliant theologian I have ever known; my mother, Barbara H. Driscoll, to whom this book is dedicated; and my advisor, Anthony B. Pinn. To quote Webbie, you're "my people," and I'm beyond grateful to have you.

I attended my first American Academy of Religion Annual Meeting in 2007 as a master's student. I met someone there who inspired and supported my decision to embark on a Ph.D. She was the most inspirational, energetic, brilliant and beautiful person I have ever met. I could not have imagined that she would see something similar in me. The significance of that first meeting, and all that has transpired between then and now, is such that to think too much on its various implications would risk deconstructing many of the propositions offered in *White Lies*. The greatest uncertainty of all, perhaps, is reckoning with the possibility of learning how to live life with the certainty felt when looking in the mirror and seeing your soul mate next to you. Her inspiration I now experience daily, her brilliance constantly keeping me in check and uncertain of my ideas. *White Lies* was, is, and remains a project, thanks to H.E.R. I love you. I thank you. Ours feels like a story that really has no end, no death. So is twilight even twilight if experienced with another? I'll leave that question for later. Seven.

Life is tragic simply because the earth turns and the sun inexorably rises and sets, and one day, for each of us, the sun will go down for the last, last time. Perhaps the whole root of our trouble, the human trouble, is that we will sacrifice all the beauty of our lives, will imprison ourselves in totems, taboos, crosses, blood sacrifices, steeples, mosques, races, armies, flags, nations, in order to deny the fact of death, which is the only fact we have. It seems to me that one ought to rejoice in the fact of death – ought to decide, indeed, to earn one's death by confronting with passion the conundrum of life. One is responsible to life: It is the small beacon in that terrifying darkness from which we come and to which we shall return. One must negotiate this passage as nobly as possible, for the sake of those who are coming after us. But white Americans do not believe in death, and this is why the darkness of my skin so intimidates them.

James Baldwin, The Fire Next Time *(1963)*

INTRODUCTION

Sighting *white* American religion in twilight times

> A nation's religion is its life, and as such white Christianity is a miserable failure.
>
> *W.E.B. DuBois*[1]

> So to answer your question, without further delay: no, I never learned-to-live. Absolutely not! Learning to live ought to mean learning to die – to acknowledge, to accept, an absolute mortality – without positive outcome, or resurrection, or redemption, for oneself or for anyone else. That has been the old philosophical injunction since Plato: to be a philosopher is to learn how to die. I believe in this truth without giving myself over to it. Less and less in fact. I have not learned to accept death …I remain impervious to learning when it comes to knowing-how-to-die, I have yet to learn anything about this particular subject.
>
> *Jacques Derrida*[2]

DEATH, UNCERTAINTY, AND A TWILIGHT SO LONG ENDURED

In his first television interview, George Zimmerman defended his killing of 17-year-old African American Trayvon Martin on the grounds that it was "all part of God's plan."[3] His only regret, that his "divine" actions polarized the nation. That polarization intensified in July of 2013 when Zimmerman was acquitted of killing Martin. Later that month, historian of religion Anthea Butler responded to the verdict by referring to the American god as "a white racist god with a problem, carrying a gun and stalking young black men."[4] In response to her accusation, Butler was called a "nigger," "cunt," "fat cow," and "special kind of fucking idiot"[5] in a barrage of online attacks. Many others assailed Butler for denigrating "god," being a race-baiter, and otherwise conflating what many regard as qualitatively distinct, the categories of "god" and "race." The commenters made little to no mention of Zimmerman's rhetorical use of god, as if his divine appeal was not even more denigrating to the idea and to those who believe in such an idea. The response to Butler proved both illogical and uneven, but helps to demonstrate a long standing feature of the American way of life: We are willing to kill but not willing to die.

Both past and present, dead black bodies still hang from Americans' lips in the tragic deaths of Emmett Till, Trayvon Martin, Michael Brown, Eric Garner, Ezell Ford, and too many others to list. Whether killed by extralegal vigilante or law enforcement officials, the real killer of these African Americans is a sort of vigilantism seemingly justified (on the front end) by a demand for safety and certainty, and vindicated (on the back end) by constant appeals to "god's plan" and "prayer." From a critical perspective, historically as much as today, on the American frontier dead black bodies (sadly) provide a canvas where race and religion collide, where any presumption that race and religion do distinct social work is called into question, exposed as a kind of *white lie*. But for many white Americans, black bodies – especially dead ones – do a different sort of work. Rather than expose white lies, these "sacrifices" allow lies to remain concealed, protected, and validated – evidenced in the backlash against Butler. Indeed, these white lies, as they are named here, provide the means for misrecognizing oneself as outside of twilight, outside of but tellingly deeply indebted to the "system," outside of a kind of existential and epistemological opacity endemic to human social life and interaction.

White Lies seeks to answer a series of three constellations of questions yet to be fully explored in a single text, or from the intellectual premise that theological correctives may do more to reinforce the "miserable failure" noted in the above epigraph by W.E.B. DuBois than to resolve it: (1) What are the functional effects, the "strategic acts of identification"[6] of race, racism, religion, and religiosity among, beneath, and within the American landscape? What might be the intellectual take-away from regarding these categories as more similar than different? African American religion (as field or data set) has never separated these terms, making possible a critical posture towards normative American religious studies and institutions. Here, I follow the lead of African American religious studies and take seriously the shared sensibilities of American whiteness and religiosity so as to expose the traditionally maintained categorical distinction between them as a white lie. (2) In what ways do the academic fields of theology and religious studies undergirded by anthropology and human interests, respectively, reinforce such a "miserable failure"? That is, how do the very ways we (as scholars of religion) seek to study such acts and functions unduly reinforce those functions? What categorical and analytical norms do these fields offer for charting or measuring such a "failure," and how might the fields – as much as their functions – be limited in their ability to fully understand and correct for the simultaneous need for such measurements, understanding these analyses as always shaky, fluid, and frustratingly uncertain? (3) What would admitting to and naming the categories of both "white Christian" and "white religion" expose about the strategic and tacit identity-formation processes at work in scholarship and social life alike? Adding to a growing body of scholarship that is beginning to suggest or treat the category of religion as a kind of identity formation[7] through processes of distinction-making and power legitimation,[8] what will the postulation of a white religious identity amongst the American religious landscape suggest to scholars and others about the limits of identity construction and the social consequences imposed on many from a *failure* to recognize those limits and consequences?

In *White Lies*, answers to these questions begin with an embrace of twilight. Twilight refers to an interpretive and thematic conceptual rubric indicative of life found in death, death in life, and the uncertainties and limitations incumbent upon sociality, identity construction, and what we can know as scholars of religion about these things. A fuller portrait of this twilight is developed over the course of the chapters, but in all of its expressions, twilight is meant to unsettle epistemological, ethical, and aesthetic foundations while also forcing recognition that the moments when such things as identity, group affiliation, safety, etc., appear to us as settled, as certain, as secure – they are not: our security, with those things, with all things, is predicated on the maintenance of white lies that insulate our senses from awareness that the world and our places in it are shaky at best. Jacques Derrida's inability to "learn-to-die," expressed in the epigraph above, is emblematic of this twilight in one of its most fundamental, embodied expressions, that which teeters between physical life and death. There is, as a twilight perspective would have it, something peculiar about the distinction posed between life and death. In the back-and-forth, a relationship is foregrounded, one that Derrida does well to play with and manipulate for pedagogical and existentially constructive reflexive censure. Indeed, Derrida tells us here that he is lying – to us, to himself, to the universe. And he doesn't know how to stop telling these *white lies*.

Stepping beyond physical life and death, another of the first, and one of the most severe, of these white lies is the suggestion seen in the verbal assault on Butler, that race and religion are somehow of different sorts, *sui generis* in their own right, distinct in themselves and thereby available for distinguishing one person or group from another. Of course, Butler, whose professional work extends far beyond one single blog posting, is censured socially – an attempted shaming and disgracing takes place with the not-so-tacit effect of reinforcing and assuming that race and religion are somehow distinct. The distinction is projected onto a black body, concealing white lies that are anything but "little" as their namesake implies.

What if a *distinction* could be posed where these categories of race and religion collided, instead, in a decidedly white religious practice or identity, focused on white bodies, made visible by Butler's reference to a white, racist, American god and inversely embodied (in part) through the murders of young black men? In light of the ongoing assault on black bodies in the U.S., these "sacrifices" necessitate a shift in focus towards (something which is rarely identified as) "white religion." This naming of white religion is the principal rationale of this book, and a hermeneutical shift towards twilight allows for the sighting, citing, and siting of white religion in some of its varied dimensions. Such a shift in explicit naming exposes a number of understudied and often denied shared sensibilities of race and religion in the American landscape explored throughout the pages of *White Lies*. Most significant here, embracing twilight (as a hermeneutical posture) illustrates "white religion" as various kinds of denial – white lies – involving social, individual, ideological, and material attempts at identity formation and supported through the threat or use of violence at the expense of brown and black others.

Both historically and today, religion shapes the economic, civic, political, social, and cultural options and avenues with which American identities and lifestyles carve out spaces of interaction and competition. Indeed, for many Americans, religion serves in an ordering, distinction-making capacity, where the uncertainties of life lived with others are mitigated through specific beliefs and practices, and through various social sanctions arising from such religious activity. Exemplified as much by historic precedents such as Jim Crow laws as by contemporary events and discourses surrounding the murders of young black men (and women), the concept of race (compounded by other forms of difference) similarly orders, sanctions, and orients social possibilities and human value in/for American society and identities. In America, race and religion appear to be up to similar identity-making functions but rarely is whiteness sited in such processes. Given this long-denied but longer still relied upon synergy, such a categorical shift towards naming "white religion" as a product of and reliant on race and religion might be in order. But what would "white religion" look like? What might it seek to accomplish? And where would analytic attention to it begin?

TWILIGHT TAKING FOCUS

My first glimpse through twilight came from a conversation once overheard between a number of individuals at one of my former institutions. One in particular, a white male scholar of Modern European History, inadvertently brought into blurry relief the ominous weight of twilight, my recognition of it, and my perception of what import such recognition of it might hold for others if only they might learn to see from within its dimly lit horizon.

The conversation involved two groups of folk with starkly antagonistic thinking: those who had seemingly internalized the importance of contextual studies (e.g., African American, African, Feminist, Queer discourses) to such an extent that there was no question that context shapes discourse, ideation, and action. And another group lamenting that context – personal stories, postmodernism, and narratives – was now, as one of them put it, "more important than fact." As one after another entered into the debate, their energy was a vivid contrast to the dismal emotional response from the professor of Modern European History who grimaced with discomfort as the conversation unfolded (or unraveled depending on one's perspective). As one person would argue for the virtues of Afrocentrism, or the brilliance of Judith Butler, another would quickly retort that much Afrocentric thought has been discounted as fallacious myth-making, and that Butler may be smart, but she's too far "out there" and her erudite writing style and tone deconstruct her concern for those in precarious situations. As yet another scholar would speak on the need for feminist correctives to racist-sexist scholarship, the next would point out the supposed biological differences between men and women.

While the debate raged on, I couldn't help but notice the one professor's pale white face, looking more like my own than those who had my head nodding in agreement. He was sad and a look of weary consternation focused attention to eyes that were fighting back tears. As the discussion subsided, Modern European History finally spoke: "I'm sad. I'm heartbroken. Because the culture I've worked my whole life to learn and understand is dying. It may already be dead. I feel like a caretaker, a mortician for something that has died."

In face of his sadness, I realized that if something about the West, or about the certainty of reason, ethics, and aesthetics sought in Modernity, had unraveled, had "died" – even if only in the minds of those who cherish such things most – then my task as a (white) scholar of the humanities and developing thinker within the academic study of religion was to learn about this death; ultimately, learning how to accept the limits and uncertainty that such a fate, perforce, requires from all its victims. At that moment I found myself caught up in what I would come to call twilight, the sense of an encroaching darkness all around me. Darkness here signifies multiple things.[9] Twilight is made of the existential angst and sullen dispositions of an affective darkness. It is an expression of uncertainty and the darkness of death that none of us escape. It marks loss, uncertain resolve, awareness of an impending end – of what sort is only decided in this twilight. The darkness of twilight is the encroaching clarity of a certain physical death marching towards us, and the uncertainties evoked from such recognition.

But where learned philosophy, the space where Modern European thought and history meet the social world – in America, at least – twilight is also colored by black bodies, black culture, black ways of knowing, being, thinking, black people enveloping – whether alive or dead – white bodies, white culture, white reason, all of these "white" things just now being made aware of their own whiteness as it is increasingly confronted, questioned, disrupted by others. These marching bodies that are encircling white bodies, encircling whiteness, are not the color of white and are increasingly confrontational – or so it is suggested by many like Modern European History who are just now being exposed to twilight but have not the eyes to see its significance, the hermeneutic it offers, focusing instead only on the fear evoked by these ever-marching black bodies. The twilight these black bodies evoke for white bodies is the result of increasing encounters not simply with black bodies, but black bodies that tell white bodies, "NO!" Whether framed in terms of the death of Modernity debated by scholars in ivory towers, or more viscerally, corporally, and violently in the "no" that one can imagine Trayvon Martin must have extolled when he refused to be surveilled (without consequence) by Zimmerman. This twilight is emblematic of black subjectivity measured not simply by "yes!" to life but "no!" to the very parameters imposed onto and truncating black life, historically. In twilight, darkness, perhaps in all of its agency, is encroaching on whiteness – exposing whiteness anew to itself, and to many for the first time. Whether celebrated or lamented, twilight is instructive, pedagogical, able to expose white Americans to a side of themselves often concealed, the "white" in white American, "white" identities that far too often go without naming.

What did Modern European History think had died? And how could I use this feeling of loss for instrumental scholarly ends? More to the point, *has* whiteness died? Or, more troubling for some, is something beginning to die that till now has gone unnamed – a kind of white religious expression rooted in the procuring of a certain identity now seemingly ceasing to do a particular sort of work for white people? I was unsettled. The other whites were shaken. All of us a little scared.

White Lies begins to address the fear, dread, and recognition of death seen in this professor's face and understands him as emblematic of much larger, more fundamental trends and shifts taking place where race and religion are concerned in the United States, for citizen and scholar of religion, alike. Some celebrate this death, others lament and fear it – leaving out the question of whether such a death has occurred or not, or what a death of certainty would even mean. Inspired by Modern European History's fear and loathing, and in hopes of cultivating a hermeneutic designed to appreciate and anticipate the death of certainty as a positive, *White Lies* begins in twilight, embracing it, and sets about in these pages to weaponize it for its ability to bring scholars of religion to greater awareness of some of the many religious dimensions of white life in America. Twilight offers an affirmatively shaky foundation for hosting discussions much needed today within and outside academic venues about *how* to embrace a shifting social significance, an impending "death," in a way that tries to not reinforce problematic insider/outsider social arrangements. Twilight only begins the discursive journey; other concepts emerge from this standpoint and are outlined in the sections that follow.

LITTLE WHITE LIES: IDENTITY-BASED EXAGGERATIONS

Why have so many white Christians in the United States been (and remain today) racist? Why does the academic field of American religion largely still ignore this ongoing legacy? However we choose to carefully define all of the terms of such methodologically "bad" questions, many would likely agree that the loose, untidy questions posed here are instructive of a certain sort of religious orientation or at least social disposition affecting a huge swath of American religious folk historically and today, both inside and outside the academic study of religion. The question can be posed differently: Borrowing the words of the great sociologist DuBois, why has *white* Christianity been such a "miserable failure?"[10] And, how would success or failure even be determined and measured?

One of the goals of *White Lies* is to answer these questions by demarcating and charting just *what* "white Christianity" and "white religion" are. The constitution of "white religion" as a category unto itself is made possible by a one-to-one parallel between its "miserable failure" and a failure to learn how to die. Indeed, white religion *is* the failure described by Derrida (in the very year he succumbed to his mortality) that cuts across, but also at times creates, social difference. And, as it turns out, the very ability to site white religion (as DuBois sees it) requires a kind of hermeneutical death, a death of one's discursively constructed existential and social orientations filtered through the denial of death, uncertainty, and limitation. Twilight begins an attempt to learn how to let go of certain ideas and patterns of social meaning-making that have given some of us a false sense of security and a very real political power, and the academic field of religious studies the option to ignore and misrecognize what is perhaps the central feature of American religion so categorized to this point – that it is *white* American religion. Some of the ideas and practices held most dear and sacred by the demographic of white people in the United States have come at a great cost to the humanity of self and those othered by a social arrangement grounded in denial, lies, and empty promises of security. Echoing the arguments of thinkers like philosopher, cultural critic, and public intellectual Cornel West and religionist, theologian, and social theorist James Perkinson, among others, the white religious failure to learn how to die has been death-dealing for us all (though for some much more than others).[11] In this regard, twilight conceptually aids in such reflection and recognition. It allows for recognition of things not typically seen, regarded – such as white religion.

So how, exactly, are we to see "white religion?" *White Lies* suggests that white religion involves the denial of human limitation and a subsequent demand for social and personal certainty procured through a denied identity – creating a presumed distance between groups and ideas based on denial of an uncertain human reality. This reality is a condition of *radical contingency*, here defined as a situation of forced reliance on others in the wake of physical death's demands. Perkinson rightly notes that "one of the very meanings of whiteness as supremacy has been an attempt to escape the terrors of contingency [that is, radical contingency] by, in effect, forcing other populations to know that particular experience of creatureliness intimately."[12] For instance, if we put such thinking to work around the murder of Trayvon Martin, someone like Zimmerman ended up a murderer precisely because of his unwillingness to face the *uncertain* trappings arising from fear of his own mortality and desire for protection of self (e.g., the "black" hoodie, the object that spawned such tragedy, posed/triggered this threat). What Perkinson suggests is that out of a denial or unwillingness to face squarely the uncertainties and limitations posed by human life, the idea of whiteness has functioned to localize those fears more acutely on certain populations, offering a sense of distance between those "terrors" and the community employing the idea of whiteness. While whiteness is specifically addressed in the first and last chapters of this book, Perkinson's words here help to ground a more fundamental white religious sensibility operative historically. Pushing this further, *White Lies* suggests that what is typically understood as the sacred/profane distinction lies at the heart of these social and existential distances posed between various groups. Just as "white" and "colored" drinking fountains reinforced a social binary of black and white, traditional theism offers a cosmic projection of a similar system, not necessarily based on white skin, but based on the same presumption of difference meant to secure certainty and ignore, fight, or deny human limitations such as our inability to overcome death, our lack of full social knowing, and our considerations of what we "ought" to do or appreciate. Such theistic offerings mark Zimmerman's appeal to "god's plan" not as a perverse rendering of divine support, but as an honest oblation to the god of white religion concealing the relation between and shared sensibilities of race, religion, violence, and white America.

White religion then functions to procure and perpetuate a demand for universal cohesion and stability in light of a human situation of radically contingent dependence necessitating humans interacting with other humans in response to their limits. Humans, more generally, are in a peculiar predicament in that their contingency is only realized through its negation. Philosopher Jean-Paul Sartre famously contended that existence precedes essence,[13] meaning that in any quest to endow existence with essence (or any failure to do so) personal concerns and interests are evaluated based on material experiences common to all humans, such as death, work, hunger, and the inevitability of interacting with other humans (in the same predicament).[14] Based on conditioning factors such as these, in Sartrean terms, every being necessitates non-being, meaning that what it means to be human is to simultaneously desire to not be human (to *not be* the thing wanting to *be*) precisely because to exist is to exist in the shadow of not existing. Humans attempt to be more than they are, attempting the impossible through science, war, art, and so on. Stated differently, humans ultimately deny their limitations and in that denial, arrive back at what they are – still limited and yet capable. And it is in this attempt to be that which is not, where humans achieve a sense of that which they are. Race and religion are not (and cannot be) removed from such an existential assessment.

Radical contingency, that *being in/as non-being*, is always the counterpoint to and the product of a prospect of "nothingness." Thought about in light of George Zimmerman's justification that the murder of Trayvon Martin was all part of "god's plan," where white religion is concerned, it is often in the process of death and destruction – what might be characterized as the exerting of power *over* another – that one's being is validated through distance *from* recognition of limits. Contingency, to this end, is radical, in that it is addressed and activated through necessary interactions with others whether or not those interactions are normatively regarded as morally good or bad. Though not all responses occur through murder, *White Lies* takes the position that these interactions, these responses to radical contingency, are *always* violent in that they involve physical, ideological, and/or discursive instances of (at least the attempt to) exerting power over another person, group, or idea (held by a person or group). At stake and up for change are the beneficiaries and victims of such violent, inevitable idolatrous responses to radical contingency, but, in twilight, we're never dealing with the prospect of "if" violence, but rather, "whose."[15]

This radically contingent portrait of the human condition suggests that the abstract, ideal notion of human freedom is ultimately bound by responsibility to others.[16] In order to make sense of their being, humans must necessarily act, responding to the situations emerging from radical contingency. Thus, twilight is not an ethical posture, but a statement about the necessary relation between being and ethics. To exist (as white) is to seemingly find oneself in relation to others for whom one's own existence is defined and oriented. There are simply no other means of definition or identity formation. In this light, the idea of self-definition is oxymoronic in that definition and awareness of being are only possible through interaction with other social actors engaged in similar circumstances. In the wake of the inability to find innate life meaning (i.e., human ability and value) on one's own terms and in isolation, it must be produced from the available contingent components – interaction with others. One of the major aims of this book is to ground these frustratingly paradoxical (and for some, out of date) existential ruminations as ethnographic and theoretical guideposts for charting and making sense of past and contemporary racial–religious–social interactions and encounters in the United States.[17]

Such a demand for cohesion and certainty is only ever adequately – albeit paradoxically – addressed through various denials of uncertainty and chaos. White religion offers adherents the perception that life has intrinsic meaning, that the social world is as it should be, and that the *bricolage* offered by human reality fits together in a manner that makes "logical" sense. At times acknowledged while at other times unquestioned and unstated, the white lies born from and sustaining white religion address the messiness of human reality by helping adherents pretend human life is neater and tidier than the available data suggest. Stated differently, white religion comes to be formed from the lies that many humans present (to themselves and others) as truth in response to any number of concerns evoking uncertainty emerging from social life, including but not limited to race, class, gender, sexuality and the like. They operate through and function as inevitable denials of reality where the "real" and what is possible is only adequately framed in terms of limit, uncertainty, and what is not possible. These denials of limit and impossibility, of radical contingency, are a kind of idolatrous "denial structure"[18] supported by constellations of white lies.

Due to such bleak options, this radical contingency produces the desire to ignore, deny, or fight directly against such a reality.[19] In light of this condition of human contingency, Sartre indicates that this need to deny is inevitable.[20] Navigating this radically contingent reality thus requires lying (e.g., justification for violence or social collateral damage), suggesting that the lies are "white" not only for the sake of who historically is telling the tales, but because their purported necessity supports their proliferation.

"Little" white lies involve processes which suggest that human uncertainty, limitation, and contingency can be overcome. Examples include Zimmerman's appeal to god, as well as his defenders who suggest that Butler's words are fallacious. They are lies meant to "conceal" other lies about human worth and ability. "Little," here, is not a judgment of impact, but a thematic means of analytically distinguishing them from their operation and function as assemblaged constellations, discussed below. These little white lies can be as seemingly innocuous as a belief in the human ability to travel to the stars, or as socially pregnant as the belief that some humans are more worthy or able to set about on such travel. Little white lies can be as mundane as they can be pervasive and powerful in shaping the social realities and existential appraisals of those within the social environment. Further, such idolatry is paradoxical in that the structure of the denial appears to be as much a product of the human situation as is the fact that no *a priori* essence presents itself. For many, "Truth" exists in the lies humans create to support these denials – little white lies.

Throughout this text, I refer to these lies as *exaggerations of radical contingency* which, taken together, amount to lies about human worth and ability, told or enacted, that reinforce various insider/outsider arrangements. Indeed, exaggerations of radical contingency are efforts at identity-based distinctions rooted in the attempt to place distance between one's self or community and the reality of death, and its subsequent expression in a radically contingent social arrangement. In short, they are lies about humans meant to reinforce the "gods" humans worship. For instance, Zimmerman's claim that the murder of Martin was "all part of god's plan" helps to keep a particular understanding and function of "god" intact. These white lies are about certain individuals or groups of humans that create a situation wherein another group (telling the lie) validates itself or its "god" as superior to another. Philosophically speaking, these exaggerations are attempts to place distance between freedom and responsibility and across various insider/outsider arrangements which skew the abilities and values of both insider and outsider groups in positive and negative ways.[21] Whereas human radical contingency exposes a necessary relation between being and ethics, exaggerations of radical contingency hide or abuse this necessary relation, presuming a disconnect between different individuals' and groups' attempts to address what is possible and valuable.

To situate these ideas in terms specific to white religious practice, justification for lynching or murder of black bodies occurs through various agreed-upon exaggerations of radical contingency, such as the concept of a black body as socially valueless, as not fully human, or some other version of suggestion that some lives are expendable. At the same time, lynchings and other murders work ritualistically, through their operation within the social environment, to reinforce and help construct a devalued and dehumanized portrait of a radically contingent person, the victim. Structuring and structured by these exaggerations, such murders materially reinforce this devalued portrait through corporeal discipline, intensifying and exposing the physical, bodily limitations of the victim, thereby *exaggerating* the radical contingency of the person, exaggerating the already present existential connection between that person and death by bringing it about prematurely.[22] This very real physical death, however, continues to ideologically exaggerate the radical contingency of other African Americans through fear shaping perceptions of choice and ability – as reminded by novelist Richard Wright's claim that his identity (as black) had been so shaped by these practices that he may as well have been lynched a thousand times over.[23] Thus, exaggerations/white lies play out in both material and ideological ways.

This process of exaggeration involves *misrecognition*, as well, in that in the constructing of black identity, white identity is as equally crafted and yet hidden and the lynching or other sort of murder is misrecognized as only substantively affecting black identity. For those whites who agree to (i.e., adhere to, worship – overtly or unknowingly) the decreased value of the black body, such a focus on the dehumanized black body diverts attention away from the "proper" object motivating the construction of the categories – white bodies and the white lies told by and about them in an unending demand for certainty. That is, the spectacle of violent assaults on black bodies amounts in this instance to a diversion tactic, the severity serving a function of misrecognizing the identitarian effects of the event on white social actors. The murders of Trayvon Martin, Michael Brown, Renisha McBride, etc., etc., more than simply reinforcing the actual perpetrators who all agreed upon – again, worshipped – the premise that black life is valueless and unable to be preserved (one type of exaggeration), reinforce the inverse as well: white bodies characterized by immanent absolute value and ability (another type of exaggeration). Where lynching and other racialized rituals are concerned, a relationship exists between the exaggeration of the radical contingency of African Americans and the existential concerns motivating the white perpetrators as well as those whites who might deny any explicit or even tacit compensatory involvement in such murders.

These exaggerations, white lies, misdirect attention towards the victim of them and away from the construction of something like whiteness taking shape as a kind of god marked by supreme value and ability – remaining as elusive to spot as a theistic god and becoming as "real" as a perceived theistic god through misrecognition of the process unfolding through the exaggerations. Like the inability to immediately "see" how an object such as a book is agreed upon as a book, an identity comes to form as whiteness is created, though it cannot be "seen" outside the hermeneutical aid of twilight. This misrecognition contributes to the creation of what I next refer to as "god-idols."

BIG WHITE LIES: FROM GODS AND IDOLS TO GOD-IDOLS

"Little" white lies are about the business of offering incremental distances between groups, and those groups' relative proximity to death and uncertainty. As structuring mechanisms, however, they also come to be structured by larger constellations of ideas and practices. These distances stem from this religious orientation towards certainty referred to as white religion, made in the image of exaggerations of a person or group's proximity to death, limitation, and uncertainty based on presumptions about that person or group's abilities and value, Imago Superlata as it were. This system produces social consequences and masks those consequences by maintaining a belief in some idea of certainty and value, be it whiteness, god, or another social centering concept. Beliefs about different (greater or lesser) abilities and values amongst different groups end up inevitably mapped onto social reality while the distance one places between this belief and human reality hides this process of social mapping.[24] This demand for certainty produces social consequences like racism and sexism, while the greater the presumed distance between human uncertainty and the beliefs used to address such uncertainty, the greater the extent to which the impact of such beliefs on that uncertain social world is concealed. In other words, this denial system is most effective when it denies its role as such a denial system. God-idols serve this function.

In an effort to uncover and make visible this denial system, the concept of a god-idol captures the functional nuances of ideas like whiteness, theism, patriarchy, and others. Appearing in countless iterations and quantities, "little" white lies come to take on a collective "believability" transmuting into an overarching functional utility, wherein various sorts of related exaggerations come to be most adequately analytically handled by recognizing them as part of larger constellations. God-idol serves in this analytic as well as social capacity, such that something like "whiteness" as a central feature of white religion, takes on the quality of a god, equal in social weight to more traditional expressions of god, yet only the sum total of the worth given to the concept by those in the social world. In like manner, traditional categories like "god" (e.g., YHWY, etc.) take on intensely social features, whereby they present themselves as little more than a storing house for the exaggerations humans make when telling lies meant to distinguish themselves from others, their life from death.

Much of this book is about letting go of the power to distinguish between certain traditionally bifurcated constellations of concepts: between white and black, between theist and atheist, between life and death, between theology and social theory, between certainty and uncertainty, between freedom and responsibility – and, most pressingly, the distinction between god and idol. Gods are ideological constructions that rely on presumed social difference for postulation of social homogeneity, and they never fully achieve what they mean to accomplish for their adherents: provide the foundation to know, to be certain, and to live without fear. Thus, gods (western ones, at least) always already have the character of idols. And "idols," like the idea of whiteness,[25] are often much more powerful than the moniker "idol" suggests. There are no "idols" or "gods," only god-idols. The category "god-idol"[26] is an attempt to hold in tension the limited possibilities of gods and the unlimited consequences of idolatrous white lies. Gods and idols, then, are here fashioned as one in the same, and distinguishing between the two simply reinforces what social theorist Pierre Bourdieu poignantly refers to as a "principle of structuration," the "(hidden) imposition" of "a system of practices and representations whose structure, objectively founded on a principle of political division, presents itself as the natural-supernatural structure of the cosmos."[27] But *White Lies* is also about charting careful, critical manipulation of distinctions so that a distinction might be posed capturing white religion in both sociological and analytical registers. The power of these god-idols is not found in any otherworldly or creator "god," but rather, in this principle of structuration that undergirds much of human social life, allowing for the transformation of a desire for certainty into the material attempt to secure it in society. "God-idol" is meant to focus attention to the structure of the relation, so that the relation between beneficiary and victim might more adequately come into focus, be made more legible and, finally, equitable.[28] Posing, then, the relation as a category unto itself, white religion appears as a flight from death, which, as it turns out, is as much a flight away from life lived equitably with others.

LEARNING TO DIE & LEARNING TO DIE WITH OTHERS

Nearly one hundred years have passed since DuBois gave us his diagnosis of whiteness and white religion; that "A nation's religion is its life, and as such white Christianity is a miserable failure."[29] In these words, DuBois essentially marked a white religious sensibility as a thing-unto-itself and noted that thing as having been a catastrophe. What if DuBois's suggestion was read, understood, and remembered in light of his having been the social scientist he very much was (rather than the "religio-theological race" critic he is sometimes treated as), not concerned with finding a theological "Truth," but exposing certain truths about human social interaction? *White Lies* regards DuBois's words as a sociological and anthropological analysis – better still, as a critique of the possibilities and limits of sociality itself. In other words, this book takes the failure described by DuBois as the starting point for analysis as well as response, and works to not reinforce this failure through unwarranted theological appeal. In so doing, this work is an attempt to add greater clarity to the weight of his words, our understanding of the weight of white religion (as an entity and a social force), and the possibilities for measuring this failure not as a theological failure but as a failure of theism (and other identity-making mechanisms, other god-idols) to allow white Americans to do the one thing incumbent upon all of us in light of our limited, finite bodies: to learn how to *live* with others by learning how to *die* with others.

The "miserable failure" described by DuBois can be understood as this failure in learning to die, a thematic entrée for one of the major aims of this book: outlining the limits of identity formation via the category of religion in guarding against recognition of individual, embodied, and social limits, as well as the consequences of such misrecognition, and the uncertainties hanging ominously above social possibilities and marking a kind of twilight of American religion in the contemporary moment. To the extent that "American religion" has for many been a proxy and code word concealing a more focused assessment of "white religion," and to the extent that white religion seems to be growing increasingly functionally inept at fashioning a "white identity" in the way it once did with ease and certitude, then twilight is not simply a conceptual entry point for this project, but additionally, offers an existential shift in orientation for those whose awareness of whiteness and white religion continues to expand. Another aim of *White Lies* is to suggest that this failure in learning to die is reinforced by a series of white lies forming white religion, where lies are indicative of the tendency to misrecognize the relationship between one person or group's means of identity formation and the social consequences imposed on other social groups and actors by that identity formation. Twilight provides the uncertain (pragmatically and philosophically oriented methodological) lens to see; exaggerations, god-idols, and white lies are what will be seen.

THE BOOK YOU HOLD: THE UNFOLDING AND STRUCTURE OF *WHITE LIES*

Twilight matters. *White Lies* journeys through this twilight, stopping to define and (re)define it at times, while in other instances pausing over the uncertainties, limitations, and shaky assemblaged identities provided by such an interpretive shift. Entering into twilight is not a jaunt into the macabre or grotesque, but towards a renewed sense for religious studies scholars of the possibilities and perils of upholding Plato's injunction, the admonition programmatized by Michel de Montaigne, lamented by Derrida, and seemingly ignored, denied, or fought against by most: that to philosophize, to critically engage, to live, to learn – about ourselves as much as others – is to learn how to die.

Part I of *White Lies* is titled "Learning to Die" and considers the work of existential and functional theorists like Émile Durkheim, Jean-Paul Sartre, and Niklas Luhmann by treating and exploring their work as ethnographically as much as theoretically instructive. I argue that these thinkers help to chart out the ideological and material expressions (respectively) of a white religious orientation – both in an affirmative and problematic/cautious sense. Handling these ethnographic examples with other contemporary social theorists such as Pierre Bourdieu, Mary Douglas, Jean-François Bayart, and James D. Faubion, Part I charts out the analytical look and function of "white lies" – how they work and function in the social arena, and how they seemingly resist awareness of their operation as well as their dismantling. Using theism as expressed in what Civil Rights era poetry collective The Last Poets refers to as "The White Man's God Complex," in the fields of theology and anthropology, in the historic practices of lynching and segregation, in the prison industrial complex, and in contemporary vigilante murders of non-white bodies in the U.S. and abroad, Part I offers an expansive interpretive apparatus designed to make social theoretical sense of white religion in the United States historically and today.

Part II of this book continues in outlining white religion by looking to possible responses to it, considering what a shift from "Learning to Die" towards "Learning to Die *With Others*" might mean in terms of how religious studies scholars understand their efforts, their craft. I chart out *uncertain* possibilities for responding to these white lies. I argue that a blurring of distinctions – that is, the production of uncertainty – between intellectual fields, between "gods" and "devils," between sacred and profane, between heaven and hell, and between life and death, begins to respond to this death-dealing demand for certainty rooted in these white lies. I look to literary and religious studies theorists such as Harold Bloom and Anthony B. Pinn, deconstructionist Jacques Derrida, and cultural theorists James Baldwin and bell hooks to frame my exploration of three figures emblematic of early (white) responses to some of these lies: anthropologist Barbara Myerhoff, and novelists Carson McCullers and Lillian Smith. Myerhoff returns to her cultural inheritance after recalibrating the significance of such inheritances through recognition of her approaching physical death. McCullers's fiction offers theoretical guidance for understanding humans and gods as homologous. Smith's racialized and economic privileges were offset by a queer identity and an early death, and complicated by her prophetic recognition of white religion as an outgrowth of fear. Such figures and their work and lives provide windows into, and offer productive possibilities for, wrestling with the manner in which they treat identity in the wake of recognition of their own death and the deaths of others and thus, the deaths their identities as "white" have seemingly caused others. To these ends, though Part II seeks to discuss possible critical rejoinders to these white lies, such a response (rhetorically) is meant to send home that these white lies are ultimately an outgrowth of an inability to accept human limits and the uncertainty posed by death. Death and uncertainty, then, stand as the final words and markers of white religion, its origins and its posterity connected to this miserable failure – here posed as a failure to "learn how to die," a failure to accept the uncertain dimensions of and limited possibilities for recognizing the relationships between seemingly different identities.

The first chapter, "In the Shadows of Whiteness: Giving Life (through Death) to a *White Lie*," begins the book by arguing that racialized lynchings come to do a very specific sort of ideological and social work in identity formation in the U.S., both currently and historically. That is to say, they produce whiteness as a racialized expression of a fundamental inability to accept human limitations and uncertainty. I turn to existentialist and functionalist theories to suggest that this whiteness reinforces a purported distance from embodied limits and uncertainties by imposing more acutely those uncertainties onto black bodies with the functional effect of creating a "white" identity marked principally by the perception of distance from these limits. I explore the multivalent rituals and practices sustaining such an identity in the wake of decreasing numbers of literal lynchings, while suggesting that this feature of identity – whiteness – might no longer be as functionally effective (as it once was) at procuring distance from uncertainty for white people. I conclude the chapter by situating whiteness within twilight, calling into question its continued functional utility.

Building from this, the second chapter, "The White Man's God Complex: Most Americans, the (White) Power of Theism, and Beginning to *Believe* in Twilight," looks to another identity-forming mechanism in theism, recast not as belief in "god," but belief in the functional utility of belief itself, with roots in the social and economic anxiety predating but "Americanized" by evangelist Jonathan Edwards and others. Whereas Chapter 1 begins with material practices and foregrounds their ability to shape identity and ideation more generally, Chapter 2 attempts the opposite, beginning with idea and belief in the power of ideas, demonstrating that such *theism* helps to materially manifest what The Last Poets referred to as the "White Man's God Complex." Moreover, this chapter suggests that for "Most [White] Americans," their purported belief in "god" works to secure the material conditions for them to act as if they were gods, undergirded by theological sleight-of-hand and the threat and use of violence.

The third chapter, "Battling White Lies: Exaggerated Identity and the Twilight of American Religion," takes a step back from whiteness and theism to look more expansively at the multiplicity of mechanisms that work to constitute a white religious sensibility. Looking to the fields of theology and anthropology as data indicative of an academic as well as social preoccupation with maintaining a sacred/profane distinction, I suggest that such a distinction might best be understood as social/existential – that is, an attempt to make use of and reinforce the "principle of structuration" sustaining this brand of identity formation. I suggest that this initial distinction is the principal "white lie" structuring and structured by various ancillary lies about the worth and abilities of various identities. I conclude by suggesting that such awareness of how these white lies function casts the very category of "identity" into uncertainty, into twilight. Here, I also note that contemporary identity politics remain so central to so many Americans' frames of reference that we find ourselves now in what Jean-François Bayart refers to as a "battle for identity"[30] waged within this ever-present, looming twilight.

The fourth chapter, "Accepting the Hell of Death: Narrating Sources, Methods, and Norms of a *Limited Religious Outlook*," begins Part II of the book. There, I turn to an extended case study in the person of anthropologist Barbara Myerhoff, whose own ethnographic work with the dying was soon accompanied by her being diagnosed with terminal cancer. Looking to her as exemplar of the limited capacity to respond fully to the consequences of white lies, I put forth a *limited religious outlook* as an analytical means of beginning to handle these uncertain dimensions. In particular, I suggest an initial recognition that white religion is marked by an awareness of the Sartrean notion that "hell is other people." Through various analytical and heuristic registers such as the concept of uncertain humanism, I argue that acceptance of this "hell" begins with learning to tell stories without exaggerations, without white lies. Ownership of one's own cultural, social, individual, and collective stories of death and dying makes possible this unexaggerated storytelling.

In Chapter 5, "Rejecting the 'Gift of Death': White Social Responsibility in Twilight Times," I put to use another case study through the literary example offered by Carson McCullers's *The Heart Is a Lonely Hunter* (1940), for what her character John Singer suggests about the relationship between "gods" and humans at centers and margins of society. Responding to a long-standing philosophical and theological tradition (inherited by white religious Americans but predating its U.S. context) wherein "god" as *wholly other* finds substitution in the *social other*, I suggest that this "Gift of Death" must be rejected. Such rejection is made possible by dismissal of claims to personal salvation in the form of everlasting life, a life after death. The chapter is not a constructive theological response to white religion, but rather, looks to theological and philosophical discourse so as to pose an anthropological litmus test: Would a willingness to give up concern for personal salvation offer the means for white Americans to determine the degree to which they are held in sway by white lies?

The final chapter, "Requiem for Whiteness: Mourning, Freedom in Uncertainty, and the Final Embrace of Twilight," considers the work of another writer – white, Southern, lesbian novelist Lillian Smith – for help in concluding the project with a thought experiment: What if whiteness died, what would such a death look like, and what would this death mean for white religion in America and the identities posed historically by such arrangements? Smith helps to frame the "former" beneficiaries of whiteness as strange *white* fruit, wherein those whose identities have been formed through white lies, have ostensibly produced the "last" other in themselves, as they've remained unable to do the one thing required – learn how to die – because they have not learned that to actually learn how to die *is*, in the end, to learn to die *with others*. The final chapter poses one exercise in such an uncertain process, and concludes with a final embrace of the uncertainties increasingly revealed behind, exposing, and confronting the white lies of white religion in America.

The final words of *White Lies* come in the form of a Postmortem. "A Warning" looks back to one of the volume's principal thematic interlocutors, Friedrich Nietzsche, and his Madman who first uttered the words that "god is dead … and we have killed him."[31] Understanding his statement as a homology for recognition of white lies in practice and increasingly called into question, the uncertainties posed by the (still uncertain) waning power of this white religious sensibility do not mark a time to celebrate but to remain vigilant. For a community just now (perhaps, if at all) learning to accept the uncertainties and limitations posed by a life lived in rejection of white lies that have insulated them from having to accept other sorts of uncertainties, the Madman's diagnosis marks analytical clarity and understanding. However, Nietzsche's prognosis that we now become gods remains an ominous warning for America as it comes to form a contemporary collective identity in the uncertainty posed by the twilight of white American religion.

A CATEGORICALLY *UNCERTAIN* APPROACH

White Lies tacks in a variety of directions and through numerous domains, impacting and impacted by a multiplicity of ideas, schools of thought, and intellectual disciplining mechanisms. The intensely interdisciplinary movement between critical social theory and poststructural theory, not to mention between the fields of theology, religion, philosophy, anthropology, and literature, may be frustrating to readers accustomed to traditional manipulations and explorations of data within an individual disciplinary housing. In one sense, I do not mean to suggest that Nietzsche, Durkheim, and Sartre (or their defenders) would agree with my characterizations of their projects, or that Luhmann or Derrida are up to the same or even similar tasks. In another sense, I cannot help but read them all as part of a long tradition of white thinkers motivated by epistemological, ethical, and skeptical demands for certainty arising from an inability to face squarely not only physical death and limitation, but the social responsibilities demanded by human dignity in light of physical death. To this extent, they work well together for painting a brief, incomplete, and certainly uncertain portrait of white American religion partially made possible by their critical theoretical distance *from* the U.S. I hope that my treatment of these figures in particular demonstrates my appreciation for the clarity their arguments afford for understanding white religion, while I work to refute the various demands for certainty and security each of their intellectual contributions espouses in its own way. Made clear through the epigraph that begins this chapter, even the deconstructionist Derrida could not learn how to die, leaving him unable to accept such an inevitable fate: "I have not learned to accept death," he says – no, "I remain impervious to learning when it comes to knowing-how-to-die. I have yet to learn anything about this particular subject."[32] I don't presume that this project could do what Derrida could not, but I do hope it might at least help to explain why learning how to die – for white Americans in particular, but for all of us, maybe – is so terribly difficult.

Notes

1 W. E. B. DuBois, "The Souls of White Folk," in *Darkwater: Voices from Within the Veil* (Cosimo, Inc., 2007).
2 Jacques Derrida, "I Am At War with Myself," *Le Monde*, August 19, 2004.
3 Anthea Butler, "The Zimmerman Acquittal: America's Racist God," accessed August 5, 2014 and January 25, 2015, http://www.religiondispatches.org/dispatches/

antheabutler/7195/ and http://religiondispatches.org/the-zimmerman-acquittal-americas-racist-god/

4 Ibid.

5 Commentary on Anthea Butler, website, accessed August 5, 2014, http://nosecretsonthenet.tumblr.com/page/2

6 Jean-François Bayart, *The Illusion of Cultural Identity* (University of Chicago Press, 2005).

7 See, for instance, Daniel Dubuisson, *The Western Construction of Religion: Myths, Knowledge, and Ideology*, trans. William Sayers (The Johns Hopkins University Press, 2003); Goldschmidt, Henry Goldschmidt and Elizabeth McAlister, eds., *Race, Nation, and Religion in the Americas* (Oxford University Press, 2004); John L. Jackson, Jr., *Thin Description* (Harvard University Press, 2013); Monica R. Miller, "Real Recognize Real: Aporetic Flows and the Presence of New Black Godz in Hip Hop," in Monica R. Miller, Anthony B. Pinn, and Bernard "Bun B" Freeman, eds., *Religion in Hip Hop: Mapping the New Terrain in the US* (Bloomsbury Academic, 2015).

8 Pierre Bourdieu, "Genesis and Structure of the Religious Field," *Comparative Social Research* 13 (1991).

9 My use of imagery reinforcing darkness/blackness as pathological is meant to foreground the interpretive posture of those to whom *White Lies* is directed. Maintaining a politically correct posture towards darkness would deconstruct its pathological social weight, but at the cost of denying the interpretive posture many hold towards darkness.

10 DuBois, *Darkwater*.

11 See Cornel West, *Hope on a Tightrope: Words and Wisdom* (Hay House, 2008); James W. Perkinson, *White Theology: Outing Supremacy in Modernity*, 1st ed. (Palgrave Macmillan, 2004).

12 Perkinson, 129.

13 Jean-Paul Sartre, *Existentialism Is a Humanism*, trans. Carol Macomber (trade paperback edition, Yale University Press, 2007), 22.

14 Jean-Paul Sartre, *Anti-Semite and Jew* (Schocken Books Inc., 1948).

15 James H. Cone, *God of the Oppressed* (rev. sub. edition, Orbis Books, 1997), 196.

16 Further, radical contingency refers to my position that humans are only free insofar as such freedom is expressed for/with others. "Exaggerated" radical contingency mischaracterizes this freedom as a freedom detached from social responsibility. The consequences of such exaggerations always come at the expense of others, as the exercise of this false freedom forsakes the individuals' radically contingent dependence on others. What's most "radical" about contingency is that it actually manifests in an abstraction that negates the contingency through embrace of social actors. See Sartre, *Being and Nothingness* (Routledge, 2003), 105.

17 By guideposts, I mean that these discourses allow for an insider's view of these social processes in practice. I treat them as ethnographic data, and as theoretically relevant to the extent that thinkers like Sartre offer an assessment of the philosophical tools at the disposal of those held in sway by white religion.

18 Ethicist James Perkinson has specifically described whiteness as a "denial structure." See Perkinson, *White Theology*, 128.

19 Although Sartre's sweeping generalities about the human "situation" are problematic in a variety of ways, I find no problem applying Sartre's insights given the particular social context of my data. That is, although Sartre's existentialism may not be universally applicable (even as he suggests it is), his ideas remain appropriate for expressing the existential concerns arising from a white, male perspective. The same is true of my usage of Émile Durkheim later, and of Niklas Luhmann and others throughout this text.

20 With technical language, Sartre defines contingency as "In the For-itself this equals facticity, the brute fact of being *this* For-itself in the world. The contingency of freedom is the fact that freedom is not able not to exist," Sartre, *Being and Nothingness*, 651.

21 Discussed in more detail in Chapter 3, exaggerations of radical contingency play out in terms of agency and value, each with a positive or negative valence. Beneficiaries and victims are both "exaggerated." The idea of exaggeration is not limited to those on the underside of social forces.
22 Perkinson, *White Theology*, 127–8.
23 Richard Wright, quoted in James H. Cone, *The Cross and the Lynching Tree* (Orbis Books, 2012), 15.
24 Bourdieu, "Genesis and Structure"; Bourdieu, *The Logic of Practice*, 1st ed. (Stanford University Press, 1992).
25 One of the first to note the relationship between racism and white Christianity in the United States is George D. Kelsey. His work inspires much of this book, as he refers to racism as a form of idolatry. Many of his suggestions are as pertinent today as they were when he published *Racism and the Christian Understanding of Man. An Analysis and Criticism of Racism as an Idolatrous Religion* (Charles Scribner's Sons, 1965).
26 Though somewhat bulky, these critical concepts like god-idol work to dislodge the conversation away from politically laden fear of identity politics, so that the "politics" behind such fear is able to be seen or measured. These terms might allow for a renewed recognition (for many) of why something like "identity politics" matters at all – and to be sure, many adherents of white religion hold a disdain for such identity politics.
27 Bourdieu, "Genesis and Structure," 5.
28 The Bourdieu scholar might ask if I am suggesting that whiteness as god-idol might operate as a homology to *habitus*. Whiteness, as its discussion unfolds in this book, is always a structuring device of one's *habitus*, but is never a one-to-one parallel. Yet, perhaps whiteness as god-idol (and as with all god-idols) is structured by and structures the overarching concept of *habitus* described by Bourdieu through the logic of practice.
29 DuBois, *Darkwater*.
30 Bayart, *Cultural Identity*, 252.
31 Friedrich Nietzsche, *The Gay Science: With a Prelude in Rhymes and an Appendix of Songs* (Vintage Books, 1974), 181–2.
32 Derrida, "I Am at War with Myself."

REFERENCES

Bayart, Jean-François. 2005. *The Illusion of Cultural Identity*. University of Chicago Press.

Bourdieu, Pierre. 1991. "Genesis and Structure of the Religious Field." *Comparative Social Research* 13: 1–44.

Bourdieu, Pierre et al. 1992. *The Logic of Practice*. 1st ed. Stanford University Press.

Butler, Anthea. 2013. "Commentary on Anthea Butler." *No Secrets On the Net*, accessed August 5, 2014, http://nosecretsonthenet.tumblr.com/page/2

Butler, Anthea. 2013. "The Zimmerman Aquittal: America's Racist God." *Religion Dispatches*, accessed November 20, religiondispatches.org/dispatches/antheabutler/7195/

Cone, James. 1997. *God of the Oppressed*. Rev Sub. Orbis Books.

Cone, James. 2013. *The Cross and the Lynching Tree*. Reprint. Orbis Books.

Derrida, Jacques. 2004. "I Am At War with Myself," *Le Monde*, August 19, 2004.

DuBois, W. E. B. 2007. *Darkwater: Voices from Within the Veil*. Cosimo, Inc.

Dubuisson, Daniel. 2003. *The Western Construction of Religion: Myths, Knowledge, and Ideology*, trans. William Sayers. The Johns Hopkins University Press.

Goldschmidt, Henry and Elizabeth McAlister, eds. 2004. *Race, Nation, and Religion in the Americas*. Oxford University Press.

Jackson Jr, John L. 2013. *Thin Description*. Harvard University Press.

Kelsey, George D. 1965. *Racism and the Christian Understanding of Man. An Analysis and Criticism of Racism as an Idolatrous Religion.* Charles Scribner's Sons.

Miller, Monica R. 2015. "Real Recognize Real: Aporetic Flows and the Presence of New Black Godz in Hip Hop," in Monica R. Miller, Anthony B. Pinn, and Bernard "Bun B" Freeman (eds.), *Religion in Hip Hop: Mapping the New Terrain in the US.* Bloomsbury Academic.

Nietzsche, Friedrich. 1974. *The Gay Science: With a Prelude in Rhymes and an Appendix of Songs.* Vintage Books.

Perkinson, James W. 2004. *White Theology: Outing Supremacy in Modernity.* 1st ed. Palgrave Macmillan.

Sartre, Jean-Paul. 1948. *Anti-Semite and Jew.* Schocken Books Inc.

Sartre, Jean-Paul. 2003. *Being and Nothingness: An Essay in Phenomenological Ontology*, trans. Hazel Barnes. Routledge.

Sartre, Jean-Paul. 2007. *Existentialism Is a Humanism*, trans. Carol Macomber. Trade paperback edition. Yale University Press.

West, Cornel. 2008. *Hope on a Tightrope: Words and Wisdom.* Hay House.

PART I

Learning to die

1

IN THE SHADOWS OF WHITENESS

Giving life (through death) to a *White Lie*

> People believe, thought Shadow. It's what people do. They believe. And then they will not take responsibility for their beliefs; they conjure things, and do not trust the conjurations. People populate the darkness; with ghosts, with gods, with electrons, with tales. People imagine, and people believe: and it is that belief, that rock-solid belief, that makes things happen.
>
> *Neil Gaiman*[1]

> There are no more ancient idols in existence… . Also none more hollow… . That does not prevent their being the most believed in; and they are not, especially in the most eminent case, called idols.
>
> *Friedrich Nietzsche*[2]

What does it mean to "believe" in an idol? How are idols produced? The first glimpses of white religion are made possible by looking to one of its most cherished idols, whiteness, exposing it by situating it as a god-idol, a centering idea produced and reinforced through various rituals which function to secure (for its adherents) a sense of personal and collective certainty and stability. As this god-idol, whiteness emerges as a particular racialized expression of a fundamental inability to accept human limitation and uncertainty. Making use of hermeneutical and functional analyses, *White Lies* begins here offering a way to interpret, to make sense of, the role and effects of whiteness in contemporary U.S. society. Although often overlooked over and against time spent on these topics by scholars of American religion, many of these racialized social activities and beliefs in the U.S. are "religious" in that they ritualistically structure and are structured by a demand for certainty and stability seemingly procured through identity formation and process. Taken as such, religion then amounts to the field through which social order is sought, created, and reinforced through maintenance of these god-idols –

centering, ultimately empty concepts employed to address demands for personal and collective certainty and security, often through attempts to ritualistically create it in the material world – thus transmuting ideas into social reality.

Whiteness is one of the "white lies," one of the "hollow" idols to borrow Nietzsche's phrase, rooted ultimately in physical death, and born in the practice of lynching. This chapter sketches whiteness in heuristic, hermeneutic form, looking first to the intense ideological work done by the practice of lynching, moving to discussions of the functional life, death, and ultimately the twilight whiteness finds itself in today. Whiteness does not materially exist, save for its conceptual expression as this racialized inability to accept limit. Conversely, neither does blackness "exist" other than as an awareness of the impossibility of ever completely accepting human limitation and uncertainty. This does not stop these empty identity markers from operating within the social environment as some of the "most believed in" of idols, whereby an imaginary idea, a lie, can bring about a kind of truth – a ground of being, an ultimate concern – as severe and enduring as the history of racialized oppression in the U.S.

As gestured towards in the Introduction, god-idols, like whiteness, are most adequately analyzable and understood through the notion of "twilight" – the doubtful clarity[3] exposed through their de/construction. Twilight as an analytical notion suggests that these god-idols are simultaneously functionally effective and, yet, seemingly break down in their effectiveness given shifts in historical circumstance, ideological commitment, and a host of other arbitrary as well as not-so-arbitrary features and trends of social life. Where white religion is concerned, this exploration of whiteness is as much made possible by the shift towards twilight as the findings from such a perspective may suggest that a god-idol born from a kind of fundamental twilight now finds itself on uncertain ground.

BLACK OFFERINGS

The journey towards this twilight begins with a stark racialized clarity cast by dead black bodies. On October 13, 1938, 19-year-old W.C. Williams hung from a tree near Ruston, Louisiana,[4] his mutilated, dead, black body casting an ominous shadow across the faces of his white murderers. For two days prior to his murder, Williams was sought for questioning about another murder, of a white man, and the beating of the white man's mistress.[5] After hiding out for days, Williams finally surrendered to a small, gun-toting, emotionally charged group of young white men. Soon, a brief confrontation ensued between Lincoln Parish Sheriff Bryan Thigpin who sought to maintain "law and order" and the ever-growing mob of white captors. With the mob threatening to shoot Williams on the spot, Thigpin struck a deal with the mob for them to "walk Williams through the woods to a side road, where they promised to meet the sheriff and surrender their prisoner."[6] Soon after the mob left with their "prisoner," Thigpin heard shots. Knowing what had happened, the capitulating sheriff drove back into town "believing there was 'nothing further [he] could do'."[7] Another "Negro" murdered – the permanence of the physical death reinforcing the fixity of black and white identity, alike.

African American humanist theologian and scholar of African American religion Anthony Pinn argues that the practice of lynching constitutes a "ritual of reference – a means of maintaining the 'truth' of a particular system and the relationship of those within that system."[8] Appealing to historian of religion Charles Long's hermeneutical thesis of the first and second creation narratives of the religions of the oppressed, Pinn argues that such rituals substantiated and reinforced the "formation of the negro." In the post-bellum period, lynching came to operate as a reinforcement mechanism, structuring and structured by the social positions developed during enslavement and needing reinforcement and reinscription in the reconstruction and Jim/Jane Crow periods. Pinn poignantly notes the significance of lynching for black identity formation: "However one conceives of lynching's place within the context of a changing U.S. society – whether as wanton expression of rage and violence or quasilegal efforts to punish criminals – it is certain that mob violence became a major mechanism of American life and a way of fixing black identity."[9]

Much has been made of this black identity formation through works as wide ranging as W.E.B. DuBois's *The Souls of Black Folk* and the fiction of James Baldwin, Richard Wright, and Zora Neale Hurston, and through the academic theological texts offered by James Cone, Dwight Hopkins, Katie Cannon, Delores Williams, Victor Anderson, Pinn, and many more.[10] Less, however, has been discussed of white identity, white religion – or more focused still, something that might be called and sited as "whiteness." Yet, such profound social events as lynchings and the participation in lynch mobs radiated outward from the lynch spectacles and had a powerful impact on white identity as well. Quoting Frantz Fanon, Pinn argues that lynching helped ensure "'the white man sealed in his whiteness, the black man in his blackness.'"[11] This first chapter picks up what Pinn only inchoately discusses: the formation of whiteness as created by and creating a false sense of group and individual security, stability, certainty, value, and ability.

What Thigpin heard was part of a cacophony of religious sounds to emerge from the sacred space created out of horror and terror – a space at once set apart and distinct from the larger surroundings, but of immense and immediate importance to how those larger surroundings are understood. What he "heard" helped to create a "vision" in his mind, of differential worth and value based on race. Elements of this particular ritual included continuous torture of Williams's body with a "red hot poker," repeated shots fired into Williams's hanging body – some accounts even indicate that blood seen dripping down Williams's naked leg suggests he had been castrated.[12] Further, a fire had been set underneath him, only to be extinguished by some "sensible" whites who reasoned that a burned body would make it impossible to compare Williams's fingerprints to those at the scene of the initial crime.[13] It is interesting that these same "sensible" folks didn't think it prudent to take Williams's fingerprints while he was still alive.

Shifting our gaze away from the black offering and to the white religious adherents and their white rituals of reference offers a heuristic for reading the birth of whiteness *as a god-idol* beginning with this "ritual" practice of lynching.[14] I refer to these lynchings as rituals in that they are understood as sacrificial offerings towards personal and collective security and certainty. Lynching is grounded in physical death. The life, then, of whiteness emerges from death through an unwillingness to fully embrace one's own death. This life, ironically, reinforces the deaths of others while never preventing the death from which it emerges and to which it will return from being overcome. They function through what religious studies scholar and social theorist Bruce Lincoln refers to as a logic of "formative negation," wherein a life "is given up for the benefit of some other group, god or principle that is understood to be 'higher' or more deserving."[15] The sacrificial victim operates as a site of formation for the group itself. In the negation of the sacrificed, the sacrificers achieve a type of identity-based reinforcement. Through lynching, black bodies were, in various ways, ritualistically sacrificed for a group of white people to "ensure not only white dominance but the larger social and moral order"[16] – a moral and social order structured by an invisible principle of whiteness deemed of central and supreme value. Such rituals provide a visual expression of an invisible idea.

The lynching of W.C. Williams was a public spectacle, with eventually around three hundred participants in the mob murder.[17] Williams's murder was the sixth reported lynching in the U.S. in 1938.[18] That year, seven lynchings occurred in the U.S.: four in neighboring Mississippi, and one (each) in Georgia, Florida, and Louisiana.[19] From 1882 to 1968, nearly 5,000 lynchings occurred in the U.S., the overwhelming majority of them in Southern states and directed against African Americans.[20] Though not all lynchings in the U.S. were directed at African Americans, the majority were. Moreover, lynchers were rarely tried or convicted of their crimes. The year Williams was murdered, none of the states where lynchings occurred sought prosecution for either the assailants or the law enforcement officials who were usually complicit in the murders. Unfortunately, such was the norm.[21] For a white citizenry who often conceived of black bodies as a problem, such lynchings operated to contain and restrain white and black modes of being and operation within society through violence and terror. These lynchings functioned to tell whites and blacks how to behave, helped to classify who was white or black, and ensured that "racialized transgressions" would not be tolerated and would be punished.

In all of its absurdity, a vicious and gut-wrenching aspect of many lynchings was the tokens and souvenirs collected from black bodies. Hair was taken and skin was flayed, many whites taking home these trinkets as reminders of the black sacrificial offering having temporarily secured a sense of fixity and order for the mob and the society its defender. Similar in their functional effect to more traditionally recognized religious artifacts such as bibles or baptismal water, these "mementos of black bodies took on a transcendent quality" for their recipients.[22] "Transfigured into powerful [religious] symbols," Pinn argues, the relics garnered in such ritualistic activities had the ironic effect of "turning the former objects of history into shapers of history."[23] Moreover, lynchings took on the character of religious pilgrimage in that many citizens would travel long distances to take part in the spectacle offered by the murder, if not to partake more viscerally in the actual killing.

These events, and these tokens of history, worked to solidify the identities of white and black in a mutually exclusive – yet symbiotic – fashion, even where lynchings had not been experienced directly. Theologian James Cone situates the effects of lynching on black identity formation by recalling the autobiographical account of Richard Wright, who says, "I had never in my life been abused by whites, but I had already become conditioned to their existence as though I had been the victim of a thousand lynchings."[24] Wright's words not only connect black and white identity to each other, but also situate the practice of lynching as instrumental to such ideological formation across space and time. Whiteness and blackness emerge together in tension – born from the material, historical ritual practice of lynching, but extending beyond specific events to shape the ideas that orient white and black identity.

Such formation began at an early age for white children. Kristina DuRocher's *Raising Racists* (2011), a study of the racist socialization of white children in the Jim Crow South, quotes one white father who brought his young son to a lynching. While viewing the brutal castration and burning of an African American named Jesse Washington who was lynched in Waco, Texas in 1916, the father remarked that "'My son can't learn too young the proper way to treat a nigger.'"[25] At once, the young boy learned the value of blackness, as well as its inverse, whiteness. Simultaneously, black bodies were overcome and rendered docile, while white participants interpolated the dead black body as an acute realization of social stability and the certainty that could be procured through white skin. Williams's dead body allowed the white perpetrators and onlookers a "temporary restoration of order" offered by the lynching as it reinforced racial codes as rigid and secure.[26] In short, it offered the white participants a moment to existentially exhale, a white religious sensibility emerging secure in the certainty afforded from an idea undergirded by skin color.

Pinn's work on lynching focuses intently on black identity formation, but his efforts also demonstrate how whites understood lynching. For the whites, lynchings were "a fight against chaos" and were "premised upon religious sensibilities… . Lynchers – many of whom were not only church members but church leaders – felt their actions had religious justification and that the process of lynching contained the ethos of church ritual and the religious re-creation of cosmic order. In short, maintenance of the social order was undertaken as a religious quest, the securing of the created order as God intended it."[27] Building on but augmenting Pinn's suggestion, these adherents' quest to find and create the social order "as God intended it" is better framed as a process of creating "god" (here understood as whiteness) through ritualized attempts to achieve social stability and certainty. Lynchings did not occur because of a divine ordinance to maintain social stability, regardless of the mob's theistic rationalizations. Rather, the attempt at social stability (the lynching) reinforced and produced the concept of whiteness as nothing less than a functional god for the white perpetrators and beneficiaries of the practice. The lynch scene marks the formation of this god-idol of whiteness, its existential and social functions for society distilled in violence.

The existential function of god-idols: What do god-idols represent?

The principal function of a god-idol is existential, working to deny personal and individual awareness of radical contingency, the situation of forced reliance on others based on the demands of limited, mortal bodies. Lynching is a material and powerful example of an exaggeration of radical contingency, an exaggeration of one person or group's proximity to death and uncertainty in relation to another person or group. These exaggerations produce god-idols that allow individuals to presume their personal concerns are disconnected from the concerns of other people. God-idols aid in this endeavor through their suggestion that, in spite of death and human limitation, life has meaning and that such meaning is secure. For instance, in her well-known memoir of life as a white girl in the racist, sexist South, Lillian Smith recounts another of these exaggerations as taught to little white children: "Your skin is your glory and the source of your strength and pride. It is white. And, as you have heard, whiteness is a symbol of purity and excellence. Remember this: Your white skin proves that you are better than all other people on this earth."[28] Smith's words are, in a sense, the "voice" of the South and much of the nation as a whole and this voice exposes the existential function of these white lies. This function produces what Jean-Paul Sartre refers to as an "inverted liberty," a fear of the freedom to be responsible to others.[29] Applying the insights of existential psychologist Otto Rank, cultural anthropologist Ernest Becker also helps to situate the consequences of this existential denial when he argues that "all the evil that men have wreaked upon themselves and upon their world since the beginnings of time right up until tomorrow" comes as man[30] "denies his true condition,"[31] a denial producing the "inverted liberty" described by Sartre and more recently couched in terms of race by scholar of religion James Perkinson. Perkinson underscores that "whiteness emerges in the colonial encounter as just such an operation of superiority, an attempt to use darker bodies as a denial structure, a medium between rocky soil and ready food, between hard labor and coveted leisure, between death and the living that inevitably lives toward such an end in the grave."[32] In a racist America, this denial has meant a bloating of white worth and value not in line with human reality. Such existential exaggerations are made possible through belief in the supremacy of one race of people over another, the belief in god or gods who purportedly respond to life's suffering and confusion, and through any idea that denies the contingency and limits of human value or ability. Whiteness comes about in the effort to fill an innate existential void, a radically contingent human reality where meaning is made rather than found. Existential exaggerations function to "fill" that void.

These existential concerns traverse what social theorist Pierre Bourdieu refers to as the "relatively autonomous religious field,"[33] bridging the existential and the abstract with the material world of society. I refer to god "-idols" because the otherworldly, cosmic story of gods and the this-worldly story of human idolaters are equally essential to the "field" of religion, wherein material realities and discursive power arrangements are navigated and, importantly, often structure and maintain their power through manipulations of the other component, (i.e., personal vs. social, this-worldly vs. otherworldly, etc.). Within this field, one person or group's "god" is in competition with another, meaning one "god" is registered as a false "idol" to those held in sway by another "god." My use of "god" and "idol" is meant to foreground that these ideas are born from radical contingency – meaning they are never the *a priori* truths they purport to be. Moreover, my use of "idol" offers a means to talk of central ideas and concepts that holds in tension the discursive power of the concepts with the malleability and contingent nature of the categories themselves. By marking such ontological markers as whiteness with the "idol" ascription, I recognize such god-idols as inadequate for addressing that which is their existential function, the denial of radical contingency, one's proximity to death and the mutual interdependence arising from that proximity. "Inverted liberty" is never *fully* achieved, which is simply to say "gods" never work well enough to kill off competing "idols," and human radical contingency is inescapable.

The social function of god-idols: What do god-idols do?

God-idols, like whiteness, maintain a social function as well, moving beyond individuals to the groups and collectivities made up of radically contingent individual humans. By "social," I refer to tangible, material people in society, people in human collectivities. The existential function is an individual idea/ideal that transmutes through a logic of practice into material reality. That is, people believe certain ideas with such certitude that they move through the world as if the ideas were unquestionable. The social world is built by such movement, while it also helps to create the ideas. Ideas shape material reality and are shaped by it. For instance, if the existential function of whiteness leads to a presumption that white people should have more money than African Americans, then the social function of whiteness is this notion playing out sociologically through quantifiable statistics. Social exaggerations of radical contingency reinforce an "appropriate" distance between individual and group concerns, and ensure that this process is misrecognized.

Lynchings emerge as social exaggerations arising from existential exaggerations. The social and existential function together, in tandem; we "see" them both in the lynching scene. This point is important, in that social and existential functions are distinguished here for the sake of analytic attention, but they amount to one shared function of staving off an awareness of human limitation and uncertainty by manipulating the ideological and material degree to which social others face such limitation and uncertainty head on. The agreement to murder W.C. Williams was not aporetic to the aims and ambitions of proper society as conceived at the time, but operated as a foundational moment reinforcing a sense of social certainty through the destruction of a black body deemed a problem for the society. Agreement to the devaluation and dehumanization of black bodies produced the ideas allowing for the lynching to take place (this is the existential function); while the lynching reinforced the produced ideas (this is the social function). In the process, society comes to be constituted in part by vicious arbitrary appraisals of value and worth that shape acute human interactions and only afterwards produce government and other institutions. American religion has followed a higher law, based on the god-idol of whiteness, trumping any legal system pre- or post-dating the United States (and safeguarding its existential failures), and motivating the mobs who administered the lynch law: a "law" based on a demand for certainty and stability. In this light, the lynchers are not the well-intentioned whites who were often described as doing the dirty work of "defying the law so as to ascertain it" for the sake of "the fundamental assertion of self-governing men, upon whom our whole social fabric is based."[34] Such justifications were common for lynch mobs, and versions of this justification are continued by those supporting George Zimmerman, Darren Wilson, and other contemporary killers of black people. These lynchers were but the priests and scribes of a sacred religious practice reinforcing and producing, structured by and structuring, a hidden yet powerful god-idol of whiteness.

MISRECOGNIZED LYNCH ROPES

How might a god-idol be seen? What is the "look" of something seemingly invisible like an idea such as whiteness? To answer this, a conceptual metaphor is helpful and is captured by the tragic lynching spectacle. Imagine a rope holding together the individual and the collective (in the abstract), the existential and the social. Williams's black body marks the existential while the tree is society. White lies are the mechanisms that determine the constitution of the rope (its length, thickness, color, etc.) and are the individual strings that twine together to produce the rope itself. God-idols, then, are the ropes produced from these exaggerations of radical contingency. Little white lies make big white lies. These ropes, like god-idols, respond to an uncertain social world. But the shape, tensile strength, and other characteristics assumed by these ropes are malleable and shapeable, meaning that these exaggerations can take a variety of forms. Also in flux are the existential and social realities held together by these god-idols, the histories and people that such god-idols hold in tension. God-idols are the entwined fibers at once binding and yet keeping at a safe distance individual and collective concerns, beliefs, and practices. Exaggerations, then, are the manipulations of this connection, the factors which form the god-idol in the image of these exaggerations: Imago Superlata.

For a more technical explication of the function of exaggerations and their relation to god-idols, Bourdieu is helpful in outlining the durability of these "ropes" and their functions through his concepts of *absolutization of the relative* and *legitimation of the arbitrary*.[35] His ideas suggest that the arbitrary and relative – the contingency of ideas and social realities – are offered as natural and eternal through a process of consecration that is, in turn, ascribed a sacred value.[36] Such structuring simultaneously appeals to the process to legitimate it and the social relations it reinforces. Worth noting in its entirety, the passage says:

> Religion [read: god-idol creation and manipulation] exercises an effect of consecration in two ways: (1) It consecrates by converting into limits of law, through its sanctifying sanctions, the economic and political limits and barriers of fact and, in particular, by contributing to the *symbolic manipulation of aspirations*, which tends to ensure the adjustment of actual hopes to objective possibilities. (2) It inculcates a system of consecrated practices and representations whose structure (structured) reproduces, in a transfigured and therefore misrecognizable form, the structure of economic and social relations in force in a determinate social formation. Religion can produce the objectivity that it produces (in structuring structure) only by producing the *misrecognition of the limits* of the knowledge that makes it possible.[37]

Misrecognition of limits is part and parcel to white religion in practice.[38] The god-idols of white religion do the work of absolutizing and legitimating such relative and arbitrary markers as skin color, gender, sexuality, and human worth or ability mapped onto these arbitrary identitarian features. But the process consecrates these connections as more than piecemeal and arbitrary.

Recognition is required (on the part of analysts) that concepts like "god" and "whiteness" originate and take their power from misrecognition of human reality – white lies allowing for misrecognition of radical contingency. Whiteness is born out of the *recognition* that humans are not alone (in a metaphysical sense; that there is a god or ordering mechanism), which is in fact a *misrecognition* of available data and a presumption that human life has innate value.[39] Worth repeating here, the ascription "-idol" exposes this misrecognition as it occurs in these "symbolic manipulations." They are white lies precisely because they are not overt fabrications, but manipulations and purposeful misrecognition of social life as it presents itself to us – as radically contingent social actors. The "idol" in "god-idol" allows for an understanding of these ideas as bound by (and to) social relations and offers a means of definition that does not perpetuate the misrecognition. Yet, these structures described by Bourdieu are very durable and not simple to overcome. As such, "god" remains an important constituent descriptor of god-idols as these centering concepts often work to "[adjust] actual hopes to objective possibilities" in such a way that the question of whether something is a "god" or an "idol" becomes moot and beside the point. More analytically useful than emphasizing these god-idols as either "god" or "idol" is holding in tension the artificial, malleable construction of these god-idols (the existential) while recognizing the intense power, durability, and weight of such misrecognized metaphysical ropes (the social).

God-idols bridge personal, existential concerns with collective, social concerns, ideas born from existential denial that structure epistemological and social relations but that are in fact structured by those same relations – the motivation for Sheriff Thigpin's capitulation. They are individually and collectively constructed ideas that take on the character of being more than the sum total of the logic of their construction – the mob mentality of Williams's murderers. They are the inexpressible behind the unthinkable. They are constitutive of the *a priori* human cognitive need for presumed *a priori* concepts – the demand of the spectators to witness the finality of a dead body. God-idols are the conceptual bridges that cross the intellectual chasms of human reason, to secure an escape from the emotional weight of death by exerting a will-to-power over death – by bringing it about for someone else. They are the presumptions of and about being that address being by suggesting it is more than fleeting, contingent, and limited – the cutting of hair and flesh for trinkets to take home. These white lies hide the initial meaningless of human existence (that meaning must be made) with claims to the contrary – the awareness of white life in the face of black death. God-idols are the always already contingent ideas that respond to human radical contingency by ignoring, denying, or fighting directly against such radical contingency – the walking dead of Ruston, LA (and elsewhere) who have not yet heard of their own death.

This formation necessitates an extended discussion of the relationship between ideas and artifacts, beliefs and practices. Holding in tension Pinn's concern that lynching be understood as religious while appealing to the social-structural theory of Bourdieu,[40] lynching as ritual constitutes an effort to simultaneously address existential and social issues through the creation and reinforcement of ideological structures geared towards social unity, order, and stability. Stated more simply, ideas and beliefs shape material, historical circumstances through the structures they impose on social possibilities; these ideas are also shaped by those possibilities. Combining Pinn's and Bourdieu's efforts helps to balance the paradoxically malleable yet rigid characteristics of these centering, structuring, and structured white lies such as whiteness. Lynchings reinforced and sought a sense of social stability that was questioned when African Americans transgressed socially circumscribed, racialized ways of being and acting. The result of addressing these transgressions through lynching produced whiteness as conterminous with the shared ideals of social order, stability, ability, and value. For many, this whiteness functioned as a central, grounding feature of white life in America.

THE LIFE OF WHITENESS

Race was a means of social oppression prior to emancipation, but the lynching of black Americans directly connects white skin to the demand for certainty and stability, giving a kind of unique hermeneutical birth and life to whiteness in the social environment. Prior to emancipation, the connection was arbitrary and involved outliers like African indentured servants and other free blacks. Lynching brings this intensification to bear, as opposed to enslavement or the auction block[41] (as alternative starting points), because from a functional perspective, slavery amounted to a social death that precluded the enslaved from participating as subjects in society.[42] During the post-bellum period, the connection becomes causal, wherein white skin and black skin come to represent a free/slave dichotomy previously sustained under the system of enslavement. Based on shifting rhetorics and grammars regarding social interests and expectations, the post-bellum period brought about a need to protect white life in a way not needed when slave and free were defined according to legal mandates and theological justifications. The birth of whiteness as a god-idol is indicative of the emerging, prescient emphasis on race to bring about the social stability once afforded through enslavement. Race, class, gender, and sexuality were (and are) always operative as structuring complexes orienting what was possible and not possible. Through the practice of lynching, race – in particular, whiteness and blackness – came to do much of the heavy lifting for the functional maintenance of society, making use of performative rituals that play out in a variety of violent ways.

Such performative violence takes shape through a demand for turning ideas into empirical artifacts. A turn to the father of functionalism, Émile Durkheim, will therefore be helpful in charting these connections. According to Durkheim,[43] ritual is where beliefs are validated and materialized while beliefs "in principle" also shape practice.[44] Durkheim's theorization of totemic religion can be deconstructed as a theorization of god-idols in practice – seeking order, stability, and security through perpetuation of a sacred object, that deconstruction proving constructive for sighting the life of whiteness. For white religion, the sacred object was and is whiteness. And this whiteness is constructed and reinforced through various rituals grounded in but extending beyond lynching. In light of Bourdieu's concerns to take into account the durability of the structuring and structured religious activities, with respect to whiteness, to talk of rituals is also to evoke the ideological cosmologies and identities produced by and producing these rituals.

Part of this process occurs through the ideological projection of these ritualistic practices onto a cosmic screen crafted through manipulation of material environments. In short, these rituals "impose [beliefs] upon us *in fact*,"[45] working to construct overarching portraits of human life in communities which explain the who, what, when, where, and why of persons, places, and things deemed sacred (things set apart) or profane (things that disrupt the thing set apart). More specifically, the profane in Durkheim's sense might on occasion disrupt the realm of the sacred, but the fundamental distinction is between things subject to norms of inviolability vs. things not subject to such norms. Through ritual practice, the system of ascription (i.e., labeling of sacred and profane) offers a cohesive, seemingly complete cosmological picture from which members of a community orient their lives.[46] Whiteness, even in its presumed absence and misrecognition, offers just such historical grounding for these cosmological constructions and points of orientation.

Sociologist and Durkheim translator Karen Fields, arguing that both witchcraft and racecraft are similarly undergirded by maintenance of invisible ontologies, suggests of race that its "practices presuppose a system of belief, [and] confirm it as well."[47] As a result, ritual not only perpetuates and validates belief (the existential function), but also reorders such beliefs (the social function). Such ordering via lynching occurred through ritualistic violence. This violence has helped to absolutize the relative and arbitrary significance of skin color while legitimating that process of absolutization. In other words, whether speaking of lynching or contemporary police execution of African Americans, thanks to the ritual qualities of past racialized murders, skin color matters in determining our temporal proximity to death. Such rites go on to shape cosmologies of participants, for instance the notion of two Americas (one white, one black), as well as the outward and inward identity markers employed by those within the society.

Ideas born from rituals are used not only for cosmological constructions, but also as a means of group identification.[48] Fields helps explain the significance of race as an outward identity marker for those in U.S. society, noting that, "in racecraft, physical features function as a visible index of an invisible essence."[49] Physical, biological differences serve as these outward emblems.[50] Racialization of bodies transmutes these bodies into their own outward identity marker wherein physical features like hands or skin color take on a "hyperphysical significance,"[51] serving as "props" reinforcing a presumption about invisible ontologies that shape group identities.[52] Police officer Darren Wilson, through such racecraft, is thus able to suggest that he killed 18-year-old African American Michael Brown because "it" looked like a demon.[53] Racialized and gendered bodies operate as modern ideo-logical emblems outwardly signaling to others where a person belongs, what that person is worth, and what he or she is able to accomplish. These outward emblems become the ideological labels with which the sacred and profane are created, defined, and maintained.[54] In effort to ensure order and stability, bodies must simultaneously belong to a group and adhere to the stipulations of that group's identity and activity – stipulations worked out and reinforced through ritual. And to press home the reference to Michael Brown's murder, much as was the case with lynching spectacles, Brown's body was left in the street for hours as a reminder that transgressions of these functional codes will not be tolerated.

Rituals in the life of whiteness work to promote inward identity construction also, in the sense that a person comes to define herself or himself through group allegiance and ritual practice. To contextualize this within the U.S., James Cone's presentation of blackness operates in this manner where an invisible ontology of blackness is presumed to exist while physical features like skin color operate as a prop proving that the invisible ontology is real. For Cone, to be black is simultaneously to be oppressed and to have one's identity fundamentally shaped through the fight against that oppression.[55] Black skin ritualistically functions as an outward identity marker where "physical features" expose an "invisible essence."[56] From this, those who have been oppressed because of this outward identity marker are inwardly shaped in response to that oppression. Such ontological blackness reinforces an essential quality for blackness based on the weight of the structuring and structured significance of historical ritualistic practices. This example helps to show that blackness can also be thought of as a god-idol, though here blackness is proxy for demonstrating the significance of its counterpoint – whiteness. White skin, thus, represents essential attributes of being duty-bound and order-driven at the expense of all else, and so many whites rely on such attributes to defend their actions, especially in moments where such social arrangements are confronted.[57] In the process of being labeled and fixed in physical and discursive ways historically, ascribed subjective identities proscribe historical options for identity formation as well. Due to the use of race as an outward identity marker, a white or black person can always be more than "white" or "black," but rarely less than those essences. Per Pinn's suggestion that lynchings effectively "seal" perpetrators and victims in their whiteness and blackness, respectively, the rituals shape not only how others treat an individual or group, but also how individuals and groups define and understand themselves, their value and ability, and their social roles based on these perceptions of value and ability. A closer turn to white identity made possible by rituals of whiteness is in order. Durkheim's well-known ritual typology offers readymade guidance: negative, positive, imitative, and piacular.[58]

Negative rites of whiteness: sacred whiteness

Signs which read "Whites Only" and "Colored" dotted the commercial landscape of huge swaths of U.S. businesses for decades. The establishment and placement of a segregation sign involves processes that reinforce beliefs about what whites and blacks are to do and be and where they are to congregate. Once placed, these signs operate interdictively for those who read them and who are exposed to their meaning. Such negative rituals make use of ideas about group identity to determine and proscribe what not to do, or be.[59] In terms of how this operates in U.S. history concerning the life of whiteness, various ritualistic interdictions amount to segregation practices (broadly understood), including specific Jim and Jane Crow laws, the "one-drop rule," and anti-miscegenation legislation.

These segregation rituals do not offer mandates on how to act so much as they "forbid certain ways of acting."[60] Whites and blacks are not told what to do, but what not to do – do not transgress the racialized borders establishing white from black. Durkheim suggests these interdictions "separate two sacred things of different species from each other"[61] or sacred things from profane things. One example of this is the "one drop rule," which sociologists refer to as "hypodescent" whereby white sacrality is deemed so susceptible to tainting that even one drop of black blood will make profane that which was once sacred.[62] As a specific example, in 1938 – the year of the Williams lynching – U.S. senator Allen J. Ellender from Houma, Louisiana – the state in which the lynching took place – famously filibustered for twenty-seven hours against an anti-lynching bill. In this and other speeches, he would exaggerate the radical contingency of white and black, extolling the importance of white purity and black profanity with quotes like "Any Negro of notable ability owes success to white blood" and "Negro blood has degraded and ultimately destroyed every white civilization where allowed to mongrelize."[63] Such statements were common on the U.S. Senate floor, and the latter is an acute example of fear of (yet blindness to) twilight. Biologically, there is no such thing as either white or black blood, and yet, such interdictions have influenced many laws in the U.S.[64] and countless cultural mores and racialized ways of being outside the legal system. Thinking of this rule in terms of the sacred/profane binary, if the "sacred" white blood comes in contact with even the smallest amount of "profane" black blood, it is marred, "blackened" and deemed corrupt. Through these and other instances of racialized interdictions like segregation laws, whiteness as god-idol is reinforced through ideological claims, and the dehumanization of African Americans exonerates the practice of lynching as somehow palatable, as part of some inevitable social Darwinism. Whiteness comes to be understood as a rubric of pristine order and certainty, and blackness that which would tarnish the certain, sacred whiteness. White lies.

In terms specific to the function of such negative interdicts in the construction of whiteness, journalist and senior advisor at the Nicolas Berggruen Institute Scott Malcomson notes that the one drop rule "made the physical metaphysical"[65] in that skin color took on significance larger than biological. Malcomson's comments help express the implication of these racist practices for the life of whiteness, in that such practices simultaneously hid the existential "essence" of white people (i.e., no essence at all) and in the process of denying such radical contingency, produced the specter of whiteness as the god-idol capable of functioning as existential and social point of orientation. Following Bourdieu, such processes allow the groups (in this case, white and black)[66] to be misrecognized as natural and absolute when they are actually a product of these ritual practices. At once, negative practices reinforce through negation and misrecognition what not to do, how not to be, and through such negations produce whiteness without direct attention to that production. In the negation, there is a presumption that the categories already exist and so these interdictions are deemed necessary to stay within proper boundaries. The negative practices actually create the boundaries through the ritual,[67] effectively isolating whiteness and blackness as distinct, real, and essential through the interdiction.

Other specific negative interdictions include anti-miscegenation laws serving as a corollary to the "one drop rule," Jim and Jane Crow laws and segregation signs such as "colored" and "white" drinking fountains, and a whole host of other negative practices involving "racial etiquette."[68] Where white religion is concerned, the most significant function of these negative rites involves the construction of racialized codes of conduct and existence. In no way an exhaustive list, a few examples of these codes include black men not talking to white women, expectations that blacks would yield their position on sidewalks to whites, that blacks would never talk "out of turn," and even the manner in which white children would refer to black adults as "boy" or "girl." Breach of such ideological norms created literal social ruptures as these transgressions called into question the ability of the functional system to reinforce and produce the god-idol of whiteness structuring and structured by the practice. Stated bluntly, the fact that women and men could have sex across racial boundaries without the cosmology being thrown asunder meant, ironically, even greater need to punish the transgressions lest the system be exposed for what it was, a façade, a system of white lies. Transgressions exposed the artificial boundaries created to evade human limits and uncertainty. Because of this, transgressions were met with punishment, often in the form of lynching. Punishment for sexual mixing of races often meant death for the African American involved.[69] But practices such as lynching were more significant than their disciplinary effects, as the practice actually functions as the central point of origin and reinforcement for whiteness.

Positive rites of whiteness: deadly offerings

Positive rites carry the weight of whiteness in the form of what Pinn sardonically labels as "rope neckties."[70] If god-idols are the ropes tying together existential and social realities with the functional denial of radical contingency, then, as noted earlier in this chapter, the lynch rope is a poignant hermeneutical tool for understanding white religion giving birth and life to whiteness. Positive rites, in one of their manifestations, see to it that the weight of whiteness is paid with black bodies hanging from ropes. Positive rites include "regulatory and organizational" ceremonies and activities for navigating the social order.[71] That is, these are rituals ultimately based on the preservation of the social system,[72] often played out as sacrifices that ensure "the prosperity of the species."[73] In the U.S., historically, lynching constitutes this type of ritual.

Lynched black bodies became a means of reinforcing, testing, and augmenting the social order, serving the function of structuring the social environment through violence. Such practices constituted and reconstituted the god-idol of whiteness through the subjugation of black bodies that carried the weight of possibility of transgressing a belief in sacred whiteness organizing the social environment. In fact, many lynchings were motivated by racialized and sexualized perceptions of transgression. One of many examples is that of Edward Coy, who in 1892 was held in a prison cell in Texarkana, Arkansas (not far from Ruston, Louisiana) charged with the rape of a white woman. With evidence mounting that Coy's relationship had been consensual, a mob grew so angry they removed him from his cell, before any trial, tied him to a tree, flayed his skin, and poured oil over his body before setting him ablaze.[74] In face of his having had sex with a white woman, or having offended the Victorian sensibilities of white women's image, or having transgressed other artificial yet powerful negative rituals, lynching was the inverse and complementary practice of reinforcing the negative interdictions and recalibrating the social order. Well-known anti-lynching crusader Ida B. Wells-Barnett's pamphlet *Southern Horrors* (1892) explains that these lynchings were not, in fact, simply motivated by vigilante concerns to punish rapists, as she notes, "They know the men of the section of the country who refuse this are not so desirous of punishing rapists as they pretend. The utterances of the leading white men show that with them it is not the crime but the class."[75] Whiteness required more from its adherents than simply telling social actors what *not* to do. Rather, through a confluence of raced, gendered, and classed concerns and decisions, lynchings reinforced an overarching white ideal, which gave way to popular slogans like "This is a white man's country and the white man must rule."[76]

Such "bloody oblations"[77] and sacrificial offerings constituted a sanctuary of violence and terror in ironic juxtaposition to the image of white people as civil, quiet, and reasonable. These sanctuaries operated as a sacralized reference point for a ritual reinforcing the dehumanization of black bodies and the subsequent exaggerations of radical contingency of white and black alike. Such "positive" practices constitute the backbone, the most functionally useful ritual of reference, organizing white religious racialized life in late nineteenth- and twentieth-century U.S. society. Indeed, lynchings were a reference point for white life.

But why did lynchings take on this referential quality? Social anthropologist Mary Douglas might offer some insights. She famously addresses Durkheim's theory of social solidarity as framed by "emotional effervescence, the idea that rituals rouse violent, ecstatic feelings, like crowd hysteria, which convince the worshipper of the reality of a power greater than and beyond the self" and which produce "the emotion of outrage, the idea of sacred contagion and consequent dangers to the community unleashed by breach of cherished norms."[78] Contextualized to the U.S., such effects offer a means of making sense of the production of whiteness. Douglas famously crafts the grid-group theory as criterion for evaluating the actual variety of functional mechanisms existing in societies across time and space, arriving at the position that the body is the locus, rationale, and canvas for such symbolization.[79] She replaces the emotional effervescence Durkheim suggests is the functional ritual mechanism for producing social solidarity with the body, and offers the grid-group model as a means of assessing the proportional relationship between bodily control and social control.

Lynching marks a moment when Durkheim's and Douglas's analyses coalesce in black bodies. The emotional effervescence of the lynch mob reinforces the certainty of the act of lynching, absolutizing and legitimating the practice by short-circuiting any ability to reflect on the practice. At the same time the forced subjugation of the black body – hanging from a tree – marks the site at which the social, material function of ritual translates individual concerns into group concerns. DuRocher notes that, within the Jim Crow South, lynching served as a ritual producing this group solidarity.[80] Lynching, understood as a positive ritual, served this dual function of situating (white) emotional effervescence at the site and sight of a (black body), aiding in misrecognition of the functional effects of the practice on those white bodies, as well as exposing – through difference and social ruptures – the dead black body, the mechanism giving birth to whiteness, as an inability to accept limits and uncertainties. This coalescence produced, gave functional life to, the god-idol of whiteness.

Imitative, commemorative, and representative rites of whiteness: white **lived** *religion*

Even one hundred years ago lynchings were not a daily occurrence, although they certainly were frequent. Sacrificial rituals did not have to take place continuously for their functional effects to continue. More rudimentary rituals could stand in as reminder of the sacrificial offering. Imitative, commemorative, and representational rites did this work – as they do today. With each enactment, the effects of previous ritualistic action are symbolically reproduced in new ways, "assur[ing] the fecundity of the totemic species" (in this case, whiteness) through rites which "serve the same end, whether they accompany the preceding ones or replace them."[81] These imitative, commemorative, and representative rites amount to different – albeit equally important – structuring and structured practices reinforcing the functional effects of the sacrificial ritual, or symbolically recreating its effects in perpetuity. These rituals do not replace lynching, but allow the effects of lynching to continue into the future even though the lynchings no longer occur as frequently or at all. They point back to, and remind of, what is learned and stabilized in the sacrifice, serving as "variations of the essential rite whereby social groups reaffirm themselves periodically."[82]

Seemingly mundane racist practices carry the weight of those lynched in history. For instance, one of the first racist jokes I ever learned (and which is consequentially ingrained in my mind) goes as follows: Q: Why do niggers always have sex on their mind? A: Because their pubic hair is on their head. Such jokes are the stuff of schoolyard fodder in many parts of the U.S. to this day. And though obviously ethically problematic and politically incorrect, they carry a functional efficacy. With this joke alone, blackness is denigrated, a "nigger" is presumed to reference a particular type of person, a person dehumanized and profaned physically through lynching. Historically, lynching served to reinforce this dehumanized status, while employing the term "nigger" reinforces the same status in a less physically violent way. Indeed, if there is a baseline definition of "nigger" in America, it must certainly be "expendable." In the telling, African Americans are hypersexualized and the commentary on hair reinforces a learned aesthetic appreciation and disdain for white and black hair textures, respectively. Such hypersexual exaggerations have an historical precedent, wherein black sexuality was not only exaggerated but the exaggeration was often used to exonerate the moral indiscretions of whites, such as one Southern white man's claim that "I don't call [miscegenation] seduction by white men, for what really happens is the Negro women seduce the white man."[83] Such jokes and quips reinforce aspects of whiteness produced during lynchings (and other possible rituals of reference such as white male rape of black women), perpetuating these white lies in an evasive fashion, offering the joke teller the ability to claim humor or ignorance.

Additional commemorative rites include nomenclature associated with arbitrary aspects of life (e.g., "nigger birds," "nigger rich," "niggertown," etc.), which further conflate black people as problematic and endangering and disconnected from white people. Theologian George Kelsey's early work on race and Christianity discusses this practice, offering an explanation and another example. Kelsey notes that "racial terms, in the racist world of thought, come to symbolize values and expectations in general. If things do not measure up to expectations, they are 'nigger' or 'niggerish,'" such "as a bad bridge, which is called a 'nigger bridge.'"[84] Here, these "arbitrary" comments rely on various exaggerations to legitimate the perspective that black people and life is of less value and ability than its inverse, white people and life.

Other rites of whiteness include defamation of property (e.g., church burnings),[85] cross burnings, and lynchings in effigy, many of these practices having taken place within the last decade. One such church burning occurred in 2009 in retaliation for Barack Obama's historic election victory. An affidavit for the case reads that the defendants "were angry about the election of Barack Obama and discussed burning the black church"[86] for some sort of racialized retribution. Another occurred in 2014 when Flood Christian Church, the church home of Michael Brown Sr., was burned to the ground on the heels of Darren Wilson not being indicted in the murder of Michael Brown.[87] As for cross burnings, the Southern Poverty Law Center's Intelligence Project found that over 200 occurred in the U.S. from 1994–1998 alone.[88] The hanging of nooses[89] and lynchings in effigy[90] have also occurred in recent years. These activities reinforce the originary positive ritual of lynching and other forms of direct bodily terror such as rape, preserving a cosmology created and sustained by negative and positive rituals working in tandem. Such imitative, commemorative, and representational rituals become the means through which the life of whiteness endures. And in fact, the seemingly mundane rituals (e.g., not as vicious as public castration) constitute a plausible deniability for those held in sway by the god-idol of whiteness. That is, when questioned, the rituals are rationalized as mere jokes, geographic descriptors like "niggertown" are explained away as "the only thing we knew to call the place,"[91] and church burnings and nooses are offered as political statements that have nothing to do with racial hatred.[92]

Though these rites may or may not always carry the same explicit ethical bankruptcy as segregation laws or the bodily terror of lynching, such rituals help to absolutize the relative idea of whiteness as sacred and to legitimate its ultimately arbitrary constitution. These rituals return attention to the memory and functional effects of lynching, effects situated over and against black death. And so whiteness as god-idol emerges out of death. To focus on death, to remember these black offerings, calls to attention the final ritual of whiteness, the piacular.

Piacular rites of whiteness: the sorrow of white religion

What is to be made of the emergence, the birth of whiteness, as springing from black bodily death? What comes of a society when it recognizes that all of the death it imposed does not prevent its own death or the death of those held in its power? The final rites of whiteness are piacular rites, understood as rites that respond to the sorrow associated with death (in an acute, individual physical sense and in a cosmic collective human finitude sense). Mourning is one example of these rites, and includes instances of both ritualistic mourning (self-immolation and forced bereavement for the deceased) and collective emotional effervescences born of the trauma experienced by a community in response to loss.[93] Piacular rites involve atonement, an attempt to set right what has (or will) come to an end.

In the context of my characterization of these ritual practices, piacular rites of whiteness might include instances that expose the damage done by whiteness as a means of responding to some sort of loss, a loss discussed below. Specific examples include the already cited Lillian Smith book *Killers of the Dream* (1949), wherein a white Southern woman tries to expose whiteness to the harm it has done and attempts to come to terms with that personal and collective legacy. Other literary works also serve this role, such as Carson McCullers's *The Heart Is a Lonely Hunter* (1940) with its portrayal of the difficulty of black and white relations in the face of the existential and social weight of racialized life in the U.S. These works are but two examples of white responses to white religion and both examples are discussed later in *White Lies*. Here, it is best to understand *White Lies* as rooted in recognition that contemporary race relations in the U.S. constitute an extended case study into the "piaculum" of whiteness and of white religion more generally – an awareness and exposure of its impending end and a subsequent demand for atonement, a renegotiation of the social order in its broadest sense. A "piaculum" contains "every misfortune, everything of evil omen, everything that inspires sentiments of sorrow or fear."[94] To the extent this book is an effort to "learn to die" in both ideological and sociological senses, it begins here with lynching and whiteness, looking to an idea that "inspires sorrow or fear." But whether the book is a piaculum in its own right remains uncertain, and is a topic returned to in more depth in the final chapter. Taking a cue from the piacular, the discussion moves next to the connection between whiteness and death and asks if a focus on death and mourning offers any insight into whiteness as it operates across various domains of power today.

THE DEATH OF WHITENESS

These various domains constitute the social – society more broadly and abstractly framed. God-idols are "real" to the extent that the society or the individual within the social reinforces them with the rituals and beliefs necessary for their structure and their structuring. Such reinforcement gives them the kind of "life" described above. But does whiteness still function in these existential and social ways for the white demographic that gives birth and life to whiteness? The contemporary moment is very different from and yet very similar to the overtly racist society marked powerfully by the *de jure* segregation and rampant vigilante justice that gave birth to whiteness as a god-idol. What are we to make of whiteness when historicized towards its seemingly waning significance? Is there a way to hold in balance continuing racist activity while recognizing that on the whole, white people today are less motivated in such explicitly racist ways? Do white Americans "worship" whiteness with less frequency or intensity than as characterized above? Or are things the same? Even without solid answers to these questions, contemporary studies at the intersection of race and religion could historicize whiteness – that is, update whiteness to meet contemporary social issues – through three heuristic lenses: the death of *whiteness's* ability to serve the function(s) of god-idol, the *death* of whiteness as the physical deaths that continue based on the legacy left from employing whiteness as god-idol, and ultimately, the *twilight* of whiteness.

The death of whiteness

The first of these heuristic frames is the death of *whiteness* as a god-idol, a functional death, and can be seen in the existential and social (dys)functions felt more and more by white people today, as something about their social position (as white) leaves them feeling encroached upon, uncertain, and limited. In effect, as the god-idol of whiteness "dies," it is made visible to its beneficiaries ironically through its increasingly limited effectiveness.

This (dys)function suggests that whiteness comes to force recognition of radical contingency in a manner contrary to the function whiteness served historically to ignore, deny, or fight against it. Though whiteness has not *actually* died ideologically or discursively, its ability to function for white people appears to have shifted significantly enough to begin questioning its longevity and deployment as a god-idol. The contemporary moment (in all its complexity) requires an interpretation of whiteness that does not give it more credit than it deserves; thinking about its functional "death" aids in such a new interpretation. White people can certainly still be racist, and many are, but my argument here is that such racism is no longer as existentially or socially useful as it once was historically. Failure to take the shifting functional utility of whiteness into account gives history too much credit and assumes historical experiences are unidimensional and fall along a narrow, oppressor/oppressed, white/black binary.

Though racism is alive and well in U.S. society, whiteness's increasing inability to function as a denial of radical contingency might signal the start of its death. Contemporary white life is not guided principally by a concern over whiteness. For many whites, white skin is no longer a significant proxy for ignoring, fighting against, or denying radical contingency. Radical contingency is still fought against by these white people, and with other yet-to-be-discussed god-idols, but in fewer and fewer instances does this demographic appeal directly to race and skin color in order to serve this function. Moreover, as discussed below, recognition of white skin evokes a growing sense of uncertainty. Yet, history does still carry much weight. Even this discussion of the death of whiteness as god-idol begins (again) with a black offering.

According to many commentators, one of the "last" U.S. lynchings occurred in 1981.[95] Nineteen-year-old Michael Donald was sought out by three Ku Klux Klan members and was murdered in Mobile, Alabama specifically because he was black. The murderers recounted at a subsequent trial that they had "put the rope around his neck and put our boots up against his face – and just pulled tight on that rope until he had no breath left in him."[96] Donald was chosen at random as the three murderers were literally looking to kill the first African American they saw. The murder was in retaliation for a recent mistrial having set free a different African American man (not Donald) who had been charged with murdering a white police officer. The racist murderers were arrested, tried, and convicted of various charges and the ringleader, Klan member Henry Hays, was sentenced to death and executed in 1997.[97]

Not only have lynching numbers decreased exponentially in the last decades,[98] the subsequent execution of the principal lyncher Hays is evidence to the fact that, in certain respects, lynchings and other racialized murders are now punished either through hate crime legislation or traditional local, state, or federal juridical means. When a ritual is no longer validated by the bulk of those within a group, its functional effectiveness must be called into question in that its efforts would no longer produce the social solidarity manipulating radical contingency. So in certain respects, the god-idol of whiteness produced from such ritualistic practices in history might be thought of as dead in the sense that, although whiteness may still operate as a discursive idea or ideal, many of its beneficiaries no longer validate the central sacrificial ritual which produced it – meaning that whiteness may no longer be the justification for or means of denying, fighting, or ignoring radical contingency ... even as these same beneficiaries *continue to benefit* from the rituals of a bygone era.

Moving past this point of social solidarity, today, lynchings and other hate-based crimes (like the murder of James Byrd, Jr. in Jasper, Texas in 1998) often no longer carry the collective justification of having transgressed a social sanction or interdictive rite. That Donald was murdered without having transgressed a racialized interdiction calls into question its ritual operation. Can this particular murder be framed in terms of a ritual of reference? Or, is it a commemorative ritual meant to hark back to the social system previously produced through societal worship of whiteness?

Unlike many lynchings historically, Donald's murderers were not using extralegal means to preserve a legal system. Rather, the transgression was their own, in that they had become alienated from the society as a whole. They perceived themselves the new outsiders of a changing society. Their crime was a similarly violent yet grotesque inversion of the violence doled out by Bigger Thomas in Richard Wright's *Native Son* as retaliation for the alienation of African Americans historically. Only this time, those alienated were the hateful whites still under the intense grip of whiteness as a god-idol, but angry over their worship of a god-idol that no longer functioned as it promised. In distinction to the bulk of historical lynchings which carried the intent to punish a transgression, the murder of Donald does not seemingly recalibrate the legal system in the manner used to justify lynching previously.

In many instances historically, this issue of transgression determined the community's acceptance of or disdain for a racialized murder.[99] Without this communal sanction, it becomes more difficult to characterize whiteness as a god-idol – even as its effects still linger to shape notions of white and black identity. Donald's murder fits within a legal system that now has (by its own *questionable* admission) expanded to include individuals and activities across race so that not only are the lynchers punished, one was even executed. Historicizing whiteness helps to foreground that the decreasing ritual activity of lynching (as punishment for transgression) has been largely abandoned and when it appears, the perpetrators (the vigilantes) are alienated from the very group they seek to benefit – an alienation also inspiring the crime. This shift does not indicate some arrival at utopian color-blindness or that other topics like police vigilantism do not deserve attention. Nevertheless, legal punishment for lynching might suggest a functional death for whiteness as god-idol, in that the central mechanism constructing whiteness, the ritual of lynching, is no longer appealed to for these functional ends. Its ritual effects are not functionally positive, but commemorative, imitating a past era still longed for (but lost) by many whites. Worth noting, this does not mean that whiteness may not exert an influence through these commemorative rituals. It simply suggests that the sum total of this influence is no longer significant enough to characterize whiteness as the central concern of the white population who created it (historically), benefitted from it historically, and continue to profit from it today.

Historicizing whiteness foregrounds that, in some respects, the existential referents produced from lynching have shifted significantly. For the killers of Donald, an inversion takes place wherein the exoneration of an African American in a court of law sent the white killers into an identity tailspin. Ironically, the court of law became its own ritual of reference in contradistinction to the ritual of lynching that for so long plugged the racist "holes" of the criminal justice system. For these white criminals, for the legal system to "benefit" African Americans through equal protection under the law, caused recognition (on the part of the criminals) that the social system created by the god-idol of whiteness had fundamentally changed. This appears to have alienated the individuals who had made a practice of alienating African Americans from the system for so long. Perhaps, this alienation experienced by the worshippers of whiteness produced in them an existential angst and awareness of their own radical contingency that white religion had not prepared them to confront. In retaliation, a commemoration ritual was in order. Only, this time the commemoration took on the quality of the initial ritual of reference, a lynching, and the commemoration was punished by the very community it sought to reassure.

For Donald's killers, the perceived referent emerging from the justice system working on behalf of African Americans reinforced their belief that now whites were no longer part of the society. The white society that lynching served to secure was no longer able to address the needs of these priests of a (now?) dead god-idol. Whiteness seemingly had died. In retaliation and for the (possible) sake of applying an existential salve to their awareness of their own radical contingency, a vicious murder was undertaken as a commemorative sacrifice to the now dead god-idol of whiteness. In a paradoxical sense, the awareness that whiteness has died forces recognition that whiteness is still alive and well, as that death reinforces the historic rituals of reference.

Such a referential quality is different today than it was historically because the norms with which white people operate have also shifted. In short, for most people, white skin's ability to deny radical contingency is no longer understood as worthy of these black offerings and murderous sacrifices. That is, white people are no longer willing to accept that whiteness is worth sacrificial murder. Lynchings, if and when they occur in the contemporary period, are investigated, prosecuted, and condemned by those (many white) in many stations of society where it was once acceptable to turn a complicit eye or participate outright in the ritual of reference. Lynchings, when occurring today, may still localize whiteness and blackness as their shared referents for the perpetrators and victims of the crime, but this racialized referent no longer trumps the demand for legal justice – meaning whiteness may still be alive but its status as god-idol is questionable because it appears to no longer serve as the last word or trump card for the society. It is no longer of *supreme* importance, even if racial justice is still not afforded for African Americans.

Donald's murder helps to frame ongoing challenges regarding the relationship between whiteness and white people, both in the popular imagination and within scholarship. Some might suggest that the growing numbers of hate groups in the U.S. is indicative of a resurgent appeal to the god-idol of whiteness. This may be historically understandable – this discussion recognizes as much, to be sure – but it does not meet a demand to understand race and whiteness as it operates today; it does not allow for a hermeneutic that would simultaneously hold in tension past and present racial atrocities and injustices with the contemporary shifting significance of whiteness as understood by the bulk of white people today. Growing numbers of hate groups including but extending beyond the KKK do not equate to an increased influence of whiteness operating as a god-idol in society, but may rather be a result of its waning influence and the subsequent existential (dys) function required for many racist whites as a consequence. In fact, these increasing numbers may suggest a functional rupture between whiteness and its status as a god-idol.

As worship of the god-idol of whiteness has diminished, statistics bear out that racial hatred groups have grown in numbers – in particular, over the last two decades. On their hate watch list, the Southern Poverty Law Center indicates that, "since 2000, the number of hate groups has increased by 67 percent." This may suggest to readers that my argument for the death of whiteness is either wrong or misguided as it ignores this increase in hate groups. Yet, the SPLC immediately follows this statistic with a rationale for the increase: "This surge has been fueled by anger and fear over the nation's ailing economy, an influx of non-white immigrants, and the diminishing white majority, as symbolized by the election of the nation's first African American president."[100] What many might initially read as an increase in race-based politics and influence from the god-idol of whiteness can actually be recognized as the loud fringe cries of those not happy with the admittedly few but important *positive* racial changes that have taken place in the country. For those left worshipping the god-idol of whiteness, their fury makes sense and they might likely be more keen to exact hate through violence, as they have already perceived a dead or dying whiteness that they are now trying to bring to life or keep alive. Whether dead or alive, what is fairly clear (to them) is that whiteness is on its functional deathbed. Rather than these groups indicating a resurgent whiteness, the rationale for their anger is what marks the functional death of whiteness, in that their perception of lost control over the economy, decreasing numbers of whites, increasing non-white immigrants, and other developments cause these fringe groups to grow as they make room for those who feel themselves alienated from the changing society. As a consequence of this perceived alienation, these fringe groups grow and emerge more loudly and in increasing numbers than when the overall society held more allegiance to whiteness as a god-idol. However, in distinction from a similar growth of the KKK during Reconstruction, these contemporary groups tend to be splintered with no collective, critical mass, unable to shape the larger society in their ideological direction. Analogically speaking, a dying whiteness screams more loudly than a healthy whiteness, meaning that these groups are not a signal of strength but of a growing awareness that they carry less and less weight in shaping society in Imago Superlata, in the image of exaggeration. White religion is beginning to recognize its twilight. Rather than making a statement about the strength of whiteness, hate groups call into question its functional effectiveness and indicate that the larger, once "white" society now alienates those who worship whiteness explicitly as much as it has alienated (and continues to alienate) many African Americans. Historicizing is not an attempt to conceal the ironies, but to reveal them.

As an example outside of race, it is helpful to move from talk of an economy of whiteness to an economy of Christian religious affiliation. In the U.S. over the last fifty years, church membership and affiliation has decreased across the board.[101] Concurrent with this decrease, there has been a growing fundamentalism and evangelicalism to the point that Christianity in popular discourse is often conflated with a fundamentalist tone and theology. Some might argue that this growth indicates a resurgent Christianity. But it is equally possible to argue that this fundamentalism is a type of religious blowback to the waning functional significance of Christianity in society.[102] Currently, fundamentalist groups may be speaking more loudly than mainline Christian communities, but those voices are not necessarily representative of the sentiments of the overall population of Christians. In parallel fashion, the contemporary murders of African Americans by police and vigilantes have brought with them a legion of defenders of such atrocities. The vociferous tone of these defenders of "law and order" are indeed reason to remain guarded about the contemporary power of whiteness, but these voices (often white) are not *necessarily* representative of all white Americans, or even most white Americans, and certainly not most Americans across demographics. Suggesting or acting otherwise is simply a logical fallacy wherein the part is taken as the whole, and the group is judged against the worst within the group, a classic prejudiced position.

Moving from Christian fundamentalism to a more focused look at race, another example of this logical fallacy involves moments when racist negative stereotypes shape perceptions of the entire black community, as in moments when all black women are presumed to be mammies or jezebels.[103] Just as it is problematic that many have employed a cultural imagination to correlate these stereotypes to the actual identities of black women, it is equally logically problematic when the opposite is undertaken – as in a conflation of members of hate groups or law enforcement supporters as indicative of the sentiments of the larger society. Going from these proxies back to whiteness, to take the part for the whole in this instance and correlate the growth or sentiments of quantitatively fringe hate groups to the sentiments of the bulk of white people is to stereotype all white people as holding a kind of transhistorical positionality regarding whiteness, without adequate evidence. The problem occurs when an overarching white population is presumed to be represented by a contemporary fringe group. In certain respects, the logical fallacy amounts to an interpretive disagreement based on generational shifts and perspectival differences based on race, age, and other social factors. Connecting a violent fringe group to a general population is easier for someone who lived through something like segregation. But for a generation of scholars who are the product of school busing and hip hop (as two of many historical differences), such a connection is less tenable as it does not take into account the shifts that have taken place in society over time. My argument emerges from the latter perspective. An historicized whiteness does not bring with it adequate evidence to suggest that whiteness operates as a god-idol in a way it once did. This does not at all mean that racism is not still a problem, nor does it mean that whiteness is not also still a problem or an operative god-idol for many, and nor does it even mean that most or many whites do not currently know overtly "racist" whites.[104] It simply, but importantly, means that whiteness is not now doing the work it once did. And that is a good thing. Assuming such connections and motivations between general white populations and hate groups gives too much weight to history, presenting it as fixed and rigid in a way that betrays very significant changes in U.S. history over the last century. This does not mean that white individuals or groups are no longer racist, and as I hope this book makes clear, my argument here is not an attempt to exonerate whites from the excruciating work that falls on us now to right so many social ships. But it might mean that in certain instances, geographies, or social settings, such racism is no longer significant enough to characterize whiteness as a centering concept for the bulk of white people – even if many of them remain "racist" and many more still hold allegiance (of one sort or another) to white religion.

Other factors also contribute to the existential (dys)function of whiteness and further situate the consequences of conflating whiteness and white people today. Historically, whiteness functioned to enable whites to ignore or deny radical contingency. Today, increasing instances exist wherein whiteness increasingly exposes whites to their radical contingency. Many whites today feel alienated because they are white. Here, I don't mean to celebrate or refute the suggestion, but to anthropologically take it as evidence that perhaps some of the tools we've inherited and that we use to talk about and make sense of race and religion must be renegotiated. For instance, in a study of the analytic implications of the concept of whiteness as employed by antiracist activist scholars, anthropologist John Hartigan uses racialized political tensions in Detroit, Michigan to show that for many whites in the area, whiteness appears to do as much to increase anxiety as it does to ameliorate it because of a presumption (by non-whites) that whites are motivated by whiteness and (to use my terms) that such a motivation is effective in denying radical contingency.[105] When these historically understandable presumptions about racist whites meet up with the acute demographics of a specific location like Detroit (which is predominately African American), whites more and more often experience both real and/or perceived alienation from certain political processes.[106] Because of this complexity, Hartigan ultimately concludes that more antiracists should "ground their insights about whiteness in an ethnographic orientation towards their subjects" rather than presume an operative whiteness where there may be none.[107] This discussion of the functional death of whiteness attempts such grounding. With social scientist Alastair Bonnett, Hartigan argues against scholarship that acts as if a "myth of whiteness"[108] continues to undergird white political motivations. Hartigan argues that much antiracist scholarship "does not recognize that today, whites are mired in fundamentally racial predicaments: trying to regain control of their identifying features, disoriented by the disjuncture between a projected social identity (as whites) and personal experience, feeling the inadequate fit of stereotyped depictions."[109] Following Hartigan, whiteness appears today to be growing existentially (dys)functional, in the sense that it often exposes whites to their own radical contingency. This inability to ignore the existential, this "death," results from a combination of legal efforts, shifting demographics, and postmodern sensibilities that question the nature of the philosophical, political, and racialized subject. Quite simply, the existential (dys)function of the god-idol of whiteness means that in the increasingly complex U.S. social context, appeals to whiteness often add to a cacophony of social chaos, exposing the radical contingency of whites even as they still benefit from white skin in other ways.

The second component of the death of *whiteness* is its social (dys)function. Here, a question is posed, a kind of thought experiment. Could it be that various shifting demographics as exemplified by Detroit, punishment and contempt for lynching (and decreasing occurrences), fewer representational, commemorative, and imitative rites (increasing political correctness), and growing disdain by many for all of these rites when they do emerge, may signal the fundamental dissolution of the "white" society itself as it has been constituted historically by this god-idol of whiteness? Could not also this dissolution be precisely what causes these fringe groups to grow and become more vocal? Might not – and it pains me to write this for fear of sounding callous – but might not the murders of African Americans by authorities over these last decades be indicative of the *decreasing* effectiveness of whiteness, even if also an expression of a renewed longing to reconstitute the god-idol? This does not mean whiteness has ceased to operate. Rather, the functional death of whiteness indicates a rupture between whiteness (as god-idol) and the white demographic that once created it, in that the contemporary period and an ever-increasing racial complexity suggests that whiteness no longer functions as a god-idol effectively ignoring and evading radical contingency. And in fact, it should be an open question if such effectiveness *ever* marked society as "white."

In terms of demographics, socially the U.S. is on the verge of a racial tipping point. According to U.S. Census Bureau reports, by 2050 those who identify as white will no longer be the statistical majority.[110] This may be welcome news to some, but based on past racism resulting from *fears of* social uncertainty and stability, these very real impending demographic shifts could intensify racial tension and violence if whites do not learn to embrace their decreasing numbers and the *possibility of* decreasing political power. The largely white Tea Party movement offers an example of anxiety playing out in the social arena as comments and election bumper stickers such as "take back America" and "Don't Re-NIG" speak to a longing for a past sense of social stability, a stability that resulted largely from overt dehumanization of and discrimination against African Americans, all women, other racial and ethnic non-whites, and sexually marginal social actors. Though politically and ethically problematic in numerous ways, this movement also signals and foregrounds white radical contingency and an attempt to deny it yet again. How analysts and scholars register such activities amounts, again, to an interpretive decision based largely on generational, racial, and other differences. Simultaneously, even as the Tea Party movement represents a collective effort to reproduce such a "white" society, it helps to diagnose the growing inability of whiteness to function as a means of denying the radical contingency of those who created the god-idol. In spite of this symptom of the functional death of whiteness, the Tea Party marks a moment to remain vigilant that such a god-idol is not resurrected.

Other examples of this social (dys)function include instances such as the recent Trayvon Martin/George Zimmerman case, and the public discussions of race and whiteness to emerge from it. Public conversations about Zimmerman's race call into question the very constitution of whiteness in the popular imagination as still an ideal-typical concept, and yet no longer exclusively "owned" by the white population having created it. It also notes an expansion (across races) of the population seeking to construct and "worship" this god-idol beyond those labeled "white."[111] Who, today, determines the connection between whiteness and white people? Perhaps, whiteness has died of its ability to serve a single racialized community as a god-idol. Echoing the concerns of Hartigan, ownership over whiteness (as a category) seems to not always fall on white people to determine. This calls into question the functional usefulness of whiteness for the white people who created it as increasing racialized complexity decreases the ability of white people to appeal to whiteness to bolster a false sense of security and certainty. This is not to say that such ritualistic acts of violence when they occur do not continue to reinforce certain ideological underpinnings within the society. That is, a future racialized murder may still reinforce whiteness but it is not clear if such murders would serve as effective a function as occurred historically with lynchings. To take a brief and specific instance, though genealogical connections between W.C. Williams's lynching discussed earlier and the murder of Trayvon Martin are easy and at times useful to make, the society has changed enough to recognize that, though such murders may do similar kinds of white religious work, their effectiveness at creating distance from uncertainty for whites is variable. There is simply a growing fluidity and malleability of the concepts, ideas, and responses produced from such violent practices. Perhaps, whiteness as god-idol "dies" when whites lose control of defining the concept and no longer have the ability to appeal to it (directly) for social stability and unity, even as violence will likely continue and may even increase as reaction to the (dys)function.

Taken together, these contemporary existential and social (dys)functions require a new way of approaching whiteness that takes into account its waning traditional functions for white people as well as the continued effects of the god-idol on everyone. Though whiteness has not died ideologically or discursively, its functional use by white people is not what it once was and these shifts should be recognized. As such, whiteness (as god-idol) might be framed as "dead" to the extent that it is neither contemporarily agreed upon by its beneficiaries and victims, to the extent that its rituals are often problematized and punished, and to the extent that it increasingly and ironically exposes whites to their own radical contingency.

And yet, the commemorative and representational rituals of whiteness persevere, even if the practice of lynching seems a (not too) distant memory. How might contemporary analyses take into account the shifts having taken place since the Civil Rights movement while remaining aware that though *whiteness's* functions may be dead or dying, its death-dealing effects still linger and necessitate a new Civil Rights movement? In the next section, I turn back to the physical deaths caused by whiteness.

The death *of whiteness*

The preceding section is meant to foreground that whiteness increasingly fails to do its functional job for its original creators. To some readers, it might seem as if this death of whiteness evokes a sense of colorblindness, an idea (rightly) held in disregard by many engaged in scholarship on the subject of race.[112] Such talk of the death of whiteness is in no way a claim about a post-racial society or a colorblind society. It is meant to situate ongoing and future ritualized racist practices as (perhaps) socially futile for those not wanting to adhere to a white religious sensibility. Though some readers may have a problem with the following suggestion, from a utilitarian standpoint, many would argue (and have done so) that the sacrifices paid by lynch victims in history were warranted and justified because of the perception that the ritual functioned to sustain the social order.[113] This discussion of the death of whiteness is meant to address those who might be callously inclined to believe a claim that "violence is necessary and justified for social stability." Written with these utilitarian, callously motivated people in mind, my comments regarding the functional death of whiteness offer a reminder that whiteness no longer offers what it once did for white people in the U.S. and so, perhaps it is time to address the ongoing very real deaths that continue today as a result of the god-idol of whiteness. Deaths that are no longer "necessary" because whiteness no longer does the functional work it once did.

In the contemporary moment, race and racism continue to produce a perilous environment for African Americans and many marginalized communities in the U.S. Ongoing racial disparities exist today that are the result of the functional effects of the god-idol of whiteness. According to law professor, attorney, and author Michelle Alexander, between 1972 and today, the numbers of those incarcerated in America skyrocketed from around 350,000 into the millions.[114]

Moreover, the overwhelming majority of those in prison are non-white. Specifically, as of 2010, 2.2 million African Americans are behind bars, followed by 960,000 Latinos, followed by 380,000 Caucasians.[115] Set in context of the larger society, 2010 U.S. census numbers indicate that African Americans make up 13.1 percent of the population, Hispanics 16.7 percent, and non-Hispanic whites a staggering 63.4 percent.[116] Such skewed prison statistics are telling. Alexander goes on to argue that "mass incarceration in the United States [has], in fact, emerged as a stunningly comprehensive and well-disguised system of racialized social control that functions in a manner strikingly similar to Jim Crow."[117] In other words, the contemporary prison industrial complex has functional parallels to the ritual function of U.S. segregation laws. Whiteness may not be "dead," after all. Those convicted of crimes are not only ghettoized and set apart from the larger society, but they also lose rights such as voting, the ability to hold adequate jobs, etc. Such efforts, Alexander notes, "do not require racial hostility or overt bigotry to thrive."[118]

The functional death of the god-idol of whiteness does not mean the dead god-idol holds no sway on the shape of society in (and at) its wake. This dead god-idol is left to cast a continued internalizing presence on the social environment. Created god-idols have a strong, material impact on society long after they have died, and this impact extends to the god-idol's former creators, beneficiaries, and victims. The previous discussion of the functional death of *whiteness* is meant to situate these contemporary ritualistic practices (such as mass incarceration) as functionally useless in that whiteness is beginning to exact its toll on everyone. Such is the legacy left by the dead god-idol.

Social scientist Loic Wacquant casts the severity of this "new Jim Crow" even more pointedly, arguing that not only have these incarcerations disproportionately affected African Americans, but that the prison industrial system has so heavily shaped black neighborhoods in the U.S. that qualitatively, mass incarceration is equally impacting African American possibilities in and outside of prisons, as both prisons and urban ghettos ultimately amount to complementary means of "purging 'undesirables' from the body politic … in an attempt to quarantine a polluting group from the urban body."[119] Again, this effectively amounts to a functioning ritualistic practice akin to segregation. Here, it would appear that although whiteness no longer achieves the stability it once did, new rituals are emerging that reinforce the god-idol.

And so the end of this god-idol's function in society as existential and social redress is not a statement about the continuance of the impact of whiteness in the contemporary moment. Rather, the *death* of the god-idol of whiteness offers a way to think through the legacy left behind from a now "deceased" god-idol, dead in the minds of many and yet alive to new possibilities for perpetuating injustices and exaggerations of radical contingency in the present. What has "died" is not whiteness, but whiteness as god-idol – whiteness as the centering concept employed to deny, fight, or ignore radical contingency. Other centering ideas and ideals have worked alongside of whiteness historically and stand ready to pick up the slack left by this death of whiteness as god-idol.

White Lies is motivated by an effort to think through these shifting and morphing racialized realities so as to more adequately analyze and mitigate these social effects, to make sense of the god-idol of whiteness that no longer functions for white people as efficiently, but continues to inflict suffering and misery (albeit in varying quantity and severity) on all members of the society, whites included. White religion seems paradoxically in decline and yet thriving. Its life, its death, the synergy between both prospects, gives way to twilight, confusion, and uncertainty.

THE TWILIGHT OF WHITENESS

When viewed through twilight, whiteness, as an idea, is not alive or dead; as a god-idol, the frame of death offers the means of holding in balance the social costs of adherence to such an idea with the functional ineffectiveness of the idea as a god-idol. That is, lynchings never achieved their goal of procuring certainty. The biggest of white lies is that our vicious lengths to obtain certainty will be justified. *White Lies* seeks to make sense of the very real consequences of ignoring the human situation of radical contingency, of living and engaging the lie of whiteness and others. God-idols do not exist, but they carry such weight as to consume the actions and ideas of those beholden to the imaginary. Such is the "twilight" of the god-idol of whiteness, a statement about and recognition of the always already virtual realities produced and producing, structured by and structuring historical human experience. According to Nietzsche, "The *lie* of the ideal has so far been the curse on reality; on account of it, mankind itself has become mendacious and false down to its most fundamental instincts – to the point of worshipping the opposite values of those which alone would guarantee its health, its future, the lofty *right* to its future."[120] The lie of the ideal and idea of whiteness has "so far been the curse on" U.S. social realities, the foundation for a white religious orientation centered on lies.

Whiteness presents itself as bound in a twilight. Not fully alive, never fully dead, whiteness continuously informs the social and existential realities of those in the U.S. through legacy effects and misrecognition. Whiteness is not something to be owned or adopted as much as it is an empty idea, an empty concept to be filled with the stuff of politics and history – a god-idol, having no intrinsic value or ability. To borrow from Claude Levi-Strauss, god-idols such as "whiteness" are floating signifiers, representing "an undetermined quantity of signification, in itself void of meaning and thus able to receive any meaning."[121] In their functional, ethereal meandering these signifiers gain such discursive power to shape the social environment that the only analytic recourse for engaging them – concepts like "whiteness" and "god" (discussed next) – is to simultaneously hold in tension such emptiness with the discursive power arrangements produced by deployment of such empty concepts in the construction of existential and social formation. Whiteness, then, is a god-idol, wherein "god" and "idol" work together to always foreground the "fictive truth"[122] of whiteness, the emptiness of the idea and the very real historical weight of such floating signifiers employed historically and today. Never fully born, yet never actually dead, whiteness exists in this twilight.

This brings the discussion back to Nietzsche's comments about "ancient, hollow idols" whose falsity "does not prevent them from being the most believed in."[123] Such idolatry is inevitable as it is a product of the limited capacity of language and society to address the existential needs arising from the human situation. To this extent, all arguments, mine included, operate according to ontological thought and action. White lies can never be fully escaped, either in overarching political arrangements or in the analytic work that breaks down and attempts to make sense of such social realities. Whiteness, in its birth and death, remains elusive, problematic – yet powerful. Analysts, and those in society, are left to do their work within the shadow cast from the god-idol as it hangs – like its black victims – in the impossible possibilities produced from the limitations of human ability and value, and the stories told in response to such limitations.

The "twilight" of whiteness is the confusion produced by adherence to floating signifiers, in an idolatrous quest to be sure, safe, certain. In both the social and academic domains, whiteness never did more – and never will do more – than obscure reality, always ignoring, denying, or fighting directly against awareness of human limitation and uncertainty. Yet, the contemporary moment finds scholars in need of recognition of this whiteness precisely because ongoing failure to take it seriously will only add to the obscurity of intellectual projects and perhaps, even, the field of American religion. In the face of what historian of religion Charles Long refers to as the "opacity of reality,"[124] whiteness has operated as a specter, exposing a false sense of certainty that is increasingly called into question in and by twenty-first century U.S. life.

"There are no more ancient idols in existence," reminds Nietzsche, his words exposing former gods as false idols and forcing recognition of the opening to uncertainty offered by awareness of radical contingency. Whiteness has served this certain function, but does it still? Alive or dead, it has not been the only white lie. Next, moving further into twilight, where human value and ability are sought and imagined, I turn to another of these lies.

Notes

1 Neil Gaiman, *American Gods* (HarperTorch, 2002), 536.
2 Friedrich Nietzsche, *The Twilight of the Idols and The Anti-Christ: Or How to Philosophize with a Hammer*, ed. Michael Tanner, trans. R. J. Hollingdale (Penguin Classics, 1990), 32.
3 i.e., uncertain certainty, impossible possibility, paradox, aporia.
4 Ruston is about sixty miles from the small Southern city where I grew up, Shreveport, Louisiana.

5 Adam Fairclough, *Race & Democracy: The Civil Rights Struggle in Louisiana, 1915–1972* (University of Georgia Press, 1999), 29.
6 Fairclough, *Race & Democracy*, 30.
7 Ibid.
8 Anthony B. Pinn, *Terror and Triumph: The Nature of Black Religion* (Fortress Press, 2003), 71.
9 Pinn, *Terror and Triumph*, 68.
10 See, for instance, James H. Cone and Gayraud S. Wilmore, *Black Theology: A Documentary History: Volume One, 1966–1979* (Orbis Books, 1993); *Black Theology: A Documentary History: Volume Two, 1980–1992* (Orbis Books, 1993).
11 Pinn, *Terror and Triumph*, 67.
12 See captions for "photo 73" at WithoutSanctury.org, an online repository of American lynching stories, accessed March 10, 2015, http://withoutsanctuary.org/main.html and http://withoutsanctuary.org/pics_73_text.html
13 "Negro, 19, Is Lynched by Louisiana Mob," *The New York Times*, October 14, 1938, 12.
14 Here, I recognize that scholars have offered other genealogical snapshots of what might be called whiteness, locating it in Modernity (Cornel West, *Prophesy Deliverance!*, Westminster John Knox Press, 2002 (1982)) or an even older theological anxiety emerging amongst the early Christians (J. Kameron Carter, *Race: A Theological Account*, Oxford University Press, 2008). But it is worth repeating that my efforts are hermeneutical and neither historical nor historicizing of the category of whiteness. I am offering a way to interpret the effects and role of whiteness in U.S. society and amongst religious studies scholarship. Readers wanting a more didactic, grounded historical account of whiteness should look elsewhere. To attempt such grounded history would be to negate my overarching concerns that we simply cannot fully know.
15 Bruce Lincoln, *Death, War, and Sacrifice: Studies in Ideology & Practice*, 1st ed. (University of Chicago Press, 1991), 204.
16 Amy Louise Wood, *Lynching and Spectacle: Witnessing Racial Violence in America, 1890–1940* (University of North Carolina Press, 2009), 6–7.
17 *The New York Times*, October 14, 1938, 12.
18 "Can the States Stop Lynching?" *The Crisis*, January 1939.
19 By the time of Williams's lynching, the practice had become so common that year after year brought growing energy in Congress for the establishment of national anti-lynching legislation. In fact, hundreds of anti-lynching bills were introduced over these same years, and every time, Southern senators trumpeted "States' rights" as a rationale for voting against the legislation. (To this day, no anti-lynching bill has ever been passed in the U.S. Congress.) Spearheaded by the NAACP and other organizations, there was outrage amongst many that lynch mobs were rarely prosecuted for their actions.
20 http://www.yale.edu/ynhti/curriculum/units/1979/2/79.02.04.x.html
21 "Can the States Stop Lynching?" *The Crisis*, January 1939.
22 Pinn, *Terror and Triumph*, 70.
23 Ibid., 71.
24 James H. Cone, *The Cross and the Lynching Tree* (Orbis Books, 2013), 15.
25 Kristina DuRocher, *Raising Racists: The Socialization of White Children in the Jim Crow South* (University Press of Kentucky, 2011), 114.
26 Ibid., 124.
27 Pinn, *Terror and Triumph*, 72, 77.
28 Lillian Smith, *Killers of the Dream* (W. W. Norton & Company, 1994), 89.
29 Sartre, *Anti-Semite and Jew* (Schocken Books, 1948), 32.
30 Here, I retain the non-inclusive language of "man" in order to emphasize that these thinkers are speaking on behalf of and for "men," even if their usage is meant to include all humans in their claims

31 Ernest Becker, *The Denial of Death* (Free Press, 1997), 30.
32 James W. Perkinson, *White Theology: Outing Supremacy in Modernity* (Palgrave Macmillan, 2004), 127–8.
33 Pierre Bourdieu, "Genesis and Structure of the Religious Field," *Comparative Social Research* 13 (1991), 8.
34 James Elbert Cutler, *Lynch-Law: An Investigation into the History of Lynching in the United States* (1905), 199.
35 Bourdieu, 14.
36 Ibid.
37 Ibid., original emphasis.
38 Bourdieu also demonstrates that religion blinds adherents to these structuring processes, such that a book about white lies can never fully know the "lies" it might be putting forth. However, I am not bound fully to the analysis of Bourdieu as anything more than illuminating of these practices. By my reading of Bourdieu, fear of rupturing his own systematicity leads him in many moments to be complicit with the very structures and structuring devices and processes he (in other moments) abhors.
39 Worth noting, my perspective means that the concept of "whiteness," denied even by those held most assuredly under its power, might wield a power to exert its influence in ways more profound and socially significant than even the idea of "god." Though both are ideas that correspond to nothing, the denial of whiteness (amongst many whites in the U.S.) seemingly legitimates the power of the idea in more severe ways than the legitimation offered by the visible and acknowledged idea of "god."
40 Pierre Bourdieu, "Genesis and Structure of the Religious Field"; Pierre Bourdieu, *The Logic of Practice*, 1st ed. (Stanford University Press, 1992).
41 The auction block is another ritual of reference discussed by Pinn. See Pinn, *Terror and Triumph*, 48–51.
42 Orlando Patterson, *Slavery and Social Death: A Comparative Study* (Harvard University Press, 1985).
43 This turn to Durkheim is the first, but not the last, instance of ethnographic theorization in this book. Durkheim's schematic helps to spell out how white religion functions in terms of whiteness, and offers a means of outlining the features, the life, of whiteness in deconstructive fashion. The turn to Durkheim offers a glimpse into the mind of an adherent to some form of white religion. I take liberty in that he is not American, nor is he referring to the U.S. In terms of the deconstruction, Durkheim's dislocation from American identity and the context of his data are helpful.
44 Specifically, Durkheim notes that, "in principle, the cult is derived from the beliefs, yet it reacts upon them; the myth is frequently modeled after the rite in order to account for it, especially when its sense is no longer apparent. On the other hand, there are beliefs which are clearly manifested only through the rites which express them." See Émile Durkheim, *The Elementary Forms of the Religious Life* (Dover Publications, 2008), 101.
45 Ibid., 14, original emphasis.
46 Ibid., 141.
47 Karen Fields, "Witchcraft and Racecraft: Invisible Ontology in Its Sensible Manifestation," in George Clement Bond (ed.), *Witchcraft Dialogues: Anthropological and Philosophical Exchanges*, 1st ed. (Ohio University Press, 2002), 283–315, 294.
48 Durkheim, *Elementary Forms*, 113.
49 Fields, in Bond, *Witchcraft Dialogues*, 299.
50 Since the U.S. example does not substitute social markers and attributes with animals and plants, instead choosing to represent the ideal type by the figure of the group in need of the totem, for the sake of space I am ignoring Durkheim's discussion of totemic symbolic representation in actual animals and plants.
51 Fields, in Bond, *Witchcraft Dialogues*, 296.

52 Ibid., 297.
53 State of Missouri v. Darren Wilson. Transcript of: Grand Jury Volume V. Date: September 16, 2014, accessed January 25, 2015, http://www.scribd.com/doc/248128351/Darren-Wilson-Testimony
54 Durkheim, *Elementary Forms*, 119.
55 James H. Cone, *A Black Theology of Liberation*, 20th anniversary edition (Orbis Books, 1990), 101. In fact, Cone's presentation of blackness as freedom seems to have him suggest that, for African Americans, the only possible "sin" is to not allow the oppressive use of outward identity markers to shape the inward.
56 Fields, in Bond, *Witchcraft Dialogues*, 299.
57 State of Missouri v. Darren Wilson.
58 Durkheim, *Elementary Forms*, 299–414.
59 Ibid., 301.
60 Ibid., 299–300, 302.
61 Ibid.
62 Kenneth Allan, *A Primer in Social and Sociological Theory: Toward a Sociology of Citizenship* (Pine Forge Press, 2010), 97.
63 Fairclough, *Race & Democracy*, 168.
64 James F. Davis, *Who Is Black? One Nation's Definition* (Pennsylvania State University Press, 2001), 9.
65 Scott Malcomson, *One Drop of Blood: The American Misadventure of Race* (Macmillan, 2000), 356.
66 Understanding that talk of racial groups might make some social theorists balk at my decontextualizing and recontextualizing, here my usage of group is more rhetorical shorthand than a specific sociological category. To the extent that I am conflating characteristics and concerns over *group* vs. *status*, such nuances will await treatment in future efforts.
67 Barbara J. Fields and Karen Fields, *Racecraft: The Soul of Inequality in American Life* (Verso, 2012).
68 Davis, *Who Is Black?*, 78.
69 Charles Frank Robinson II, *Dangerous Liaisons: Sex and Love in the Segregated South* (University of Arkansas Press, 2006), 77.
70 Pinn, *Triumph and Terror*, 52.
71 Durkheim, *Elementary Forms*, 326.
72 Ibid., 351.
73 Ibid., 327–9.
74 Robinson, *Dangerous Liaisons*, 77.
75 Ida B. Wells-Barnett, "The Black and the White of It," in *Southern Horrors: Lynch Law in All Its Phases* (1892).
76 Ida B. Wells-Barnett, "The New Cry," in *Southern Horrors: Lynch Law in All Its Phases* (1892).
77 Durkheim, *Elementary Forms*, 351.
78 Mary Douglas, *Natural Symbols: Explorations in Cosmology*, 3rd ed. (Routledge, 2003), xv.
79 Douglas, *Natural Symbols*, xxxvii.
80 DuRocher, *Raising Racists*, chapter 5.
81 Durkheim, *Elementary Forms*, 351.
82 Ibid., 387.
83 George D. Kelsey, *Racism and the Christian Understanding of Man. An Analysis and Criticism of Racism as an Idolatrous Religion* (Charles Scribner's Sons, 1965), 39.
84 Ibid., 39.
85 "Affidavit Provides Details of Macedonia Church Fire Probe," *The Republican – Masslive.com*, accessed April 10, 2013, http://www.masslive.com/news/index.ssf/2009/01/affidavit_provides_details_of.html

86 *The Republican*, accessed May 10, 2013, http://www.masslive.com/news/index.ssf/2009/01/affidavit_provides_details_of.html
87 "Outspoken Ferguson Pastor Who Had Church Burnt Down Defiant in the Face of Death Threats," *The National Post*, November 27, 2014, accessed January 25, 2015, http://news.nationalpost.com/2014/11/27/pastor-who-had-his-church-burnt-down-in-ferguson-reflects-with-his-family-on-thanksgiving/
88 "Cracking Down on Cross Burnings | Southern Poverty Law Center." In *Intelligence Report* Summer 1999 Issue 95, accessed March 12, 2015, http://www.splcenter.org/get-informed/intelligence-report/browse-all-issues/1999/summer/intimidation. Southern Poverty Law Center Website, accessed April 9, 2013, http://www.splcenter.org/get-informed/intelligence-report/browse-all-issues/1999/summer/intimidation
89 "Two Arrested in Noose Incident Near Jena, Louisiana," September 21, 2007. Cnn.com, accessed April 9, 2013, http://www.cnn.com/2007/US/09/21/car.nooses/
90 "Lynched Effigies Shock Many," September 21, 2012. Abclocal.go.com, accessed April 2, 2013, http://abclocal.go.com/wtvd/story?section=news/local&id=8820026
91 Personal auto-ethnographic experience, Shreveport, Louisiana, 2012.
92 "North Carolina Man Travels Country in Truck with Hanged Effigy of President Obama," November 2, 2012. Complex.com, accessed April 2, 2013, http://www.complex.com/city-guide/2012/11/north-carolina-man-travels-country-in-truck-with-hanged-effigy-of-president-obama
93 Durkheim, *Elementary Forms*, 390.
94 Ibid., 389.
95 Important to make clear, Donald's murder might be understood as one of the last literal lynchings, as he was hung from a tree, but not the last metaphoric/figurative "lynching" of black bodies. Other examples of similar racialized bodily terror would include the murder of James Byrd, Jr. in Jasper, Texas in 1998, and countless more like Trayvon Martin and others.
96 The National Geographic Channel, "A Modern Day Lynching," accessed March 12, 2015, http://channel.nationalgeographic.com/channel/videos/a-modern-day-lynching/
97 ExecutedToday.com, "1997: Henry Francis Hays, Whose Crime Cost the Klan," accessed April 11, 2013, http://www.executedtoday.com/2008/06/06/1997-henry-francis-hays-ku-klux-klan-michael-donald/
98 University of Missouri, Kansas City, online database, Lynching Statistics, by year, accessed February 11, 2013, http://law2.umkc.edu/faculty/projects/ftrials/shipp/lynchingyear.html
99 DuRocher, *Raising Racists*, 127.
100 "What We Do-Southern Poverty Law Center," Southern Poverty Law Center website, accessed May 10, 2013, http://www.splcenter.org/what-we-do/hate-and-extremism
101 "'Nones' on the Rise," October 9, 2012. Pew Research Center's Religion & Public Life Project, accessed March 12, 2015, http://www.pewforum.org/2012/10/09/nones-on-the-rise/
102 Grant Wacker, "The Rise of Fundamentalism," accessed May 15, 2013, http://nationalhumanitiescenter.org/tserve/twenty/tkeyinfo/fundam.htm
103 Emilie M. Townes, *Womanist Ethics and the Cultural Production of Evil* (Palgrave Macmillan, 2006).
104 For more on the complications of contemporary race relations and sentiments, see: "Poll: Most Americans See Lingering Racism – In Others," December 12, 2006, assessed June 20, 2014, http://edition.cnn.com/2006/US/12/12/racism.poll/index.html?eref=yahoo
105 Whether or not these whites are or are not "racist" is beside the point. My point is simply that whiteness is cast back on these whites in a way that short-circuits the functional utility of whiteness.

106 John Hartigan, *Odd Tribes: Toward a Cultural Analysis of White People* (Duke University Press Books, 2005), 239.
107 Ibid., 241.
108 Ibid., 238.
109 Ibid., 240–1.
110 "Minorities Expected to be Majority in 2050," August 13, 2008. Cnn.com, accessed January 12, 2013, http://www.cnn.com/2008/US/08/13/census.minorities/
111 Erik Wemple, "Why Did PBS Call George Zimmerman 'White?'," *Washington Post*, April 11, 2012, accessed March 12, 2015, http://www.washingtonpost.com/blogs/erik-wemple/post/why-did-pbs-call-george-zimmerman-white/2012/04/11/gIQAZsC4AT_blog.html
112 Michelle Alexander, *The New Jim Crow: Mass Incarceration in the Age of Colorblindness* (The New Press, 2010).
113 Personal auto-ethnographic experience and conversation with thirty-year-old white male, Many, Louisiana, March 15, 2013.
114 Alexander, 8.
115 "Incarceration Rates by Race and Ethnicity – 2010," Prison Policy Initiative, accessed March 12, 2015, http://www.prisonpolicy.org/graphs/raceinc.html
116 "U.S. Population Statistics," February 2015. U.S. Census Bureau website, accessed March 12, 2015, http://quickfacts.census.gov/qfd/states/00000.html
117 Alexander, *The New Jim Crow*, 4.
118 Ibid., 14.
119 Loic Wacquant, "Deadly Symbiosis: When Ghetto and Prison Meet and Mesh." *Punishment & Society* 3, no. 1 (2001): 95–134.
120 Friedrich Nietzsche, *On the Genealogy of Morals and Ecce Homo, Edited with Commentary by Walter Kaufmann*, trans. Walter Kaufmann (Vintage Books, 1969), 218, original emphasis.
121 Claude Lévi-Strauss, quoted in Jeffrey Mehlman, "The 'Floating Signifier': From Lévi-Strauss to Lacan," *Yale French Studies, French Freud: Structural Studies in Psychoanalysis 48* (1972): 10–37, 23.
122 Charles H. Long, *Significations: Signs, Symbols, and Images in the Interpretation of Religion*, 2nd ed. (The Davies Group Publishers, 1999), 184.
123 Nietzsche, *The Twilight of the Idols*, 32.
124 Long, *Significations*, 207.

REFERENCES

"Affidavit Provides Details of Macedonia Church Fire Probe." 2013. *The Republican – Masslive.com*, accessed April 10, 2015, http://www.masslive.com/news/index.ssf/2009/01/affidavit_provides_details_of.html

"Cracking Down on Cross Burnings | Southern Poverty Law Center." 1999. In *Intelligence Report* Issue 95, accessed March 12, 2015, http://www.splcenter.org/get-informed/intelligence-report/browse-all-issues/1999/summer/intimidation

"Henry Francis Hays, Whose Crime Cost the Klan." 1997. *ExecutedToday.com*, accessed April 11, 2013, http://www.executedtoday.com/2008/06/06/1997-henry-francis-hays-ku-klux-klan-michael-donald/

"Incarceration Rates by Race and Ethnicity – 2010." 2010. *Prison Policy Initiative*, accessed March 12, 2015, http://www.prisonpolicy.org/graphs/raceinc.html

"Lynched Effigies Shock Many," September 21, 2012. Abclocal.go.com, accessed April 2, 2013, http://abclocal.go.com/wtvd/story?section=news/local&id=8820026

"Minorities Expected to be Majority in 2050," August 13, 2008. Cnn.com, accessed January 12, 2013, http://www.cnn.com/2008/US/08/13/census.minorities/

"'Nones' on the Rise," October 9, 2012. Pew Research Center's Religion & Public Life Project, accessed March 12, 2015, http://www.pewforum.org/2012/10/09/nones-on-the-rise/

"North Carolina Man Travels Country in Truck with Hanged Effigy of President Obama," November 2, 2012. *Complex.com*, accessed April 2, 2013, http://www.complex.com/city-guide/2012/11/north-carolina-man-travels-country-in-truck-with-hanged-effigy-of-president-obama

"Poll: Most Americans See Lingering Racism – In Others," December 12, 2006, accessed June 20, 2014, http://edition.cnn.com/2006/US/12/12/racism.poll/index.html?eref=yahoo

"Two Arrested in Noose Incident Near Jena, Louisiana," September 21, 2007. Cnn.com, accessed April 9, 2013, http://www.cnn.com/2007/US/09/21/car.nooses/

"U.S. Population Statistics," February 2015. U.S. Census Bureau website, accessed March 12, 2015. http://quickfacts.census.gov/qfd/states/00000.html

Alexander, Michelle. 2010. *The New Jim Crow: Mass Incarceration in the Age of Colorblindness*. 1st ed. The New Press.

Allen, James and John Littlefield. 2015. "Without Sanctuary." Historical Archive, accessed March 12, 2015, http://withoutsanctuary.org/pics_73_text.html and http://withoutsanctuary.org/main.html

Allan, Kenneth D. 2010. *A Primer in Social and Sociological Theory: Toward a Sociology of Citizenship*. Pine Forge Press.

Becker, Ernest. 1997. *The Denial of Death*. Free Press.

Bourdieu, Pierre. 1991. "Genesis and Structure of the Religious Field." *Comparative Social Research* 13: 1–44.

Bourdieu, Pierre et al. 1992. *The Logic of Practice*. 1st ed. Stanford University Press.

Carter, J. Kameron. 2008. *Race: A Theological Account*. Oxford University Press.

Cone, James H. 1990. *A Black Theology of Liberation*. 20th anniversary edition. Orbis Books.

Cone, James H. 2013. *The Cross and the Lynching Tree*. Reprint. Orbis Books.

Cone, James H. and Gayraud S. Wilmore. 1993. *Black Theology: A Documentary History: Volume 1 1966–1979*. Orbis Books.

Cone, James H. and Gayraud S. Wilmore. 1993. *Black Theology: A Documentary History: Volume 2 1980–1992*. Orbis Books.

The Crisis. 1939. "Can the States Stop Lynching?," January.

Cutler, James Elbert. 1905. *Lynch-Law: An Investigation into the History of Lynching in the United States*.

Davis, James F. 2001. *Who Is Black? One Nation's Definition*. 10th anniversary edition. Pennsylvania State University Press.

Douglas, Mary. 2003. *Natural Symbols: Explorations in Cosmology*. 3rd ed. Routledge.

Durkheim, Émile. 2008. *The Elementary Forms of the Religious Life*. Dover Publications.

DuRocher, Kristina. 2011. *Raising Racists: The Socialization of White Children in the Jim Crow South*. University Press of Kentucky.

Fairclough, Adam. 1999. *Race & Democracy: The Civil Rights Struggle in Louisiana, 1915–1972*. University of Georgia Press.

Fields, Barbara J. and Karen Fields. 2012. *Racecraft: The Soul of Inequality in American Life*. 1st ed. Verso.

Fields, Karen. 2002. "Witchcraft and Racecraft: Invisible Ontology in Its Sensible Manifestation," in George Clement Bond (ed.), *Witchcraft Dialogues: Anthropological & Philosophical Exchanges*. 1st ed. Ohio University Press.

Gaiman, Neil. 2002. *American Gods*. HarperTorch.

Hartigan, John. 2005. *Odd Tribes: Toward a Cultural Analysis of White People*. Duke University Press Books.

Kelsey, George D. 1965. *Racism and the Christian Understanding of Man. An Analysis and Criticism of Racism as an Idolatrous Religion*. Charles Scribner's Sons.

Lincoln, Bruce. 1991. *Death, War, and Sacrifice: Studies in Ideology & Practice*. 1st ed. University of Chicago Press.

Long, Charles H. 1999. *Significations: Signs, Symbols, and Images in the Interpretation of Religion*. 2nd ed. The Davies Group Publishers.

McCullers, Carson. 2004 [1940]. *The Heart Is a Lonely Hunter*. First Mariner Books.

Malcomson, Scott. 2000. *One Drop of Blood: The American Misadventure of Race*. Macmillan.

Mehlman, Jeffrey. 1972. "The 'Floating Signifier': From Lévi-Strauss to Lacan." Yale French Studies, French Freud: Structural Studies in Psychoanalysis 48: 10–37.

The National Geographic Channel. n.d. "A Modern Day Lynching," accessed March 12, 2015. http://channel.nationalgeographic.com/channel/videos/a-modern-day-lynching/

The National Post. 2014. "Outspoken Ferguson Pastor Who Had Church Burnt Down Defiant in Face of Death Threats," November 27, accessed January 25, 2015, http://news.nationalpost.com/2014/11/27/pastor-who-had-his-church-burnt-down-in-ferguson-reflects-with-his-family-on-thanksgiving/

The New York Times. 1938. "Negro, 19, is Lynched by Louisiana Mob," October 14.

Nietzsche, Friedrich. 1969. *On the Genealogy of Morals and Ecce Homo Edited with Commentary by Walter Kaufmann*, trans. Walter Kaufmann. Vintage Books.

Nietzsche, Friedrich. 1990. *The Twilight of the Idols and The Anti-Christ: Or How to Philosophize with a Hammer*, ed. Michael Tanner, trans. R. J. Hollingdale. Penguin Classics.

Patterson, Orlando. 1985. *Slavery and Social Death: A Comparative Study*. Harvard University Press.

Perkinson, James W. 2004. *White Theology: Outing Supremacy in Modernity*. 1st ed. Palgrave Macmillan.

Pinn, Anthony. 2003. *Terror and Triumph: The Nature of Black Religion*. Fortress Press.

RobinsonII, Charles Frank. 2006. *Dangerous Liaisons: Sex and Love in the Segregated South*. University of Arkansas Press.

Sartre, Jean-Paul. 1948. *Anti-Semite and Jew*. Schocken Books Inc.

Smith, Lillian. 1994 [1949]. *Killers of the Dream*. W. W. Norton & Company.

Southern Poverty Law Center. n.d. "What We Do—Southern Poverty Law Center," Southern Poverty Law Center website, accessed May 10, 2013, http://www.splcenter.org/what-we-do/hate-and-extremism

State of Missouri v. Darren Wilson.Transcript of: Grand Jury Volume V.September 16, 2014, accessed January 25, 2015, http://www.scribd.com/doc/248128351/Darren-Wilson-Testimony

Townes, Emilie M. 2006. *Womanist Ethics and the Cultural Production of Evil*. Macmillan.

Wacker, Grant. "The Rise of Fundamentalism," accessed May 15, 2013, http://nationalhumanitiescenter.org/tserve/twenty/tkeyinfo/fundam.htm

Wacquant, Loic. 2001. "Deadly Symbiosis: When Ghetto and Prison Meet and Mesh," *Punishment & Society* 3(1): 95–134.

Wells-Barnett, Ida B. 1892. *Southern Horrors: Lynch Law in All Its Phases*. Project Gutenberg.

Wemple, Erik. 2012. "Why Did PBS Call George Zimmerman 'White?'." *Washington Post*, April 11, accessed March 12, 2015, http://www.washingtonpost.com/blogs/

erik-wemple/post/why-did-pbs-call-george-zimmerman-white/2012/04/11/gIQAZsC4AT_blog.html
West, Cornel. 2002 [1982]. *Prophesy Deliverance!* Westminster John Knox Press.
Wood, Amy Louise. 2009. *Lynching and Spectacle: Witnessing Racial Violence in America, 1890–1940.* University of North Carolina Press.
Wright, Richard. 2014 [1940]. *Native Son.* Harper Perennial.
University of Missouri, Kansas City. Online database. Lynching Statistics, by year, accessed February 11, 2013, http://law2.umkc.edu/faculty/projects/ftrials/shipp/lynchingyear.html

2

THE WHITE MAN'S GOD COMPLEX

Most Americans, the (white) power of theism, and beginning to *believe* in twilight

> Who's gonna die next?, 'cause the white man's got a god complex
>
> *The Last Poets*[1]

> God ain't good all of the time. In fact, sometimes, God is not for us. As a black woman in a nation that has taken too many pains to remind me that I am not a white man, and am not capable of taking care of my reproductive rights, or my voting rights, I know that this American god ain't my god. As a matter of fact, I think he's a white racist god with a problem. More importantly, he is carrying a gun and stalking young black men.
>
> *Anthea Butler*[2]

In 1971, The Last Poets gave name to a psychosocial system of belief prevalent in the United States, in which race, gender, wealth, and other factors cause some people to act as if they are gods and others to become sacrificial offerings to these "gods." They asked: Who's gonna die next?, 'cause the white man's got a god complex.[3] Their lyrics describe in ethnographic fashion the precarious living conditions faced by black folk across the United States. "Silent niggas scream for help" as social options run scarce and people turn to gambling, drug dealing, and other avenues of the underground economy to get by in impoverished conditions. Dying as consequence of direct alienation from the "white man's" resources, or through the social maladies enacted as a need to make a little scratch, in every direction turned, black folk are getting killed by this god complex. The Last Poets saw death all around them, poverty and racism suffocating any possibility of flourishing, and all of it, they said, was "'cause the white man's got a god complex."

Fast forward over forty years, the complexities of this complex are still not overcome, and black people continue to bear a disproportionate brunt of the negative effects of things white Americans believe. This chapter takes up the task of outlining certain features of this complex, including that it is maintained by many if not most Americans; it has a longstanding historical precedent in the founding of American society and religion; it unifies socially by dividing; it cultivates social power or the sense of it; it reproduces itself automatically; it allows those who believe in god to try and act like god; violence and death are always necessitated by it; it operates and functions as a system – and perhaps, it also might not be working as effectively as it once did. But the violence it brings shows no signs of slowing.

This chapter first empirically and demographically situates *White Lies*' primary data set as "white," often "male," and "theistic." I then focus attention on defining theism as belief in the idea of "god," where I underscore the contextual and shifting nature of theism in the United States. The fact that the meaning and usefulness of the idea of god shifts over time and space, from my vantage point, suggests that "god" for white theists is best understood as an ideological placeholder for society. This would also suggest that theism, then, is not belief in god, but is belief in the idea of god. That is, theism is belief in the functional utility of belief. I then apply the social systems theory of Niklas Luhmann to unpack certain significant features of white theism operating within (and as) the white man's god complex. These features include the effects of belief *in belief*, and the requirement of second order observations for understanding and protecting society as god. That is, believing in belief (instead of "god") makes the idea of god appear to correspond to reality. Such functions, it becomes aware, require sacrifices, rooted in the ultimate sacrifice – physical life. Sighting these functions requires taking a "god's eye view" of the system, of the white man's god complex, which reinforces belief as able to impact the social world. In light of these findings, I conclude by arriving at yet another instance of twilight, this time the twilight of theism, where it grows apparent that sacrifice is inescapable – what will be sacrificed remains to be seen.

GODS IN THE CROSS-HAIRS

As noted already, on February 26, 2012, in Sanford, Florida, 17-year-old African American Trayvon Martin was accosted, assaulted, and murdered by George Zimmerman. Martin had been walking through his (own) neighborhood in the rain and was policed and surveilled by a vigilante, Zimmerman, who sought to oversee neighborhood goings-on for the sake of safety and security of property. Zimmerman believed he was doing the right thing in his surveillance. Seeing Martin walking down the street, Zimmerman believed the young man out of place, a sort of invader. Fearful that Martin didn't belong, Zimmerman chose to confront him. Only, the confrontation was met with something unexpected. Martin told Zimmerman "No! You will not surveil me without consequence!" In more abstract terms, it might be said that two warring belief systems engaged in battle that day – one based on the belief in a particular sort of "god" and a certainty of self and safety aptly described by The Last Poets as a god complex; the other based on a naming and rejection of idolatry. Martin, to the best I can fathom, and hoping these words give honor to the young man, embodied and comported himself with a different kind of confidence, one that believed in the worth of himself, and rejected any action or belief that would question or give pause to black – no, human – agency. At this point, we all know how the day ended. Zimmerman, "carrying a gun and stalking young black men," eventually killed the object of his fear. Trayvon was murdered in his own neighborhood, gunned down for having rejected Zimmerman's beliefs.

On November 23, that same year, in nearby Jacksonville, another 17-year-old African American male, Jordan Davis, was riding around town in a car listening to rap music with three other friends. The boys ended up parked at a convenience store. Moments later, 45-year-old white male Michael Dunn pulled up to the same store. While the occupants of both cars waited for their companions to come back from the store, an argument broke out. Dunn was angry that loud rap music coming from the kids' car was rattling his windows. Davis is reported to have grown frustrated over this strange white man trying to police what these four young black men could or could not do. By all accounts, Davis was angry and yelling – he should have been. Likely, his whole life he had been hearing white people, white men in particular, not only telling him what to do, but doing so with a pompous confidence that seemingly justified the directives – an arrogance made possible by a certain sort of belief in oneself, a "god complex." Rejecting this "god," Davis and the other boys cranked the music. Many readers might know how this story ends, too. In response to a young black man telling him "No!" Dunn pulled out a handgun and began firing at the boys' car. Davis was hit three times as the boys sped away while Dunn continued to fire. Despite the shooting, Dunn did not think enough of the altercation or the safety of the boys to contact authorities. Davis died that day and Dunn didn't seem to care until police arrived to arrest him two days later at his home. Dunn did not seem phased at his taking of a black life. He had resented the "noise" – rap music – coming from the car in which Davis was a passenger, and that resentment, coupled with the belief that no black man could or should chastise or threaten a white body, was grounds for murder.

Martin and Davis are two of countless examples of young black men (and women) killed by white vigilante citizens with guns and vendettas of one sort or another. Add in the murders of black people at the hands of police and law enforcement, such as Michael Brown in Ferguson, Missouri and Eric Garner in New York City, The Last Poets' words are as applicable today as when first spoken. Who will die next because of this god complex? Violence is a principal component of this complex, and I seek to sketch this reliance in the pages that follow. But this complex is also oriented around and by *belief*, a particular sort of belief with historical roots in American Protestantism, a longstanding functional utility in the United States.

In July 2013, George Zimmerman was acquitted of killing Trayvon Martin. The verdict rocked the nation and left to fester racialized wounds unable to heal because the crimes of racism remain out of control. As mentioned in *White Lies'* opening pages, in response to the not guilty verdict, Anthea Butler, Associate Professor and Graduate Chair of Religious Studies at the University of Pennsylvania, went on the rhetorical offensive in a short essay written for *Religion Dispatches* titled "The Zimmerman Acquittal: America's Racist God." In the essay, Butler rails against the American god, describing it as "a white racist god with a problem, carrying a gun and stalking young black men."[4] Butler and many others (including me) were furious at the verdict, but also disgusted by Zimmerman having claimed in a television interview that the murder of Martin was part of god's plan. Qualitatively speaking, where white America is concerned, our god is and has been a white racist with a gun, just as Butler described. Prof. Butler merely told the truth behind Zimmerman's white lie.

Effectively, Butler gave voice to a major component of the god complex: its reliance on violence, racism, and denial. And for her honesty, many sought to punish her. In various online venues, comments, and emails received after the *Religion Dispatches* piece was published, Butler was called a "nigger," "cunt," "fat cow," and "special kind of fucking idiot"[5] in a barrage of online attacks. Many white Americans were furious at her. The backlash was so severe that Butler created a social media page dedicated to cataloging the hate mail and hate speech. The responses to Butler's essay demonstrate, more or less, the other dimensions of this god complex, and serve as data indicative of the lengths to which white people will go to defend their "god." As a result, vigilante murders and those done by law enforcement (including the Executive Branch of the government), in tandem with the public conversation emerging from Butler's essay, serve in this chapter to cast light on a few primary features of this god complex: it relies on violence, it seeks to reproduce itself in perpetuity, and this violence and reproduction are made possible by white conceptions of god and white American *belief* in god.

At what or whom these people were furious is an open question. Were they angry that their god had been assaulted? Or, were they angry that a black woman had been the accuser? Many were definitely *not* angry that a young black life had been taken. If online comments were any indication, like Zimmerman and Dunn before, these whites wanted black blood. The god complex does not tolerate being told "No!" by a black woman any more than a black man, but it is designed to address and exterminate those who would dare question the sacred social order.

In effort to add to the public discussion, *Religion Dispatches* followed up one week later with essays by Willie James Jennings and J. Kameron Carter, two towering contemporary theologians who also happen to write on the intersections of race and theology. Jennings's essay provided a strong qualification of Butler's argument, ostensibly saying that those who would defend Zimmerman or find fault with Butler's essay were worshipping the *wrong* god, a "god who is powerful, flexible and moves around America as if he owns it."[6] Though not as sharp as

Butler's talk of god carrying a gun, Jennings' point was largely the same. Many Americans act like gods all the while claiming to believe in god. "That god," most assuredly, "is a white racist."[7] Carter's essay purported to be a sort of counterpoint to Jennings, celebrating the larger aims of both Jennings and Butler, but suggesting instead that "The Only Response Worth Its Salt to the Zimmerman Verdict" is one of "Christian Atheism."[8] His point was not to celebrate some contemporary remixing of death of god theology, but to use the language of theology to suggest that Christians should – and must – reject any ideology, belief structure, or complex that allowed some to act like gods "with the power of death and under the protection of law."[9]

As many might expect, Jennings and Carter faced criticism, too. The most popular comment left under Carter's essay called the piece "nonsense" and went on to suggest that Zimmerman is not racist and that "I'm not a racist, but people clearly choosing to ignore facts in order to perpetuate the version of the story they wish were true in order to fuel their race baiting is crazy wrong."[10] The comments left under Jennings's essay largely sought to vindicate god from the charge of "divine racism," while others sought to remind us that Butler was wrong because "god sees no color of skin."[11] Most of the comments, whether defending or rebuking Butler, showed a strange combination of ignorance of theological discourse paired with a certitude that the commenters knew who "God" really is. Whatever this American god was or is, it was not "my God" was their constant refrain. All involved in the debate left room for their own theologically oriented plausible deniability. Indeed, Jennings and Carter had also taken time in their essays to qualify that there was a difference between the American god they were talking about and accusing, and God.

The race-based, gendered, and other *ad hominem* attacks faced by Butler are easy enough to see and understand as reactions to two central notions valued supremely by most white Americans, god and whiteness. Furthermore, second in quantity only to these defenses of god were defenses of white people, who were claiming to not "be" racist. Most (white) commenters were sure of two things: that god was real and that they were not racist. These many vindications of god, the protecting of god, and the protecting of white bodies in response to Butler's black rage are instructive of the complexities associated with understanding the white man's god complex. For the whites involved in the discussions, there seemed to be a connection between their identities as "white" and their identities as "believers." In other words, their responses to Butler's argument only proved the merit of her argument – that white people have incredible difficulty disassociating their beliefs in god from their beliefs in their own identity.

Whatever may or may not be made of non-white exonerations of "God" while looking down the barrel of the white racist god's gun – the discussion's forebear, William Jones, was, after all, an atheist – this chapter looks to both the racialized killings of African Americans by vigilantes and law enforcement officials, and other killings as well, along with the conversations unfolding from these atrocities, to begin making sense of two of the most cherished of American pastimes, believing in god and feeling like god. Such beliefs about god and self are constituent parts of a white man's god complex that has wrought havoc on many in the United States and abroad. We white Americans are not gods, and no amount of killing or lying will ever vindicate our devilish desire to be gods.

I want to suggest that Butler's words be taken more literally than most would want to *believe*. Functionally speaking, the American god *is* "a white racist"[12] murderer. Thinkers like James Cone, James Perkinson, and many others such as Butler, Carter, and Jennings have articulated a more or less cohesive (albeit at times inchoate) rendering of a "white" theological or religious sensibility/identity operative historically in the United States or shaping the brand of Christianity that found fertile soil here in the U.S. Building on their efforts, I present an apparatus for understanding *how* a white man's god complex works and *why* it persists. I argue that this complex is structured by theism functioning as what Niklas Luhmann refers to as "a contingency formula,"[13] structuring society as god, and procuring a sense of certainty for some through the sacrifice of others. The connection between the murders of young black men and the verbal assault on Butler are more than situationally related; rather, they exemplify the two principal features of the white man's god complex in practice, its self-reproduction and its reliance on violence.

Keep in mind that whiteness is only one feature of what I characterize as a larger, incredibly durable religious disposition, where structured and structuring distinctions produce semblances and senses of secure identities. Another is theism, the belief in *the idea of* god. This belief in the idea of god – working with the god-idol of whiteness – has come to produce and sustain the white man's god complex. I define the white man's god complex as the (conscious and unconscious) posturing disposition of oneself and/or community as absolute in value and ability, wherein society (the projection of the self) functions *as* god so that social actors might act like gods, rejecting or denying radical contingency. That is, the white man's god complex is a thought/embodied structure projected onto society in such a way that it creates the necessary conditions and contexts that enable the functional realization of that projection. The white man's god complex functions as a system, where multiple god-idols (groupings of exaggerations of radical contingency) come together in a way that casts society as god, and death/limitation as false idol. God-idols, remember, are the demigods, the half-gods that operate to secure society as god. In this securing, they're able to maintain an enduring power over and control of others.

My argument brings together existential and functional perspectives to suggest that within this complex, society functions as ultimate concern.[14] God, understood here in a Tillichian sense as one's "ultimate concern,"[15] and the history of theism operative amongst U.S. whites indicates that the white ultimate concern has been and remains society – an expression of the social divine, "that aggregate force which is the basis of any society or association."[16] Stated differently, most whites remain only concerned with themselves, and this solipsism is deadly for those outside the white man's god complex. This oxymoronic social solipsism, with its dangers for others, characterizes the "god complex." Theologian Paul Tillich girds my understanding of the idea of god and the anxiety of meaninglessness felt by many white theists historically and today.[17] Durkheimian functionalism offers a theoretical assessment of society *as ultimate concern* by speaking of society as god and god as society.[18] From within the white man's god complex:

> Society is not an empirical fact, definite and observable; it is a fancy, a dream with which men have lightened their sufferings, but in which they have never really lived. It is merely an idea which comes to express our more or less obscure aspirations towards the good, the beautiful and the ideal. Now these aspirations have their roots in us; they come from the very depths of our being … thus it would seem that the ideal society presupposes religion.[19]

Where this god complex is concerned, existential wrestlings find material expression in society.[20] Society is, in this regard, a sort of functioning center, a thread that ties and binds social life as it exists and social life as a collectivity thinks it should exist.

If god is society, then at some level, theism would involve believing in society. But this isn't exactly the case, as theism functions to secure society as god through belief localized elsewhere. Society achieves ultimate concern as those within it register other ideas or processes as that ultimate concern. Whether evangelical and concerned with the justice of god, or liberal Protestant and characterizing god as love, or a nationalist who connects god to race, land, and material resource, the adherents of the white man's god complex hold such a variety of beliefs that society's functioning emerges as the "one true god" within this complex. Thus, god becomes that which centers a community's concerns, beliefs, and actions.

As many would have it, following a Lockean economist theory of the genesis of the social, the actors in the complex operate out of the notion that society is a collection of individuals who come together (through and using communication) to ward off natural and other social dangers and risks arising from growing complexity. Such perspectives presuppose something called an "individual" existing prior to collectivities, and rely on this assumption that societies function to guard against physical death and limitation.[21] Though Durkheim went to great lengths to assault this thin perspective on the social, it still seemingly carries much purchase with white people and echoes of it might even be heard by those defending social tragedies as collateral damage of one sort or another. Though white people are not alone in guilt regarding this tendency, my focus here is on understanding this willingness as expressed in the white man's god complex.

The lyrics from The Last Poets foreshadow and remind, however, that this god complex comes at a social cost. History demonstrates that many white people are willing to kill to guard against such limits and ensure the survival of a society, which has as functional aims the reduction of complexity, physical danger, and risk. Each stanza from the spoken word poem ends in a couplet that warns of an impending death blamed on the "white man's god complex."[22] Why do The Last Poets place such blame on the "white man?" Simply stated, perhaps because white people respond to their limits by imposing them on others. Where race is concerned in the United States, the imposition of these limits has come in a variety of forms, such as enslavement, Jim and Jane Crow laws, and a current assault on black life through the prison industrial complex and through vigilante and socially sanctioned (law enforcement) murders. The list of these death-dealing social limits extends beyond these well-known forms of racial oppression.

These limits, this "radical contingency," consist of what we can know, the choices we make based on what we know, our limited time alive, and our interactions with others. Within the white man's god complex, such limits are responded to when "the white man plays out the god complex as a control freak who has been socialized to believe that he must dominate and be the lord of the world, supervising the planet."[23] The exaggerated claims white U.S. citizens make and beliefs they hold about gods and humans, claims which deny human limitations by imposing such limits onto others,[24] have social consequences. These consequences, these sacrifices, lead religious studies scholar Theodore Trost to directly refer to the white man's god complex as "a system of violence, an order of power *over* African Americans."[25] This system of violence occurs through the exaggeration of one group's radical contingency by another group. Such exaggerations embellish human value or ability as perceived by many and as manifest in society through sacrifice. The "stock ingredients" for such a complex include the confluence of whiteness and theism working together so that society might be created in the image of exaggerations of human ability and value, Imago Superlata.

As hinted at in the previous chapter, my interest isn't theological or metaphysical, but is to anthropologically isolate, illumine, and make sense of what has been labeled a "god complex," the "white man's god complex," this attempt to know and control all information and values, an effort in omnipotence and omniscience that seeks to secure society as god by responding to uncertainty and limitation through imposing such uncertainty and limits onto others. Responding to the complex, then, will require transforming oneself into the sacrificed – here a euphemism for seeing oneself as the exaggerator, the "liar," and reflection on what such a posture demonstrates about interpretations and assumptions about social possibilities. So who are we, the liars? Who exactly is guilty of the white man's god complex?

MOST AMERICANS

In an effort to make very clear both *who* I am talking about and *what* I am talking about, it is important to situate this book's primary demographic, data set, and audience by grounding my discussion of white people, noting the variety amongst them, discussing the social sameness afforded by white skin, and then finally moving to situate "white theists" as a more or less cohesive group for analysis. Though demographic trends are shifting in the United States, historically and today the bulk of those operating according to such a god complex are disproportionately white, disproportionately theists, and disproportionately Christian.[26] I use "white theist" to indicate a group of people who have ostensibly practiced and/or benefitted from (at least) two complementary means of securing the false sense of certainty and subjectivity offered by god-idols.[27]

When I make claims about "whiteness," its effects or its constitution, I am not talking about "white people," and when discussing theism, I am not referring to the essential feature of a theist. Nor am I talking about the primary characteristic with which to define any particular group of people.[28] Whiteness and theism are god-idols, discursive ideas – conglomerates of exaggerations of radical contingency – that work to shape society in the image of those exaggerations. "Whiteness" derives its name from "white people," but whiteness and theism (as god-idols) are worshipped by many people across race, space, and time. White people are not the sum total of the worship of the god-idol of whiteness, though they are never fully removed from it.

My use of "white people" refers to the overarching statistical demographic in the United States who, by virtue of certain physiological markers and the meaning of those markers in relation to these god-idols operating in the social world, check off "Caucasian" or "White Hispanic" on census reports.[29] "White people" refers to the community of those phenotypically and sensorially labeled "white" or "Caucasian" by virtue of a number of different (initially) arbitrary physiological and social factors. The meaning and significance of those physiological markers shift over time. Accordingly, so do definitions of white people. Here, I rely initially on self-ascription on census reports to ground my definition of white people. I find this sufficient because relying on the idea of "whiteness" and its privileges afforded to many white people has the tendency of reinforcing whiteness as something necessarily connected to white people, which it is not.

According to the 2010 Census Bureau numbers, non-Hispanic whites make up roughly 65 percent of the U.S. population.[30] Taking into account Hispanic whites, that percentage jumps to just under 80 percent.[31] These "white people" make up well over half of all active voters, although the 2012 national elections saw the number of these voters decrease from 2008.[32] Approximately 46.5 percent of these "white people" hold some sort of job[33] and 6.1 percent are considered "working poor," indicating that they "are persons who spent at least 27 weeks in the labor force (i.e., working or looking for work) but their incomes still fall below the official poverty level."[34]

In contrast to these "white people," in 2011, 13.3 percent of African Americans and 12.9 percent of Hispanics were counted in this same group of working poor.[35] Though these percentages explain how poverty disproportionately effects black and brown communities, they also show that there are nearly 7,000,000 working poor white people, meaning that these whites make up the overwhelming majority of poor people in the United States.[36] A similar point may be made with respect to poverty more generally, with nearly 12 percent of white people falling at or below the poverty line, while African Americans face a poverty rate of nearly 26 percent.[37] On the completely opposite end of the socioeconomic spectrum, of the 1 percent who are the wealthiest in the United States, nearly 95 percent are white people.[38]

These white people also accounted for over seven million arrests nationwide in 2009, with African Americans accounting for over three million arrests.[39] Staggeringly, of all of these arrests, where whites represent over half of total arrests (they also account for nearly 100,000 more violent crime arrests than blacks),[40] whites represent only 11 percent of the total incarcerated population, compared with approximately 27 percent Hispanic inmates and 62 percent African American.[41] These arrest and incarceration statistics indicate that white people are arrested at a rate roughly 2:1 compared to black and brown people, but face prison at a rate of 1:10 relative to their black and brown counterparts.

These quantitative statistics explain two crucial qualitative characteristics of white people: a) that there is extreme diversity amongst this group, and that, despite this diversity, b) whites share considerable social privilege (even while many are economically disadvantaged), a privilege that connects them as a cohesive (albeit porous) group.[42] Therefore, when I describe white people, I want to present this demographic in its complexity and variety.[43] I have included these figures to note that no ideal-typical portrait of "white people" can be gleaned from actual, empirically determined statistics. By "ideal-typical," I borrow social theorist James Faubion's use of the Weberian idea, where it refers to a theoretic guidepost, a stereotype if you will, used to reinforce certain social theories as effectively "closed" or correct in every moment.[44] For instance, The Last Poets' use of the term "white man" presumes a type of shared experience amongst these whites. This is an "ideal-typical" portrait, both analytically incomplete and yet useful. In deference to the usefulness of The Last Poets' ideal-typical description, subjective assessment affords an ideal-typical framing of white people. Whites across socioeconomic class derive benefit from white skin, be it interpersonal, structural, or otherwise. If an ideal-typical image is possible at all, it would then include the advantage wrought from white skin, what some label white privilege.[45] This privilege cuts against the variety of the group, but does not alone justify a dismissal of the social variance amongst the group.

Religious commitments also hold together many of these white people as an ideal-type. Within the United Sates, 2012 Pew Research data show that 78.4 percent of the entire U.S. population considers itself Christian (of one sort or another).[46] More than this claimed ideological or church affiliation, 92 percent of Americans "believe in God or the idea of a universal spirit."[47] Nearly 70 percent are certain of this god's existence, even though what this god looks like takes a great number of shapes in the United States. Beliefs held by whites are as diverse as these white people. Worth noting, of these American believers, six out of ten understand themselves to have some sort of "personal relationship" with god and/or conceive of god anthropomorphically.[48] Despite the suggested rising numbers of non-believers, nearly half of all Americans feel that increasing atheism is problematic for America. No doubt, the bulk of those holding the view that atheism or non-belief is problematic are believers in "god." I regard this believing group's fear of non-believers as an indication that their ultimate concern seems to be a smooth, effectively functioning society in "America."[49] Even the framing of such questionnaires relegates religious belief to an undercurrent of a more important ideological marker: U.S. Citizenship. Effectively, this suggests that a white person does not have to be a traditional "theist" to worship the god of society. Nevertheless, the bulk of those within the complex ascribe to traditional belief in "god." This is an important point, as my definition of theism (unpacked below) does not require belief in god. Any ultimate concern will suffice, even belief in belief. Nevertheless, theism as traditionally defined plays a huge role in the lives of many of these white people, and so I give attention to traditional theistic and Christian ideas overlapping with more non-traditional cultural and social instances.

Though Caucasians make up a sizeable and disproportionate percentage of non-theists and atheists as well, the majority of Americans believe in god or a higher power and the largest single racial group in the United States is Caucasian, meaning that a sizable and influential percentage of the overall American population are white theists, and so theism offers another component of an ideal-typical white American.

This belief connects them.[50] So does their racial privilege: the social, cultural, and economic advantages afforded white people, and by dehumanizing non-white people. In fact, if I might invert the argument regarding double or triple jeopardy suggested to occur amongst African American women as a result of the oppression felt because of sexism, racism, and poverty,[51] white theists are *doubly advantaged* because of their whiteness and their theism, and where economic advantage is found, *triply advantaged*.[52] These markers of an ideal-type are not simply arbitrary means of analytic social stratification. God-idols do the work to actually procure these advantages, the complex transmuting an ideal-type, a norm which is actually an exception, into a quantifiable group. They function to secure this privilege. And this function is yet another connective feature binding these white theists as a cohesive unit within this project.[53]

Theism connects most Americans at the level of my analysis, yes, but it is also used to connect them with one another. It offers an ideological foundation, grounded in an ultimate concern for society, from which Civil Religion[54] and institutional religious practices emerge with immense variety. Despite such variety of belief and practice, belief in belief connects them. Though white theists range in wealth, education, social options, and religious commitment, theism grounds many of their understandings of themselves and others.

Appealing to Pierre Bourdieu, I want to label this theistically grounded group as a white theistic petit bourgeois,[55] meaning that their theism – their belief in the idea of god (however constituted, even as belief *in* belief) – produces a centering ideal from which white theistic variety radiates outward. For these white theists, variety is responded to by ideologically agreeing across a vast array of stated possibilities of belief. I do not mean to suggest that there are no limits to this agreement, but that even those limits are fundamentally based on social differences.[56] Belief in the idea of god brings this variety together, and it is recast as a concern for the society centered on this white theistic petit bourgeois. For example, in more explicit terms, believing in their belief in god, white Baptists find commonality with Methodists, Methodists with Pentecostals and Catholics, etc., etc. For instance, when meeting new people, white theists are often interested to ask the newcomer "What church do you attend?"[57] The presumption is that a white theist can learn a lot about a stranger if they know where, and if at all, the stranger attends church. As equally important as any specific answer is that an answer is offered at all. The question posed has *everything* to do with belonging and sameness, specifically with respect to sect or denomination, and generally in terms of a larger theistic (and usually "white") way of life. Further, activities like dinner-time prayer, church attendance on Easter, and a host of activities (born of disparate theological positions) work to reinforce a white normativity constituted through the various god-idols (whiteness, theism, etc.) working within the god complex. That is, presumptions about ideological normativity are not "determined" through these questions so much as they are produced in the very asking. The concern over what is said in churches, for many of these white theists, is less important than whether church was attended or not. Worth recalling, the question of "What church do you attend?" asks if one has participated in a U.S. social activity that Dr. Martin Luther King, Jr. described as "the most segregated time in America."[58] The question of theistic orientation, in the U.S., is always racialized even if tacitly, the god-idols working in tandem to determine various sorts of affinity or social acceptability. The questioning says more about the questioner than it does the questioned, in terms of the white theist's values and commitments. Couched in light of theism, these questions outline insiders from outsiders. Belief in the idea of god is central to these efforts. More generally, theism unites, and unites through distinction. This concern over theism operates as a unifying idea through the distinctions it imposes and presupposes. Questions about "god" or "church" have more to do with humans – they are questions about human group allegiance.[59]

Formative sociologist Max Weber helps to contextualize the utility of theistic allegiance with his treatment of Protestant sects in the United States. His basic thesis argues that sect (e.g., Baptist, Methodist, Quaker, etc.) membership was a basic requirement for entering into entrepreneurial and business ventures. The logic behind the need for membership involved responding to unscrupulous businesspeople who would easily swindle unsuspecting settlers on the American frontier. God, and by extension church membership, allowed different parties who did not know each other to trust the other was honest by virtue of church allegiance. To be a member of a sect meant one was an upstanding citizen and therefore allowed access to a certain amount of economic and social capital. To be a member of the same sect would mean, then, perhaps even greater access to resources. To the extent that church membership is on the decline today, other mechanisms are in place to ensure such honesty among and across various economic parties. Weber puts it this way: "It is not the ethical *doctrine* of a religion, but that form of ethical conduct upon which *premiums* are placed that matters."[60] That is to say, and acting as a proto-form of the Bourdieusian theories grounding much of this book, on the American frontier, god has always been a euphemism for a particular sort of belief in the social common good, and sectarian membership (which emerged as congregational and denominational affiliation in the U.S.) was but a proxy for grace or trust extended to various social actors so they might not swindle one another. This arrangement, as many will no doubt recognize, is what leads to the "spirit" of capitalism.[61]

Of interest here are the economic ends guiding such memberships and affiliations, and the way that a concern to determine one's identity on moral or ethical grounds – that is, based on what they do/did – ended up the exact opposite. Rather than determine the worth or value of individuals based on specific actions, such actions were transmuted into a group acceptance that was then extended as membership into a much broader middle-class ethos. Effectively, these white members of these sects invariably had to do very little for such membership. All that was required was *belief*: a professed belief in a god that connected across sectarian lines, and in the mandates of one's sect that ensured moral righteousness, all along having as its functional goal the "breeding of ethically qualified *fellow believers*."[62] Weber makes it plain:

> Today the kind of denomination [to which one belongs] is rather irrelevant. It does not matter whether one be Freemason, Christian Scientist, Adventist, Quaker, or what not. What is decisive is that one be admitted to membership by a 'ballot,' after an *examination* and an ethical *probation* in the sense of the virtues which are at a premium for the inner-worldly asceticism of Protestantism and hence, for the ancient puritan tradition. Then, the same effect could be observed.[63]

Weber's final comment about the "ancient puritan tradition" foreshadows another important component of this religion of "most Americans," that being sin and violence as punishment for sin. However, notable here is Weber's suggestion that "what" one *is* doesn't matter, so long as there is membership of some sort. He elaborates that such membership is not as simple as professing allegiance, but involves a community underwriting their commitment to the individual that may then extend to others who would seek to judge or interact with the member. Are not pastors' classes and catechisms also means of examination of the moral worth of prospective members of the community? If direct racial affiliation is not the mandate for membership, it at least remains an open question whether or not the moral or ethical turpitude thus determined dictates the degree to which racialized bodies might be willing to support or sustain a certain sort of status quo. Further, with membership in belief sects serving as entry into the economic sphere, we can note the impact of contemporary segregated church services on many racial and economic disparities, past and present. Essentially, pastors' classes and the like amount to theological disciplining mechanisms, and professions of faith end up outward signs of one's willingness to be disciplined, to toe a particular line in order to receive access to goods and services of a social and economic sort. By this method, theological affiliation provides a proxy for race-based identities to be at once denied and yet secured.

Following from Weber's efforts, various versions of secularization theses might then demonstrate the waning significance of not simply theological or ecclesial disciplining techniques, but also the decreased effectiveness of theological or racial identity to do the functional work they once did to secure the middle class. While denominational affiliation might be on the decline, such decline might simultaneously be the result of an increasing trust in the laws and governmental parameters ensuring ethical business transactions and opportunities, and it might explain why belief in "god" today serves as a shorthand version of the sectarian memberships necessary for access to capital in years past.[64] Weber's thesis involving demystification and secularization connects explicitly to economic capital, in particular the establishment (and one might infer, the eroding) of the middle class. In either case, secularization discourses might then be a proxy equivalent to theology for many trying to make sense of a social order and identity once secured for "most Americans" and perceived by many as in decline today. It might also be noted and acknowledged that many white Americans tend to blame black people (e.g., desegregation, integration, affirmative action, social services, rap music, etc.) for the decimation of the middle class and its values, when, in fact, to the extent the middle-class has been eroded at all, it is more likely an effect of a nearly forty-year assault on business regulations. For their part, legislated business regulations took the place of theistic sectarian moral policing that waned in the twentieth century. Heuristically speaking, at about the same time The Last Poets gave us a name for understanding white relationships to state, god, and blackness, politicians legislated into effect the ability for economic actors to lie in the marketplace. To this extent, most white Americans are as victimized by some of these lies as they are (also) themselves the liars and beneficiaries of such deregulation.

Of great curiosity to me is how Weber's thesis of sectarian identity formation and secularization might have something to say of the manner in which different "gods" emerge on different sides of racial divides. Thinking back to the efforts of Carter and Jennings noted in this chapter's introduction, and looking ahead to a discussion in chapter 4, there are grounds here to demonstrate that there are, indeed, multiple "gods" operative across (or perhaps even within) racial groups. Carter's or Jennings's distinction between the American racist god and whatever "God" they profess allegiance to, may be more appropriate than a critical assessment might first want to admit. Granted that the god early white settlers and immigrants brought to the American shores was as thoroughly enmeshed with economic concerns as Weber postulates, and given that the enslaved could own no property until after emancipation, then qualitatively, there are *at least* two "gods" operative in America today – an inherited American god of economic privilege and violence and a god of the margins, social peripheries, and of those victimized by the American god. By this I intend to suggest two means of enacting the social power of belief. I will leave it for those more qualified and justified to wrestle with these gods of the black American experience.

Significant for this talk of the white man's god complex, of the white American experience, however, there are not here the multiple options for "god" that are found in black religious expression. Of course, the manner and mode of theological belief and expression are today even far more varied than as described by Weber (in large part corroborating Weber's own ideas about the secular devolution of this particular brand of American Protestantism) – but despite their diversity they remain *mono*theistic. That is, for white Americans, belief in god only does one thing: secure our proximate distance to social centers. How else are we to make sense of, or take responsibility for, Darren Wilson, the Ferguson, MO police officer who murdered Michael Brown in 2014, becoming a millionaire in the wake of the grand jury decision not to indict him?[65] In the wake of finding ourselves within a god complex wherein race and masculinity, theism and economics cohabitate to such a degree that there is no way to parse them from each other, bearing responsibility for the god complex may necessarily involve rejecting any and all belief in god. The only options involve either embracing the only god ever known by white Americans, the god of the white man's god complex, or rejecting this god through some form of atheism that would ensure one did not believe in oneself or the racist society. For most Americans, the American racist, violent god is our "God." Upper or lower case, however it is described, if it relies on belief, white belief, then it supports the white man's god complex.

Marking a functionally similar, though seemingly disconnected sociological trend regarding taste-making amongst a particular social class in France, Bourdieu offers some further analytic guidance. Though Bourdieu was speaking of sanctioned aristocratic and academic distinctions of the French petit bourgeois, his comments are applicable to white U.S. theists. He writes:

> The official differences produced by academic classifications tend to produce (or reinforce) real differences by inducing in the classified individuals a collectively recognized and supported belief in the differences, thus producing behaviours that are intended to bring real being into line with official being.[66]

As argued by Bourdieu, "official being" suggests that the petit bourgeois do not find a home in any specific stratified class, they teeter on the anxious edge between the proletariat and the bourgeois. They are homeless and classless, in the sense that their economic variety suggests they do not belong to any socioeconomic demographic and their ethnic origins have often been blurred genealogically to such an extent that they can no longer adequately profess membership as "Polish" or "French" or "Irish," etc. "Academic classifications" in the form of census reports and the like that ask about "white" racial groups "produce (or reinforce) real differences by inducing … a collectively recognized and supported belief in the differences." The category of "white," even as it serves to track socio-economic and other trends, ends up helping to reinforce the sorts of social anxiety that have worked in the establishment of "most Americans" *as white*. Moreover, where white theists are concerned, there is the sense that they do not have the luxury of "belonging" to any cohesive ethnic group, and theological or denominational affiliation works to fill this void. Whites certainly are a racial group, but because of their variety, they often feel themselves "homeless" in this sense.[67] The irony, of course, is that they feel this homelessness while at home in a largely white society. Irony aside, many contemporary white theists often feel this homelessness directly or find a sense of belonging in the notion that their home has been taken over (i.e., they have lost/are losing their country).

Much Tea Party rhetoric is indicative of this homelessness sentiment, and certain cultural products emerging out of this rhetoric help to exemplify the feeling. Appealing to myself as auto-ethnographic data, I turn now to an example of this sensibility as it presented itself to me in the form of an email forward I received – where talk of god gives way to direct presentation of the white theist's ultimate concern, the intent to bring actual society into line with their ideal image of society by "produc[ing] behaviors that bring real being in line with official being."[68]

A number of years ago, I received an email forward that included a painting by conservative Jon McNaughton titled "The Demise of America."[69] I reached out to McNaughton seeking permissions to reprint the image here, but as white lies are wont to protect themselves, my request was rejected. So allow for a summary. The painting is ominous and dark, showcasing a conflagration of the halls of Congress. Washington D.C. is on fire. Seated in a chair at the front of the painting is Barack Obama, somberly playing a fiddle.

The email forward also includes two brief paragraphs of political prose, situated under the painting. The first line tells the reader the name of the painting. The next few lines argue that "many Americans" are dismayed and horrified by the "downward spiral" of America's economic, moral, and political situation. McNaughton then suggests that the country is facing "ruin" due to President Obama's "indifferent attitude." The last lines of the email draw a parallel between Nero's persecution of Christians whilst Rome burned, to the contemporary moment in America wherein "Obama fiddled, while the people witnessed the demise of America."[70]

Though the words and perspective are attributed to McNaughton, by virtue of its inclusion as a mass email forward, I want to suggest the first paragraph may genuinely describe the sentiments of "many Americans," "dismayed" at the "indifference" of President Obama. While in the second paragraph, these sentiments are connected to a quasi-historic example of Nero's persecution of Christians indicating that those who feel this dismay (today) seem to understand themselves as persecuted, and that such persecution is the result of an American, Christian, theistic religious orientation. From the sentiments exposed here, the anxiety casts them thrutching in a variety of directions in an effort to find points of social sameness that might operate as a type of capital. In the United States, theism is a type of social and cultural capital as it operates to address such uncertainty and limitation by artificially producing sameness and order, whether through moral maintenance or racial identity – which, in the end, amount to the same thing for American religion.

The import of this photo passed around through email forwarding suggests it represents the sentiments of many of these white theists, meaning that the image speaks not only specifically to a particular interpretive posture on the part of one person, but being passed along through email, repeatedly, suggests the expressed sentiments are shared by the "many Americans" discussed in the paragraphs underneath the image. In short, though it is impossible to know the exact numbers of people who share the sentiments expressed in the email, there is enough of a critical mass of individuals for whom it appeals that the content of the email offers a way to understand some of the motivations of these "many Americans." Other features of this class-less class of white theists include "an ethos of restriction through pretension, the voluntaristic rigour of the 'called' but not yet 'chosen,' who base their pretension to embody one day what 'ought to be' on a permanent invocation of 'ought.'"[71] The god-idol of theism, for the white U.S. theist, is this "ought," belief in the idea of god as a means of reinforcing a largely white society as god. In the image, where incomplete history, racialized social animosity, and secularization's economic edge collide, white theistic sentiments are exposed – not as accurate or grounded, but as an expression of their sense of connection rooted in a belief in the idea of god as safeguarding a more fundamental belief in the idea of a white society. If it is the sense of many of these white theists that their society is in "demise," then it stands to reason that one way they might respond to the feeling of encroaching demise would be to embrace it more fully, metaphorically "learning to die," in the sense of learning to accept this (perceived) loss of power and certainty rather than fight against it. Instead, they blame the black man.

To help explain this point, as well as how I am situating theism and its social operation, in the United States historically, theism offers a type of social and cultural capital that operates to address human uncertainty and limitation by artificially producing sameness and order. In short, the quantity and diversity of social anxiety and experience amongst white theists requires the postulation and adherence to a sameness offered by *different* ideas about god – a sameness that localizes in society.[72] That is, sameness is sought and limitation responded to not by god (i.e., society) – their god is in "demise," after all – but by belief in the idea of god (theism) as a means of (re)securing society as god. This sameness comes about by the imposition of difference as a corrective for difference's casualties. It is not enough that the painting includes a burning Congress, it also includes an image of a black president, unconcerned – even happy – about the conflagration. His inclusion signals to white theists that the problem is not theirs, allowing them to find unity in their exoneration and their vilification of Obama as distinct from them. In this effort, the painting exemplifies (in the twenty-first century) what Noel Ignatiev explored in relation to the nineteenth, the use of black stereotypes to produce and reinforce an ideal-typical white identity and society.[73]

In certain respects, my point about theism is similar to Ignatiev's conclusion that whiteness was embraced by Irish American immigrants in an effort to align themselves with older English residents and to distinguish themselves from blacks.[74] In this sense, whiteness is less of a thing and more a strategic use of identification. Theism functions in a similar capacity, only on a larger scale and cutting across insular ethnic communities. Theism is the bridge between existential yearnings and functional, material acquiescence. Evidence for this is also to be found in the comments leveled against Butler, where many sought to vindicate or exonerate "god" as they presumed themselves to be talking about the same thing ("god"). These vindications relied on vilification of Butler, suggesting that god's defenders were not worried about "god" but were defending various contextual expressions of theism functioning together to reinforce society as god. Society *is* their god. Theism makes it so, and allows social actors to act like god.

Theism extends beyond a concern over otherworldliness or cosmic forces. But complicating my argument is that theism – as understood and defined by white theists (as I've characterized them) – is part and parcel with reinforcing society as ultimate concern. White theists employ "theological" language, adhering and appealing to "god" to undergird their actual operative god as society. The following offers a final brief anecdotal example of this theological appeal as it works to reinforce the sense of society as god protected by and defining this white theistic petit bourgeoisie:

> For most Americans, the blessings of God have been the basis of our liberty, prosperity, and survival as a unique country.
>
> For most Americans, prayer is real, and we subordinate ourselves to a God on whom we call for wisdom, guidance, and salvation.
>
> For most Americans, the prospect of a ruthlessly secular society that would forbid public reference to God and systematically remove all religious symbols from the public square is horrifying.[75]

Allowing for minor theological tweaks to Newt Gingrich's theo-political aphorisms, and applying Bourdieu's conception of the petit bourgeois to Gingrich's characterization of "most Americans," white theists are the "most Americans" described here by Gingrich. His words not only suggest this theistic connection among whites, but describe theism and whiteness working together within the white man's god complex. The comment that "we subordinate ourselves to a God" and Gingrich's vehement disdain for secularism expose and foreshadow the social function and significance offered by this belief in the idea of god in the United States. His comments seem to suggest that those who hold sway over belief in the idea of god, or of theism, do not simply find themselves on the right side of Pascal's wager,[76] but find themselves the recipient of social privileges that come about from the sacrifices required by adherence to theism.

This white man's god complex is not limited to evangelical or fundamental theists, nor is it only operative amongst white theists who might fit the popular image of an "extremist" or a "racist." In historical context, Gary Dorrien's extensive history of liberal theology paints this white theistic need through different imagery, as he argues that liberal theology develops as a means of balancing an expanding modern, rational quest for knowledge with an ongoing preoccupation with finding ways to keep the idea of god relevant while on this quest.[77] Dorrien's statement about liberal theology's progenitors seeking god's preservation undergirds the use of theism in this same capacity albeit within a white theistic constituency that tended to appreciate education, the arts, progressive culture, and the like. Here, my point is simply to note that, though the contemporary instances used here suggest I am relegating all white theists to one political and theological position, the white man's god complex has affected far more than contemporary conservatives worried over the loss of their country. I also don't mean to suggest that Dorrien is interested in (or would even agree with) the ideas I present here. Rather, his brilliant analysis of liberal theologians does well to demonstrate that the ultimate concerns of classically liberal white (and even black) Christian leaders in the United States is the effective functioning of an ideological system thought to undergird social cohesiveness. Dorrien notes that liberal theology is largely "defined by its openness to the verdicts of modern intellectual inquiry … its conception of Christianity as an ethical way of life; its advocacy of moral concepts of atonement or reconciliations; and its commitments to make Christianity credible and socially relevant to contemporary people."[78] The liberal or conservative demands to keep or protect "god" or "Christianity" overlap and are blurred. Ostensibly, "god" for most (white) Americans, and "theology" or "Christianity" for white Christians specifically, was and always has been a proxy for social concern. Dorrien's analysis shows equal anxiety on the part of many white liberal theistic leaders in terms of the ideas of god and religion cohabitating. But such synergy is judged, it appears, according to social reality, marking the social world as of supreme value and ability, not any particular theistic tradition. Contemporary conservative positions posit a loss of both religion and society, directly; liberal whites often fear this same loss of social function, but rely on a different lexicon to express the fear. Many white Americans, falling on either side of a political continuum, when they talk about "god" are actually talking about and wrestling with, ultimately, a shared god complex employing theism (as a god-idol) as a means of securing society as god so that human limitations can be ignored or denied. I challenge anyone to find an example of white American appeal to god or other theological or identity-based categories that cannot be reduced to a concern that the social world remain intact or function more equitably or efficiently. Prayers are always directed ultimately to society.

This preoccupation with "God" has a powerful radiating effect of securing certain distinctions and realities for these "most Americans." As I conclude below, this security comes at a cost. In fact, this idea of god, played out amongst these "most Americans," has assured that they follow an "ethic of noblesse oblige" (an ethic based on artificial social impositions) that often reinforces their anxieties as they work to curb them. Sending along the email of "The Demise of America" is a physical expression of theism's social function. That is, continuing to believe in a god's preferential option for America does more to reinforce the anxiety that the social notions of American Exceptionalism, for one example, seek to assuage than it does to actually produce contentment or social belonging.[79] The idea of god (1) allows these "most Americans" to pretend they have life better than their actual circumstances allow, while it (2) also works to prevent these "most Americans" from arriving at the life they already perceive themselves to hold. By this token, the white man's god complex ensures that white theists live their lives as a lie. This is Imago Superlata, made in the image of an exaggeration, and theism works to ensure this exaggerated lifestyle. Moving now to a more focused discussion of why belief in the idea of god operates in this fashion, perception and the power of belief are shown as key to these attitudes of "most Americans."

THE (WHITE) POWER OF THEISM

> One person with a belief is a social power equal to 99 who have only interests.
>
> *John Stuart Mill (Quoted by Forrester, a commenter on Stormfront, a white supremacy website)*[80]

Theism offers a particular type of social weight and power based on the inherent paradox of the idea of god. As society changes in look, form, and need, so too will images of "god," always a parallel projection to and of various images of the social world, but the preoccupation with society as actual ultimate concern remains constant.

Contrary to popular belief/normative definitions of theism in the study of religion – that is, belief in some sort of "god" existing in some (or all) place or time – as I argue above, theism is best defined as belief in the idea of god, or belief in the power of belief, that is, belief in the functional utility of belief itself.[81] Theisms emphasizing god's wrath, providence, justice, or love are all various expressions relying on the same belief in an idea. Questions about "god" or "religion" involve human identity and group allegiance[82] – an allegiance in service to society. Though beneficiaries and victims of this god complex vary from one person or group to the next, the run of the mill theisms operative within the United States have played a role in maintaining this god complex, as explored above. Understanding theism as belief in the utility of belief helps to explain this relationship more precisely.

While engaging in some online "fieldwork" my efforts have taken me to a number of explicitly racist online hotspots. One of these is Stormfront,[83] a white supremacist website that has been around since 1995. They define themselves as "a community of racial realists and idealists. We are White Nationalists who support *true* diversity and a homeland for *all* peoples. Thousands of organizations promote the interests, values and heritage of non-White minorities. We promote ours. Yet we are demonized as 'racists.' We are the voice of the new, embattled White minority!"[84] Immediately, any explicit discussion of "god" or "religion" is absent, and, yet, their claims regarding "nationalism and homeland" echo the white theistic disposition discussed above. What, then, could this suggest about theism?

Started as a bulletin board and clearing house for the organizing of racist people and ideas, they deem their prejudice justified by an awareness of the anxiety that society is no longer theirs, such that they perceive themselves a "minority." (Parenthetically, this founding date means that before Amazon.com and Google, before AOL, the proliferation of pornography, and our ubiquitous acceptance of the Internet, white supremacy made quick use of the innovative technology we now rely on daily.)[85] While examining this site, I came across one prolific commenter on the website named Forrester, whose signature line within his comments included the following quotation from John Stuart Mill: "One person with a belief is a social power equal to 99 who have only interests."[86]

Why does such a statement about belief matter to a white nationalist? Seeking background, I traced Mill's statement to explore his position on religion and society. Mill says,

> Yet so natural to mankind is intolerance in whatever they really care about, that religious freedom has hardly anywhere been practically realized. ... In the minds of almost all religious persons, even in the most tolerant countries, the duty of toleration is admitted with tacit reserves. Wherever the sentiment of the majority is still genuine and intense, it is found to have abated little of its claim to be obeyed.[87]

Mill's words come through as musings of a man troubled by an ineffective and hypocritical social arrangement. Mill finds religion to promote intolerance, and he clearly has a problem with such religion. In light of his chosen Internet activities, it appears Forrester also notes the possibilities that religious freedom might promote intolerance. Having thought long about the significance of Forrester's appreciation of Mill's idea – such was the poignancy of Forrester's attaching it as the intellectual foundation for his comments on Stormfront's website – I have become aware that ideas do not have to meet with material reality to have dastardly consequences for the social world. That seems Mill's implied point, as well, as he demonstrates the disconnect between the notion of religious tolerance and the actual practice of religious intolerance. Belief in the idea of tolerance allows for the actual expression of intolerance, precisely because the rhetoric undergirding the beliefs and practices suggests otherwise. Theism, to this effect, functions effectively when it acts as if it is doing something other than what it is actually doing, reinforcing society as god made in the image of a white man. A belief, alone, is enough to do much damage, even if practically speaking, no white man can *really* be thought of as "god." Functionally speaking, there is little reason to distinguish the belief from the social reality, as one brings about the other. To use myself and this book as an example, I *believe in* the idea of god as a person or group's "ultimate concern," and that belief offers me a second-order viewpoint allowing me to analyze a group of people who have believed in the idea of god as useful for them. Applying a Feuerbachian twist to this, then, I *believe in* the utility of the idea of god as ultimate concern so that I might register theism as belief in the idea of god, as opposed to belief in god. Believing in the idea of god gives the effect of producing a perception of oneself as god or god-like. This is as true of my writing of *White Lies* (and the decision of what to include/leave out, as well as how to arrange the book) as it is of the white lies I seek to describe. The ethical impact of this process is severe and discussed at other times in the book. For now, it is enough to simply note the effect of certainty or security produced by the process of belief. This process is a central feature of the white man's god complex. One might define this as an ontologizing process, when an idea takes on the character of existing by virtue of the choice to presume said existence.

Well-known ethicist and philosopher Alasdair MacIntyre helps to explain this subtle but important point. And it is this distinction that Forrester seems to have registered and is seeking to exploit. Delivering the Bampton Lectures at Columbia University in 1966 (along with Paul Ricoeur), MacIntyre noted that "theistic belief" is something new in history and that it is paradoxical.[88] Simply put, belief is a choice made and, in that choosing, it signals the options inherent in that choice. As argued by MacIntyre, prior to Pascal's wager, god was presupposed to such an extent the idea hardly gave rise to detractors. With the (relatively) modern period and the Enlightenment, both theism and atheism emerge at the same time.[89] God became an option. This move positions the belief itself, not the object of belief, as the unquestioned and most taken-for-granted concept. As such, belief has taken god's place as "god," as history has unfolded over the last centuries. This has produced a series of theistic crises from which modern theology (as a field) has emerged. The result is that a word like "theism" now evokes as many different definitions as are imaginable, and most importantly, a stated belief in the idea of god requires a dismissal and an intolerance of its counterpoint, atheism.

Aside from this historical trajectory, however, is the suggestion that such shifts in definitions and adherence to them are contextual.[90] MacIntyre makes the suggestion that Paul Tillich's "decipherment [of theism] was reasonably similar to Feuerbach's," in that both assessments of god and theism hinged on psychological projection, but Tillich saw no need to characterize his position as atheistic.[91] Basing their divergent perspectives on cultural changes,[92] MacIntyre concludes that one time and place's atheism is another's theism. In terms of society, MacIntyre's position sums up my own: "When religion is only thus able to retain its hold on society, religious belief tends to become not so much belief in God as belief in belief."[93] With this operative definition of theism in place, as belief in the functional utility of belief, Forrester's quoting of Mill implies that a connection exists between the social power of belief and the white man's god complex and serves as a warning that if this complex is not understood by those who want to dismantle it, then those seeking to keep it intact will surely believe it possible.

THE WHITE MAN'S GOD COMPLEX AS A SYSTEM

Understanding god as society, and theism as belief in the belief of god, here I argue that the white man's god complex might be understood in terms of a self-creating and self-sustaining social system. I bring into this project certain ideas of social theorist Niklas Luhmann, whose preoccupation with understanding society as a system represents a distillation of the mindset and disposition amongst white theists from which the white man's *god complex* derives its name.[94] That is, Luhmann is locked inside the god complex and so reliance on him offers an honest rendering of how others – like myself – within this system can begin to make sense of themselves in it. Luhmann's theory combines elements of Durkheimian and especially Weberian notions of functional differentiation with a heavy influence from cybernetics research that promotes the idea of a closed feedback loop. At its core, social systems theory attempts to provide a type of unified field theory for society, in that it seeks to account for the smallest of social events across space and time, while also accounting for the most complex.[95] It represents an effort to address growing complexity by having that complexity teach the system how, when, and where to expand so that it remains intact. To wit, it is a stab at a theory of everything. Grandiose in its ambition, if not quixotic to its core. From my vantage point, the parallels between systems theory's attempt to make sense of all the social world, and the white man's god complex's penchant to embark on the impossible, are unmistakable.

Society can be thought of as a system, a closed feedback loop that defines itself through the communication provided by the feedback obtained from the same society. That is, society self-perpetuates and self-defines. This social system, in effort to address the needs of humans in various sizes of community, slowly differentiates its functions as society grows. Every interaction or moment of feedback increases the sum total of "complexity" existing within the system. As a result, systems theory argues that societies expand in light of this added complexity, defining further subsystems in the process and reinforcing the existing systems as well.[96] As the system expands, complexity increases. Stated differently, as society grows and differentiates activities in specialized form, it grows more complex. Yet, the system, like the god complex, has the "reduction of complexity" as its aim.[97] The focus on complexity is pronounced, and one way to shorthand describe systems theory is that it offers a theory of what we can know, how knowing always reminds us of what we do not (yet) know, and how we respond to that reminder in more and more expansive ways, considering that with every decision, "There must always be something excluded" and "that [exclusion] is the result of system formation."[98] So "knowing" relies on the exclusion of data unknown (data we know we know nothing about) and unknown data (data we do not recognize as missing).

As expansion occurs, so too does exclusion. As an outgrowth of expansion, the system develops more and more subsystems that address growing and expanding needs of humans as a result of the formation of the society. This expansion of subsystems amounts to the functional differentiation of society.[99]

Theism as a subsystem

God-idols like theism and whiteness, working within the complex, can be thought of as subsystems.[100] Characterizing each as such a subsystem helps to explain the self-reinforcing constitution of theism and casts light on why the god complex seems to require death and sacrifice. Translated into English in 2013, Luhmann's volume *A Systems Theory of Religion* finds him, among other things, theorizing religion as a system, in the sense of a biological or eco-system. He theorizes the idea of god as an ideological "contingency formula" that transforms uncertainty, limitation, and radical contingency into the foundation for denials of this uncertainty. His discourse makes use of the term "god" in this capacity, wherein it secures and seeks to guard against disrupting the society, the system. As such, his use of god is akin to my term god-idol, and his talk of society or "system" characterizes my functional definition of god as society. Theism's variety of expression is a kind of functional differentiation aimed at the initial function, the reduction of complexity, indicating that the function of theism is simple: to presuppose a solution to complexity that proffers cohesion and wards off competing possible solutions.[101]

Where religion is concerned, Luhmann notes that its "initial problem" is that of "negotiating meaning,"[102] where meaning is achieved by choosing what to include within the system. Meaning is made through the insulation of society as communicable,[103] that is, as closed and (therefore) real. Meaning ends up paradoxical because it sacrifices information so that manageable information can be understood as "meaning."[104] God-idols are required for overcoming this paradox of decision. Theism makes this closure possible, a theological sleight-of-hand wherein belief in the idea of god is presumed enough to make it so; such an approach considers belief as a kind of contemporary ontological argument taking place at the borderlands of the social and existential but without the concern over perfection (of object). Meaning-making and understanding, for Luhmann's grounding in communication as the distinction-making apparatus and connective tissue of all systems, is the Occamist[105] cross from which religious functions hang. In more existential language, this amounts to projecting exaggerations of radical contingency onto a cosmic screen transforming them into grounds for their own denial, another way of sighting the theistic god-idol in practice.

With reference to white U.S. Christians, the god-idol of theism functions as a communication of the incommunicable, in that there is no existentially honest way to make a claim like "God bless America." Required in the stead of this honesty regarding the paradox, then, is a lie, or what historian of religion Charles Long has referred to as a "fictive truth." In theorizing religions of both oppressed and oppressor, Long argues that "the oppressed must deal with both the fictive truth of their status as expressed by the oppressors [those under sway of the white man's god complex], that is, their second creation, and the discovery of their own autonomy and truth – their first creation."[106] Theism and other god-idols like whiteness take shape from these "fictive truths," exaggerations of radical contingency[107] based on things like black inferiority, white superiority, American exceptionalism, or claims that tragedies are the result of "god's will."[108] Where white theists are concerned, talk of god's will does little but reinforce the will of the white theist.[109] "Theistic appeals" allow the system to expand when new information confronts it. Through this simplicity, orientation is achieved, noting the same orientation described by Long as "ultimate orientation" from which he defines religion. For Long, religion amounts to the process whereby "one comes to terms with the ultimate significance of one's place in the world."[110] Reading Long through a functionalist lens, where race and god meet in the United States, this orientation process amounts to determining if one is to be a beneficiary of the sacrifices demanded by the god of society, or whether one will be sacrificed. On this point, I agree with Long, but what Long suggested as a relatively vague description of ontological "opacity," I suggest is more aptly considered as limitation, radical contingency, and physical death. Both options are taken into account by the complex, making response to it difficult.

To elaborate my example, in his first television interview, George Zimmerman told the world "I do wish that there was something – anything – I could have done that wouldn't have put me in the position that I had to take his life." He then qualified his actions and his comments with a statement that "It was all god's plan." Theism, as a contingency formula, is one of these "fictive truths." The "second creation" (i.e., society as god) requires a negotiation of meaning made possible by "god's plan."[111] In the same interview, Zimmerman appeals to a belief in the [justice] *system*, and concludes with his only regret: that he had helped to polarize the nation, to set it at odds with itself.

Surely, Zimmerman's sentiments ring as egregious to many. To those who would suggest he's just doing it wrong – theism, I mean – I contend that *functionally*, he's doing it right. And per systems theory, disagreement as to how to "be a theist" follows from the functional differentiation of theism as this contingency formula, therefore refutations of Zimmerman's theological appeal that rely on other theological appeals reinforce the functional efficacy of his claims. Theism makes the incommunicable (the senseless killing of Martin) communicable (that it was part of god's plan). Luhmann suggests this function involves "substituting the 'how' (religion or society works) for a 'who or what.'"[112] Zimmerman's own agency is reclaimed as if *he were* god. Thus, one "theism" cannot be rejected by another. Theism follows this logic of believing something the case, and making it the case through that belief. As a functionally differentiated contingency formula, theism works to keep the social system closed, *making god over in the image of society, and society over in the image of a white man.*

The deployment and implementation of "god" amongst these white theists occurs through a basic psychological Imago Dei reversal, as noted so long ago by Feuerbach.[113] If "god" is a homology for "meaning," remembering that meaning is in flux and contingent on agreement and yet other communications, then theism is crafted through a similar agreement to respond to the unknown or meaninglessness by presuming it not to be the case. As the white man's god complex is a psychical representation of society as god, then "God" – however characterized theologically – is actually a representative for society, and god-idols, the mechanisms that reinforce the "fictive truths."

In the United States, for white theists, "the observer God had offered a security of orientation that was nearly unequalled. If that idea of him is given up, 'orientation' becomes a problem (and a buzzword too)."[114] Theism works to provide this orientation and is responsible for many of the exaggerations of reality keeping the god complex sustained and protected. This securing of orientation is the take away from a functionalist assessment of theism as a subsystem and contingency formula used to stave off the recognition that, at the end of the day, our white, theistic "worldviews rest on pudding."[115]

Autopoiesis of the system

How does this negotiation of meaning occur? Negotiating meaning requires "transferring indeterminability into determinability" and "infinite burdens of information into finite ones."[116] Applying Luhmann's position to the terms of my argument, god-idols "transfer" radical contingency into exaggerated radical contingency by taking the sum total of human interactions and imposing limits upon them. That is, the experience of radical contingency arises out of a feeling of limit in the face of absolute possibility, and is offset by imagining successful navigation of that possibility by imposing limits onto self and others. These latter limits refer to exaggerations of radical contingency, and the former (existential limits) such as death, incommunicability, and uncertainty foreground radical contingency. God-idols are the transference devices used to respond to limits by imposing other limits that produce the sense that one has no limits. The system can only be presumed to encompass all of society if "noise" from the environment is bracketed out of analysis, and god-idols work as these noise-cancelling ideas. White men, in their god complex, can only reinforce that complex by bracketing out other voices and other data. Where theism is concerned, belief in *the idea of* god is registered by believers as belief in god, thus "substituting the 'how' … for a 'who' or 'what.'"[117] This is the paradox. My suggestion that theism is a god-idol is meant to expose this paradox, reinforcing "how" such a white man's god complex ends up so blind to its own function.

This solution to complexity is achieved through the idea of autopoiesis. Autopoiesis refers to self-production, or self-reproduction. Autopoietic systems are systems that "reproduce themselves from within themselves."[118] One feature of the white man's god complex is that it affords audience to no external data, and this complex's defenders are legion. The belief in the idea of god works to ensure an autopoietic process, operating as the hinge or door opening (and/or closing) the possibility for any real socio-political results to develop. That is, if the white man's god complex is understood as a psychical system, then that system's demand for the complex to remain "closed" signals an entry-point into its dismantling through hermeneutical and interpretive means – a shift in orientation.

This "closure" plays out epistemologically, ethically, and aesthetically, in terms of time, quantity, space, and other categories. Ostensibly, these are the categories outlined by Kant; the god-idol, an expression of the transcendental subject shown in its shortcomings.[119] Stated with a basic philosophical bent, *White Lies* argues that Kantian rationality (that is, using a transcendental subject) is seemingly necessary, but every usage requires the very real, material shedding of blood. God-idols are the concepts that fill in for such a transcendental subject, concepts made possible by social manipulations of one's proximity to death, limitation, and uncertainty. On this point, the consequence and cost of reason, knowledge, certitude of thought or deed, is human blood. Certainty comes at a cost.

Belief in the idea of god must act as if it is belief in god, so that new data and options are guarded against. Theism is an option, but relies on a choice of orientation that denies itself as optional. Hence, uncertainty becomes certainty – and a paradox of choosing between first-order uncertainty and second-order certainty presents itself. Restated in a different but important light, humans remain outside the system through a process of distinction.[120] An observer can remain within society, leaving it open, and unable to attend to each event. Or, one can take this second-order, god's eye view position, bracketing the data in such a way that the system appears closed, that the observer can act omniscient. Many traditional ethnographies are example of this, wherein a "society" or "culture" is effectively closed and presented within the pages of a monograph as if fixed in time and space.[121] The white man's god complex functions in this anthropological fashion, and this example is borne out through the subjective turn in anthropology ushered in largely by scholars at Rice University. Such "god's eye" second-order positioning, which the "subjectivists" would later assault, came to characterize much of the Enlightenment project, as guided by Cartesian rationalism, where "clear and distinct" ideas juxtaposed observer from observed.[122] Distinction between first- and second-order observations, then, bears out as the *sine qua non* of understanding human responses to the world in which they live. To understand society, one must act as if distinct from it. And as Luhmann remarks of religion, belief in the idea of god plays an integral role in this distinction-making process.

Due to the immense complexity of modern society, uncertainty produces a paradox of distinction of paramount order, where knowing constantly reminds of unknowability.[123] Though it might appear as if this material is a tangent to my talk of theism, functionally speaking, society is the only "god" functioning at all, precisely because it suggests otherwise through a second-order abstraction occurring within theism as practiced. As a corollary to the notion that theology is a second-order enterprise,[124] theism is as much a second-order effort to describe society in its ideal definition and expression as a cohesive, whole system. Belief in god, which MacIntyre suggested went by the wayside with Pascal, is a first-order observation. Belief in the idea of god, however, is as much a second-order enterprise as is theology as a discipline, as noted by theologian Gordon Kaufman[125] and many other thinkers. Belief in the idea of god, theism, like theology, addresses unknowability through a kind of distinction that presumes a "clear and distinct" idea is enough to bracket out other data. By these measures, contemporary belief in god, ironically perhaps, *requires* "believers" to act like gods.

Playing "god" through appeals to "god" ... a prelude to violence

White people aren't gods. So what happens when we try to act like gods? The white man's god complex is structured and is structuring based on two primary features, two central psychosocial activities that need to be achieved or are required within the white man's god complex so that its autopoietic reproduction is made possible. First, the god complex is largely unacknowledged in its actual function; its logic goes unexposed and unexplored by the very actors within the system who act as if they are distinct from it.[126] Such hidden logics undergirding the god complex allow us to subsume all beliefs in the idea of god into one "theism" (as I have done in this chapter) so as to position those differences as a sameness marking society as god, and setting in motion the social conditions that allow some within such a society to act like gods. This structure of misrecognition is obtained through purportedly first-order beliefs in god that actually situate the believer as a second-order observer.

Second, because increasing social complexity militates towards exposure of this logic, more drastic (and violent) structuring of sacrifices is necessitated so that the god complex remains intact. The god complex requires the continued functional need for human sacrifice as a corrective to the limits of belief in the idea of god. Simply stated, if "god" existed in the scope suggested by many adhering to the complex, there would be no reason for social expressions of power over any group. These functions, then, point ultimately to the paradox lodged within the interpretation of society's function by those within the god complex: society is relied on to protect against death and limitation, but it does so through god-idols that justify the death and limitations of those on the borders of or outside society. These features allow for the autopoietic reproduction of the complex, and both are witnessed in the murders of Martin and Davis, and the verbal attack on Butler.

The white man's god complex follows this structured logic in that it entertains no external data, meaning those within the system "reproduce themselves from within themselves."[127] They end up working to maintain the system. Theism is used by those within the complex to ensure it remains "closed" in this fashion, unable to see itself in operation and thus able to reproduce itself in perpetuity. Again, belief in the idea of god must act as if it is belief in god, so that alternative narratives and competing visions of life and humanity are guarded against. Hence, we see Zimmerman appeal to god, tricking himself and others into thinking he isn't playing god. For society to function as god, allowing those in it to act like god, those actors must act as if distinct from it – thus, society's functioning as god *requires* a god complex.

For Bourdieu, distinctions subsist in structure, which is imposed onto (and by) society in a more or less unilateral sense shaping individual and group logics of practice and habitus, etc. This structural foundation makes Bourdieu's theory rigid, and requires that the social effects of the existential demand for certainty (e.g., attaining money, power, and long life, or poverty, early death, etc.) be realized in the social environment. Luhmann's theory, though equally focused on distinctions, begins this distinction with a *psychical distinction*, an idea that autopoietically defines and redefines systems and subsystems. From this psychical starting point, material actualization of certainty or ability need not occur for the god-idol to be produced and reproduced, nor for said god-idol to exert considerable influence on the system or society. Whereas Bourdieu is helpful in examining whiteness as a god-idol born out of material expressions of a demand for certainty – that is, white skin as a visible "totem"[128] or sign of an invisible essence – Luhmann's psychical starting point helps to theorize the "invisibility" of the idea of god, as noted by MacIntyre,[129] and the variety of "god" in which adherents claim belief. Deconstructing this variety as psychological projection is necessary, as appealing to the actual experiences or thoughts of those maintaining the white man's god complex will not offer anything more than a) diffusive appeals to that variety and b) a constant defense of the god believed in by the white theist, even to the point of violence and sacrifice.

The principal defense against those who attack the white man's god complex or the vision of society as god to which it appeals comes in the form of sacrifice. Theism affords a façade of "reality," "truth," and the "ultimate orientation" theorized by Long and underscored by Luhmann. But such orientation never brings with it a total certainty; truth has never been agreed upon. Only the perception of it has been agreed upon, as evidenced in the efforts of Descartes, Kant, and others.[130] Out of this anxiety, other orientations or refutations of the white man's god complex must be actively fought against. Take, for instance, George Zimmerman's murder of Trayvon Martin, wherein Zimmerman posits himself as clear and distinct from Martin, thus positioned outside of or above the bounds of society, so as to protect that society. Zimmerman, through his actions, takes a second-order, god's eye view position, bracketing the data in such a way that the system appears closed, allowing himself to presuppose a certainty afforded by a qualified omniscience. In making appeals to "god," the "believers" actually situate themselves as "gods." The white man's god complex functions in this fashion, translating the incommunicable (i.e., god as an entity) into communicable (i.e., god in flesh). Zimmerman is that incarnation. Trouble is, this sleight-of-hand tactic has incredible social consequences.

Biologist and noted scientific theorist Humberto R. Maturana developed the idea of autopoiesis on which Luhmann's theory rests. Maturana has this to say on the matter of violence:

> Just because certain people think that they are in the possession of truth, the situation frequently arises that everything unfamiliar and extraordinary will appear as an unacceptable and insupportable threat. The possible consequence of such an attitude is that people feel justified to use violence because they claim to have privileged access to reality or the truth, or to fight for a great ideal. This attitude, so they believe, justifies their behavior and sets them apart from common criminals.[131]

In response to the acquittal of Zimmerman in the murder of Martin, Butler openly criticized the American god as "a white racist god with a problem, carrying a gun and stalking young black men."[132] Such a "god" seems to be what Maturana is describing here when talking of these "certain people." The attacks on Butler are efforts to dismiss information that might change the nature of the system, of society. Such vehement *ad hominem* assault against Butler provides examples that the society protects itself through belief in the idea of god, and the exclusionary framework it provides. To protect the white man's god complex, and the god-idols that constitute it, such people will go to great lengths, name call and even kill, in order to flee from accepting complexity, uncertainty, or physical death. Not only do social actors within this system act like "god," they echo the Puritanical, wrathful god of Jonathan Edwards. All who would confront the system are "sinners" looking down the barrel of an angry god's gun. Hence, such processes indeed subsist in structure – structuring actions and ideas to be sure – but they are as equally structured by a particular vision of the American god ideologically held as violent and undergirded by economic concerns. Zimmerman was suspicious that Martin was a thief, after all, someone who would disrupt the social order by disturbing who had access to resources. In steps "god," Zimmerman, to determine and sustain a racialized moral binary. Martin says no to this binary, and to the functional suggestion that Zimmerman is god. When Zimmerman is unable to psychologically handle Martin questioning his authority, he kills Martin.

Theism brings with it an interesting feature worth noting. The god-idol of theism (with this flexibility) allows for sacrifices to be executed away from the United States so that the white theistic petit bourgeois remains the center. Appeals to god or economics are made during war and colonial expansion, justifying the use of force so as to protect the interests of the society. Justifications of lynching and justifications of American foreign war campaigns have certain parallels. For instance, white men in America justified the dropping of atomic bombs on Japan in WWII on the grounds that it would shorten the war, ultimately saving more (American) lives, as if the bombing victims were sacrificial offerings. Where lynching was concerned, its justification often came in the form of protecting a false sense of white womanhood that required guarding against being tainted by African American men. These seemingly disconnected sacrificial offerings were happening in American history at the same time, events seldom held in tension, except perhaps through visual art.[133]

The god complex always requires sacrifice, but not necessarily in proximity to the social center of the white theistic petit bourgeois.[134] Translated, no longer does the white man's god complex require the lynching of African Americans in proximity to the spaces where white theists live. This doesn't mean such sacrifices (and murders) do not continue, but simply that theism as god-idol allows that they not occur in the same spaces where whiteness demanded such sacrifices. Theism affords the continued existence of structural racialized oppression in the United States through even such seemingly disconnected domains as foreign relations and domestic racial relations. Sacrifices are still required for theism, but not with the same situational "totemic" requirements as whiteness. The sacrifices move outward from the social center of white society to the margins. For instance, a war on terror (spoken of in terms of U.S. national interest) undergirded by an ideological war between Islam and Judeo-Christianity leaves the domestic racial stratification and white theistic petit bourgeois center intact through the sacrifices of soldiers, enemy combatants, and innocent bystanders who live and work at the metaphoric borders of American imperial expansion. Understanding that systemic expansion as the expansion of white theistic society, theism necessitates sacrifices and seems to be functioning effectively even as whiteness appears in twilight.[135] Is there a way, then, to cast this theism into twilight?

"WHO'S GONNA DIE NEXT?"

The white man's god complex emerges as a model and representative of personality, situating adherents in the image of *their image of god* (i.e., in the image of an exaggeration). Understandably enough, white theists' images of god, historically, look a lot like the white theists whose demand for cohesion and the answering of questions is so great that the questioner – the observer – is turned into the answer. I don't mean to suggest that adherents always carried a physiognomic image of god or Jesus. Edward Blum and Paul Harvey's *The Color of Christ* effectively argues that such racial binary suggestions amount to a "myth rendering material, social, and cultural power meaningless."[136] On this point, I agree. Here, I am noting something more fundamental. The shared attributes of white believer/god involve existential concerns, such as knowledge, hopes, aspirations, safety, possibility, and love. Even still, such existential redress is never fully offered by god-idols, as this paradoxical, second-order abstraction is never fully attainable. In consequence of the practice, sacrifice corrects for this limitation.

The structuring feature of this complex comes in the form of justified sacrifice through governmentally sanctioned warfare, murder by law enforcement, and vigilante justice, alike. On the former point, Cornel West is correct in characterizing Barack Obama as a "global George Zimmerman" in response to the drone strikes that continue to kill innocent people in the name of self-defense – 221 at the time of West's first suggestion.[137] These killings mark Obama as *defender-in-chief* of this white man's god complex, rationalizing the murder of children in the name of security and national defense.[138] The irony, of course, is that he's not afforded full access to its perks. Recall Maturana's suggestion that for those within an autopoietic system, their assumed "privileged access to truth … justifies their behavior and sets them apart from common criminals."[139] Such "privileged access" is made possible by military intelligence in Obama's case, by closed grand juries and corrupt police forces in the case of domestic law enforcement, and by the god-idols of whiteness and theism functioning as a system in the case of vigilantes and governmental representatives alike. Murderous behavior becomes justified as "self-defense" or "standing your ground" with the perpetrators not even being registered as criminals (Zimmerman) or, in the case of Michael Brown's murderer, Officer Darren Wilson, with a grand jury deciding he would not even face trial. Such justification is also evidenced in NYPD union leader Pat Lynch – his name a metonym[140] for his actions – coming to the defense of NYPD Officer Daniel Pantaleo, who killed unarmed African American Eric Garner using a chokehold – illegal by the NYPD's own standards of conduct. Lynch not only defended Garner's murder as justified because Garner resisted arrest, but suggested that because Pantaleo was an "Eagle Scout,"[141] he could not possibly be guilty of Garner's murder. Harking back to the moral mechanisms of sectarian association, it is worth remembering that the Boy Scouts of America is a theistic organization, and "Eagle Scout" represents the highest badge of moral respectability.

Lynch went on to celebrate the grand jury for "listening to every bit of evidence" in the case, evidence the authorities say justifies Pantaleo's actions. Here we see how this "privileged access to truth" functions in precisely the capacity described by Maturana, separating those who seek to act like gods from those who would cause disruption to such a system.

In a discussion of Luhmann, anthropologist and social theorist James Faubion helps to situate the source of such continued threats:

> The modern or functionally differentiated social system depends for its ongoing autopoiesis on the capacity of its subsystems to 'recognize themselves' in terms of the binary codes that are specific to each of them. The recognition and maintenance of those codes is a necessary condition of the effective functioning of the subsystems jointly and severally.[142]

Trayvon Martin, Jordan Davis, Michael Brown, Eric Garner, and so many more, went unrecognized, that is, they were regarded as functionally and morally corrupt, a threat to the effective functioning of the system. Worth reiterating, Luhmann suggests that negotiating meaning requires "transferring indeterminability into determinability" and "infinite burdens of information into finite ones."[143] At times, Luhmann even refers to indeterminability as "noise," an apt descriptor remembering that Jordan Davis was killed over "noise." Second-order appeals to "god" justify such closures, but the more significant and destructive means of negotiating meaning within the complex involves killing those who cast doubt on the efficacy of the system, on *god*.

In the eyes of Zimmerman, Martin seems to have been breaking these codes. He was out of place, a "space invader" to borrow the term from sociologist Nirmal Puwar.[144] Likewise, Michael Dunn presumably did not "recognize himself" in the "noise" of rap music, and such a breach of coding resulted in Davis's murder. Garner's "crime" is reported to have been selling "loosies," individual cigarettes. His true crime seems to have been the rupture to the system wherein his black body presented itself as an expression of shame that the white man's god complex does not work for all, and has never worked for many.

Recognition of these codes comes at a cost. Here, Luhmann serves as data as well as theorist, in that his systems theory rejects any such code that would prevent the effective functioning and autopoiesis of the system, the society. And more specifically, choosing the "right" code seemingly requires cancelling out the "wrong" codes. Luhmann, in effect, offers a mirror from which a second-order observation of the white man's god complex appears as possible, but breaks down in its appearing. This mirror takes shape partly through Luhmann's (famous) disdain for moralizing. In regards to overall systems and subsystems within the group, Luhmann notes that distinctions based on morals "cannot be pressed into a moral scheme, so that real moralizing is only an auxiliary technique, which is at the same time a feverish immune response of the society for problems they cannot solve otherwise. And as physicians know, fever is not undangerous."[145] Luhmann's demand to preserve the closed system of his theory, his valorization of system-qua-system and order, stability, and certainty, require that the binaries characterizing each system and subsystem be preserved at the expense of moralized binaries destroying or risking the systematicity and order.

Faubion goes on to describe Luhmann's sentiments regarding morality, and such disdain has everything to do with the ability to recognize appropriate social codes:

> It is incompatible with 'the moral integration of society' because, as Luhmann emphatically puts it, it 'excludes the identification of the code values of the function systems with the positive/negative values' that typically constitute the apparatus of justification or 'program' of the moral code.[146]

Faubion underscores that systems theory's disdain for morality is a result of it being more concerned with certainty and *verstehen* than with human beings. It is "rational." For Luhmann, understanding the system is, simply, more interesting than attention to those social actors within/constituting the system. Indeed, systems theory removes "humans" from its analysis altogether, relegating what we typically understand as "humans" to raw communication of information. The imagery of "fever" is a testament to his position that he cares more for his own intellectual certitude than he does for those who might be hurt through his efforts. Effectively, high theory is here a proxy and metonym for the function of belief in the idea of god within the white man's god complex. There might be another reason behind Luhmann's concern. Thinking back to Weber's suggestion that sectarian membership allowed for a sort of shorthand rendering of moral and ethical passage, then any moralism that seeks to rupture the order of things would necessarily undercut the ability of such coding to serve in this manner. In short, Luhmann does not appreciate moralism or ethics because they are functionally inefficient. However, they also risk deconstructing a system wherein identity serves as the only ethical and moral foundation. By this token, within the white man's god complex, only white men are considered "moral" because we have fashioned ourselves above morality. Any suggestion otherwise is taken as unsophisticated or dangerous. Whether social theorist or social actor – there is really only the illusion of this distinction, anyway – those who act like god don't like to be told that they aren't gods.

Similarly, Butler was attacked for exposing the logic of the god complex through her moralism. The *ad hominem* attacks make awful sense in light of her words that called into question the antiquated and "fictive" assumptions that society is in the service of all. Butler disrupted the binary codes. Epithets levied against her amount to a kind of prayer – an ideological oblation – suggesting her concerns are "noise," marking her as outside the system. When the codes are broken, exposing the façade of certainty – which is to say, exposing god as a lie – which is to expose social actors to an awareness of their death – which is to expose the complex as murderous rather than life affirming – history demonstrates that black people are attacked and often murdered.[147] But why is there such a concern over moralizing? What, exactly, is this ultimate function of the white man's god complex?

The ultimate function of the white man's god complex is an impossible self-preservation. In colloquial terms, one must fake it in order to make it. That is, humans respond to uncertainty by presuming the sense of certainty they seek is enough to provide it, transforming the lack of certainty into a sense of certainty. I understand this process as that which traditionally is referred to as rationalism. Theism provides a bridge across this paradox, a bridge "built" with black bodies historically, concealing the logic of this existential paradox wherein a believed in sense of certainty materializes in the social environment. An actor, social agent, person, subject, theist or other religious adherent (choose your identity marker, the "idol" of idols for the anthropologist, according to Faubion)[148] must constitute herself or himself as such by deciding a course of arbitrary, radically contingent options.[149] God-idols become the mechanism through which the logic of the paradox of distinction is constituted and through which that logic is concealed. They provide the sense that no second-order observation is necessary, but again, they actually provide the means for such an observation, and they hide their involvement in this process. These god-idols distinguish group from group, affecting the sense of the god's eye view, and hide the fact that they distinguish in that way through both fear and the use of actual violence.

Theism, as operative within the white man's god complex, then, is about the business of inclusion and exclusion as the means for transforming "the indeterminable into the determinable."[150] The indeterminability of god, then, becomes the foundation for belief in belief that is rooted in indeterminability, uncertainty. Theism, then, is an attempt to deny, overcome, or fight against the limits of human intelligibility by faking what can be known in such a way that it becomes the actual narrative adopted and definition employed for the system as it radiates from its center. It is believing that belief is enough, and being willing to kill to ensure believers remain justified in those beliefs.

The quintessential gap posed by indeterminability and uncertainty, spanned by theism functioning as a contingency formula, is the gap between biological life and biological death. The uncertainty does not arise from death directly, but from an existential awareness that the thing positioned to protect against death – society – will ultimately fail. Society holds its citizens hostage through an anxiety reinforcing itself and comes to be constituted as the one, true god – paradoxically staving off death (temporarily) for some by requiring it of others more expeditiously. Death takes on the character of an idol, a means of self-deception – to be feared, dismissed as inauthentic, and destroyed.

Given that one of the complex's most basic sociological propositions is that society functions as an aide in offsetting death,[151] two existential possibilities emerge for those of us within the system. One either travels in the direction of society, leaning on it and trusting in it as the white theist believes in the idea of belief, "Loving the Lord, your god, with all your heart, all your strength and all your mind,"[152] or one must focus on death, and begin to believe in the impossibility of overcoming it. The ultimate function of the white man's god complex is to ensure that white men remain as far away from (their own) death as possible, which makes the following ominous words from Luhmann useful for determining what can be done about this complex:

> If one wishes to proceed in the other direction, using the negative side of the distinction as a symbol for the distinction, one would come close to a symbolism of death, negating all distinctions [à la Ricoeur, Derrida, Becker, Camus, and others]. This reflection shows that the (interest-laden) figure of life after death integrates two logical impossibilities in a single paradox, indicating the unity of every distinction either from its negative or positive side – that is, either as death or God.[153]

Between death and society are the god-idols, ready to span the unknowable for a group of people who work very hard to ignore existential limits by socially inscribing limits on others and themselves. Embracing death, Learning to Die, for those in the white man's god complex, will thus mean the "death" of belief in the idea of god.[154]

The white man's god complex seems ill-prepared to march towards such an existential conclusion. To wit, the system (per its own terms) does not allow for its own death. Its death is overcome as society is deemed eternal, even as its individual constituents die themselves. So how would one begin to disrupt the white man's god complex? How does one "kill" something that cannot die? How does one respond to a system, whose ancillary function is to protect against responding to that system? The answer begins by taking a tautological look at the central feature of many of these white theists' religious tradition, the scene at Golgotha – of a social outsider sacrificed to preserve society, whose body and cross foreshadow the twilight of theism and the ethical chasm now required of those of us who have adhered to the white man's god complex.

BEGINNING TO *BELIEVE* IN THE TWILIGHT OF THEISM

When white U.S. theists (as Christians) appeal to a biblical passage like John 3:16 that claims "So god so loved the world that he gave his only son so that whoever believes in him will not perish but have eternal life," they are transmuting the uncertainty posed to us by the story of Jesus's life into the certainty afforded by the scandal of his death. This sacrificed "only son" is a victim of the god complex in an earlier expression as well as today, in that the meaning many contemporary white Americans make of his death has become a major justification for this complex. In terms of both the New Testament and systems theory, these victims are required due to the precept that the believer's life is worth more than Jesus's own life. To state it bluntly, those who believe in god as a personal savior through the sacrifice of Jesus Christ have blood on their hands. They are murderers. The biblical narrative serves then not as a theological promise, but an anthropological, existential diagnosis. Such is the god's perspective, constructed in the image of the perspective of the believer. John 3:16 is effectively a tautological analysis of society, combining a traditional definition of society as recognized amongst many within it historically, as well as an ethical statement about the sacrifices required by society so conceived.

Through this tautological lens, Jesus Christ is understood as a real victim of the functional maintenance of society, only the sacrifice is not simply localized in space or time but like the function of lynchings, this sacrifice of Jesus takes on a transhistorical, structuring impact. We sacrifice those at the margins – geographically, temporally, ideologically, ethically. These margins include space and time. Just as African Americans were lynched to preserve a white society, or innocent children are killed (collaterally) to "protect and defend" the United States, so Jesus Christ was lynched in effort to preserve a social order. Those that celebrate his death, his dying "for us" or for themselves, are as guilty of this god complex as they would be when suggesting or feeling like a murdered African American (by law enforcement or otherwise) makes America safer or better. Theologian Serene Jones reminds us that "Christianity is the story of a black body being killed by the most powerful nation in the world."[155] What we do with such wisdom will involve whether or not we reject or celebrate our god complex. If the ritual effects of lynching produce whiteness as a functional god-idol, the ritual commemorations of Jesus Christ's life and death reinforce theism as a similar functional god-idol, perpetuating certain dimensions of a skewed understanding of social reality wherein we turn a paradox into the means of overcoming it.

The historical invisibility of whiteness (that is, the god-idol is not discussed openly or its worship recognized by adherents) is made possible by theism. The clear admission and discussion of a panoply of theistic expressions of "god" amongst this group of white theists suggests that theism hides whiteness, as if hiding contingency, suggesting to me (from my attempted second-order location) that the connection between whiteness and theism is intimate, to say the least. Stated differently, theism leaves people blind to their own uncertainty and limitations. Theism bastardizes the significance of the story of Jesus' death into a hopeful narrative, rather than as a warning about the perils of society and the sacrifices it demands to function effectively. Theism blinds adherents to the fact that it and all other god-idols (and the society they work to create) do not ever fully deny or defend against physical death. Logically parallel to MacIntyre's point that theism and atheism emerge together, god-idols bring with their construction the constant awareness of death. The ethical question arises, then, of who will die for the sake of a god – a belief in whom leads, inevitably, towards the asking: "My god, my god, why hast thou forsaken me?"[156] In ethical response to this existential axiom about god having forsaken humans, owning up to the white man's god complex requires denying theism, denying belief in the idea of god.

These words spoken by Christ during his crucifixion help to produce the cross/lynch tree as a tautological myth for recognizing the connection and radical contingency posed by the relationship between the metaphysical world and the social world. What I mean is that the weight of such moments (for victims and perpetrators, alike) – the "sacredness" of the moment – has everything to do with what it suggests about the relationship between "gods" and society, and who counts as worthy of that society. Moreover, many theologians and scholars of religion argue that the crucifixion amounted to an attempt to preserve the social order in a way that did not cause undue harm or concern to either the insular Jewish community of the time or to the larger Roman state.[157] In systems theory, Jesus is a threat of uncertainty packaged within an abundance of complexity. He was too complex for the system to risk allowing his voice to continue to be heard. He was, in this way, threatening; his death a protective measure for the society – not a means toward "our" salvation. Jesus, as prophet, was a threat, an outsider in terms of his ideological commitments. Understanding the white man's god complex as a psychical or ideological "complex," Jesus' death offers the same warning as posed by the Last Poets: "who's gonna die next, 'cause the white man's got a god complex."[158]

As an adherent of the white man's god complex, I want certainty – for the world, for myself, and for this book. So who will die next? How can we white Americans begin to respond to our own god complex, and to what extent, if at all, might we escape the system? The ability to "see" theism in twilight, to *believe* in its unraveling, requires making whiteness visible, grounding an approach to belief with the constant reminder that we live as uncertain humans. Theism functions within this god complex as belief in the idea of this god producing and sustaining society. Here, I now move to the ethical implications of the contingency formula in practice. Belief in the idea of god, or belief in belief, if its collateral damage is to be avoided or offset, requires an embrace of whiteness as a marker of the impossibility of belief. That is, I must situate myself within and am guilty of propagating white lies, but also I am trying to recognize and shed light on the damage done to many by these lies. This vantage point, then, provides an ironic "god's eye view" of theism as having masked the consequences and functions of whiteness and all other possible god-idols.

These sacrifices are demanded of those who do not adhere to the white man's god complex. Theism requires sacrifice from those on the margins or outside the society and not beholden to the god-idols. Who dies, and what differences are posed between opposing societies or groups is of little consequence here, as the white theistic petit bourgeois vision of normativity determines offerings. The exclusion of the other is the sacrificial moment, though it often occurs as material, embodied sacrifice of physical life. To this end, the body count of sacrificial offerings made on behalf of the white man's god complex is immense, and includes not only African Americans, but Native Americans, immigrant Japanese during WWII, *all* women, and many, many others across the globe thanks to an effort to not only use these sacrifices to insulate and define U.S. borders, but to work diligently so that these sacrifices occur near those borders. Such borders extend beyond geography and include both time and space, cross even into myth and biblical history.

My analytic construction of the white man's god complex is my attempt at a second-order observation. It is my attempt to "be god" in the form of a distant observer as I construct a particular world with words and seemingly distance myself from that world. Scholars like bell hooks have suggested that it is socially and politically possible for white people to shift locations, to "see the way whiteness functions to terrorize without themselves feeling locked into denial or guilt."[159] But hooks's comments seem to fail to consider that the task of sighting whiteness requires the second-order observation methods learned from the white man's god complex. There is no escape from the guilt or shame of the white man's god complex, even if the attempt addresses hooks's concern over denial. The attempt requires "the master's tools," and recognition of whose tools these are and from where they emerge must always be kept in sight during their use. This situates me, the observer of a white man's god complex, in the tension-filled twilight experienced by those who attempt to break free from a system, be it a social or psychical system.

Forcefully inserting me into these data is an effort to guard against the allochronic discourse (i.e., manipulating space and time so as to construct an ethnographic data set as closed) of second-order anthropological observations, which in light of Luhmann's systems theory is one expression of the god complex held amongst white theists. In other words, so that my argument does not reinforce (to the extent that it is possible to not reinforce such things) whiteness or theism, I seek to expose them both through the explicit inclusion of my own voice in the argument. Following Johannes Fabian on this point, the "authorial 'I'" offers the "constitutive organ of ethnographic intersubjectivity"[160] and guards against the temporal hijacking and mythmaking that results from the god-complex playing out in intellectual enterprise. In short, the god-complex is expressed in the traditional anthropological constitution of the other as fixed in space and time, distinct from the ethnographer or analyst, such that "the Other's empirical presence turns into his theoretical absence."[161] Such a process gives explanation to how Jesus's death might be appropriated antithetically from its tautological significance, as well as why the story remains illuminating for my argument seeking to dispel a god complex by rejecting belief in god.

Will I worship from within the white man's god complex, or register the wealth of sacrifices that have undergirded the complex, and respond to their voices? Only by recognizing myself within the data is it possible to offset this "conjuring trick"[162] of the Imago Superlata, the presentation of an "ought" as an "is" through the careful, calculating constitution of a first-order experience as a second-order observation. Perceived as ironic or fitting, our ability to see whiteness with a second-order lens provides the ability to own up to our first-order experience of relying on whiteness and theism.

I have crafted the term "god-idol" for precisely this purpose, to "cross" the paradox of distinction. Believing in the idea of god transforms existential uncertainty into the foundation for the appearance of certainty. Yet, such belief comes at the cost of sacrifice, and brings with it the reminder that it is little more than a choice. God-idols, then, are the proper name I give to theism so as to foreground the certainty and uncertainty constituent of it as a paradox. Whiteness, theism, and all god-idols, unduly rely upon a dualism and bifurcation sedimented in uncertainty for the production of certainty that can then work to maintain society and social order, as such. The original signs "god" and "idol" are metaphorically held together by the "-" cross, binding certainty and uncertainty in tautological tension. Stuck between positionalities of "god" or "idol," I choose intellectual and ethical idolatry in the form of the term "god-idol," indicative of the confusion and uncertainty and limitations as well as the possibilities exposed at Golgotha, between death and life. Responding to the white man's god complex requires this tension posed by the cross and marked by the sign "-" between "god" and "idol." In effect, the god-idols responsible for so many sacrifices are now the crosses that we must bear as our shame at having lived under the lie of the white man's god complex. My use of the term "god-idol" is a constant reminder of the responsibility I bear for the sacrifices faced by others as a consequence of the beliefs I have maintained.

Philosophically speaking, whiteness and theism are expressions of an inability to accept human limitation and uncertainty, the inability to accept self-sacrifice (broadly and metaphorically understood); blackness, then, ends up not the ability to accept such limitation and uncertainty, but recognition and awareness of the impossibility of ever fully accepting that limit; the inability to accept having to sacrifice oneself for the sake of another. Responding to the god complex requires an embrace of whiteness through a prism of blackness, coming to terms with life as a paradox.

White Lies is about me and the many others like me in the United States who want to understand how my life – a life lived as a lie, lived in the truth of the death of others – might work to offset the damage done by this lie, my life as a white man with a god complex. After two chapters exploring the functional interworkings of these things I've called god-idols, these denial mechanisms, what I have found is that whiteness and theism are not unique and are only two of many such god-idols, functioning side by side within the white man's god-complex. Even now, such a complex finds me wanting to believe in the power of belief even as I arrive at the conclusion that such beliefs produce too many consequences for others. At this point, I can only reorient myself towards a belief in the impossibility of belief, believing in the twilight of theism.

Notes

1 The Last Poets, "White Man's God Complex," *This is Madness*, 1971.
2 Anthea Butler, "The Zimmerman Acquittal: America's Racist God." *Religion Dispatches*, July 14, 2013, accessed August 24, 2013, www.religiondispatches.org/dispatches/anthea butler/7195/the_zimmerman_acquittal_america_s_racist_god/.
3 The Last Poets, "White Man's God Complex."
4 Butler, "The Zimmerman Acquittal."
5 http://nosecretsonthenet.tumblr.com/page/2, accessed March 10, 2015.
6 William James Jennings, "What Does It Mean to Call 'God' a White Racist?" *Religion Dispatches*, July 17, 2013, accessed December 12, 2014, http://religiondispatches.org/what-does-it-mean-to-call-god-a-white-racist/
7 Jennings, "What Does It Mean."
8 J. Kameron Carter, "Christian Atheism: The Only Response Worth Its Salt to the Zimmerman Verdict." *Religion Dispatches*, July 23, 2013, accessed December 12, 2014, http://religiondispatches.org/christian-atheism-the-only-response-worth-its-salt-to-the-zimmerman-verdict/
9 Carter, "Christian Atheism."
10 Carter, "Christian Atheism."
11 Jennings, "What Does It Mean."
12 William Ronald Jones, *Is God a White Racist? A Preamble to Black Theology* (Beacon Press, 1997).
13 Niklas Luhmann, *A Systems Theory of Religion* (Stanford University Press, 2013).
14 Paul Tillich, *The Courage to Be* (Yale University Press, 2000), 47. Existentialism and functionalism are, in fact, closely connected. Durkheim is usually taken up as a functionalist/social constructionist by critical approaches yet those who do so often fail to see his more existential, self-evident, and *sui generis* moments; and vice versa for those who are working from existential and phenomenological frames of analysis.
15 Ibid.
16 Michel Maffesoli, *The Time of the Tribes: The Decline of Individualism in Mass Society* (SAGE, 1996), 21, 38.
17 Tillich, *The Courage to Be*.
18 Émile Durkheim, *The Elementary Forms of the Religious Life* (Dover Publications, 2008), 16, 412, 420.
19 Ibid., 420.
20 The sheer variety of beliefs in god suggest that most images of god are "dreams" of society in an ideal form, as "aspired" and "rooted" in the "very depths" of a person or community's "being."
21 See, for instance, "John Milton Yinger," in William H. Swatos and Peter Kivisto, *Encyclopedia of Religion and Society* (Rowman Altamira, 1998). Also, see Niklas Luhmann's distinction between danger and risk societies, where he notes "that modern society is designated with good reason as a risk society." Niklas Luhmann, Interview, "Niklas Luhmann – Beobachter im Krähennest," 1973, accessed March 10, 2015, http://www.youtube.com/watch?v=qRSCKSPMuDc
22 The Last Poets, "White Man's God Complex."
23 Eugene Rivers, *The Gospel in Black and White: Theological Resources for Racial Reconciliation*, ed. Dennis L. Okholm (InterVarsity Press, 1997), 23.
24 James W. Perkinson, *White Theology: Outing Supremacy in Modernity* (Palgrave Macmillan, 2004), 128.

25 Carolyn M. Jones and Theodore Trost, *Teaching African American Religions* (Oxford University Press, 2005), 232, original emphasis.

26 Pew Forum, Religion and Public Life Project, "Chapter 1: The Religious Composition of the United States," 2013, accessed March 10, 2015, http://religions.pewforum.org/reports

27 For the sake of space, this chapter does not address "men" or "masculinity" though it is very much a part of the white man's god complex. Masculinity and/or patriarchy amounts to another god-idol. I focus on white and theist to show the relation between two god-idols, and to include white women, who have also benefitted from and adhered to this god complex even as they too have been victimized by it and other god-idols.

28 Many scholars analytically conflate this god-idol with those who gave rise to it and benefit from it. This conflation makes some political sense, as the signifier "whiteness" is derived from the use of white skin by white people to do the work of exaggerating radical contingency. This move is not exactly wrong, historically, but today is anachronistic as the complexities of race require greater specificity. But this very significant social and political connection does not justify analytic conflation of real people with the god-idol. Incidentally, this conflation functions as an inverse adherence to the god-idol, but discussing such a connection would detract from my principal concern to sight *white* Americans. See Chapter 1 for a bit more on this analytic conflation.

29 Though self-selection is surely not the only criteria determining who counts as white, it is the only reliable, empirically grounded means of discussing "white" people without appealing heavily to qualitative or subjective analysis. These people *are* afforded substantial privilege from their skin color, but as a data set, initially defining them against their privilege relegates the definition to the mere subjective opinion of the analyst. Though I arrive later at such a position, I want to first empirically ground this group without making assumptions about privilege, to the extent this is possible.

30 U.S. Census Bureau, Statistical Abstract of the United States: 2010, "Table 12. Resident Population Projections by Race, Hispanic-Origin Status, and Age: 2010–2015," accessed March 10, 2015, http://www.census.gov/compendia/statab/2012/tables/12s0012.pdf.

31 Ibid.

32 U.S. Census Bureau, "The Diversifying Electorate – Voting Rates by Race and Hispanic Origin in 2012 (and Other Recent Elections)," (May 2013), accessed March 12, 2015, http://www.census.gov/prod/2013pubs/p20-568.pdf

33 U.S. Department of Labor, "Labor Force Characteristics by Race and Ethnicity, 2011," (August 2012), accessed March 5, 2014, http://www.bls.gov/cps/cpsrace2011.pdf

34 Ibid.

35 Ibid.

36 Ibid.

37 U.S. Census Bureau, "Appendix Tables A-1–24: Poverty Rates for Specific Race or Ethnic Populations by State: 2007–2011," accessed March 10, 2015, http://www.census.gov/hhes/www/poverty/publications/Appendix_Tables1-24.pdf

38 "Wealth of Top 1 Percent Varies by Race." *The Duke Chronicle*, December 1, 2011, accessed March 10, 2015, http://www.dukechronicle.com/articles/2011/12/01/wealth-top-1-percent-varies-race

39 U.S. Census Bureau, Statistical Abstract of the United States: 2012, "Table 324 and 325: Arrests by Sex, Age, and Race: 2009," accessed March 10, 2015, http://www.census.gov/compendia/statab/2012/tables/12s0325.pdf

40 Ibid.

41 Michelle Alexander, *The New Jim Crow: Mass Incarceration in the Age of Colorblindness* (The New Press, 2010).

42 The actual demographic of white people is far removed from the single image of an affluent white male with a wife and 2.5 children who never see trouble, the prototype of "whiteness" if you will. Though affluent white people obviously exist, statistics bear out that white people are much more economically diverse than that.
43 It is important to keep in mind that this added complexity does not translate to exoneration for the oppression of non-whites.
44 James D. Faubion, *An Anthropology of Ethics* (Cambridge University Press, 2011), 115, 258.
45 Many scholars continue to employ the language of privilege, though I err on the side of Lewis Gordon who has argued that these so called white "privileges" are better characterized as rights, so that the effects of them (i.e., adequate jobs, housing, food, etc.) are registered as human rights, making the fight for them a matter of parity rather than vying for privileges not guaranteed in the first place. See Lewis Gordon's chapter "Critical Reflections on Three Popular Tropes in the Study of Whiteness," in George Yancy, *What White Looks Like: African-American Philosophers on the Whiteness Question* (Routledge, 2004). Privilege, from my perspective, has more to do with mechanisms of denial of responsibility. By this token, *White Lies* is deeply interested in these mechanisms of denial, though I rarely discuss "privilege" so as to not confuse readers who may have different operative definitions of it.
46 Pew Forum, Religion and Public Life Project.
47 Ibid.
48 Ibid.
49 "Growth of the Nonreligious." Pew Research Center, July 2, 2013, accessed March 10, 2015, http://www.pewforum.org/2013/07/02/growth-of-the-nonreligious-many-say-trend-is-bad-for-american-society/
50 I am not concerned to be sensitive to the variety of stated beliefs in god. I am interested to describe all of these beliefs as rooted in a more fundamental structural and functional position that situates society as god, and death as a false idol.
51 Margaret C. Simms and Julianne M. Malveaux, *Slipping Through the Cracks: The Status of Black Women* (Transaction Publishers, 1986).
52 I do not mean to ignore other forms of oppression or advantage, such as economic, gendered, sexual preference, and the like, but simply to foreground that theism as belief in the idea of god affords a particular type of utility that interconnects and works with racial advantage and other forms of advantage or oppression. Even with this caveat about economic oppression, theism cuts across economic diversity to posit an interpretive sameness. It is different than actual economic advantage. It replaces or fills in for whites who are economically disadvantaged.
53 This cohesiveness does not necessarily correspond to these white theists' own impression of themselves, but operates as an analytic bracket for my project.
54 Robert Neelly Bellah and Phillip E. Hammond, *Varieties of Civil Religion* (Harper & Row, 1980).
55 Pierre Bourdieu, *Distinction: A Social Critique of the Judgement of Taste* (Harvard University Press, 1984), 25.
56 I follow Bourdieu who follows Marx on this point.
57 Personal auto-ethnographic experience.
58 Lewis V. Baldwin, *There Is a Balm in Gilead: The Cultural Roots of Martin Luther King, Jr.* (Fortress Press, 1991), 51.
59 Ludwig Feuerbach, *The Essence of Christianity* (Prometheus Books, 1989).
60 Max Weber, "The Protestant Sects and the Spirit of Capitalism," in Max Weber, Hans Heinrich Gerth, and C. Wright Mills, *From Max Weber: Essays in Sociology* (Oxford University Press, Galaxy, 1958), emphasis original.
61 Weber, "The Protestant Sects."
62 Weber, "The Protestant Sects," emphasis original.

63 Weber, "The Protestant Sects."
64 Weber's thesis on secularization might also have much to tell us about deregulations on Wall Street and the eroding of the middle class.
65 "Killing Michael Brown Has Made Darren Wilson a Millionaire," December 10, 2014. *Popular Resistance*, accessed December 12, 2014, https://www.popularresistance.org/killing-michael-brown-has-made-darren-wilson-a-millionaire/
66 Bourdieu, *Distinction*, 25.
67 Though registered by many as an "extreme" voice, Glenn Beck helps to characterize my point about homelessness. See, for instance, "'No More Lies': Glenn Beck's Powerful Speech at Tea Party Washington, D.C. Rally," June 19, 2013. *Teaparty.org*, accessed March 10, 2015, http://www.teaparty.org/we-will-no-longer-accept-the-lies-glenn-becks-powerful-speech-at-washington-d-c-rally-25595/
68 Bourdieu, *Distinction*, 25.
69 The painting can be seen at http://www.jonmcnaughton.com/the-demise-of-america/, accessed March 10, 2015.
70 Personal email received. For the image or background on McNaughton, see https://www.facebook.com/pages/Jon-McNaughton/157211518652 and jonmcnaughton.com. For an example of the actual email forward, see http://www.freezonemediacenternews.com/2013/08/the-demise-of-america.html, accessed March 10, 2015.
71 Bourdieu, *Distinction*, 339. The quote continues: "However, as soon as the analysis is refined, it is seen that this system of dispositions takes on as many modalities as there are ways of attaining, staying in or passing through a middle position in the social structure, and that this position itself may be steady, rising or declining."
72 This sameness localizes in society, and the different expressions of theism provide plausible deniability of function. Recent public and scholarly interest in "irreligion" and "unbelief" and the "Nones" serves as an example – at the center is this obsession with belief however it can be garnered, even and including belief in no deity or no tradition or institution.
73 Noel Ignatiev, *How the Irish Became White* (Routledge, 2008).
74 Ibid.
75 Newt Gingrich and Callista Gingrich, *Rediscovering God in America: Reflections on the Role of Faith in Our Nation's History and Future* (Thomas Nelson, 2009), 9.
76 Pascal's wager refers to the metaphysical wager posed by believing or not in god's existence. All things equal, to not believe when god does exist sets one's afterlife up for hardship; to believe does no harm in this world, so why not believe. Pascal was wrong on this point. Belief has immense consequences for this world.
77 Gary Dorrien, *The Making of American Liberal Theology: Imagining Progressive Religion, 1805–1900* (Westminster John Knox Press, 2001).
78 Gary Dorrien, *The Making of American Liberal Theology: Crisis, Irony, and Postmodernity: 1950–2005* (Westminster John Knox Press, 2006), 2–3.
79 Bourdieu, *Distinction*, 24.
80 Stormfront Website Forum, (n.d.), accessed December 13, 2014, http://www.stormfront.org/forum/
81 I'm talking about arrogance and justification, the fundamental inability to ever accept limited value or ability, based on the sheer force of belief in that certainty.
82 Ludwig Feuerbach, *The Essence of Christianity*.
83 Stormfront Website Forum, (n.d.), accessed December 13, 2014, http://www.stormfront.org/forum/
84 Ibid., original emphasis.
85 Southern Poverty Law Center, "Extremist Files: Stormfront," (n.d.), accessed March 10, 2015, http://www.splcenter.org/get-informed/intelligence-files/groups/stormfront.
86 Stormfront Website Forum, (n.d.), accessed March 10, 2015, http://www.stormfront.org/forum/t584083/

87 John Stuart Mill, *On Liberty* (Blackwell, 1863), 20.
88 Alasdair MacIntyre and Paul Ricoeur, *The Religious Significance of Atheism* (Columbia University Press, 1969), 13.
89 Also, by page 28, MacIntyre arrives at one of his theses: theism, as understood by those at any given moment, changes with the times. Hence, Tillich is deemed a "theist" in 1950, while Feuerbach is considered an atheist in the previous century, when they both rely on the same relegation of the god idea to psychology. As do I. Perhaps, then, my argument looks to contemporary race relations to define theism/atheism as much as it does the opposite, looks to theism and theology as a means of addressing and analyzing contemporary race relations.
90 Interestingly, MacIntyre discusses Durkheim's functional limits in the United States, though I do not agree with his findings. Ostensibly, MacIntyre argues that totems are visible, and as such, their parallel to the idea of "god" is limited, as theism defies all appearances. MacIntyre concludes: "The gods of the heathen are partially visible; the God of Abraham is wholly invisible." See MacIntyre and Ricoeur, *The Religious Significance of Atheism*, 19–21.
91 Ibid., 27–8.
92 Ibid., 28.
93 Ibid., 21.
94 Worth noting, Luhmann counts himself amongst those who *believe* in the idea of god. See Niklas Luhmann, *A Systems Theory of Religion*, 130, emphasis added.
95 My allusion is to a unified field theory searched for in physics, sought since at least Einstein's general theory of relativity effectively addressed the physical states of the large. A unified field theory would combine the general properties of Einstein's theory with the immensely small physical properties of quantum mechanics. Where society is concerned – better still, theology and god – Luhmann seeks to ultimately address the god (the immensely large/Einstein's theory) with death (the immensely small, quantum mechanics) where society is the systematicity developed in response to the tension posed between the two poles, god and death, metaphysics and the physical world, ideology and materiality.
96 Niklas Luhmann, "Niklas Luhmann – Beobachter Im Krähennest," 1973, accessed June 20, 2014, http://www.youtube.com/watch?v=qRSCKSPMuDc
97 Ibid.
98 Ibid.
99 Ibid. Durkheim and Luhmann could not be much farther removed from the Lockean notion of individuals coming together to form society. For both Durkheim and Luhmann, the social precedes (logically and temporally) the individual, and the economist individual is a product – never the foundation – of a particular social order. Ironically, when defending the closing and excluding of the system, as noted earlier, Luhmann's comments seem to, ever tacitly, rely on anthropological and sociological positions that suggest society develops as human dangers push people into closer proximity and into greater reliance on each other.
100 I focus primarily on theism, but whiteness is also a subsystem. The line between them blurs within the system, remaining distinct and yet overlapping. They are identity-making god-idols, so they exert a similar function, but each has its own "job" within the system.
101 Luhmann, *A Systems Theory of Religion*, "The Contingency Formula God," 107.
102 Ibid.
103 Not only are the god-idols the ideas which undergird communication, they hinge on the presumption and presentation of themselves as communicable. Hence, racial discourse often occurs as two people talking past each other; a white person assuming a shared god-complex will register their idea of god as communicable to someone outside the complex. The assumption does more to foreground (to others) that

said white person is held sway by the god-complex than it does to communicate across social context.

104 In certain respects, Luhmann's theory is in accord with Anthony Pinn's position on and definition of religion as a "quest for complex subjectivity," but it might be noted that they depart on the point of *verstehen*, or understanding. Luhmann wants to "understand" complexity by making it simple; Pinn wants to interpret the complex in a way that exposes the complexity hidden by social expressions of Luhmann's position on religion. Pinn arrives at his standpoint starting with William James and experience, and Luhmann through systems theory and its structural and functional underpinnings and implications, innovatively registered through the psychical domain. They appear in accord that religion is a negotiation of meaning, but have very different vantage points for how to analytically or existentially handle that meaning.

105 Faubion, *An Anthropology of Ethics*, 57–60.

106 Charles H. Long, *Significations: Signs, Symbols, and Images in the Interpretation of Religion*, 2nd ed. (The Davies Group Publishers, 1999), 184.

107 Rather than reuse Long's notion of the "fictive truth," I have created the idea of exaggerations of radical contingency to situate the ideas as rooted in existential anxiety, and to express that they are more "real" than the "fictive" disclaimer provided by Long.

108 Butler, "The Zimmerman Acquittal: America's Racist God."

109 Religion is about the business of responding to the complexity of too much or not enough meaning by presupposing that the "too much" or "not enough" of meaning offers a foundation for moving forward, for existing in complexity and yet responding to it through various distinctions and ideological compartmentalizations. That is, religion qua religion is the process of calling the unknown known, of labeling complexity as simplicity. In Pinn's work, however (and this point will play out in later chapters more extensively), black religion hinges around the same paradox but attempts to present in complexity what has been deemed simple by the system's distinction. From this point, and in terms of the idea of god, Luhmann's words speak to the nature of god-idol construction for white Americans.

110 Long, *Significations*, 6.

111 Butler, "The Zimmerman Acquittal: America's Racist God."

112 Luhmann, *A Systems Theory of Religion*, 105.

113 Feuerbach, *The Essence of Christianity*.

114 Luhmann, *A Systems Theory of Religion*, 130.

115 Cornel West, *Hope on a Tightrope: Words and Wisdom* (Hay House, 2008), 34.

116 Luhmann, *A Systems Theory of Religion*, 107.

117 Ibid.

118 David Seidl, "Luhmann's Theory of Autopoietic Social Systems," published presentation, Munich School of Management, Munich Business Research (2004).

119 Roger Scruton, *A Short History of Modern Philosophy: From Descartes to Wittgenstein*, 2nd ed. (Routledge, 2001), 142–3. Here, my suggestion is not direct, but I mean to use Kant's concept of the "transcendental unity of apperception" as an example of the categorical work done by god-idols. Per my argument, Kant was right that the idea of god does not translate into god's existence. Kant was shortsighted, however, in relegating religion to morality and presuming that the space left between the concept of god and the concept of the existence of god would not cause calamity if not understood as equally artificial.

120 Niklas Luhmann, *Theories of Distinction: Redescribing the Descriptions of Modernity* (Stanford University Press, 2002).

121 For two, of many, texts on these concerns, see Johannes Fabian, *Time and the Other: How Anthropology Makes Its Object* (Columbia University Press, 2002); and Claude Lévi-Strauss, *The Savage Mind* (University of Chicago Press, 1968).

122 René Descartes, in Benedict de Spinoza, Gottfried Wilhelm Von Leibniz, and René Descartes, *The Rationalists: Descartes: Discourse on Method & Meditations; Spinoza: Ethics; Leibniz: Monadology & Discourse on Metaphysics* (Random House, 1960).
123 Niklas Luhmann and Stephan Fuchs, "Tautology and Paradox in the Self-Descriptions of Modern Society,"*Sociological Theory* 6, no. 1 (Spring 1988): 21–37.
124 Stanley J. Grenz, *Theology for the Community of God* (Wm. B. Eerdmans Publishing, 2000), 11.
125 Gordon Kaufman, *In Face of Mystery: A Constructive Theology* (Harvard University Press, 1995), 478. Here, Kaufman easily breaks down his earlier argument from *An Essay on Theological Method* and explains a bit about why the first/second order issue matters.
126 This brings into question the efficacy of calling such a complex a "lie," as those who are doing the lying most often genuinely do not think they are lying. However, as I hope is clear, I mean to rupture any such suggestions that ignorance exonerates liars. Later chapters engage how such normative judgments (mine) are possible and what consequences come with holding certain norms.
127 David Seidl, "Luhmann's Theory of Autopoietic Social Systems," published presentation, Munich School of Management, Munich Business Research (2004).
128 Durkheim, *Elementary Forms*, 102 – though in light of Augustine of Hippo's famous definition of sacrament as "the visible form of an invisible grace," this might mean that whiteness as god-idol has a sacramental quality, marking the benefits of white skin as a sign of "grace." See Joe R. Jones, *A Grammar of Christian Faith: Systematic Explorations in Christian Life and Doctrine* (Rowman & Littlefield Publishers, 2002), 659.
129 MacIntyre and Ricoeur, *The Religious Significance of Atheism*, 19–21.
130 William James, *The Will to Believe: And Other Essays in Popular Philosophy* (Longmans, Green, and Company, 1921), 15.
131 Humberto R. Maturana, quoted in Bernhard Poerksen, *The Certainty of Uncertainty: Dialogues Introducing Constructivism* (Imprint Academic, 2004), 48.
132 Butler, "The Zimmerman Acquittal: America's Racist God."
133 See, for instance, Eric J. Sundquist, *Strangers in the Land: Blacks, Jews, Post-Holocaust America* (Harvard University Press, 2009); and Dora Apel, *Imagery of Lynching: Black Men, White Women, and the Mob* (Rutgers University Press, 2004).
134 This is not to indicate that such localized sacrifices as lynchings do not occur in the geographic places and times where theistic sacrifices are doled out for the sake of the white man's god complex. On this point, no doubt, aspects of the white man's god complex extend to other communities and groups. My comments here simply situate the differential function of theistic sacrifices as they emerge from adherence to the god-idol of theism and are perpetuated by the white theistic petit bourgeois.
135 Luhmann helps to demonstrate how these god-idols continue to function within their own twilight – that is, god-idols continue to operate powerfully even if they do not appear to bring about the materialized, social expression of the exaggerations of radical contingency. In fact, their power seemingly hinges on this twilight.
136 Edward J. Blum and Paul Harvey, *The Color of Christ: The Son of God and the Saga of Race in America* (The University of North Carolina Press, 2012), 19.
137 "Cornel West: 'Obama Is a Global George Zimmerman'," July 22, 2013, accessed March 10, 2015, http://www.huffingtonpost.com/2013/07/22/cornel-west-barack-obama_n_3635614.html
138 Ibid.
139 Maturana, quoted in Bernhard Poerksen, *The Certainty of Uncertainty*, 48.
140 Christopher Driscoll, "On the Journey to White Shame," accessed December 13, 2014, http://marginalia.lareviewofbooks.org/mrblog-journey-white-shame-christopher-driscoll/

141 "Chokehold Cop is 'Eagle Scout' Blameless in Death, NYPD Union President Says," *Huffington Post*, December 4, 2014, accessed December 13, 2014, http://www.huffingtonpost.com/2014/12/04/pat-lynch-eric-garner_n_6272738.html
142 Faubion, *An Anthropology of Ethics*, 108–9.
143 Luhmann, "Niklas Luhmann – Beobachter Im Krähennest."
144 Nirmal Puwar, *Space Invaders: Race, Gender and Bodies Out of Place* (Berg, 2004).
145 Luhmann, "Niklas Luhmann – Beobachter Im Krähennest."
146 Faubion, *An Anthropology of Ethics*, 108–9.
147 Black people, here using the term in an ontological sense rather than one based on phenotype, are sacrificed so a lie, a "fictive truth," can be maintained. In stark terms, this means all who hold such belief in the idea of god are either directly or tacitly guilty of reinforcing the white man's god complex and by extension, the murders of Martin, Davis, Brown, Garner, and countless more.
148 Faubion, *An Anthropology of Ethics*.
149 Luhmann, at times, even characterizes this move as a response to the inadequacies posed by Talcott Parsons' theory of "double contingency," which refers to the contingent nature of communication. Intelligibility, order, certainty between the sender and receiver is made possible not only by the actual communication, but by the influence of the receiver/sender's reception on the communication. Luhmann takes aim at the shaky foundation provided by Parsons' theory, and addresses it through the asymmetry posed by moving outside of the society, taking a "god's eye" view.
150 Luhmann, *A Systems Theory of Religion*, 111.
151 For precision's sake, I don't mean to suggest that social theorists within the white man's god complex hold to this Lockean position, but that it remains a feature of the complex whether contemporary social theorists agree or disagree with the proposition.
152 Mark 12:30.
153 Luhmann, *A Systems Theory of Religion*, 115.
154 Stated differently and unpacked in Part II, adequate response to the white man's god complex seemingly requires learning to approach white society as idol, and death as god, inverting the trajectories and functions of god and death.
155 "How a New York Seminary Became a Hub for Eric Garner Protests," December 7, 2014, *Think Progress*, accessed December 13, 2014, http://thinkprogress.org/justice/2014/12/07/3600539/faith-leaders-seminarians-protest-garner-decision/
156 Matthew 27:46. King James Bible.
157 Robert M. Royalty, *The Origin of Heresy: A History of Discourse in Second Temple Judaism and Early Christianity* (Routledge, 2013), 157. Countless other examples of this argument exist within contemporary liberal theological writings.
158 The Last Poets, "White Man's God Complex."
159 bell hooks, quoted in Perkinson, *White Theology*, 133.
160 Johannes Fabian, *Time and the Other: How Anthropology Makes Its Object* (Columbia University Press, 2002).
161 Fabian, *Time and the Other*, xli. Fabian even refers to this practice as a type of bad faith, which foreshadows my argument in Chapter 3.
162 Ibid. Not only is theology better understood as anthropology but, paraphrasing Fabian, anthropology is very much involved in theology and myth-making second-order endeavors.

REFERENCES

"Chokehold Cop is 'Eagle Scout' Blameless in Death, NYPD Union President Says," December 4, 2014. *Huffington Post*, accessed December 13, 2014, http://www.huffingtonpost.com/2014/12/04/pat-lynch-eric-garner_n_6272738.html

"Cornel West: 'Obama Is a Global George Zimmerman,'" July 22, 2013. *Huffington Post*, accessed March 10, 2015, http://www.huffingtonpost.com/2013/07/22/cornel-west-barack-obama_n_3635614.html

"How a New York Seminary Became a Hub for Eric Garner Protests," December 7, 2014. *Think Progress*, accessed December 13, 2014, http://thinkprogress.org/justice/2014/12/07/3600539/faith-leaders-seminarians-protest-garner-decision/

"Killing Michael Brown Has Made Darren Wilson a Millionaire," December 10, 2014. *Popular Resistance*, accessed December 12, 2014, https://www.popularresistance.org/killing-michael-brown-has-made-darren-wilson-a-millionaire/

"'No More Lies': Glenn Beck's Powerful Speech at Tea Party Washington, D.C. Rally," June 19, 2013. *Teaparty.org*, accessed March 10, 2015, http://www.teaparty.org/we-will-no-longer-accept-the-lies-glenn-becks-powerful-speech-at-washington-d-c-rally-25595/

"Wealth of Top 1 Percent Varies by Race," December 1, 2011. *The Duke Chronicle*, accessed March 10, 2015, http://www.dukechronicle.com/articles/2011/12/01/wealth-top-1-percent-varies-race

Alexander, Michelle. 2010. *The New Jim Crow: Mass Incarceration in the Age of Colorblindness*. 1st ed. The New Press.

Apel, Dora. 2004. *Imagery of Lynching: Black Men, White Women, and the Mob*. Rutgers University Press.

Baldwin, Lewis V. 1991. *There Is a Balm in Gilead: The Cultural Roots of Martin Luther King, Jr.* Fortress Press.

Bellah, Robert Neelly and Phillip E. Hammond. 1980. *Varieties of Civil Religion*. Harper & Row.

Blum, Edward J. and Paul Harvey. 2012. *The Color of Christ: The Son of God and the Saga of Race in America*. The University of North Carolina Press.

Bourdieu, Pierre. 1984. *Distinction: A Social Critique of the Judgement of Taste*. Harvard University Press.

Butler, Anthea. 2013. "Commentary on Anthea Butler." *No Secrets On the Net*, accessed August 5, 2014, http://nosecretsonthenet.tumblr.com/page/2

Butler, Anthea. 2013. "The Zimmerman Aquittal: America's Racist God." *Religion Dispatches*, accessed August 24, 2013, religiondispatches.org/dispatches/antheabutler/7195/

Carter, J. Kameron. 2013. "Christian Atheism: The Only Response Worth Its Salt to the Zimmerman Verdict," July 23. *Religion Dispatches*, accessed December 12, 2014, http://religiondispatches.org/christian-atheism-the-only-response-worth-its-salt-to-the-zimmerman-verdict/

Dorrien, Gary. 2001. *The Making of American Liberal Theology: Imagining Progressive Religion, 1805–1900*. 1st ed. Westminster John Knox Press.

Dorrien, Gary. 2006. *The Making of American Liberal Theology: Crisis, Irony, and Postmodernity: 1950–2005*. Westminster John Knox Press.

Driscoll, Christopher. 2014. "On the Journey to White Shame," accessed December 13, 2014, http://marginalia.lareviewofbooks.org/mrblog-journey-white-shame-christopher-driscoll/

Durkheim, Émile. 2008. *The Elementary Forms of the Religious Life*. Dover Publications.

Fabian, Johannes. 2002. *Time and the Other: How Anthropology Makes Its Object*. Columbia University Press.

Faubion, James D. 2011. *An Anthropology of Ethics*. Cambridge University Press.

Feuerbach, Ludwig. 1989. *The Essence of Christianity*. Prometheus Books.

Gingrich, Newt and Callista Gingrich. 2009. *Rediscovering God in America: Reflections on the Role of Faith in Our Nation's History and Future*. Thomas Nelson.

Grenz, Stanley J. 2000. *Theology for the Community of God*. Wm. B. Eerdmans Publishing.

Harvey, Jennifer. 2007. *Whiteness and Morality: Pursuing Racial Justice through Reparations and Sovereignty*. 1st ed. Palgrave Macmillan.

Ignatiev, Noel. 2008. *How the Irish Became White*. 1st ed. Routledge.

James, William. 1921. *The Will to Believe: And Other Essays in Popular Philosophy*. Longmans, Green, and Company.

Jennings, Willie James. 2013. "What Does It Mean to Call 'God' a White Racist?" *Religion Dispatches*, July 17, accessed December 12, 2014, http://religiondispatches.org/what-does-it-mean-to-call-god-a-white-racist/

Jones, Carolyn M. and Theodore L. Trost. 2005. *Teaching African American Religions*. Oxford University Press.

Jones, Joe R. 2002. *A Grammar of Christian Faith: Systematic Explorations in Christian Life and Doctrine*. Rowman & Littlefield Publishers.

Jones, William Ronald. 1997. *Is God a White Racist? A Preamble to Black Theology*. Beacon Press.

Kaufman, Gordon D. 1995a. *In Face of Mystery: A Constructive Theology*. Harvard University Press.

Kaufman, Gordon D. 1995b. *An Essay on Theological Method*. 3rd ed. An American Academy of Religion Book.

King James Bible. N.d.

The Last Poets. 1971. "White Man's God Complex," This is Madness.

Lévi-Strauss, Claude. 1968. *The Savage Mind*. University of Chicago Press.

Long, Charles H. 1999. *Significations: Signs, Symbols, and Images in the Interpretation of Religion*. 2nd ed. The Davies Group Publishers.

Luhmann, Niklas. 1973. "Niklas Luhmann – Beobachter im Krähennest," accessed March 10, 2015, http://www.youtube.com/watch?v=qRSCKSPMuDc

Luhmann, Niklas. 2002. *Theories of Distinction: Redescribing the Descriptions of Modernity*. Stanford University Press.

Luhmann, Niklas. 2013. *A Systems Theory of Religion*. Stanford University Press.

Luhmann, Niklas and Stephan Fuchs. 1988. "Tautology and Paradox in the Self-Descriptions of Modern Society." *Sociological Theory* 6(1): 21–37.

MacIntyre, Alasdair and Paul Ricoeur. 1969. *The Religious Significance of Atheism*. Columbia University Press.

Maffesoli, Michel. 1996. *The Time of the Tribes: The Decline of Individualism in Mass Society*. 1st ed. SAGE.

McNaughton, Jon. N.d. *The Demise of America*, accessed March 10, 2015, http://www.jonmcnaughton.com/the-demise-of-america/, http://www.freezonemediacenternews.com/2013/08/the-demise-of-america.html, and https://www.facebook.com/pages/Jon-McNaughton/157211518652

Mill, John Stuart. 1863. *On Liberty*. Blackwell.

Okholm, Dennis L., ed. 1997. *The Gospel in Black and White: Theological Resources for Racial Reconciliation*. InterVarsity Press.

Perkinson, James W. 2004. *White Theology: Outing Supremacy in Modernity*. 1st ed. Palgrave Macmillan.

Pew Research Center. "Growth of the Nonreligious," July 2, 2013, accessed March 10, 2015, http://www.pewforum.org/2013/07/02/growth-of-the-nonreligious-many-say-trend-is-bad-for-american-society/

Pew Forum. 2013. Religion and Public Life Project, "Chapter 1: The Religious Composition of the United States," accessed March 10, 2015, http://religions.pewforum.org/reports

Poerksen, Bernhard. 2004. *The Certainty of Uncertainty: Dialogues Introducing Constructivism*. Imprint Academic.

Puwar, Nirmal. 2004. *Space Invaders: Race, Gender and Bodies out of Place*. Oxford University Press.

Rivers, Eugene. 1997. *The Gospel in Black and White: Theological Resources for Racial Reconciliation*, ed. Dennis L. Okholm. InterVarsity Press.

Royalty, Robert M. 2013. *The Origin of Heresy: A History of Discourse in Second Temple Judaism and Early Christianity*. Routledge.

Scruton, Roger. 2001. *A Short History of Modern Philosophy: From Descartes to Wittgenstein*. 2nd ed. Routledge.

Seidl, David. 2004. "Luhmann's Theory of Autopoietic Social Systems," published presentation, Munich School of Management, Munich Business Research.

Simms, Margaret C. and Julianne M. Malveaux. 1986. *Slipping Through the Cracks: The Status of Black Women*. Transaction Publishers.

Southern Poverty Law Center, "Extremist Files: Stormfront," (n.d.), accessed March 10, 2015, http://www.splcenter.org/get-informed/intelligence-files/groups/stormfront.

Spinoza, Benedict de, Gottfried Wilhelm Von Leibniz, and René Descartes. 1960. *The Rationalists: Descartes: Discourse on Method & Meditations; Spinoza: Ethics; Leibniz: Monadology & Discourse on Metaphysics*. Random House.

Stormfront Website Forum, (n.d.), accessed December 13, 2014, http://www.stormfront.org/forum/

Stormfront Website Forum, (n.d.), accessed March 10, 2015, http://www.stormfront.org/forum/t584083/

Sundquist, Eric J. 2009. *Strangers in the Land: Blacks, Jews, Post-Holocaust America*. Harvard University Press.

Swatos, William H. and Peter Kivisto. 1998. *Encyclopedia of Religion and Society*. Rowman Altamira.

Tillich, Paul. 2000. *The Courage to Be*. 2 Sub. Yale University Press.

U.S. Census Bureau, "Appendix Table A-1–24: Poverty Rates for Specific Race or Ethnic Populations by State: 2007–2011," accessed March 10, 2015, http://www.census.gov/hhes/www/poverty/publications/Appendix_Tables1-24.pdf

U.S. Department of Labor, "Labor Force Characteristics by Race and Ethnicity, 2011," August 2012, accessed March 5, 2014, http://www.bls.gov/cps/cpsrace2011.pdf

U.S. Census Bureau, *Statistical Abstract of the United States: 2010*, "Table 12. Resident Population Projections by Race, Hispanic-Origin Status, and Age: 2010–2015," accessed March 10, 2015, http://www.census.gov/compendia/statab/2012/tables/12s0012.pdf

U.S. Census Bureau, *Statistical Abstract of the United States: 2012*, "Table 324 and 325: Arrests by Sex, Age, and Race: 2009," accessed March 10, 2015, http://www.census.gov/compendia/statab/2012/tables/12s0325.pdf

U.S. Census Bureau, "The diversifying Electorate – Voting Rates by Race and Hispanic Origin in 2012 (and Other Recent Elections)," May 2013, accessed March 12, 2015, http://www.census.gov/prod/2013pubs/p20-568.pdf

Weber, Max, Hans Heinrich Gerth, and C. Wright Mills. 1958. *From Max Weber: Essays in Sociology*. Oxford University Press, Galaxy.

West, Cornel. 2008. *Hope on a Tightrope: Words and Wisdom*. Hay House.

Yancy, George. 2004. *What White Looks Like: African-American Philosophers on the Whiteness Question*. Routledge.

3

BATTLING WHITE LIES

Exaggerated identity and the twilight of American religion

> They believed their words. Everybody shows a respectful deference to certain sounds that he and his fellows can make. But about feelings people really know nothing. We talk with indignation or enthusiasm; we talk about oppression, cruelty, crime, devotion, self-sacrifice, virtue, and we know nothing real beyond the words. Nobody knows what suffering or sacrifice mean – except, perhaps the victims of the mysterious purpose of these illusions.
>
> *Joseph Conrad*[1]

> Today nothing threatens the 'stability of the social order' more than the illusion of cultural identity. It needs, as never before, to be contested by a modern philosophical *ethos* that unravels the roles of the contingent and the universal, now that political parties in Europe and elsewhere have seized the initiative in what they call the 'battle for identity.'
>
> *Jean-François Bayart*[2]

Joseph Conrad's "An Outpost of Progress" (1897) is about two white men left in the expanse of colonized Africa who go crazy and die as a consequence of no longer having the ability to register themselves over and against their colonial peers or the Africans they deemed savage. White people "believe their words."[3] They believe their illusions of grandeur, and as Conrad's story exposes, the tragedies of *not believing* in such illusions are seemingly as problematic for white people as are the consequences for others.

The two white men were named Kayerts and Carlier. Kayerts was a short and fat man, the chief in charge of the trading station owned by the Great Trading Company. Carlier was the assistant, tall and thin. They were dropped off at a trading post three hundred miles from the next nearest post, and the steam boat they arrived on would not return for six months. As Conrad writes of the two men, "they were two perfectly insignificant and incapable individuals, whose existence is only rendered possible through the high organization of civilized crowds."[4]

Away from the society and civilization they knew, their efforts at growing accustomed to difference (and more importantly, to their own limits and uncertainties) merely ended in heightened fear and suspicion. Conrad tells us that "they lived like blind men in a large room, aware only of what came in contact with them (and of that only imperfectly), but unable to see the general aspect of things."[5] Really, they had lived this way before, only unknowingly, shielded from their tears and limits by civilization. Africa exposed these often denied features of their white life. As described by Sven Lindqvist, author of *Exterminate All the Brutes* (1996), a book that tries to site the essence of colonialism (and of white people), "it is just the distances, the climate, and the solitude that break down the two Europeans. Most of all the solitude, for that entails an inner abandonment, Conrad writes; they lost something that previously 'had kept the wilderness from interfering with their hearts.'"[6] Africa exposed them to themselves.

Among their possessions was a collection of books and a newspaper. Lindqvist suggests that Conrad's inclusion of the newspaper in his story was a veiled reference to the very publication in which "An Outpost of Progress" first ran. Conrad was telling white people something about ourselves. The newspaper celebrated "Our Colonial Expansion" and "spoke much of the rights and duties of civilization, of the sacredness of the civilizing work, and extolled the merits of those who went about bringing light, and faith and commerce to the dark places of the earth."[7] Blurring the line between fiction and reality, the newspaper represents more words to be believed, more lies to be ingested in the name of sacred civilization.

Five months passed with the two men effectively doing nothing of substance. They would engage in frivolities of one sort or another, they turned the natives into curiosities for ridicule and amusement, ominously ignoring that their white predecessor lay under the dirt not far from their trading post. One day in their sixth month, a group of blacks with guns and a clear command of a language foreign to Kayerts and Carlier arrived in the camp. These gun-toting blacks began treating the outpost as if they were at home. These strangers caused Kayerts and Carlier to grow even more fearful. Loading their own guns, Kayerts and Carlier asked Makola, their black servant, to tell them to leave. The strangers left the following afternoon, with Makola guiding them a ways before he returned to the camp acting in a manner that confused the two white men. Over a sleepless night filled with drum beats and gunshots heard off in the distance, Kayerts and Carlier grew restless.

Ten other black men had worked at the company post for nearly two years in what had been promised to them as six-month work rotations. Kayerts and Carlier come to learn that Makola, both in a quest for ivory and in an effort to make some use out of the workers at the post, had traded the men to the strangers, for ivory. The trade was how Makola convinced the strangers to leave. Kayerts and Carlier were furious with Makola, for "slavery is an awful thing" as Kayerts suggested with "unsteady voice."[8] More words believed by Kayerts and Carlier, or at least they thought themselves believers of such words. Soon the white pair would discover that their "words are nothing but 'sounds.' The sounds lack content outside the society that created them."[9] To this extent, Conrad's clumsy, tragic white protagonists say something of all white life that knows "nothing real beyond the words" we hide behind and use to conceal our reliance on a vision and promise of society and civilization … turning ourselves into victims of ineptitude and stalled humanity as we pay no mind to the actual victims of "these illusions." Not a full day passed before the men came to deny their hypocritical disdain for slavery, and they embraced the ivory as belonging to the company.

The sixth month passed with no sign of the steam boat. Growing wearied of their surroundings, and with no wherewithal of ability or compassion, Carlier grew increasingly frustrated with Africa and Africans and "talked about the necessity of exterminating all the niggers before the country could be made habitable."[10] More words. More to be believed.

Their steam boat was at least two months past due, and with rations running out, the two men lost their faculties. A quarrel between them ensued over Carlier demanding some of the last of their sugar, and Kayerts's subsequent anger at Carlier's having called him a "slave-dealer." Kayerts's refusal to accept the truth, that civilization had indeed turned him into a slave-dealer, was enough to make him grab a gun. Running in circles around their house, both men momentarily collapse, and Conrad tells the reader that Kayerts suddenly perceived "that death and life had in a moment become equally difficult and terrible." Swiftly upon this awareness, Kayerts hears a stirring. Thinking Carlier has grabbed a weapon and is out to attack, Kayerts shoots. He kills his partner and only afterwards realizes Carlier had been unarmed. Remorse filling his body, Kayerts grows pensive and his perspective shifts: "He [now] found life more terrible and difficult than death." Unable to break free from the sorrow of progress, he thought about death and Carlier and "in a very few moments he became not at all sure who was dead and who was alive." As dawn arrived, on the horizon were heard horns from the steam ship here to save these civilized men. When the Company Director and others landed on shore, they found Kayerts hanging in the twilight of early morning, by a leather strap from the cross that stood atop the grave of their predecessor, his lifeless body sticking out a "swollen tongue" at civilization and progress.

WHITE LIES

Conrad's brief story is a political statement about the impending end of colonialism, and the psychological and social anomie[11] that might result when white colonizers eat the poisonous fruit (i.e., the inability to accept difference) harvested from colonialism – what Malcolm X referred to as "chickens coming home to roost."[12] This poisonous fruit comes in the form of "believing" cultural identity as verifiable, as more than an illusion, leading ultimately to an inability to accept difference, an acceptance which would force recognition of the unverifiability of identity, the uncertain dimensions of any identity. Social theorist Jean-François Bayart, citing Michel de Certeau, suggests culture refers to an open tradition, constantly rupturing upon itself, following a dialectic of "permanence and change."[13] But for these adherents to white religion, there is reason to believe Conrad's ironic protagonists, Kayerts and Carlier, have no cultural identity because they have no culture, no means of coming to terms with limits or difference. As a result, their identities are constructed partially through the "borrowing" of other cultural "emblems."[14] But such borrowing brings with it the "suffering and sacrifice"[15] noted by Conrad. "An Outpost of Progress," then, offers a window into white identity formation as it emerges not simply in Europe or Africa, but in the Americas as well.

Already discussed at length in previous chapters, white "identities" are constructed through exaggerations of radical contingency, ideological beliefs or practices that coalesce to produce god-idols that refute human limitations by imposing those limits onto others in the form of physical and social suffering and sacrifice. These exaggerations are white lies, subterfuge and falsified representations of human possibility – not exactly "wrong" to the extent that they manipulate real human possibility, but false exaggerations and dismissals of the details involving the impact of these exaggerations on others.

The exaggerations I have in mind are identity-based, the ideas people hold about their own and other groups' values and abilities, in terms of both limitation and possibility. These exaggerations produce various polarizing us/them, insider/outsider, sacred/profane arrangements, securing such us/them thinking through the illusory promise of identity. The most fundamental lie told, the quintessential "white lie": that one's own identity or actions are not inextricably linked to the identities and experiences of others, that a distinction exists between the expression of human freedom (as identity-formation) and ethical responsibility to others. By responsibility, I mean awareness that expressions of human freedom are made possible through dependence on other humans. Exaggerations of radical contingency, exaggerations of this relationship between freedom and responsibility, reinforce the illusion of distance between human freedom and responsibility by offering the illusion of identity. Conrad, in "Outpost," casts this lie (and subsequent lies) in their ugliness, distilling them in one powerful passage:

> Few men realize that their life, the very essence of their character, their capabilities and their audacities, are only the expression of their belief in the safety of their surroundings. The courage, the composure, the confidence; the emotions and principles; every great and every insignificant thought belongs not to the individual but to the crowd: to the crowd that believes blindly in the irresistible force of its institutions and of its morals, in the

> power of its police and of its opinion. But the contact with pure unmitigated savagery, with primitive nature and primitive man, brings sudden and profound trouble into the heart. To the sentiment of being alone of one's kind, to the clear perception of the loneliness of one's thoughts, of one's sensations – to the negation of the habitual, which is safe, there is added the affirmation of the unusual, which is dangerous; a suggestion of things vague, uncontrollable, and repulsive, whose discomposing intrusion excites the imagination and tries the civilized nerves of the foolish and the wise alike.[16]

This chapter characterizes all such thinking that relies on the relationship between individuals and groups so as to deny that reliance as "sacred/profane" thinking, because it follows from a social demand for solidarity and security truncating social responsibility for certain groups based on illusory identities. I label all such traditional talk of the sacred or profane as exemplary of exaggerations of radical contingency because it hinges on acting as if it were more than its impact on the social world. God-idols are produced by conglomerates of exaggerations and rely on and make use of this principal sacred/profane distinction. Pushing this further, here I try to sight and site these invisible exaggerations from within the privileged exaggerations afforded to me. Here, we begin to "see" white religion in its expansiveness, as the Imago Superlata, white identity made in the image of an exaggeration of itself – a white lie.

Conrad seems to register this white lie in the form of colonialism. His short story does well to note the victims of such belief in illusions, and suggests that the illusions mask the initial victims and transform beneficiaries into victims, themselves. Conrad's words above, and his entire story, suggest there are no outposts of "progress"; there is no progress where colonialism, ideological exaggerations, or the god-idols they fashion are concerned, as belief in "progress" and society ultimately exact justice on the protagonists who are left for dead, "civilization" arriving too late if it *really* arrived at all. Kayerts and Carlier understand their identities in light of progress, yet Conrad seems to be telling his readers that these illusions and beliefs are not what they appear to those who benefit from them. White lies, taken as truth, appear only to end in death for the believers, and in their wake they leave the blood of countless "others."

Bayart's ominous description of the "battle for identity"[17] contextualizes Conrad's sociological diagnosis for the contemporary moment, where the protagonists of Conrad's story (and their deaths) have not taught others how to live in a less harmful way, but only how to adapt so that their illusory beliefs remain intact, still believing the white lie yet aware of its danger. Today, the white liars appear to have learned from those who have sought to expose them as liars, registering themselves as victims.

Take for instance the story of president George W. Bush who writes in his memoir that the lowest point in his presidency was the moment when Kanye West told the world that "George Bush doesn't care about black people."[18] Bush was more concerned to defend a white lie about his own identity as "not racist" than he held guilt about having literally lied to the world about weapons of mass destruction in Iraq.

These illusory identities continue to be worshipped now as they are manipulated in a "battle for identity," set afire by "the spectre of difference vanishing [from and] haunting the modern world."[19] The god-idols people worship have been registered as illusions or as problematic by many beneficiaries and victims alike (e.g., "racism" is regarded as morally wrong by most today), but white lies remain in place. Kayerts and Carlier still have much to teach us about our (white) selves today. Whether or not it too often goes unnamed such as whiteness, or over-named in the case of blackness, our preoccupation with identity remains a defining feature of contemporary American social life, as do the continuous casualties it imposes on human bodies as it works to respond to the limits of human bodies in what Bayart characterizes as this "battle for identity."

THE "THEOLOGICAL" SENSIBILITIES OF KAYERTS AND CARLIER

If identities are illusory, and the things theology and anthropology tend to discuss rest on such illusions, then theologians and anthropologists are cast directly into this battle. And it is precisely this battle, the back and forth, the constant antagonisms, which reinforces the believability and viability of identities as they are materially absolutized and legitimated[20] through the pain and suffering brought about by the antagonism. Society – god – is death dealing, and through such deaths produces and reinforces the "white lie" of a sacred/profane distinction used to ground "operational acts of identification"[21] as more than that, as cohesive, demarcated identities.

In the first two chapters, I have charted two of the more significant god-idols worshipped by white Americans, whiteness and theism, respectively. I suggest that, taken together, these god-idols work to constitute the cohesion of this group as an *identity*, understood as an ideological marker of distinction that has material effects in space and time. God-idols are projections of identities, the interests that solidify and make identity possible, centering concepts that work to concretize a person or group's sense of distinctiveness through various arbitrary, relative, and ultimately illusory distinctions. Here, I take a step back seeking to theorize this broader process and begin to offer an initial response to it. For many white Americans, an emptiness of identity is responded to by crafting a false sense of identity through the implementing of various distinctions, undergirded by a sacred/profane distinction. This orientation is the Imago Superlata, the process of forging "identities" in the image of exaggerations about human worth and ability, identity-based and focused exaggerations, a rhetorical means of dislodging the "white" from white religion (analytically), so as to see the abstract operation working to constitute the "white" in white religion. Imago Superlata is somewhat of a synonym for white religion, but also emphasizes the more abstract, quasi-fundamental dimensions of white religion.

Much of what follows schematizes this orientation by looking to figures such as existentialist philosopher Jean-Paul Sartre, whose location in relation to privilege makes him useful for understanding the Imago Superlata, while also serving as a warning that escape from it is difficult. Despite this difficulty, in response to the social suffering brought about by this orientation, Sartre's ethnographic, troubling perspective is responded to with social theorists Jean-François Bayart and Mary Douglas, arguing for a blurring and breakdown of "identity," beginning with a methodological breakdown of the identities and distinctions guiding the fields of theology and anthropology.

The term Imago Superlata is meant to evoke (and revoke) the notion of the Imago Dei, that we are made in the image of god. Adherence to the Imago Dei seemingly relies on an arbitrary sacred/profane distinction, and manipulations of "the contingent and the universal."[22] Such reliance allows that certain identities can be concretized and thus believed or realized, such as a "white" or "black" or "gay" identity. The scope of data is here broadened to consider some of the theologians and anthropologists who, by my reading, have studied or maintained sacred/profane distinctions as they studied the identities formed through such distinctions, such as Thomas Altizer, David Tracy, Marshall Sahlins, and others. Though exceptions exist to every rule or generalization, I am persuaded that particular formulations of these fields typically model and are undergirded by a distinction between sacred and profane which, socially and politically, reinforces identity as an often hidden "telos" for both disciplines, and especially for theology. Because both fields are so central to the intellectual heritage of and methodological tools employed in the academic study of religion, attention to them here serves as shorthand appraisal of the field of religious studies. But attention to these fields is also meant to trouble any presumptions about lines of demarcation between theological/anthropological methods and data, blurring the assumed parameters seemingly separating the two fields by casting both as preoccupied with that very distinction, the sacred/profane binary.

This blurring is accomplished through focused attention to the "ethical domain,"[23] where "anthropological" methods are used to examine theology/theologians as data, and "theological" methods are applied to further examine anthropology/anthropologists as data. In the process, I trouble any distinction between "who" and "what" count as data, and "how" we handle those data. An open-ended, loose hermeneutical characterization of these fields is employed, as more thorough attention to subfields of theology and anthropology (such as feminist or womanist theology or anthropological discourses extending beyond a preoccupation with humans) would detract from my larger argument and inadvertently privilege distinctions and classifications in a way that further reinforces the "operational acts of identification" that *White Lies* exposes.

In what follows, the major features of the Imago Superlata are outlined. These features include its reliance on the sacred/profane, its relationship to suffering and bodies, its secondary exaggerations, and its existential roots in the suffering of human bodies. The following sections think through how the academic study of religion might respond to the "twilight of the god-idols" – the contemporary inability of god-idols and the exaggerated identity claims that produce them to make good on a false promise to address human limitations.

FIGHTING ETHICAL BATTLES WITHOUT "ETHICS"

The "battle for identity"[24] described by Bayart is waged as much by white people as anyone else. But by virtue of history and the functional, dubious "effectiveness" of god-idols like whiteness and theism at procuring materialized expressions of the false claims made about human identities, white people largely remain in a position to wield disproportionate and varied capital and power within the social system. Clarity as to how the system operates is easier to obtain[25]; changing the system is more elusive, and yet is demanded both empirically, as identity is illusory, and morally, as these illusions create a social and cultural climate that skews the life options of those within such settings.

In light of having been thrust into such a "battle," the only means of understanding or disrupting the Imago Superlata involves attention to the same field where white existentialist Sartre's *Being and Nothingness* [26] leaves off, and which grounds the admonition offered by Bayart that follows his diagnosis: ethics. I don't suggest such a focus offers the means for a white, straight male like myself to fully escape the Imago Superlata, and this chapter concludes on a note about that inescapability. Attention to ethics, however, offers a methodological reflexivity and the possibility for renegotiating who bears the brunt of the effects of white lies. Human life in relation to other humans produces suffering necessarily, but through attention to such relations, certain suffering might be mitigated even if other unknown and known forms of suffering emerge in its place. In answer to the question of what to do about suffering, the simple and popular answer remains most appropriate: we fight it.

From normative ethics to the "ethical domain"

God-idols are big white lies, akin to the cultural imaginaries described by Bayart. They're "big" insofar as the work they do is expansive and multivalent. They are characterized by alleged appeals to universal truths that bring with them meanings "convey[ed] in *specific historical contexts*."[27] Whether the lies told involve anthropological claims about gods and devils or theological claims about humans, all of them appear as various exaggerations (i.e., "lies") of human/divine worth and ability, or a combination of both, which signals a necessary concern for the ethical dimensions of the Imago Superlata, not simply on moral grounds but on epistemological ones as well. These god-idols are imaginary cultural identity markers, concepts and categories that people and communities use to make sense of and navigate a reality and a history inherited from and by yet other people engaged in this "battle." This reality and history vary by individual and community, characterized by peril and tragedy as well as joy and prosperity. Not all face the same amount of suffering, or kind of suffering, but all know something of loss, emotional and physical pain, suffering and tragedy. The weight of one's circumstances weighs heavily regardless of calamity or entitlement, even as that weight often feels different and presses down on the motivations and actions of each person in a multiplicity of ways.

Following Bayart, who finds reason to study such ideas even while registering them as imaginary, no one is excused by god-idols (or one's recognition of them as such) "from making ethical judgments."[28] But ethics, historically, is fraught with problematic normative claims that valorize and co-opt assumptions about social homogeneity,[29] meaning that many if not most iterations of traditional ethics historically exemplify the Imago Superlata through normative moral judgments arising from one context and prescribed or proscribed for those outside that context or identity. Attempting to guard against this legacy while admitting to the limits of fully escaping the epistemological or ethical need for norms, here, normative claims extend only to those within the same category of constructed identity in which I find myself.

This talk of ethics is not necessarily a means of normative moral censure, but is instead grounded in terms of identity formation, focusing my attention on the relationship between one identity and the next. Talking of "lies" does not presume a "truth" exists, but notes that there is no "Truth," merely versions and interpretations of social life as likely to be elucidated by traditional Christian myth as by Bourdieusian social theory. Where identity is the object of scholars' attention, the line between myth and theory unravels, such that "scholarship is myth with footnotes."[30] Many claims towards "identity" hinge on manipulations of the notion of "Truth," such as teleological belief in "progress" demonstrated in Conrad's story. Meanwhile, as social theorist Bruce Lincoln reminds us, theorization is never removed from a vested identity-based interest. If identity is to be deconstructed, then Lincoln's suggestion about theorizing myth offers guidance for any efforts to discuss the mythic dimensions of identity: "the story I would tell – and like all others, it is a story with an ideological dimension, conditioned by its author's interests and desires …"[31] With this in mind, scholars of religion have never strayed far from their theological roots.

This attention to ethics includes the various dimensions involved in the social and self-policing and disciplining of bodies as charted by anthropologist James Faubion in his *Anthropology of Ethics*.[32] Following Faubion, the attention here is on the "ethical domain"[33] wherein ethical actors are constituted through their motivations in fashioning themselves as subjects, the evaluative criteria for living into that subjectivity, the training required to achieve such subject status, and the "telos" or end point of an ethical actor's striving towards a "subject position."[34]

Building on this attention to the ethical domain, "identity" is here understood to be an outgrowth of this quest for subject positionality, and the "subject" (whether philosophical, social, etc.) as bound by this same arrangement. This subject-focused framework is equally applicable to the field of theology as it is to anthropology and most academic study of religion. More generally, religion refers here to the arbitrary and relative[35] beliefs and rituals (i.e., distinction-making mechanisms including scholarship) humans use to make meaning – that is, social power and capital – where there is none intrinsically. It amounts to a process whereby limits are imposed so as to deny other limits through appeals to these identities demarcated by this imposition. Thus, religion is this process of identity formation contingent on illusory identities imposed on outsider groups projecting back a false identity on the insider. Those whom we as scholars refer to as "adherents" are as reliant on this process as are we, the scholars, as we arbitrarily distinguish ourselves (or our roles as scholars) as distinct from *their* role as practitioners. Religion is constituted at the place where language responds to limited human bodies, particularly when such language meets an embodied "quest for complex subjectivity"[36] through various claims of and about relative and arbitrary identities.

Faubion's schematic of the ethical domain offers a way to situate the dimensions of ethics without being fearful of the normative claims[37] that are part and parcel of so much talk of religion and identity. Ethics is present even in its "absence" within ethnography and theology alike, so attention to it remains important even if this attention means more work necessary in qualifying normative claims so they do not hijack analysis. For Bayart, attention to ethics requires a dose of liberalism:

> Let us judge knowing what we are about, not on the basis of scanty information; let us not allow the wool to be pulled over our eyes; let us take care to consider as productive events (*événementialiser*) the matrices of symbolic action through which the imaginary figures of politics are constituted and condensed.[38]

God-idols fall within these matrices, as does ethical consideration, and Bayart's words align nicely with Pierre Bourdieu's characterization of religion as a structuring and structured symbolic medium.[39] Ethics becomes an understandable and consequential feature of registering these matrices of symbolic action as loaded with constructed human meaning (understanding "meaning" itself as little more than a distinction-laden, arbitrary place-holder), and structuring possibilities for deciphering such meaning. Indeed, the god-idols are ideas that provide humans with a sense of meaning – understood as a sense of "identity" facilitating a certain sort of social power and capital – meaning wrought as other humans serve as fuel for the forge. This question of meaning brings the discussion back to two chief intellectual arenas that have wrestled with the ways humans make meaning: theology and anthropology.

Situating theology and anthropology within the "ethical domain"

Traditional theology and anthropology can be imagined as data, in that they fall within this ethical domain through their shared preoccupation with identity, as identity structures *and is structured by* the perception of meaning.[40] Obviously enough, both areas might easily serve as sources of data for many endeavors – that is, picking and poaching specific people or projects within these fields to elucidate particular trends, etc. And I do this in what follows. But I also purposefully generalize the bulk of these fields as "entities," data in their own right, to demonstrate their preoccupation with identity, and to purposefully allow my argument to mimic the very tendency analyzed. In this hermeneutical light (admittedly leaving out many exceptions to this generalization), some of the ways each of these two methodologies informs the other are revealed. As data, they tell us something about how they – as methods – might begin to treat *their own* data. Further, loose though my characterization of these fields may be, examining them in such a (twi)light allows them to also serve as proxy and example of the manner in which individuals and groups cultivate a sense of meaning by crafting a particular "identity" over and against other constructed "identities."

My turn to these fields is the result of their having served as my primary theoretical and methodological training grounds. I am, to this extent, trained in religious studies, theology, and anthropology, and so by virtue of my own anxieties about this intellectual heritage – white, theistic, etc. – I am instead projecting such anxieties onto the fields I have chosen to examine. Here, I am not concerned to vindicate my chosen methods of analysis, but to demonstrate the process of taking stock of the various aspects of the ethical domain. My argument seeks to model identity construction. Lastly, as a traveler on a Bourdieusian path, I turn to that social theorist to underscore another feature of my focus on theology and anthropology:

> The strategy of taking as one's object the very tradition one belongs to and one's own activity in order to make them undergo a quasi objectification – a common practice among artists, since Duchamp – has the effect of turning commentary ... into a personal work suitable for publication in avant-garde reviews, by a further transgression, scandalizing the orthodox, of the sacred frontier between the academic field and the literary field, i.e., between the 'serious' and the 'frivolous.'[41]

In other words, turning myself and my training into data, through a "quasi-objectification," has the effect of dismantling any "orthodox" distinction between academic and literary (here meaning crass or ordinary) investigation. Bourdieu gives vocabulary able to expose such a "sacred frontier" organizing many distinctions across fields as a white lie, and so my turn to these two fields follows the transgressive logic he describes. To proceed with a transgression, then, what follows is an initial example of theology and anthropology, as data, speaking back to theology and anthropology, as method.

In 1895, African Methodist Episcopal Bishop Henry McNeal Turner suggested that "god is a negro."[42] Turner scholar Stephen Angell helps to couch the significance of Turner's claim as a sociological statement, meant to do a specific kind of work: "Turner's affirmation of a black God ought to be primarily understood as the strongest response he could fashion to the idolatry of whiteness that he saw all around him."[43] One way to understand this "idolatry" is by recognizing it as a combination of racialized exaggerations of radical contingency working in tandem with a more fundamental exaggeration that presumes god as distinct from human/humanity. Yet, failure to acknowledge the synergy of theology and anthropology where identity is crafted causes difficulty in registering Turner's comment as "anthropological." Privileging the ethical domain exposes and clarifies the claim "god is a negro" as actually suggesting that "negroes" are fully human, and even possibly intimating that Turner may have been suggesting that the "negro" is "god." The theological pronouncement is implicated in the need to make such an anthropological statement to begin with, as his words reinforce a human/divine distinction undergirding the racialized distinction from which Turner sought recourse.

These constructed ideas, at face value isolated "illusions believed"[44] about god/gods, enter into the "relatively autonomous religious field"[45] wherein political, social, and existential needs meet and compete with yet other ideas that transmute in and across a sacred/profane line. Each idea relies on the tension posed by the other, and the structure imposed by the distinction. Because "god" carries a certain social and cultural capital – a "religious capital"[46] – the claim "god is a negro" offers a litmus test for recognition of black humanity and contributes to a growing ability for social actors to register that full worth. Like Turner, Anthea Butler's essay on the George Zimmerman acquittal manipulates similar tensions between who is a human and who is a god, so as to foreground black humanity.[47] Bourdieu states the process this way: "This simultaneously leads to the heart of the system of production of religious ideology, that is to the most specific (but not ultimate) principle of *ideological alchemy* by which the transfiguration of social relations into supernatural relations operates and is therefore inscribed in the nature of things and thereby justified."[48] Religious capital, thus, has the function of transferring a supernatural claim into a "natural" claim working to secure human subjectivity or maintain social power.[49] Exaggerations of radical contingency hinge on the efficiency of this ideological alchemy.

This ideological alchemy, witnessed in Turner's pronouncement by transforming theological discourse into anthropological data, and Butler's use of anthropological concerns taken up in/as theological critiques, makes a rather simple methodological and theoretical point, as if the theologian as data is speaking up telling the scholar of religion: "Wait, you're doing it wrong!" To know god is to know human, and human, god. Aside from being a powerful anthropological statement that African

Americans are fully human, Turner's claim that "God is a negro" – if read with a deconstructive or Feuerbachian hermeneutic – also theologically pronounces "God is a human." In terms of the meaning offered by/to each, they are equal, though socially unequal based on the "ideological alchemy" taking place thanks to the sacred/profane distinction. Methodologically considered, where white adherents to god-idols are concerned, an ethical demand arises to identify and explicate theology as anthropology and only then is greater epistemological clarity even offered, much less the possibility of social or political shifts in power. Analysis of white religion necessitates such attention and shift toward treating theological pronouncements as anthropological claims. Through such a shift, scholars might better see (and reflexively respond to) the manner in which claims made by people about "god" offer a wealth of information about how they see people.

An anthropological reading of Turner's pronouncement is not to say that anthropology as a field has fared any better on the question of its involvement in white lies. Worth expressing forcefully, the break here between theology and anthropology is not where they fall on "god" or the "sacred" as understood in terms of ontology or metaphysics, but is a break between human identity construction and the impositions placed on other humans, a failure to register that this ideological alchemy does not require "believing" in god; it's enough to believe human identities distinct. As argued in Chapter 2, theism is belief in belief, the proper name for believing in the social utility of and ontological veracity of distinctions. This latter break, the one I'm interested in, is exposed by how each field has fallen on ontological claims about "god" or the "sacred." As data, both fields appear equally guilty of diminishing their commonality by privileging either the "sacred" or "profane" dimensions of their own data.

Where anthropology is concerned, much has been made of the ethnographic imagination constructing the "primitive"[50] or the "other."[51] The "subjectivist turn"[52] has sought to address this imagination as historically problematic, and has been helpful in fostering a reorientation. But this turn has often reinforced a particular construction of "identity" in effort to refute many problematic features of a western identity. Theology may offer certain tools for the charting of social motivations and consequences of these anthropological constructions of "primitives" or "gods," constructed through direct claims to identity or academic attempts to study such claims.

For instance, how might the well-known Marshall Sahlins/Gananath Obeyesekere debate[53] over the rationality of indigenous peoples and the tension and power dynamics between indigenous and dominant ethnographic presentations of such rationality be read as theological data? For background, anthropologist Marshall Sahlins reinforced in 1983 a long-held anthropological "belief" that upon Captain Cook's arrival on the Polynesian island shore in 1779, the inhabitants (of the islands we today call Hawaii) revered Cook as their returned god, Lono. Sahlins suggests that Cook was subsequently treated as a god and summarily executed because he was a god. Another anthropologist, Gananath Obeyesekere, refutes the idea that the "natives" believed Cook a "god" by claiming that all cultural groups (e.g., these early Hawaiians as well as westerners) have the same practical rational faculties.[54] For Obeyesekere, this anthropological belief in the natives believing Cook a god was empirically ridiculous and offensive to the "rational" sensibilities of non-Europeans. It is likely not that the natives created Cook as god, but that Europeans created the narrative of Europeans as god.[55] Sahlins later writes that Obeyesekere's refutation is problematic as it ironically reinforces a Eurocentric rationality as normative, and because it relies heavily on the category of Obeyesekere's own experiences as non-European. Sahlins ends up suggesting that "Obeyesekere's anti-ethnocentrism turns into a symmetrical and inverse ethnocentrism."[56] Here, the debate played out in and over theological rhetoric, is essentially one over identity – that of the object of the field's investigation, and that of the field itself.

Thinking back to the example of Conrad's "An Outpost of Progress," nothing about the presentation of Kayerts and Carlier suggests they'd be taken for gods; presumably, as Obeyesekere makes clear, neither would Captain Cook on the Hawaiian Islands have looked like a "god." Again, the debate as well as the contents of the debate hinge on ideological alchemical manipulations which "derive their structure" from "the same principle of division."[57] Both scholars appear to make use of a principle of structuration to sight and site identities – Sahlins even poses Obeyesekere's refutation as an anti-anthropology, meaning loosey-goosey "generation of historical and ethnographic fables."[58] Essentially, he's claiming that Obeyesekere is thinking theologically to kill the idea of a white god operative in black minds. Sahlins relies on meaning made from temporal/historical and sacred distinctions to facilitate his effort at a structural approach to history, writ large. Obeyesekere relies on a structural reversal so as to refute social distinctions. Their disagreement is actually over technicalities involving method, a euphemism here for mode of meaning-making/identity-making – *meaning* their arguments are both ostensibly "theological" with anthropological "ends" in mind. Each, that is both the anthropological and theological, actually hides behind the category of experience in his own way, couched as either a "rigorous" scholar or a Sri Lankan-born anthropologist. At the end of the "day," they look a lot like George W. Bush and Kanye West.

Applying theological methodologies to anthropological conversations (and vice versa) might expose the ideological/theological interests at work on both sides of such a debate in a way similar to the anthropological examination of Turner's theological pronouncement. How does Turner's (or Obeyesekere's, or West's) theological defense of black humanity reinforce the dominant culture's ability to use the idea of "god" even more effectively than before? Can both Obeyesekere and Sahlins be "right"? Moreover, where Sahlins's work informs the political complications of my own, what political stakes are involved in being proven empirically or ethically "right" when it comes at the expense of reinforcing the social inequalities making the stakes of such conversations important at all?

In short, we can learn a lot by studying the beliefs people hold and the social values those beliefs expose and engender as emblematic of both anthropological and theological distinctions. If Obeyesekere and Turner are left to respond to dominant cultural identities by employing the tools of that dominant identity – namely, "rationality" and "god," respectively – is there any escape from the Imago Superlata? Within white religion, groups marginalized *by it* often respond *to it* through appropriation of its organizational techniques. But as a member of the dominant group within that framework, I'm left to either reinforce it by following the assertions and ideas of the marginal, reinforcing my social privilege by relying on the epistemological privilege of the margins, or I can argue more fundamentally against white lies and risk marking all identities as equally illusory, again reinforcing my privilege. How might this paradox find response? Is there a way to escape the distinction between sacred/profane, theology/anthropology that makes this paradox possible?

"TO FREE OURSELVES" FROM KAYERTS AND CARLIER

Traditionally, the *distinction* between theology and anthropology seems to involve the sacred/profane distinction, wherein theology (and religious studies, to a large degree)[59] sifts meaning in and through the lens offered by the "sacred" against that of the "profane," while anthropology postures as employing a profane or dis-interested (i.e., "social scientific") lens in order to talk about people, and at times, their beliefs and practices often involving the "sacred." Both, however, often creatively manipulate their own vantage points and in that manipulation frequently reinforce the beliefs of their data through the ideological alchemy made possible by the distinctions they use to define themselves and their data, not to mention forging their own academic identities (critical or confessional) on the maintenance of this distinction.

For a cursory example, I might unpack the shared sensibilities of, say, Clifford Geertz's methodology of "thick description" and *The Interpretation of Cultures* [60] and Karl Barth's systematic *Church Dogmatics*,[61] in that both efforts "denote an attempt at – and ambition for – rich, rigorous, and even *full* social knowing."[62] This is seen in Geertz's attempt at robust examination of text, subtext, and interpretive meaning of such relationships, and in Barth's systematic efforts that, in my estimation, seek to outline each possible avenue of human social interaction by way of a cosmic projection. "God" is not the only cosmic projection, but ecclesiology, missiology, eschatology, and other subfields of theology arise out of projections as well. Though not all theologians and anthropologists follow precisely the precedent set by these two texts, I wonder just how far removed contemporary ethnography and contextual theology really are from these early discipline-defining ventures. We tend to talk a good postmodern game of relativity, reflexivity, and unknowability, but do we really walk it? Following anthropologist John Jackson's claim that "identities rely on archives,"[63] meaning that identities require storehouses of information for their formation – storehouses where meaning is ascribed so as to be used in the construction of identity – then ethnographic thick description and theological exercise (whether systematic or contextual/constructive) may well amount to the archives holding the "stuff" of the ethical domain, those ideas and practices that constitute and serve as the "operational acts" forming identity. In other words, theology and anthropology – explicitly or covertly interested in the topic of identity – are intimately culpable in perpetuating white lies. By that measure, religious studies' influence from these fields finds it often and increasingly explicitly exploring the topic of identity against a backdrop of tools and social arrangements organized around a white lie based on disciplinary, as much as "ontological," distinctions.

Attention to the ethical domain necessitates, then, that the sacred/profane distinction, distinguishing the two disciplines, be dissolved in a political/social as much as an existential sense. However, such political efforts will not occur until the proper object of investigation is understood to rely on, and in fact to be, this distinction. Where anthropology becomes its own data on this point, Claude Lévi-Strauss aids in foregrounding this distinction when he argues that "the truth about man resides in the system of their differences and common properties."[64] This structuralist axiom may have something to tell about whatever "truth" is to be unearthed about the academic study of religion. Lévi-Strauss is most accurate if we read him as his own data: "the truth about [the anthropologist] resides in the system of their differences and common properties." And yet, even as Lévi-Strauss critiques Sartre on the grounds that existentialism "merely exchanges one prison for another"[65] (i.e., one god-idol for another), structuralism ultimately reinforced the inability to dismantle these distinctions by virtue of the intellectual security seemingly offered by structuralism and the distinctions upon which it rests.

Lévi-Strauss's structuralism remained too disinterested in the violence enacted through his own distinction between culture and nature.[66] That is, structuralism's ability to theorize distinctions hinged on a distinction between nature and biology, and human cultural production arising out of a fight against such natural risks, dangers, limits, and the like. Perhaps, post-structuralism emerges largely from an increased attention to the ethical dimensions of subject positionalities, exemplified in the very need for an anthropology of ethics as offered by Faubion, who notably is running with a baton passed to him by the incomplete work of Foucault.[67] Part of what makes exaggerated radical contingency *exaggerated* is that it hides the social consequences of responses to human contingency, the effects of the "illusions" and "cultural imaginaire" exposed by both Joseph Conrad and Jean-François Bayart, respectively. These illusions are our most intensely believed ideas, such as structuralism, the scientific method, or god-idols. God-idols and identities hide their own social effects. Indeed, they are designed to do so as their function is to ignore, deny, or fight directly against death and human limitations through division.

This taxonomic impulse is as much present among religious "practitioners" and anthropologists and philosophers who theorize such practices, like Lévi-Strauss and Sartre, as it is among those who theorize such activity in a more "interested" fashion through theology and religious studies. Indeed, there is no disinterested scholarship. One expression of the sacred/profane distinction involves the distinction between scholar and data. In the same way theologians and anthropologists study "god" or the "other," they are telling us much about themselves. Scholars are social subjects themselves, where Bourdieu notes that what is true of taste is true of "social subjects, classified by their classifications, [who] distinguish themselves by the distinctions they make."[68] Failure to dissolve both the scholar/data distinction and the methodological distinction (both structure and are structured by the other) reinforces blindness to contemporary power exerting itself on us and our arguments. Responding to this blindness marks my turn to theologians and anthropologists as data not as a choice, but a necessity. Any uncertainty brought about by the loose, playful breakdown of these distinctions, I hope, is indicative of my effort to foreground the uncertainty hidden behind white lies.

Though emerging with very different aims and intellectual inheritances, but also with ties to the University of Chicago, theologians Thomas Altizer and David Tracy both are arguably remembered as shapers of contemporary theology. Their works *imply* that, have the effect of suggesting that, the unstated (though central) role of theology is to maintain its preoccupation with identity or with the idea of god. Though differences between their ideas are notable, in functional terms, both Altizer and Tracy reinforce particular versions of the "sacred" as distinct from the "profane." These scholars' theological efforts are instructive insomuch as they both have been influential in shaping the field, because both of them inform my own ideas in substantial ways, and, lastly, because they are well-known for attempting to move theology beyond its narrow preoccupation with god and tradition. In many respects, both can be celebrated for having worked hard to refute particular constellations of white lies. Yet, for all their innovations, neither escapes the charge that the protection of certain identity/identities is the ghost that most pressingly haunts their ambitions.

Thomas Altizer, though seemingly close to using his lens of the death of god to see the deaths caused by "god,"[69] never seems to finish the task even as he proclaims that theology must be "reborn" by killing god, killing itself through dissolution.[70] Altizer celebrates the death of god, understanding this death as the freedom from tradition[71] more than as causing rigorous reflection over what to do with awareness of god's death as it would relate to non-white, marginal groups.[72] His writings are filled with moments where he feels secure that the death of god provides the freedom "from the alien power of all moral law," liberation "from the threat of external moral judgment," and "release of the burden of a transcendent source of guilt."[73] Such goals tug at my Nietzschean sensibilities, but they also suggest this death marks a freedom from social responsibility rather than towards it; how such flight from responsibility plays out in a social setting where white men often act like gods or believe others see them as gods is never interrogated. For Altizer, it appears the death of god is also the death of anyone else's context and any identity save his own, even calling himself "the last theologian."[74] Such a claim does the functional work of precluding anyone else's opinion, even if his point was to historicize the death of (a) tradition. If the reader finds my suggestions mere *ad hominem*, the following example should demonstrate that the social stakes of these arguments run deep and personal for Altizer. In a way that perhaps awaits its own book, Altizer ends up emblematic of white life lived in contemporary twilight.

Altizer recounts in his 2006 *Living the Death of God: A Theological Memoir* – with deathly seriousness – the time when historian of religion Charles Long set an African curse upon him at the 1989 American Academy of Religion Annual Meeting, a curse Altizer blames for ruining much of his life, including his marriage. According to Altizer's version of events (foil here to Sahlins), Long justified his curse on the grounds that Altizer "refused to offer the sustenance that Chuck [Charles Long] had once so needed."[75] While colleagues at the University of Chicago, in a time of crisis Long once went to Altizer for some sort of help and Altizer did not provide any. Altizer assumes Long maintained a grudge from this slight, such that it required a curse years later, at the AAR meeting of all places.

Functionally speaking, is not the death of god little more than the securing of white men as god? But if Altizer is to be believed, then god can be harmed and killed, indeed, and scholars of African American religion are indeed engaged in the death of "gods." It is telling that Altizer proclaimed the death of god rather than asking the question of whose god has died. Failure to begin asking such a question, especially when he had seemingly developed the tools for such engagement, is in the end its own curse.

In the case of David Tracy, his effort at underscoring a fundamental theology holding together the field's variety[76] is admirable, and his theorization of religion as a series of limits to and limits of human expression[77] loosely informs my focus on religion as involving the manipulation of limits. It might also be noted that Tracy is an American Roman Catholic and so his personal relationship to white American religion and its roots in a particular sort of Protestant economic anxiety (or economy of anxiety) are grounds for further study elsewhere, as both white American Catholics and white American Jews have a long and complicated relationship with being both victimized by white religion while in other moments, beneficiaries of it. But here, Tracy's production of a fundamental theology proves useful for underscoring another aspect of theology's preoccupation with identity. Though recognizing that "the modern Christian theologian cannot ethically do other than challenge the traditional self-understanding of the theologian,"[78] his reflexivity ends up more focused on preserving the theological task through pluralistic and fundamental claims than deconstructing the god-idols reinforced by theology historically. Ostensibly, his pluralism gives needed space to recognize competing god-idols (making his "modern Christian" qualification a bit confusing), but does little to chart the consequences of them.

Tracy's interest in pluralism might have been the actual "death of god" in the form of the death of theology as a discipline, in that difference continuously calls into question claims to divinity in tending to foreground (someone's) limitation. Here, difference (understood loosely as pluralism's point of origin) begets difference, not unity, meaning it undercuts the possibility of a functional social god, as attempts at group cohesion always come unraveled. Difference brings focus, then, to limitation and uncertainty. Hence, the fanciful story of Long's curse on Altizer might bear a tautological truth more biting than any individual curse. This "truth" involves recognition that the "gods" worshiped across time and space gain their identities, abilities, and utilities from a social world wherein sameness and difference collide. We truly learn about metaphysics – that is, what is *really* real – when difference ruptures what we think we know about ourselves and others. To these ends, theology (as a method) "dies" when theologians begin to privilege difference as opposed to orthodoxy, sameness, or any other synonym for social ideological agreement and affinity. Yet, instead of this methodological death of theology occurring (as tellingly argued for by Long in *Significations*),[79] Tracy worked to usher in a fundamental theology appealing even more explicitly to shared features of human experience – again, an effort to mitigate the impact of difference through acceptance of the veracity of different identities so long as they can be captured, categorized within a fundamental project, canonized, homogenized – with Tracy as the medium transmuting difference into sameness. Both of these thinkers quickly give life back to difference destroying "sacred" apparatuses they initially seek to trouble; Altizer becoming "god" by marking Nietzsche's proclamation that "god is dead" as an historical event,[80] and Tracy through a continued methodological appeal to fundamental theology.

Pushing this further, the story from Altizer offers a kind of embodied, interpersonalized, racialized example of the Imago Superlata in practice – in other words, Altizer's argument for god's death in tandem with bitterness at having been "cursed" by Long for having not aided him in a time of need – serves as an analogy for race relations where whiteness and theism are operative categories (meaning, everywhere in the U.S.). Of course, the details of what actually happened are as elusive as any claims about "god," but as an analogy, Altizer's frustration speaks to and embodies a similar frustration likely felt by those for whom I have authored this book. Just as Altizer privileges his own moral failing in the time of Long's need, Altizer seems more concerned about the damage Long may have done to him as a response. Altizer echoes the same sensibility seen in Sahlins, Bush, and the white men in Conrad's story, and, by extension, Tracy offers a softer emblem of the white preoccupation with white identity theologically transmuting difference into sameness.

But I don't think these are exceptional perspectives, only exceptional examples of a sacralizing tendency much more pervasive among white religion. I suggest that many whites hold a similar sense of the recognition of adherence to a god-idol of whiteness historically, even as the affective responses to contemporary black frustration and even "rage" are what is often rhetorically privileged by these whites hermeneutically. To this extent, Altizer ends up a mirror held up to white Americans where their feelings attached to the god-idols of whiteness and theism collide and are called into question. The "curse," in effect, is the accursed state of recognizing that there are no more theological tricks to employ. What Altizer deems a curse is none other than his own increasing recognition of his own radical contingency – a position he, and many others have trouble accepting without looking for an excuse. These excuses often take shape through various versions of "blame the victim" thinking. How could this social milieu be regarded as anything but a "curse"; the source of our fears and anxieties now planted as the seeds of our undoing? Indeed, the atheist Altizer seems here more keen to reify an otherworldly spiritual realm than submit to and take full ownership of his/our social actions. To this extent, otherworldly and this-worldly are both used, by Long and Altizer alike (according to Altizer, at least), to address more basic postures towards difference, its embrace or its abandonment. For Altizer – and here he embodies white adherence to whiteness as well as theism – the curse is a black man calling into question white worth simply by calling attention to the racialized curse white Americans conjured against black peoples for centuries.

As white theologians, Altizer by analogy, and both Tracy and Altizer by methodology exemplify white religious expression in the sense that a preoccupation with sacred identity or methodological identity – whether alive or dead – deafens them to the cries of the victims of god-idols, and blinds them to their own victimization through this process. To these ends, seen as data, Altizer, Tracy, and many of us look a lot like Kayerts and Carlier. The "battle for identity" described by Bayart and enacted in Conrad's story is not a euphemism, but a tautology, a "distinction that does not distinguish."[81] The anecdote of Long having cursed Altizer serves the same tautological ends – an expression of limits exposed as imposed differences fight back exposing real, embodied limitations and human failings.

Dissolving the distinction between theology and anthropology

How am I able to cast these thinkers as my data, while critiquing their theoretical efforts in the same breath, without relying on bad faith, deconstructing my own argument in the process? Surely, some will dismiss this book as little more than its namesake, white lies, sweeping *ad hominem* assaults against some of the academy's "idols." But such reactions would require ignoring that we are all locked in this "battle for identity." To call it a battle is no exaggeration or white lie. Given my position that theology and anthropology are preoccupied with questions of identity, and my suggestion that identity is constructed in and through social and political "battle" – or at best, a kind of cultural theft[82] – then both disciplines either address ethical interests of actors (requiring all scholars to turn themselves into their data along with their traditional data), or they reinforce the illusory identity of the group studied as well as their own. Attention to the data within the ethical domain, and to the voices ignored by Kayerts and Carlier, requires that we maintain a "distinction that does not distinguish,"[83] arguing for a dissolution of such methodological, sacred/profane distinctions.

The historical misrecognition that theology and anthropology are up to similar tasks has produced a general failure to provide attention to the relationship between what is studied by each and the question of who/what subjects and ideas live or die as "subjects" are constructed from the god-idols worshipped within the communities studied or explored. The failure is, ironically, a failure to see the anthropological dimensions of theology and the theological dimensions of anthropology. Deconstructing some of the "methodological" tools of each against the other exposes such a failure and helps to understand why the misrecognition has occurred and why it continues today – because illusory identities have a lot to say about how and by whom power is wielded across various arbitrarily crafted domains of distinction.

Admittedly, not all theologians and anthropologists (or all white) scholars of religion look like Kayerts and Carlier, and my characterization here is not meant to be a strawman (to the extent such is avoidable at all). But all of us (white scholars of religion) do find ourselves within the system from which Kayerts and Carlier emerge and die, and which they personify. Attention to ethics seems understandable. In fact, attention to the ethical domain blurs the distinction between each of these disciplines and social rhetorical strategies in ways that have not fully been recognized or attempted by many in the field of religious studies, and, more generally, the white American public. The following example, paraphrased from theologian James Cone, expresses my outlook on both disciplines:

> [Asked of Theology]
>
> The ethical question "What am I to do?" cannot be separated from its theological source, that is, what God has done and is doing to liberate the oppressed from slavery and injustice.[84]
>
> [Asked of Anthropology]
>
> The ethical question "What am I to do?" cannot be separated from its [anthropological] source, that is, what [I/My Community] has/have done and is/are doing to liberate the oppressed from slavery and injustice.[85]

Both questions are actually posed simultaneously, arising together in any instance where human or "divine" identity is described or discussed. Attention to the ethical domain foregrounds this simultaneity, and such attention is mandated by a white academic context. The simple difference is that the bulk of non-white academics have already made easy intellectual sense of the weight of such context. When will we?

The dissolution of the theoretical and methodological distinction between anthropology and theology is also foregrounded by the typical data of religion, adherents. Recent debates waged in the wake of George Zimmerman's acquittal about the role of "god" in the tragedy of Trayvon Martin's death inchoately reinforce not only why ethics is important, but how it offers a roadmap for analysis. If Cone's words situate the impact of an ethical lens in an abstract sense, then rhetorical data coming from popular culture offer a grounded example of the same thing I have in mind. Discussed already in Chapter 2, the *ad hominem* assault against religious studies scholar Anthea Butler, who argued that the American god is "a white racist god with a problem. More importantly, he's carrying a gun and stalking young, black men,"[86] works as an instance where the data of religion force recognition that there is no distinction between scholar and adherent where religion is concerned. In Chapter 2, I mentioned some of the specific language used to assault Butler in response to the claim about god, such as her being labeled a "fat cow," "cunt," and "nigger," all various explicit assaults against her humanity.[87] These verbal assaults experienced by Butler – and continuing even now at the time of this writing – expose the projected desires and goals of those who felt it necessary to defend themselves (and their god) against her. Such a defense of god actually is rooted in a personal slight, a personal assault on their "illusions believed," the charge that a person or group is lying. That the chosen recourse of adherents to the Imago Superlata when their god is attacked is to attack the humanity of adherents to other gods, attacking features of human or divine worth or ability, speaks volumes about the limits of ideological alchemy. If "god" were more than an "illusion," then there would be little need for censure. There is a reason Bourdieu calls it "alchemy," because it takes just the right ingredients of belief, quantity, and social moment to produce meaning. Because of this censure, because of the normative claims it exposes and reinforces, such discussions foreground the damage inflicted by belief in illusions. Situating ethical interests first analytically indicates that anger at "god" being criticized exposes "god" as a psychosocial illusion, but with very "real" effects. God's identity can only be defended by claims made by and about human identities. Theological language, then, is ethnographic terrain. So how might theology (as a method) move forward in auto-ethnographic fashion, able to respond to having heard itself speaking as data – which, of course, is another way of expressing Kayerts and Carlier having finally heard the voices of their victims by having registered themselves as victims.

Social anthropologist Mary Douglas, whose interest in issues of social power and control mark her writing as foreshadowing the need to break down these methodological distinctions, demands more of theologians than solipsistic naval gazing. In fact, she offers a statement about what theologians (and, by extension, white people more generally) ought to do in light of recognizing that a claim like Durkheim's – that "society is god"[88] – says much about the "relation of self to society."[89] For Douglas, theology and anthropology are connected – and the connection is exposed ethically:

> The theologians who should be providing for us more precise and original categories of thought are busy demolishing meaningless rituals and employing the theological tool chest to meet the demands of anti-ritualists.[90]

As a method for producing such "precise and original categories of thought," Douglas suggests theologians use the tools of social theory to

> [t]urn round on themselves and inspect their values, to reject some of them, and to resolve to cherish positional forms of control and communication wherever they are available. This would seem to be the only way to use our knowledge to free ourselves from the power of our own cosmology.[91]

Douglas' admonitions remain understudied in light of their contemporary utility. They may just hold wisdom for scholars of religion learning to live in the twilight of white religion.

CULTURAL EMPTINESS AND THE CONSTRUCTION OF IDENTITY/OTHER

White religion appears to arise out of an absence of culture, with "culture" being understood as the ideological and physical locations where traditions are retained and recast.[92] Kayerts and Carlier seem not to have had their own culture, and their actions – colonialism, generally, perhaps – might arise from a cultural emptiness, akin to what bell hooks has noted using Sam Keen's idea of "cultural anhedonia" – "the insensitivity to pleasure, the incapacity for experiencing happiness"[93] – making cultural identification an "illusion." Western colonialism and "culture" seems to subsume other cultures as if to poach them for the gifts offered by their otherness. But if all cultures are subsumed within a western culture marked by its operation as what Lévi-Strauss calls a "coalition of cultures,"[94] what relationship does western culture have to these constituent "others," whom Joseph Conrad refers to as "the victims of the mysterious purpose of these illusions?"[95] It appears that the *actual* "other" within the Imago Superlata is the dominant group with no cultural identity, and that out of this emptiness, the "other" – as typically understood – is created as the first and last "other" (i.e., white Americans) takes the identities of the constructed "others" while pretending that no such theft has taken place.

This "coalition of cultures" is crafted, constructed, and made real through the construction of these victims as "the other." Filling a perceived void of culture, the result of poaching all cultures as one's own, the "other" ("Blacks, Gays, the poor, Jews, Allah") is constructed as ideas that are then mapped onto real people and communities. As explained by Sartre, "If the Jew did not exist, the anti-Semite would invent him."[96] Beneficiaries and victims arise coterminously with the creation of their "identities." I follow Bayart that there are no "identities," only "operational acts of identification."[97] These identities are formed through adherence to god-idols that span the distance between perceptions of what is and what ought to be, often overlapping.[98]

In my estimation, few have outlined this cultural emptiness better than Sartre, while his efforts to address it leave many wanting more. Engaging Sartre allows for a more sympathetic interpretation of white existential sensibilities. To the extent possible, *White Lies* tries to be intellectually honest in suggesting that Kayerts and Carlier represent countless scholars, whose ideas exist and matter, including mine – while responding thoughtfully to the perils brought about by those concerns. Sartre offers a line in the sand, of sorts, on this point of descriptive vs. prescriptive response. For instance, Sartre's problematic suggestion that the answer to racism is to stop being black[99] ends up helpful in characterizing the limits of white religion and remains a warning that white attempts to solve the "problem" of difference will always fail if beginning from the premise that difference is a problem to be solved. At the same time, Sartre's more thoughtful response to Anti-Semitism indicates that not all god-idols carry the same social weight, meaning one might have the race issue worked out but promote homophobia, or one might think one has the answers to the race question, but reinforce the problem in other areas.[100] Or in Sartre's case, extend a certain sort of agency to Jews that was not equally extended to blacks. Ultimately, Sartre's focus on paradox, manipulations of such paradox, and interest in the race question give him a usefulness underscored by Lévi-Strauss who argues that Sartre's existential phenomenology "affords a first-class ethnographic document … essential to an understanding of the mythology of our own time."[101] Sartrean existentialism is emblematic of Conrad's imagined moment when Kayerts and Carlier finally hear their "othered" victims because they briefly recognize themselves as victims, those without an identity.

Originally written in French and published as *Réflexions sur la Question Juive* (Reflections on the Jewish Question) in 1946, Sartre's *Anti-Semite and Jew* offers a kind of grounded ethical addendum to his famous *Being and Nothingness* published three years earlier, but which did not appear in English until 1957.[102] Sartre argues that anti-Semitism is a "comprehensive attitude" and "passion" that orients not only how anti-Semites see Jews, but how anti-Semites navigate the entire world.[103] Anti-Semitism arises out of what Sartre describes as a "fear of being free,"[104] a fear of the human condition. From Sartre's perspective, anti-Semitism is intellectually easy, lazy, as well as death-dealing and marking a flight from human responsibility.[105] Arguing that "hate is a faith"[106] and that metaphysics (i.e., concerns over sacred/profane) are the privilege of the "Aryan governing class,"[107] the anti-Semite is guilty of this fear, this flight made possible by the anxiety produced from within a class-based society.[108] Inspiring my own constitution of the white theistic petit bourgeois discussed in the previous chapter, Sartre suggests that anti-Semitism is "a poor man's snobbery," used by the "'white-collar proletariat' to distinguish itself from the real proletariat."[109] Though I disagree here with Sartre's apparent elitism[110] and his overreliance on freedom as *sui generis* – both examples of god-idols in their own right – anti-Semitism is produced through these denials. In a desire for identity, where no culture is available to help constitute an identity other than the cultures of others, the void is filled by way of illusory beliefs about others producing equally illusory identities that have the power to shape material circumstances. Though Sartre's reliance on freedom situates it as the sacred object in his project, reinforcing the Imago Superlata, that very problematic feature of his work offers model and blueprint to chart how many god-idols are produced, including homophobia, sexism, classism, etc. To this extent, such reliance on freedom lends to Sartre's writings the ethnographic import suggested by Lévi-Strauss, in that it both brilliantly outlines the Imago Superlata and offers a useful warning to those who seek to disrupt it from within.

THE PRINCIPAL WHITE LIE

God-idols are expressions of something basic, something human: a demand for identity in the face of the illusion of cultural identity. Anti-Semitism and other god-idols within the Imago Superlata are identity-based quests for solidarity and ideological agreement. What does such a push for solidarity (or the belief in it) accomplish? Ironically, it allows for imaginary individual identities to be cultivated, but prevents actual social solidarity in modern society. Imago Superlata takes an existential concern over the limitations of real, embodied bodies, and imagines resolutions in a disembodied, illusorily sacred, social realm. This bears unpacking.

The first and foremost feature of white religion is that it constitutes a social/existential paradox as a sacred/profane distinction. Radically contingent cultural identity, the illusion of it as more stable than an illusion, is responded to by constructing society as functionally sacred, and this is the first exaggeration of radical contingency, its initial white lie. Society is an ideal-typical concept situating group homogeneity as "sacred." "Society is god."[111] Within the Imago Superlata, the paradox of illusory, empty identity is responded to by creating distances between the two poles of the paradox, an awareness of self and an awareness of other selves.

Among adherents to white religion – a system that even this project is a part of – the distinction suggested between sacred and profane is believed, allowing for society to function as god, and offering the grounds for further exaggerations. More white lies. This is usually couched in traditional "sacred" terms such as metaphysics and otherworldliness involving questions of knowledge and being, but emerges far below such traditionally theistic markers in that the sacred/profane distinction is any first distinction arising out of the "principle of structuration" described by Bourdieu.[112] Because typical understandings of "sacred" and "profane" rely on this distinction, the distinction is the actual object of interest, where distinction (in the abstract) is homologous to identity (in the abstract). The effects of this first distinction, this structural propensity, is that the binary described by Émile Durkheim has the function of hiding a person or group's relationship and responsibility to another person or group.[113] Applying a hermeneutic of reversal to Durkheim's work among totemic groups in Australia, I argue that his famous distinction of the sacred/profane actually indicates more about the way such distinctions operate within the religious orientation I'm describing, an orientation to which I consider him an adherent. "Totemism" theorizes the theorist far more than it theorizes any group or data set "out there." Durkheim argued that religious beliefs can be ordered into "sacred" and "profane" which "divides the world into two domains" and of which the division can be presupposed as prior to humans in community.[114] The first white lie is justified through another white lie, that the sacred is more real than its arbitrary, rhetorical, and discursive construction. The "sacred" is the exaggeration undergirding all other exaggerations because it teaches us how to exaggerate and reinforces the efficacy of exaggerations.

Durkheim also writes that "beliefs, myths, dogmas and legends" offer the means of charting sacred from profane.[115] Culture orients the margins and borders between society (as god) and those on the margins between and away from sacred social solidarity and homogeneity. From his study of these features, Durkheim concludes that the sacred/profane binary has at least three characteristics. First, its construction is largely arbitrary. That is, the distinction between sacred and profane things amounts to an arbitrary, yet "absolute,"[116] division. Those things marking the division are also largely arbitrary in the sense that there is no intrinsic quality attached to any object marking it sacred or profane. Bourdieu's suggestion that religion functions to "legitimate the arbitrary" should come to mind here.[117] Second, the sacred and profane are marked by a radical heterogeneity that often produces a "veritable antagonism,"[118] such that a "battle for identity"[119] as suggested by Bayart is inevitable. From this absolute arbitrary distinction, and through the antagonism between the two poles, the sacred/profane binary functions to produce, reinforce, and legitimate social homogeneity. It creates a sense of social belonging through the process of marking and division. Yet, this homogeneity is never fully achieved. The "outposts" of progress[120] (i.e., outposts of society) always deconstruct this homogeneity through the deaths/sacrifices occurring on those margins, explained at length in the first two chapters with respect to whiteness and theism. In a perpetual process, social solidarity is sought through a plucking out/sacrificing/removal of people who would question this homogeneity, with the process being reinforced and justified on sacred/profane grounds. That is, the process is justified through religious claims holding no intrinsic weight but the extrinsic weight offered by the very thing seeking homogeneity. Distinction, here the sacred/profane distinction, functions antagonistically and of necessity as a sleight-of-hand tactic. The antagonism produced gathers momentum in the social world. *White Lies* hinges on this point, in that my argument recreates the Imago Superlata as it theorizes it. Such is the paradox this book describes and does not try to escape: that by partial virtue of benefits gleaned from my privileged illusory identity – or Bayart's – I'm left to tell the story of illusory identities to my counterparts and everyone, reinforcing the privilege in a larger attempt to usurp and undermine the privilege. This seems akin to the challenge faced by Sahlins, as well. Identity, though illusory, is inescapable, leading to a paradox wherein the only response to identities – real or imaginary – is a battle, an *ad hominem* assault one against the next. If identities are illusory, and things theology and anthropology talk about rest on such illusions, then theologians and anthropologists are cast directly into the battle. And it is precisely this battle, the back and forth, which reinforces the believability and viability of identities as they are materially absolutized and legitimated through the pain and suffering brought about by the antagonism. The sacred – god – is death dealing, and through such deaths and attempted murders produces the "white lie" of grounded, ontologically viable identities.

Radical contingency is thus caustic and ever frustrated, in that its response to itself, exaggerations of radical contingency, rests on illusions requiring antagonism, as only *ad hominem*-styled justifications are available for validating things artificially constructed. We respond to white lies with … more white lies. Where meaning-making is concerned, *ad hominem* attacks might just have their roots in *ad* "homonym" – that is, violence erupts in the social world between two like objects or signs due to an ascription of or confusion about different meanings. Because society is both in need of homogeneity and is serving as its own justification for that homogeneity, precisely because of its intrinsic heterogeneity, it must remain perpetually antagonistic, working towards sameness by killing difference.

This antagonistic heterogeneity (distinct, itself, from theism discussed in Chapter 2) is the precondition of god-idols to be constructed, because it functions to produce the need for god-idols to span the distance sited by the sacred/profane distinction. The paradox is transmuted into two opposing halves, and adherents seek to orient themselves according to only the "positive half" of this radical contingency that is no longer registered as artificial, arbitrary, or relative. The principle also creates this distance, as it is an illusory distance believed in so that acute expressions of cultural identity might also be believed in. Whiteness or theism become "absolute," queerness becomes "biological" out of a need to absolutize and legitimate the god-idols constructed through this distinction-making apparatus. This first "distance," the constructed distance between social and existential positions vis-à-vis the sacred/profane binary, offers the foundation appealed to by constructed god-idols to justify other "us/them" distances, other exaggerations of radical contingency and other god-idols. But lies are always about something. The white lies of the Imago Superlata are about bodies.

PROJECTING IDENTITIES ONTO MATERIAL, LIMITED BODIES

White religion responds to an existential problem of embodied limitation by projecting illusory identities onto other bodies. Though my turn to Sartre might cause some to suggest I reproduce a justification of this arrangement as I work against it, I am not seeking any such "unity" of the sort he demanded, and I am of the opinion that Sartre's theorizations in proximity to social centers and privilege are helpful for their hermeneutical offerings even if his philosophical musings are all too often disembodied. What they help to make sense of is this constant and chronic attempt to resolve a paradox of radical contingency by exaggerating the possibilities of escaping it, only to arrive back at paradox through the sacrificial offering of individual or "social" bodies in the process. Here, I'm not seeking to solve this problem of social weight, only to understand it in relation to the ideas held by those in that arrangement and to which they adhere.

What Durkheim calls this "veritable antagonism"[121] emerges as ideological battles are waged between, within, and across "imagined communities"[122] composed of enfleshed bodies. All exaggerations of radical contingency take place on real, limited physical bodies. Yet, those constructed exaggerations – reinforced by a disembodied notion of society as god – remain discursive and thereby unable to address an embodied existential problem. As a result, these disembodied (i.e., illusory) group allegiances (societies, social collectivities) localize onto bodies of those perceived outside the group. In every instance, parts are sacrificed for maintaining illusory conceptions of the whole.

Physical, materially limited, radically contingent bodies respond to those limits by projecting an illusory social body onto real bodies, and judging the material body against the social body. In fact, Douglas makes this point even more forcefully:

> The physical body can have universal meaning only as a system which responds to the social system, expressing it as a system. What it symbolizes naturally is the relation of parts of an organism to the whole. Natural symbols can express the relation of an individual to his society at that general systemic level. The two bodies are the self and society: sometimes they are so near as to be almost merged; sometimes they are far apart. The tension between them allows the elaboration of meaning.[123]

Limited bodies are judged to belong or not based on an unlimited ideal in the form of god-idols, such as whiteness, heteronormativity, etc. The ethical domain helps to show that social actors are embodied actors. Sacred and profane appear in physical form as bodies, limited bodies, radically contingent bodies. My argument is not that the sacred *is* the profane but that both sacred and profane are components and outgrowths of human complexity and embodied as much as disembodied limitations and uncertainties. Society is cast as sacred while individuals become profaned, expendable, sacrificable, because of the meanings elaborated by the division.

This embodied focus suggests that what a person says or does to their own body is proportional to what they say or do with/to other bodies. Further, adding a dimension to this relationship, ideological projections of bodily concerns are also proportional to other projected bodily concerns. Further still, ideological projections are also proportional to direct embodied statements, meaning a person can say something about "god" and it impact the bodies of adherent and non-adherent alike. Hence, the ideological effects of belief produce material consequences for adherent and sacrificial victim because material bodies are used in the crafting of these illusory identities. Exaggerated claims and images of self and others – projected onto the bodies of self and other – come to produce the image one holds of one's own and others' identities. All identities, human or "divine," are formed through this process.

The Feuerbachian[124] cosmic screen is bodies – material bodies – of others. The projector: radically contingent humans; the projection: an exaggerated image of a limited physical body. This seems to be what Mary Douglas has in mind when arguing that bodies are canvases for symbolization.[125] Where whiteness is concerned, Chapter 1 explored this process through the spectacle of lynching, wherein the cosmos localizes onto hanging, mutilated, dead black bodies, constructing exaggerated images of blackness (as death) and whiteness (as safety from death) in the minds of white and black alike. Lynchings mark instances where individuals are sacrificed physically, so that the social margins can be reorganized. Black bodies out of place, what Nirmal Puwar calls "space invaders,"[126] bring the margins to the center, rupturing the sense of stability, and are eradicated, sacrificed, reordering that stability through the death of the offering. Trinkets and tokens cut from black flesh, as well as the attendance of children, function to ensure the memory lives on of the costs associated with – as well as how to respond to – momentary recognition that sameness doesn't really exist.

Complementing such vicious murders, but no less significant in the use of bodies as screens for exaggerations of radical contingency, the segregation that is so part and parcel of U.S. Christian worship services suggests churches are veritable as well as metaphoric social centers where homogeneity is sought and determined. Where physical sameness is weak, ideological sameness increases. That is, racial diversity can be more easily achieved (in an Evangelical church, for instance) where a premium is placed on belief. Where physical sameness is strong, as is common in mainline liberal white denominations, greater ideological/theological diversity is afforded. Rather than belief shaping who is in attendance, the physical bodies in attendance shape belief. In both instances, however, difference is sacrificed in the promotion of social sameness, and bodies function as the mechanism, the "screen," whereby a façade of sameness masks a depth of difference.

Ostensibly, these Feuerbachian projections, coming from and onto bodies, map out rhetorical and cultural distinctions between sacred and profane terrain and say something of the power and control exerted in effort to believe in identity, with the viciousness of any given ritual being determined by perception of the proximity of one illusory group to the next. That is, bodies are deemed sacred or profane through the adherence to a sacred/profane distinction transmitted through disciplinary mechanisms like discursive language and embodied feeling. Stated succinctly, "sacred" and "profane" localize onto material bodies, humans creating god-idols from their wrestling with their own bodies.

Because of this embodied, cosmic mapping – bodily canvases are limited, after all – a god-idol always brings with it both dimensions of the sacred/profane binary distinction localized on the bodies of adherents and outsiders. God-idols are produced from individuals in groups and in response to and with the tools offered by the paradox of radical contingency. This suggests god-idols are limited because they are never stronger than the screen upon which their projection rests – limited bodies. This paradox of human response to limit and contingency remains constant; the paradox cannot be escaped. Exaggerations in the direction of more (e.g., the white man's god complex) or less (e.g., nihilism) than the paradox reinforce the paradox. Necessary, then, is to find a way to pay attention, to expose the limits of god-idols by exposing embodied limits hidden by the Imago Superlata and the "opacity" (of theology and reality)[127] reinforcing this misrecognition. In short, because theology is made of the stuff of limited bodies, it is limited in seeing its own limitations, in seeing itself as an exaggeration – its paradoxical origins and preoccupation with limited human bodies responded to through illusory identities. The next section offers a schematic and interpretive lens to analytically "see" these exaggerations in practice.

LITTLE WHITE LIES: AGENTIAL AND VALUATIVE EXAGGERATIONS

Douglas's call to offer "more precise and original categories of thought" might be responded to by offering here a tendential,[128] partial framework for analyzing the exaggerations that localize onto physical bodies, ultimately creating god-idols as they coalesce. Here, specific examples are suggested as vehicles for the schematic, but the examples in what follows are not exhaustive, but rather representative and are meant to be useful for analyzing a variety of exaggerations.

The Imago Superlata reacts against the human paradox of radical contingency, a position which registers human freedom as bound by its expression in another person. Illusory god-idols are structured by the various exaggerations that skew this balanced relationship. The sacred/profane distinction, as the first exaggeration, works to suggest that such distance is achievable. It also works to ensure the inevitability of sacrifices in the production of that distance. But following behind this first distinction, these god-idols also structure two secondary exaggerations to give shape to identities and god-idols: (1) agential exaggerations, which exaggerate human/divine abilities, and (2) valuative exaggerations, which exaggerate divine/human worth. In bad faith, they presuppose value and ability without sufficient evidence, as their building blocks – limited bodies – suggest otherwise. More white lies. These are the two "theological" mechanisms that turn illusory human cultural and social identities into functional god-idols. This framework is not meant to be exhaustive, but open and the start of my efforts to chart the relationship between idea and action, individual and group, the small and the large.

Agential exaggerations allow for the anthropomorphic projection of the human desire for identity onto a cosmic, embodied screen where such desires are suspended until such time as they are realized. This temporal dimension might suggest god-idols function teleologically, wherein the promise of human ability or human value, if not found immediately, will be secured at some point. These agential exaggerations manipulate human abilities so as to outline group belonging, solidarity, and protection. In complementary fashion, valuative exaggerations presuppose the worth of particular individuals and groups often through things like belief in a soul, the "sacred," and/or the veracity of an achievable identity. That is, they mark and manipulate human value – who has it, who doesn't, arbitrarily ranking value in an effort to hide ability. Such white lies foreground a human arrogance, a bloated sense of worth and ability that does not correspond to the intrinsic possibilities offered by human finitude, bodily limitation, mortality, and social life. Two examples are in order.

For one example from recent years, well-known televangelist Pat Robertson said on The 700 Club that a trend among gay men involves wearing rings on their fingers able to cut skin, so that these men are able to transmit HIV/AIDS to others.[129] Of racialized exaggerations, I can offer my own personal, auto-ethnographic example. At age twenty-two, working as a lifeguard instructor during a camp that one week per summer hosted mostly African American boys, white men would come up to talk about why so few of the black boys could swim. Repeatedly, I heard suggestions that "black people were less buoyant" and that "black bones were heavier," with one decidedly certain white man adding that the strong bones were also "why 'they' were so good at sports." Series of these exaggerations working together autopoietically produce/are produced by homophobic and racist (respectively) god-idols shaping the identities of those who adhere to them. Concomitantly, these exaggerations victimize others (the signified) as those negatively impacted by them are forced to square with the social options cultivated from adherence to these illusory exaggerations and their god-idols, and the variable quantity of agreement/belief in these social and ideological exaggerations.

Agential exaggerations involve exaggerated statements about human/divine ability. They come in positive and negative varieties, and always bring a benefit and deficit moral valence indicative of the exaggeration as a response to the paradox of radical contingency and the flight from responsibility. In the case of the myth of the gay AIDS rings, the agency of gay men is elevated in an effort to characterize them in this or that way, while adherents of homophobia (as a god-idol) find their own agency mitigated (a negative exaggeration) so that the homophobic god-idol might endure through the narrative that gays are dangerous. A trade-off is made in this moment, the adherents accepting their own limits so as to reinforce their ultimate victory over limits. Agential exaggerations are akin to theologian David Tracy's characterization of religion as various "limits to" and "limits of" human existence.[130] In this case, limits to an exaggeration of gay male agency (via pathology and technology) are offered so as to reinforce a god-idol of homophobia that responds to the empirical and ethical limits of social life. The positive or moral valence refers to who ethically or politically benefits from the exaggeration, and its normative grounding is determined by a person or group's power within and proximity to social centers. In this case, homophobes (the signifier) are benefited socially and existentially while gay men (the signified) receive a social and existential deficit. The exaggeration works to reinforce heterosexual relations as a marker of social homogeneity, and homosexual relations are sacrificed (as profane) for the sake of the (sacred) society.

Belief in the inability of or difficulty for African Americans to float (as efficiently as whites, presumably) is another agential exaggeration. Here, African American limitations are exaggerated, situating the signified group "black people" in the negative, while an implicit story finds "white people's" abilities exaggerated positively. In this case, unlike the first example, the moral valence follows the exaggeration, with the negative exaggeration about African Americans also producing a social and existential deficit for African Americans, while the same exaggeration offers an identity-based benefit to the story-teller (the signifier) through other exaggerations (always) related to black bodies.

The next secondary exaggeration involves responsibility, the awareness that expressions of human freedom are made possible through dependence on other humans. What one registers as one's responsibility to another is a question of value, of worth. Valuative exaggerations cover this ground. For instance, "transvestites are an abomination"[131] is a valuative exaggeration marking a "trans" person as outside of society. It is a statement of worth, where the dehumanization of the signified within the exaggeration reinforces a false sense of worth held by the adherent to the exaggeration (the signifier), akin in certain respects to Erving Goffman's discussion of some of the links between "virtual and actual" identities,[132] in that assumptions about the false or "real" identity, by those who hold it or those who do not, are bound to each other in a social and existential dance over identity.

These valuative exaggerations also carry a valence, only it is an agential valence. To suggest that a "trans" person is outside of the group – in this case, the human group – prevents this person from exercising the agency and abilities offered intrinsically within the ethical domain. Limited bodies are still capable of a vast array of ideas and actions. The signification of queer bodies or African Americans as worth less than the signifier prevents even the abilities of those making the claims to situate their own existence as cohesive or complete, in that the exaggeration guards against full possibility within the social group. The believer in such an exaggeration validates themselves as worthy of inclusion within humanity, also reinforcing that whatever their agency, it will be afforded in this grouping. At the same time, the person so labeled as an abomination is deemed unworthy and, through that exaggeration, their agency is taken away as they are alienated from the group in such a way that they no longer have the ability to freely express their actual abilities.

Corresponding to the existential paradox of freedom in responsibility,[133] exaggerations work to manipulate freedom away from responsibility so that it appears the paradox of radical contingency can be avoided by way of identity. Sartre situates the stakes of exaggeration in theological terms:

> Every human reality is a passion in that it projects losing itself so as to found being and by the same stroke to constitute the In-itself which escapes contingency by being its own foundation, the *Enscausa sui*, which religions call God. Thus the passion of man is the reverse of that of Christ, for man loses

> himself as man in order that God may be born. But the idea of God is contradictory and we lose ourselves in vain. Man is a useless passion.[134]

Sartre's position speaks to the inescapability and yet futility of these exaggerations of radical contingency as they create god-idols and yet, those god-idols remain "idolatrous" in that they never fully achieve their function. Here, note that I am not celebrating Sartre's position, but using it as ethnographic data; Sartre helps to describe the Imago Superlata, which relies on exaggerations. Agential exaggerations are the "not yet" of having recognized that such attempts to be more than human through truncating the choices and abilities of others never find fertile soil. Those worshipping such god-idols negate even their own value and ability in this process, in that exclusion of human possibilities from the social world literally and simply undercuts any actual social progress and relies on assumptions about shared norms guiding conceptions of "progress." To this end, there are no "outposts of progress" because the Imago Superlata does not allow for it thanks to these exaggerations. It *exaggerates* false possibilities, thus truncating real possibilities.

White religion crafts identity out of a complex arrangement of these exaggerations and they gain their power as god-idols through the number of adherents to such beliefs and the number of exaggerations that shape the life options and arrangements of those who are the subject of the exaggerations. Again, power comes from the limited bodies needing power. Labeling each a "god-idol" is meant to situate them as a response to the paradox of radical contingency and to offer a way of talking about such identity-based constructs as they interact with, and are impacted by, the social environment. Finally, these god-idols are never fully disconnected from one another and operate intersectionally, in that they "do not function independently but, rather, act in tandem."[135] God-idols are syncretic, moving as function and pragmatic concern shape the abilities and demands placed upon them, such that differently cast god-idols (patriarchy, whiteness, theism, etc.) employ difference to militate towards social sameness. Ironically, their function guards against tautological recognition of social sameness only and always offered, through radical contingency, our limited and limiting relationship to other limited, limiting bodies in space and time.

I offer the following schematic meant to help organize such exaggerations, and to assess the severity and social effects of them:

Two types:

1. Agential Exaggerations (Freedom)
2. Valuative Exaggerations (Responsibility)

Four manifestations:

1. Signifier Positive/Signified Negative[136]
2. Signifier Positive/Signified Positive

3. Signifier Negative/Signified Positive
4. Signifier Negative/Signified Negative

Two modifiers (whose identity benefits):

1. Moral Valence→Abilities within the Group (points to linguistic, embodied code)

   [The social actor's "worth" determines what that social actor is allowed to do]

2. Agential Valence→Sense of Belonging (points to morality – personal or positional)

   [The social actor's "abilities" determine where that social actor belongs]

With certain exaggerations, either the signifier or signified is implicit and determined by social norms and the operative god-idols worshipped by the parties involved in the exaggerations. Moreover, the two modifiers must be stipulated more carefully. Each modifier serves to attach a valence to these exaggerations. One lie involving ability will carry with it a corollary tacit assessment of value, and vice versa. Agential exaggerations stretch and skew perceptions about abilities so as to determine who does or does not "belong" in a group, that is, their value. Valuative exaggerations guard against the already existing, intrinsic abilities of those inside and outside of groups. They work in concert; my schematic offered here is heuristic and analytic, meant to offer a way of understanding what happens in these exaggerations, but the two types do not show up in isolation. Abilities are always judged, to this extent, just as worth is always predicated on presumptions about ability – at least within this Imago Superlata.

The sacred/profane distinction, as it constructs for adherents an empty, invisible god-idol and identity, offers the blueprint for these secondary and tertiary exaggerations. Each exaggeration, each of these white lies, follows the initial pattern, where radical contingency is exaggerated with empty, illusory markers as varied as the human minds that create them and the limited bodies that are the screen for their projection. Thus whiteness and theism, as I understand them, are made from groupings of exaggerations of radical contingency. The sacred/profane divide/distinction, in its practical and theoretical distinctions, is the principal exaggeration making possible more specific exaggerations that produce god-idols.

SACRIFICE, CAPITAL, AND THE SACRIFICE OF POWER AND PRIVILEGE

The consequences of these exaggerations emerge in the form of sacrifice, a forsaking of physical bodies to physical and social death. Indeed, these exaggerations function to produce and justify such sacrifices as necessary and to determine who will be sacrificed. The first two chapters have extensively engaged such sacrifices as they structure and are structured by the god-idols of whiteness and theism. Here, I present a brief note about the Imago Superlata's demand for sacrificial offerings, and in this Sartre remains a guide:

> It seems to all these featherbrains that by repeating with eager emulation the statement that the Jew is harmful to the country they are performing a rite of initiation which admits them to the fireside of social warmth and energy. In this sense anti-Semitism has kept something of the nature of human sacrifice.[137]

The sacred/profane distinction, ostensibly, is this first distinction, the distinction getting the taxonomical ball rolling. But "imagined communities,"[138] societies and social groups (dominant or marginal) must localize somewhere and they end up localizing in/on other bodies, necessitating "something of the nature of human sacrifice" described by Sartre. This "something" seems to come in the form of individual and group alienation from society, or in the form of physical bodily sacrifice, or in the form of forced ideological agreement. The point is to keep difference at the geographic and metaphoric margins of society, where antagonistic battles are fought. Due to this demand, it is impossible that the other not be artificially produced and subsequently sacrificed – as this production "secures" the unstable, illusory borders of identity.

The irony of forsaking bodies for identity is that god (as society) functions to produce the very thing it cannot accomplish, a genuinely cohesive social life devoid of social risks and physical dangers for the bodies that make up each community. Because of this inability, "social warmth and energy"[139] ends up being cultivated through exaggerations that produce human sacrifice either directly or through in-group/out-group marginalization, producing a type of sacred "capital" which, when spent for the sake of identity-construction, has an externalizing effect on/in the construction and sacrifice of "others." "Sacred" capital, or what Bourdieu calls "religious capital,"[140] is transferrable into economic, symbolic, and political capital. Capital is thus procured by governing other bodies while pretending to be interested only in governing one's own through illusory constructs in the form of invisible god-idols. Contemporary U.S. foreign policy, discourses over domestic safety, and the construction of the "terrorist"[141] as an ideal-typical category (in my terms, a god-idol) exemplify this tendency.

White religion always exposes (in its concealing) a prescient reminder of human suffering, limitation, and disorder because god-idols materialize through ideological constructions of their inverse, limitation. The problem has been, as Conrad points out in the epigraph beginning this chapter, that not many of the believers take time to listen to the victims of their belief long enough to register that they, too, are victims (or could become victims). Imago Superlata is sustained by inattention and misrecognition of the ethical domain from which emerges all talk of humans, gods, and sacrificial offerings. And actually, it appears the difficulty of listening might have something to do with the "production" of the groups who will serve as sacrificial offerings. In effect, society is treated as a temporary flight from death occurring at the expense of those on the margins of that flight. In this functionally inept arrangement, society is death-dealing as it requires the deaths of those on its margins so that it might appear to be that which it never is, homogenous. By death, I mean both physical and social varieties, but here underscore the nature of death as the (in)ability to wield power and capital. Sacrifice is not about killing the weak, but the strong: those who would disrupt the social order. Understood as a white lie, "god" as the "social divine" is a murderer, who kills by promising eternal life and security for those who can or will capitulate to the false sense of social certainty provided by god-idols who kill the strong to protect the weak. God-idols, and the identities shaping and shaped by them, determine *when* one group lives and when another dies.

Physical death is of course very real, and I do not mean to be read as downplaying its significance. Indeed, contemporary social life largely hinges on the social effects of fear or threat of physical death. But death needs to be understood within its social context – it is an end to power. On this point, as example, someone like Tupac Shakur remains socially alive to the extent that the power of his memory continues to shape the power afforded those on the margins of society, those victimized by white religion, to work against it. To be discussed much more fully in Part II, my argument necessitates a discussion of whether death and suicide are ever possible, given these functional parameters. Death surely. Individual suicide is possible but is best understood not as physical death, but ultimately as a total embrace of the Imago Superlata, in that the physical suicide is a result of succumbing to the weight of the Imago Superlata through having had one's radical contingency exaggerated (to its end) by self or others. Part II of *White Lies* suggests that rather than suicide as a response to the Imago Superlata – one can't kill what is already dead,[142] after all – the only adequate response to the Imago Superlata by those within it is learning to die with others, with those on the margins. Where responses to the Imago Superlata are concerned, death is mandated for its beneficiaries in the form of relinquishing capital and power. For theology, this begins through a methodological shift, giving up the power of the sacred/profane binary and what it has (purportedly) offered in the way of social knowledge about self and other.

THEOLOGY AS A *LIMITED* HUMAN SCIENCE

> I believe the ultimate goal of the human sciences is not to constitute, but to dissolve man.
>
> *Claude Lévi-Strauss*[143]

Despite the contemporary assessment of identities as cultural constructions offered here, identities still hold a vast amount of psychological and social merit, but given what we know of them, how we undertake to make sense of them and their social impact becomes an important question to consider. At once, for white men working from within this battle for identity and impacted by the pantheon of god-idols created within it, it is incumbent upon us to learn more about ourselves. Yet, one thing we already know about ourselves is that we've often assumed a bloated sense of self and our ability to know. If within the Imago Superlata individuals worship themselves through worship of the god-idols spanning the illusory space between the social and existential, then we might be able to apply tools crafted in the study of societies towards greater understanding of these ideological structures and the relations between them. And we might also be able to learn from past failures at full social knowing about the impossibility of such knowing.

If in fact we worship our own illusory identities created by flights from responsibility that always do damage to those in flight, then how might we move forward with Douglas's desire to "free ourselves from the power of our own cosmology"[144] while not remaining lodged so firmly within a cosmological assumption that we are able to know fully how to escape? A partial answer might involve recasting the theological task as an endeavor to escape from this arrangement while augmenting our arrogance by remembering that theology is undertaken by limited, limiting humans.

Wilhelm Dilthey's early efforts at a philosophy of the human sciences and Ernst Troeltsch's later characterization of theology as a human science is telling of our limited capacity to escape from a proportional relationship between what we know of another (or *the* other) and what we can know of ourselves. How we respond to our worship of god-idols correlates to one's reflexive ability and exposes the limits of one's critical field of vision. In Dilthey's case, as articulated by Paul Ricoeur, those limits led Dilthey to relegate the foundation of the human sciences to a positivistic psychology, and though Troeltsch tried to move away from the positivism, he also retained the focus and assumptions about shared human psychology.[145] "Human science," wrote Ricoeur (parenthetically explaining that by this term Dilthey meant "every modality of the knowledge of man which implies an historical relation"), "presupposes a primordial capacity to transpose oneself into the mental life of others."[146] Understanding knowledge as lodged in history is not helpful if we assume all people understand or interpret that history the same way. By asking the question of whether theology is a human science, I mean to trouble the notion that one person or group's mental representation is enough to allow them to make sense of another person or group's representations. Taking seriously past and contemporary theological endeavors as a "human science" allows the scholar to chart and analyze the tendency of theology to rely on the crypto-positivist move made by Dilthey. Theology, as argued in this chapter, has the quality of an identity-making process. Our examination of its specifics, its actual god-talk (norms employed, assumptions glossed, identity-based axioms relied upon) of any particular theological project is a constant reminder that we can't have full access to the vast array of information and modes of meaning-making that go into any such project. We are able to learn more about ourselves by actually realizing that what we know about others demonstrates we know even less about ourselves (and those we study) than we realized or than we would likely want to admit. That is, the greater our assumptions about the identities of others, the farther and farther away from self-knowledge we travel. Our efforts at thick description are always thinner than we think. As Jackson makes clear, "thick description can be complicit with the more unproductive occultings of anthropological [and theological] research, especially since seeing through another person's eyes is not the same thing as actually seeing that person."[147] Our past efforts at seeing others have often reinforced our inability to see them in any capacity other than "the other." We have been telling *ourselves* white lies, tricking us into thinking we "know" the object of our inquiry. Hence, this chapter's attention to theology is tragically playful. As scholars of religion – many of us fearful of the baggage we carry from our theological inheritance – we have remained theologians indeed. Confessional not necessarily to our belief in "god," but to our god complex marked by an arrogance that we might distinguish ourselves as much from the failures of our predecessors as from our "data." Here, too, we have been Bush refuting the charge of racism, Altizer killing god only to act like god, and Kayerts and Carlier blind to our impending death.

By extension, our very efforts to relate to "the other" and to one another (within a field, academic or social) on "human" scientific grounds alienates us from our object of investigation and actually creates the condition that we remain unable to see them, our relation to them, and ultimately, the "operational acts" that (by another order of magnitude) prevent us from seeing that our own identity is artificial and determined only through objectifying relationships.

Groups can be seen, detected, made aware of their (own) presence; individuals can be seen; death can be seen. That is, human gods and idols are visible, even, if often, claims to the contrary are made by adherents. But how are beliefs, invisible claims (e.g., that "god" exists – as pantheism, otherworldliness, personality, etc.) that point back to god-idols, able to be detected? In particular, how are the beliefs that undergird such god-idol construction (such as white supremacy, male dominance, and the like) to be made visible when adherents to such beliefs often readily deny their adherence?

Claude Lévi-Strauss realized the stakes involved with exposing such invisibility, as his desire to "dissolve man"[148] was an effort to expose the hidden structure behind "man," and is indicative of the costs required to expose invisible ideas. In this moment, that which is "sacrificed" is the identity marker, this illusory belief of men as an ideal. Structuralism then sought to dissolve this god-idol so that its "properties be better studied,"[149] exposing, sighting, the structural distinction making such valorization of "man" possible. The visible and invisible meet in sacrifice. Thinking of Lévi-Strauss's comments from the vantage point of Sartre's suggestion that anti-Semitism carries with it "something of the nature of sacrifice,"[150] Lévi-Strauss sought to sacrifice or "dissolve" man in the abstract, so as to constitute the tautological truth of structuralism. Yet, structuralism came to operate in this space that it exposed, acting as a god-idol precisely because the distance(s) it presupposed are actually as illusory as the perceived identities on either side of the structure(s). In Bourdieusian language, Lévi-Strauss failed to dissolve the "principle of structuration"[151] as he worked to "dissolve man."

The sacred/profane distinction is a white lie. Structuralism is also a white lie. There are no distinctions in any "ultimate" cosmological or ontological sense. But due to the lie, sacrifices are the moments where cosmic recognition of this lie is ordered while the lie is maintained by adherents of it. By cosmic recognition, I mean that certain forces or energies exist in the cosmos that find a way to coalesce. To offer one of the few "metaphysical" positions found in these pages, like gravity – really, gravity is a physical expression of what I mean – these energies seek a balance currently inaccessible to humans. Here, I am suggesting a simple monist position. We are all of and in energy, and there is a certain poetry that many contemporary physicists call this energy "dark energy" – a beautiful reminder that in the contemporary twilight of white religion, recognizing darkness, blackness, may be our only salvation. Because of the practice and belief in the illusion of dualism, sacrifices *appear* to function as a necessary cosmic response to the lie of any sacred and profane distinction. For the exaggeration of the distinction to be maintained, there must be an externalized point or object where the two come together. In this instant, a lynched black body is both expression of the profanity of finality and uncertainty, and is the sacred object worshiped and demanded of adherents – so that those adherents can maintain the distinction between the sacred and profane so that their ancillary distinctions might also be upheld.

In response to the dualism of the Imago Superlata, I want to "dissolve" human and god into the same category – sacrificing the veracity of identity as anything more than illusion – so as to foreground the ethical domain resting beneath the structural distinction exposed by Lévi-Strauss. And I want to begin with the methodological identities that inform my work. I'm not seeking to "dissolve man" so as to arrive at the truth of structure; Lévi-Strauss has helpfully and problematically accomplished as much. Neither am I seeking to recast "man" in the vein of Frantz Fanon's demand for a new humanism.[152] Rather, I mean to dissolve the sacred/profane structural distinction, understanding both "humans" and "gods" as illusory, so that such god-idols would not block or impede the necessity of ethical consideration to the social impositions required by certain forms of human identity formation. In short, I respond to Lévi-Strauss's concern with the tools gleaned from Mary Douglas's efforts to chart the proportional relationship between bodily control and social control.[153] Stated as clearly as possible, because this proportional relationship exists between body and society, then it stands to reason that a relationship also exists between cultural perceptions of bodies and cultural perceptions of societies; that is, between illusory identities and the god-idols they create. To talk of identity is to talk of god-idols; illusions believed in whose adherence controls many of the life options of humans within the ethical domain.

This perspectival shift offers the benefit of analyzing god-idols and the space between them as fictive but retaining the meanings made from them and their intersectionality as "true," to the extent that these meanings function to shape social and cultural life options of those within this "battle for identity."[154] Having learned from my hermeneutical treatment of theology and anthropology as data, I want to suggest that by hermeneutically treating each god-idol as a religious tradition or society – that is, treating an idea born *from* groups *as a* group methodologically – it is possible to get a sense of the impact of various god-idols on our own identities and the identities of others. In a sense, this move is an inversion of the arrangement suggested by Troeltsch: that what we know about those we study tells us that we *cannot* know the mind of another. Such a perspectival shift does not rely on a psychological foundation, but one rooted in embodied human limitation and the shared situation of mortality. Through such a move, it might also be possible to chart scholars'/social actors' own culpability in constructing such god-idols. Understanding theology as a limited/limiting human science might prime scholars of religion to learn more about how to respond to whiteness, sexism, homophobia, and so on, if those social ills are not simply treated as modifiers to insular, cohesive religious traditions, but are treated as "religions," where god-idols are worshipped as meaning is made, identities formed over and against the constructed other. Situating these god-idols as such, theology might then begin to *see* that these god-idols materialize through manipulation of elaborated and restricted codes,[155] "constraints of structure ... such as rules, classifications, compartments"[156] (i.e., social and cultural codings), reinforcing and reinforced by agential and valuative exaggerations. Accordingly, through focus on such codes, scholars might better understand the impact of these god-idols on the various established "traditions" we study as foils and proxies for the study of our own identity. These codes are placed in tandem with personal and positional[157] moral disciplining mechanisms, "constraints on the individual imposed by group memberships"[158] (i.e., moral suasion), and reinforced by adherence to the sacred/profane distinction, the distinction between human freedom and ethical responsibility. Given these parameters offered by Douglas, not only does studying theology in this manner open up new avenues for understanding the relationships between what is believed about god-idols and believed/assumed about "humans," but this complementary focus on limitation and "thinness" will help scholars and adherents of white religion understand the relative difficulty of "freeing ourselves from our own cosmology"[159] – that is, the difficulty of learning to not lie.

Exaggerations of radical contingency localize onto real bodies in space and time, as insider language and rituals reinforce outsiders through exaggerations of value that shape the guilt, shame, and sense of duty[160] a person holds in any given social setting, including scholars. Exaggerations of value and ability create god-idols which discipline bodies into accepting an illusory identity for themselves based on presumed existential need and social options. Willingness to address – or reshape – these dynamics is only possible after having given up the first illusion, the illusion that something "sacred" does exist, that god is society, that society is god, or that distinctions – as god-idols and identities alike – are necessary in the social world at all. Understanding the impact of shame and guilt might have something to say about the difficulty many scholars might have at thinking of their *discipline* – a poignantly brilliant name describing just what it does – in this new (but actually old) limited light.

Theologian Anthony Pinn appears to have inchoately called for such a shift early in his career, stating "I believe that human liberation is more important than the maintenance of any religious symbol, sign, canon, or icon."[161] Pinn's early work did well to describe the "what" of this necessity even if his rhetorical use of the term "liberation" caused some to miss his point. In other words, even "liberation" works as a god-idol for many, causing continued confusion regarding the significance of Pinn's *Why Lord* (1994) to this day. In company with Douglas, Pinn sought to free theology from its preoccupation with itself, so that an uncertain sort of human freedom might reunite with an uncertain sort of responsibility, a reunion that might begin to tell the truth about radical contingency and how so many of us respond to it.

THE TWILIGHT OF (WHITE) AMERICAN RELIGION

This is the "battle for identity"[162] today, as registered from within the twilight it has posed. In 2013, online news outlet Gawker held a "Privilege Tournament," where the bracket depicted below sought to chart the privileges afforded by various identities, identities I've sought in this chapter to cast as illusory, and yet socially bound to and by white religious sensibilities. Online viewers spent a number of days voting for their choice of least privileged. The dubious winners were the homeless. Today, as many arrive at recognition of the illusion of identity, constant calls of "reverse racism" and other instances where the traditionally privileged express feelings of their own alienation, privilege is often registered through an inversion of victims as beneficiaries. Many suggest that (or feel like) the racially privileged are ending up the real victims of this battle. In many respects, we white Americans *are* victims of this battle, in that the contemporary moment marks a period where those who have been on the margins for too long are fed up and those margins have grown large enough to at least be offering a constant reminder to those at social centers that our days are numbered. Further, this battle for identity, as it plays out in the political theatre, leaves young Americans (many of them white, no doubt) so jaded and sardonic that Gawker deems such a "tournament" appropriate, and its viewers are left to giggle and be entertained through a reinforcement of the existential and social toll brought about by a religious orientation creating these identities as competing and defined over and against others.

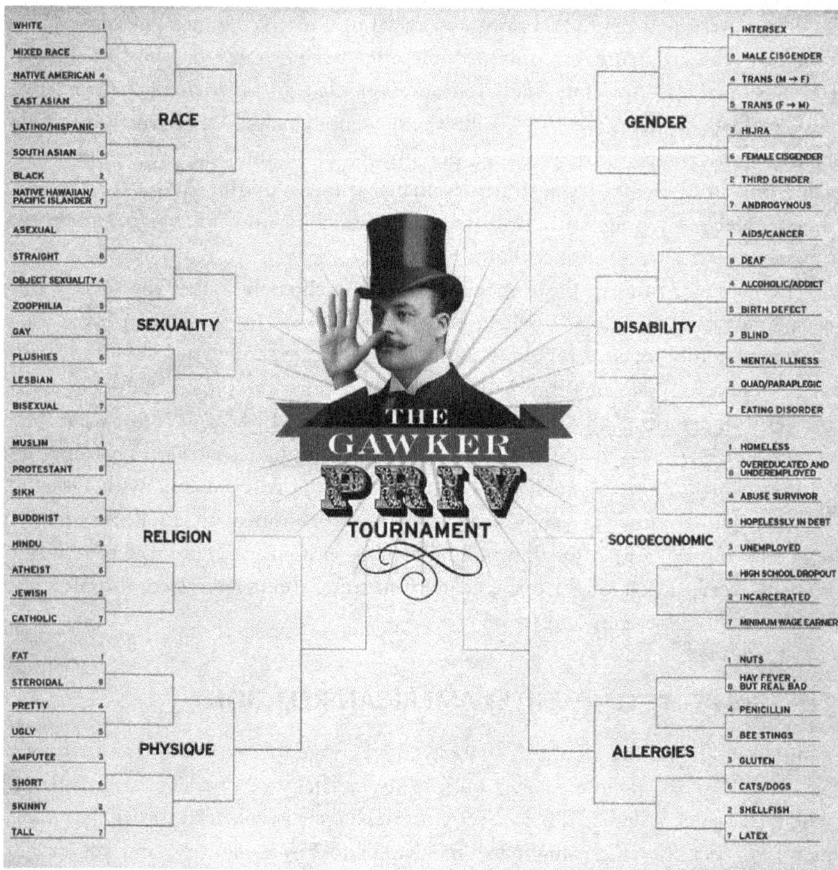

FIGURE 3.1 Photo of the Gawker Privilege Tournament Bracket. Image by Jim Cooke. Available at: http://gawker.com/the-privilege-tournament-1377171054. (Reprinted here with permission from Gawker Media Group.)

This "battle for identity" and this image are representative of the twilight of the god-idols. This twilight is characterized by the proliferation of god-idols, their ability to be hijacked and manipulated to a degree that outsider and insider (to social centers, to privilege, to resources) are increasingly in flux, and such fluctuation is increasingly feared by many white Americans. This white fear suggests that this twilight is also marked by growing recognition that these god-idols cannot achieve their functional mandate. They do not respond adequately (for anyone) to the paradox of radical contingency. The lies we have told are coming to haunt us, our "chickens are" indeed "coming home to roost."[163] All of these identities fall into the pantheon of god-idols, a twilight cast as much by their inability to function as by the sheer volume of options and the recognition that responding to one god-idol (e.g., whiteness or theism) seemingly requires the construction of another.

How might one come to address the twilight of the god-idols as framed by this image representing the contemporary moment, knowing such an orientation fails to function but unable to escape it? If the "illusions believed"[164] by Kayerts and Carlier led to their deaths – their physical deaths, yes, but more importantly, remembering death as their loss of power – and if the panoply of cultural identities and god-idols worshipped today find most within a tournament, a "battle for identity," then what is next for white Americans?

The Imago Superlata is an exaggeration of life in the *wake* posed by death. How might white Americans, white people, and white scholars battle against a white lie? This chapter has sought to answer the question of "why" so many continue to ignore these calls for something new, and interrogate "how" to move forward, generally, but more importantly, how white scholars of religion might take stock of their data, understanding themselves as part of that data, and cultivate new methodologies responsive to the paradox of finding oneself within a death-dealing social context, inside of a "battle for identity" that seemingly has no end in sight.

Having learned to die by learning that death and sacrifice is a stock ingredient in the society and identity in which whites find themselves and exert considerable privilege, will they choose to live knowing that their lives and identities come at the cost of others, or will whites learn how to live more dangerously,[165] with more uncertainty, by embracing a willingness to die – to let go of power and privilege – so that others might live more fully? And would such an embrace be possible without relying on a white heroism that would merely reinforce the swollen self-worth we already hold as white people? As *White Lies* transitions into Part II, I begin such a response by arguing that learning to live within the twilight of the god-idols requires learning to die with others.

Notes

1 Joseph Conrad, "An Outpost of Progress," in *Tales of Unrest* (Scribner's, 1898), 178.
2 Jean-François Bayart, *The Illusion of Cultural Identity* (University of Chicago Press, 2005), 252.
3 Conrad, "An Outpost of Progress," 178.
4 Ibid.
5 Ibid.
6 Sven Lindqvist, *Exterminate All the Brutes: One Man's Odyssey Into the Heart of Darkness and the Origins of European Genocide*, trans. Joan Tate (New Press, 1996), 26.
7 Conrad, "An Outpost of Progress."
8 Ibid.
9 Lindqvist, *Exterminate All the Brutes*, 12.
10 Conrad, "An Outpost of Progress."
11 Robert J. Franzese, *The Sociology of Deviance: Differences, Tradition, and Stigma* (Charles C. Thomas Publisher, 2009), 34.
12 Robert Terrill, *Malcolm X: Inventing Radical Judgment* (Michigan State University Press, 2007), 117–21.
13 Bayart, *The Illusion of Cultural Identity*, 65–67.
14 Ibid., 68.

15 Conrad, "An Outpost of Progress," 178.
16 Ibid.
17 Bayart, *The Illusion of Cultural Identity*, 252.
18 "George W. Bush: Kanye West Attack Was Worst Moment of Presidency," June 26, 2010. *The Guardian*, accessed February 7, 2015, http://www.theguardian.com/music/2010/nov/04/george-w-bush-kanye-west
19 Bayart, *The Illusion of Cultural Identity*, 7.
20 Pierre Bourdieu, "Genesis and Structure of the Religious Field." *Comparative Social Research* 13 (1991), 14.
21 Bayart, *The Illusion of Cultural Identity*, 92–93.
22 Bayart, *The Illusion of Cultural Identity*, 252.
23 James D. Faubion, *An Anthropology of Ethics* (Cambridge University Press, 2011), 3–4.
24 Bayart, *The Illusion of Cultural Identity*, 252.
25 See Chapter 2 for discussion on Luhmann and systems theory for background on the theorization of society as a system and the difficulty of changing the functions of such a system.
26 Some might suggest that since Sartre renders freedom the new sacred, why not turn to Camus? I think Sartre remains so useful precisely because he makes this problematic move. My point is not to celebrate every aspect of Sartre's existentialism, but to think with him – as a marker of the Imago Superlata reinforced *even by* someone interested in disrupting it. Sartre, in his failings, ends up more helpful for this project.
27 Bayart, *The Illusion of Cultural Identity*, 251, original emphasis.
28 Ibid.
29 Christine M. Korsgaard and Onora O'Neill, *The Sources of Normativity* (Cambridge University Press, 1996), 8.
30 Bruce Lincoln, *Theorizing Myth: Narrative, Ideology, and Scholarship* (University of Chicago Press, 2000), 209.
31 Lincoln, *Theorizing Myth*, 216.
32 Faubion, *An Anthropology of Ethics*, 3–10.
33 Ibid., 3.
34 Ibid., 3–4.
35 Bourdieu, "Genesis and Structure," 14.
36 Anthony B. Pinn, *Terror and Triumph : The Nature of Black Religion* (Fortress Press, 2003), 157.
37 Faubion, *An Anthropology of Ethics*, 108–111
38 Bayart, *The Illusion of Cultural Identity*, 251.
39 Bourdieu, "Genesis and Structure," 2.
40 Ibid., emphasis added.
41 Pierre Bourdieu, *Distinction: A Social Critique of the Judgement of Taste* (Harvard University Press, 1984), 497.
42 Henry McNeal Turner, quoted in Stephen Ward Angell, *Bishop Henry McNeal Turner and African-American Religion in the South* (University of Tennessee Press, 1992), 261.
43 Angell, *Bishop Henry McNeal Turner*, 261.
44 Conrad, "An Outpost of Progress."
45 Bourdieu, "Genesis and Structure," 7.
46 Ibid., 9.
47 Anthea Butler, "The Zimmerman Acquittal: America's Racist God." *Religion Dispatches*, July 14, 2013, accessed November 20, 2013, http://www.religiondispatches.org/dispatches/antheabutler/7195/
48 Bourdieu, "Genesis and Structure," 5, original emphasis.
49 Ibid.

50 Gananath Obeyesekere, *The Apotheosis of Captain Cook: European Mythmaking in the Pacific* (Princeton University Press, 1997), 143; Claude Lévi-Strauss, *The Savage Mind* (University of Chicago Press, 1968).
51 Johannes Fabian, *Time and the Other: How Anthropology Makes Its Object* (Columbia University Press, 2002).
52 Grant Evans, "Indigenized Anthropology in Asia," in Jan Van Bremen, Eyal Ben-Ari, and Syed Farid Alatas (eds), *Asian Anthropology* (Routledge, 2005), 52.
53 Marshall Sahlins, *How "Natives" Think: About Captain Cook, For Example* (University of Chicago Press, 1996).
54 Gananath Obeyesekere, *The Apotheosis of Captain Cook: European Mythmaking in the Pacific* (Princeton University Press, 1997), 228–30.
55 Obeyesekere, *Apotheosis of Captain Cook*, 3.
56 Sahlins, *How "Natives" Think*, 8.
57 Bourdieu, "Genesis and Structure," 3.
58 Sahlins, *How "Natives" Think*, 9.
59 William Edward Arnal and Russell T. McCutcheon, *The Sacred Is the Profane: The Political Nature of Religion* (Oxford University Press, 2012), xi, 22–23.
60 Clifford Geertz, *The Interpretation of Cultures: Selected Essays* (Basic Books, 1973), 3–30.
61 Karl Barth, *Church Dogmatics: Pts. 1–2. The Doctrine of the Word of God* (T. & T. Clark, 1960).
62 John L. Jackson, Jr., *Thin Description* (Harvard University Press, 2013), 13, original emphasis.
63 Jackson, *Thin Description*, 11.
64 Lévi-Strauss, *The Savage Mind*, 249.
65 Ibid.
66 Jacques Derrida, *Of Grammatology* (JHU Press, 1998), 106–8.
67 Faubion, *An Anthropology of Ethics*, 3.
68 Pierre Bourdieu, *Distinction*, 6.
69 Thomas J. J. Altizer, *Living the Death of God: A Theological Memoir* (State University of New York Press, 2006), 44–47.
70 Thomas J. J. Altizer and William Hamilton, *Radical Theology and the Death of God*, softcover edition (Bobbs-Merrill Company, 1966), 15.
71 Thomas J. J. Altizer, *The Gospel of Christian Atheism* (Westminster Press, 1966), 25.
72 By this token, I am also frustrated that the work of Mark C. Taylor, perhaps the heir apparent to Altizer where death of god theology is concerned, seems more interested to pronounce the death of the subject than to engage critically with the multiplicity of subjective options arising from recognition that the only dead god to discuss is a god of certainty and possibility that whiteness and theism (even in these god-idols' "deaths") have helped to procure historically. For an example of Taylor's work, see Mark C. Taylor, *Erring: A Postmodern A/theology* (University of Chicago Press, 1987).
73 Altizer, *Gospel of Christian Atheism*, 147.
74 Altizer, *Living the Death of God*, xi.
75 Ibid., 46.
76 David Tracy, *Blessed Rage for Order: The New Pluralism in Theology* (University of Chicago Press, 1996), 4–8.
77 Tracy, *Blessed Rage for Order*, 98–109.
78 Ibid., 7.
79 Charles H. Long, *Significations: Signs, Symbols, and Images in the Interpretation of Religion*, 2nd ed. (The Davies Group Publishers, 1999). See "Chapter Twelve: Freedom, Otherness, and Religion: Theologies Opaque."
80 Altizer, *Radical Theology*, 11.

81 Niklas Luhmann and Stephan Fuchs, "Tautology and Paradox in the Self-Descriptions of Modern Society," *Sociological Theory* 6, no. 1 (Spring 1988): 21–37, 34.
82 Bayart, *The Illusion of Cultural Identity*, 68.
83 Luhmann and Fuchs, "Tautology and Paradox," 34.
84 James H. Cone, *God of the Oppressed*, rev. sub. edition (Orbis Books, 1997), 180.
85 Ibid., 180.
86 Anthea Butler, "The Zimmerman Acquittal: America's Racist God." *Religion Dispatches*, July 14, 2013, accessed November 20, 2013, http://www.religiondispatches.org/dispatches/antheabutler/7195/
87 Anthea Butler, *No Secrets on the Net*, accessed November 20, 2013, http://nosecretsonthenet.tumblr.com/
88 Mary Douglas, *Natural Symbols: Explorations in Cosmology*, 3rd ed. (Routledge, 2003), 173.
89 Ibid., 153.
90 Ibid., 167.
91 Ibid., 169–170.
92 Bayart, *The Illusion of Cultural Identity*, 65–67.
93 bell hooks, *Black Looks: Race and Representation* (South End Press, 1999), 26–27.
94 Claude Lévi-Strauss, *Race and History*, UNESCO Report (1952), 45–6.
95 Conrad, "An Outpost of Progress,"178.
96 Jean-Paul Sartre, *Anti-Semite and Jew* (Schocken Books Inc., 1948), 13.
97 Bayart, *The Illusion of Cultural Identity*, 92.
98 Ibid., 93.
99 See, for instance, Frantz Fanon, *Black Skin, White Masks*, revised edition (Grove Press, 2008).
100 Other thinkers, such as Albert Camus and Frantz Fanon, are not as helpful in theorizing the Imago Superlata (from within it – as I am forced to do). To my mind, Camus's Rebel isn't rebellious, in that it borders too heavily on nihilistically, automatonically assuming nothing will change, and I don't think all people perpetually engage in the Sisyphean task equally, if at all. Some social actors own yachts, or make decisions affecting the life options of others. My project seeks to shift who is forced to roll the rock up the hill, what this "rock" would even mean for different groups, and who has access to yachts and decisions. I seek parity, not revolution. Of Frantz Fanon, his new humanism is new indeed, but is a call for something outside the Imago Superlata, and so I have intentionally limited my reliance on Fanon so as to work through how such an exaggerated and exaggerating life orientation offers (or does not offer) internal tools for dismantling it.
101 Lévi-Strauss, *Savage Mind*, 247.
102 The choice of the French title is significant, in that "The Jewish Question" was largely framed as such by the anti-Semite, as in "What can we do about this problem?" Contextualized to the U.S., his title choice would be akin to me titling this book "The Black Problem," localizing the problem of racism onto the shoulders of its victims.
103 Jean-Paul Sartre, *Anti-Semite and Jew*, 17.
104 Ibid., 28.
105 Ibid., 43, 50, 53–4.
106 Ibid., 19.
107 Ibid., 133.
108 Ibid., 149.
109 Ibid., 26.
110 Here, I want to underscore that Sartre's ethical failings end up theoretical benefits, as his use is predicated on his proximity to social centers. I am working against the perspective he offers, part of it at least, but need him – like Luhmann and Durkheim

in previous chapters – in order to be intellectually honest about the interpretive consequences of those near social centers.

111 Émile Durkheim, quoted in Douglas, *Natural Symbols*, 173.
112 Bourdieu, "Genesis and Structure," 13.
113 Ibid., 12–13.
114 Émile Durkheim, *The Elementary Forms of the Religious Life* (Dover Publications, 2008), 37.
115 Ibid.
116 Ibid., 38.
117 Bourdieu, "Genesis and Structure," 14.
118 Durkheim, *Elementary Forms*, 39.
119 Bayart, *The Illusion of Cultural Identity*, 249.
120 Conrad, "An Outpost of Progress," 187.
121 Durkheim, *Elementary Forms*, 39.
122 Benedict Anderson, *Imagined Communities: Reflections on the Origin and Spread of Nationalism* (Verso, 2006).
123 Douglas, *Natural Symbols*, 91.
124 Ludwig Feuerbach, *The Essence of Christianity* (Prometheus Books, 1989); Alan Richardson and John Bowden, *The Westminster Dictionary of Christian Theology* (Westminster John Knox Press, 1983), 471.
125 Mary Douglas, *Natural Symbols*, xxxvii.
126 Nirmal Puwar, *Space Invaders: Race, Gender and Bodies out of Place* (Oxford: Berg, 2004).
127 Charles H. Long, *Significations*, 204–7.
128 Faubion, *An Anthropology of Ethics*, 273.
129 "CBN Covers Up Pat Robertson's Claim that Gays Spread AIDS on Purpose," August 27, 2013, *Gawker.com*, accessed March 10, 2015, http://gawker.com/cbn-covers-up-pat-robertons-claim-that-gays-spread-hiv-1209996528
130 Tracy, *Blessed Rage for Order*, 104–5.
131 As with exaggerations regarding same-sex marriage, examples of this adage abound. Here is one: "What Does the Bible Say about Cross-Dressing/Transvestism?," (n.d.), *Gotquestions.org*, accessed March 10, 2015, http://www.gotquestions.org/cross-dressing-transvestism.html
132 Erving Goffman, *Stigma: Notes on the Management of Spoiled Identity*, reissue edition (Touchstone, 1986), 135.
133 Jean-Paul Sartre, *Being and Nothingness: An Essay in Phenomenological Ontology*, trans. Hazel Barnes (Routledge, 2003), 531–52, esp. 544–47.
134 Ibid., 636.
135 Carol Hardy-Fanta, *Intersectionality and Politics: Recent Research on Gender, Race, and Political Representation in the United States* (Routledge, 2013), 175.
136 The language of signification is borrowed from Charles Long, but I find that his work – brilliant as it is – reproduces the distinction between sacred and profane in ways my talk of exaggerations seeks to avoid; or at least, I try to localize any such binaries onto bodies themselves.
137 Sartre, *Anti-Semite and Jew*, 51.
138 Anderson, *Imagined Communities*.
139 Sartre, *Anti-Semite and Jew*, 51.
140 Bourdieu, "Genesis and Structure," 9.
141 Jasbir K. Puar, *Terrorist Assemblages: Homonationalism in Queer Times* (Duke University Press, 2007).
142 Effectively, this marks adherents to the white man's god complex as living dead; zombies whose demand for murder is sustained by feasting on the margins of the society they worship.

143 Lévi-Strauss, *The Savage Mind*, 247.
144 Douglas, *Natural Symbols*, 169–70.
145 Wolfhart Pannenberg and Francis McDonagh, *Theology and the Philosophy of Science* (Westminster John Knox Press, 1976), 104.
146 Paul Ricoeur, *Hermeneutics and the Human Sciences: Essays on Language, Action and Interpretation* (Cambridge University Press, 1981), 49.
147 Jackson, *Thin Description*, 15.
148 Lévi-Strauss, *The Savage Mind*, 247.
149 Ibid., 247.
150 Sartre, *Anti-Semite and Jew*, 51.
151 Bourdieu, "Genesis and Structure," 13.
152 Frantz Fanon, *Black Skin, White Masks*, revised edition (Grove Press, 2008), 200–206.
153 Douglas, *Natural Symbols*, xxxiii, 101.
154 Bayart, *The Illusion of Cultural Identity*, 252.
155 Douglas, *Natural Symbols*, 25.
156 Ibid., xix.
157 Ibid., 29.
158 Ibid., xix.
159 Ibid., 169–70.
160 Ibid., 64–71.
161 Anthony B. Pinn, *Why, Lord?: Suffering and Evil in Black Theology* (Continuum International Publishing Group, 1999), 11.
162 Bayart, *The Illusion of Cultural Identity*, 252.
163 Terrill, *Malcolm X*, 117–21.
164 Conrad, "An Outpost of Progress,"178.
165 Friedrich Nietzsche, *The Gay Science: With a Prelude in Rhymes and an Appendix of Songs* (Vintage Books, 1974), 228.

REFERENCES

"CBN Covers Up Pat Robertson's Claim that Gays Spread AIDS on Purpose," August 27, 2013. *Gawker.com*, accessed March 10, 2015, http://gawker.com/cbn-covers-up-pat-robertons-claim-that-gays-spread-hiv-1209996528

"George W. Bush: Kanye West Attack Was Worst Moment of Presidency," June 26, 2010. *The Guardian*, accessed February 7, 2015, http://www.theguardian.com/music/2010/nov/04/george-w-bush-kanye-west

"What Does the Bible Say about Cross-Dressing/Transvestism?," n.d. Gotquestions.org, accessed March 10, 2015, http://www.gotquestions.org/cross-dressing-transvestism.html

Altizer, Thomas J. J. 1966. *The Gospel of Christian Atheism*. Westminster Press.

Altizer, Thomas J. J. 2006. *Living the Death of God: A Theological Memoir*. State University of New York Press.

Altizer, Thomas J. J., and William Hamilton. 1966. *Radical Theology and the Death of God*. Softcover edition. Bobbs-Merrill Company.

Anderson, Benedict. 2006. *Imagined Communities: Reflections on the Origin and Spread of Nationalism*. Verso.

Angell, Stephen Ward. 1992. *Bishop Henry McNeal Turner and African-American Religion in the South*. University of Tennessee Press.

Arnal, William Edward and Russell T. McCutcheon. 2012. *The Sacred Is the Profane: The Political Nature of Religion*. Oxford University Press.

Barth, Karl. 1960. *Church Dogmatics: Pts. 1–2. The Doctrine of the Word of God*. T. & T. Clark.

Bayart, Jean-François. 2005. *The Illusion of Cultural Identity*. University of Chicago Press.
Bourdieu, Pierre. 1984. *Distinction: A Social Critique of the Judgement of Taste*. Harvard University Press.
Bourdieu, Pierre. 1991. "Genesis and Structure of the Religious Field." *Comparative Social Research* 13: 1–44.
Bremen, Jan Van, Eyal Ben-Ari, and Syed Farid Alatas (eds). 2005. *Asian Anthropology*. Routledge.
Butler, Anthea. 2013. "Commentary on Anthea Butler." *No Secrets On the Net*, accessed November 20, http://nosecretsonthenet.tumblr.com/
Butler, Anthea. 2013. "The Zimmerman Aquittal: America's Racist God." *Religion Dispatches*, accessed November 20, religiondispatches.org/dispatches/antheabutler/7195/
Cone, James. 1997. *God of the Oppressed*. Rev Sub. Orbis Books.
Conrad, Joseph. 1898. *Tales of Unrest*. Scribner's.
Derrida, Jacques. 1998. *Of Grammatology*. JHU Press.
Douglas, Mary. 2003. *Natural Symbols: Explorations in Cosmology*. 3rd ed. Routledge.
Durkheim, Émile. 2008. *The Elementary Forms of the Religious Life*. Dover Publications.
Evans, Grant. 2005. "Indigenized Anthropology in Asia," in Jan Van Bremen, Eyal Ben-Ari, and Syed Farid Alatas (eds), *Asian Anthropology*. Routledge.
Fabian, Johannes. 2002. *Time and the Other: How Anthropology Makes Its Object*. Columbia University Press.
Fanon, Frantz. 2008. *Black Skin, White Masks*. Revised ed. Grove Press.
Faubion, James D. 2011. *An Anthropology of Ethics*. Cambridge University Press.
Feuerbach, Ludwig. 1989. *The Essence of Christianity*. Prometheus Books.
Franzese, Robert J. 2009. *The Sociology of Deviance: Differences, Tradition, and Stigma*. Charles C. Thomas Publisher.
Geertz, Clifford. 1973. *The Interpretation of Cultures: Selected Essays*. Basic Books.
Goffman, Erving. 1986. *Stigma: Notes on the Management of Spoiled Identity*. Reissue edition. Touchstone.
Hardy-Fanta, Carol. 2013. *Intersectionality and Politics: Recent Research on Gender, Race, and Political Representation in the United States*. Routledge.
hooks, bell. 1999. *Black Looks: Race and Representation*. South End Press.
Jackson Jr, John L. 2013. *Thin Description*. Harvard University Press.
Korsgaard, Christine M., and Onora O'Neill. 1996. *The Sources of Normativity*. Cambridge University Press.
Lévi-Strauss, Claude. 1952. *Race and History*. UNESCO Report.
Lévi-Strauss, Claude. 1968. *The Savage Mind*. University of Chicago Press.
Lincoln, Bruce. 2000. *Theorizing Myth: Narrative, Ideology, and Scholarship*. 1st ed. University of Chicago Press.
Lindqvist, Sven. 1996. *Exterminate All the Brutes: One Man's Odyssey Into the Heart of Darkness and the Origins of European Genocide*, trans. Joan Tate. New Press.
Long, Charles H. 1999. *Significations: Signs, Symbols, and Images in the Interpretation of Religion*. 2nd ed. The Davies Group Publishers.
Luhmann, Niklas and Stephan Fuchs. 1988. "Tautology and Paradox in the Self-Descriptions of Modern Society." *Sociological Theory* 6(1): 21–37.
Nietzsche, Friedrich. 1974. *The Gay Science: With a Prelude in Rhymes and an Appendix of Songs*. Vintage Books.
Obeyesekere, Gananath. 1997. *The Apotheosis of Captain Cook: European Mythmaking in the Pacific*. Princeton University Press.

Pannenberg, Wolfhart and Francis McDonagh. 1976. *Theology and the Philosophy of Science*. Westminster John Knox Press.

Pinn, Anthony B. 1999. *Why, Lord? Suffering and Evil in Black Theology*. Continuum International Publishing Group.

Pinn, Anthony B. 2003. *Terror and Triumph : The Nature of Black Religion*. Fortress Press.

Puar, Jasbir K. 2007. *Terrorist Assemblages: Homonationalism in Queer Times*. Duke University Press.

Puwar, Nirmal. 2004. *Space Invaders: Race, Gender and Bodies out of Place*. Oxford.

Richardson, Alan and John Bowden. 1983. *The Westminster Dictionary of Christian Theology*. Westminster John Knox Press.

Ricoeur, Paul. 1981. *Hermeneutics and the Human Sciences: Essays on Language, Action and Interpretation*. Cambridge University Press.

Sahlins, Marshall. 1996. *How "Natives" Think: About Captain Cook, For Example*. 1st ed. University of Chicago Press.

Sartre, Jean-Paul. 1948. *Anti-Semite and Jew*. Schocken Books Inc.

Sartre, Jean-Paul. 2003. *Being and Nothingness: An Essay in Phenomenological Ontology* trans. Hazel Barnes. Routledge.

Taylor, Mark C. 1987. *Erring: A Postmodern A/theology*. University of Chicago Press.

Terrill, Robert. 2007. *Malcolm X: Inventing Radical Judgment*. Michigan State University Press.

Tracy, David. 1996. *Blessed Rage for Order: The New Pluralism in Theology*. University of Chicago Press.

PART II

Learning to die *with others*

4

ACCEPTING THE HELL OF DEATH

Narrating sources, methods, and norms of a *limited religious outlook*

> For the poet is condemned to learn his profoundest yearnings through an awareness of other selves. The poem is within him, yet he experiences the shame and splendor of being found by poems – great poems – outside him. To lose freedom in this center is never to forgive, and to learn the dread of threatened autonomy forever.
>
> *Harold Bloom*[1]

> Lord, what is man, that Thou has regard for him?
> Or the son of man, that Thou takest account of him?
> Man is like a breath,
> His days are as a fleeting shadow.
> In the morning he flourishes and grows up like grass,
> In the evening he is cut down and withers.
> So teach us to number our days,
> That we may get us a heart of wisdom.
>
> *Jewish burial poem*[2]

Transitioning from a white religious outlook to something more equitable, life-affirming, and humble requires coming to terms with the "shame" and "dread" described above by literary theorist Harold Bloom as much as it requires learning to "number our days." Following the efforts of anthropologist Barbara Myerhoff, numbering our days means learning to accept death in all its iterations, opening oneself to the wisdom that such an embrace might offer for reassessing the value of others and recalibrating the cultural artifacts we have inherited (and have often rejected) as means of limiting ourselves in the face of death. This chapter tacks between poetry and narrative, finding and unraveling the uncertain loose ends provided by stories told in the face of death. Perhaps, through such story-telling, we who worship with white religion might begin to "number our days."

For many white Americans, much shame is attached to momentary recognition of having worshiped an exaggerated image of oneself. Thinking of tragic social injustices like racism as "poems," shame and splendor collide in a demand to finally take responsibility for oneself and one's cultural heritage. These "poetic" features of white life often prevent the telling of a new narrative where the costs of social life are more equitably distributed. Stories transmit partial and at times inaccurate cultural memories, offering "cultural mirrors" able to "present collective knowledge"[3] about a community. Now, and in the face of death – what Malcolm X began to understand as "the white man fast losing his power to oppress and exploit the dark world … the white man's world was on the way down, it was on the way out"[4] – narrative offers a means for the "white man" to cope with and accept that loss. White Americans can teach ourselves to "number our days" by beginning to tell the stories of how our days are numbered. That is, acceptance of a loss of perceived or actual power and certainty in social centers is made possible using a methodology offered by physical mortality.

This chapter "loses the freedom" of thinking white American cultural heritage is empty of tools for responding to the most perilous aspects of that heritage, and moves towards the responsibility demanded by the relinquishing of the idea of freedom from physical or social death. Such responsibility might be thought of as the courage to never forgive or exonerate lynching, Jane Crow, gender discrimination, homophobia, the list goes on – as well as moving towards a response that offers a new way to live with the "shame" and "splendor" that comprise white American culture and lead many on the social margins of that culture to characterize or maintain that "the white man is the devil."[5] Surely not all non-whites think or talk in terms of the white man as a devil, and though many whites have turned such talk into yet another black stereotyping mechanism, the notion of white devils is instructive. Malcolm X spoke often of white devils, and helps to ground the charge. Asked by Louis Lomax in 1963 why he called white men devils, Malcolm responded this way:

> Because that's what he is. What do you want me to call him, a saint? Anybody who rapes, and plunders, and enslaves, and steals, and drops hell bombs on people … anybody who does these things is nothing but a devil.
>
> Look, Lomax, history rewards all research. And history fails to record one single instance in which the white man – as a people – did good. They have always been devils; they always will be devils, and they are about to be destroyed. The final proof that they are devils lies in the fact that they are about to destroy themselves. Only a devil – and a stupid devil at that – would destroy himself![6]

Such words are hard for white Americans to swallow as anything more than overgeneralized, race-based essentialisms: crazy talk. But Malcolm was by no means crazy; he was angry. And as white Americans we might learn from such anger, if for no reason other than the selfish concern to make sense of what Malcolm X meant when he said that we were "about to destroy [our]selves." In the wake of increasing racial tensions, and what seems an ever-increasing governmental and social dysfunction matched by the eventual end of the quantitative white statistical majority, we might do well to understand this destruction as rooted in a failure to see or learn from the sinister side of ourselves and adjust our actions in the wake of our penchant to act like devils. Where, and how, will we "white devils" find methodological escape from the "hells" we have created for ourselves and others? How can white people in the United States escape their complicity in reinforcing injustice? Is escape even possible? Here, I respond to this anxiety of destruction through a focus on the narratives told by the dying. Through such focus, sources, norms, and methods of a limited religious outlook are offered as a "possible" means of escaping this shameful legacy. Through such stories, told and written from a limited religious outlook, human ability and worth might be recalibrated to offset the exaggerations posed by white religion. Perhaps, we might finally no longer be regarded as "devils" when we take ownership of our status as devils, and begin to focus on transforming our white heritage, white culture, white community.

Such a new life would be lived understanding the dangers of society functioning as god. And it would come to live in the uncertainty posed by death. In short, white Americans might learn how to produce and embrace their social death if they tell, and listen to, the stories connected to physical death, theirs and those caused by them, and the deaths of others. This focused attention is no panacea for social problems, but will likely evoke greater awareness that death is incumbent upon all people, and that in its unavoidability, we are offered a justification for and a ground to begin to learn to live more equitably in community.[7] Here is what I mean.

In the previous chapter, I argued that god-idols (e.g., such as whiteness, or theism, or heteronormativity) emerge through a process of identity formation referred to as the Imago Superlata, a system of religious belief and worship of exaggerated images of self and others, such that society functions as god and one's responsibility to others is ignored, fought against, or denied. This denial is reinforced and made possible through a reliance on others as sacrificial offerings and victims. How might scholars' efforts and their oft chosen data – "religious" people – not unduly reinforce white religion? Better still, how can this religious process be fought against while stuck inside of it? Such a dilemma might find resolution through white acceptance of and movement toward embrace of uncertainty and human limitations cultivated through what I call a *limited religious outlook*.

I offer a limited religious outlook and outline some of the methods, norms, and source materials for such an outlook. Here, I want to make clear that I do not have in mind, nor am I influenced by, something like Stanley Hauerwas's idea of narrative theology.[8] I am not trying to use the tools of narrative or literary or poetic theory to unpack the many dimensions of Christian theology or any other form of theology, but to use certain tools of literary theory to offer the start of a religious outlook that privileges uncertainty and limitation.

Specifically, a limited religious outlook works to recalibrate human ability and worth that have been skewed by white lies. With "religious" here continuing to be read as practices and beliefs that seek to fashion identity through the imposition of exaggerated distinctions on others, this outlook seeks to limit such distinction-making. It forces confrontation between two versions of oneself or one's community: the self, undergirded by white lies, and the self, facing death.

A limited religious outlook has three important components: (1) It is *religious* to the extent that white religion as a process of identity formation is never fully escapable. Neither is full social escape from god-idols possible. Hence, it remains a religious outlook recognizing the limits of escaping religion. As an outlook, an epistemological and existential "line in the sand," it functions *religiously.* (2) It is an *outlook*, or vantage-point, a hermeneutical point-of-orientation that sees no principal distinction between a scholar's data and a scholar's personal commitments. It registers such artificial and arbitrary distinctions as exaggerations of human worth and value. Freed from the desired maintenance of such distinctions, "focus" is not wasted on preventing distinctions either, as all distinctions are admitted to break down upon close scrutiny (even – and especially – ones employed here rhetorically). Distinctions help us all to see the world, but they are not the world, and the image they provide is always an uncertain outlook at best. (3) Most importantly, it is *limited.* It is limited in what conclusions it can draw with certainty. It is limited in its capacity to work (or function) as efficiently as arrangements within the Imago Superlata. By this, I mean it does not have a smooth functioning society in mind, or society at all. It is reflexive and focused on not only individual limitations of selves, but limitations of possibilities for those selves to contribute or participate in society without doing harm to another self or group. Therefore, it foregrounds humility, insofar as this humility is a product of reflection that the benefits many experience at different times and places in the social world always come at the expense of other humans. But with that caveat, it also foregrounds the limits of religion's usefulness as an epistemological category, as an ethical mediator, and as a social institution that has ceased to function effectively (if it ever really did). A limited religious outlook is a limiting of the scope of religion's functional use, and a limiting of appeal to such functions. Finally, it limits any expectations that very many will be able to limit their own religious outlook. It is a crash course in epistemological and ethical humility, not out of intellectual laziness, but based on the ontological inability to fully achieve certainty, security, or immortality. It is a partial blueprint for "numbering our days" as the physically dying beneficiaries of a dying and death-dealing social arrangement. And it limits its assumptions that such a blueprint – or narrative – will appeal to those most in need of the teaching.

For a white, theistic petit bourgeois aggregate that has long been death-dealing in its flight from a variety of human limits, narratives and stories told by the physically dead and dying might say something about how to embrace death. Inchoately started in the previous chapter through a focus on the blurring of methodological and identity-based distinctions, a limited religious outlook learns from and leans on narrative and storytelling as a concession to existential limitation and epistemological/analytical limitation. That is, in the wake of such vast limits, stories offer salve as we come to terms with those limits and fill in the epistemological gaps posed by academic accounts that tend to privilege didactic precision and analysis. Modern critical scholarship, like the Modern poetry that is the focus of Harold Bloom's appraisal, is a microcosmic expression of white religion, as it deals in precision, critical distinction, and qualification. Scholars, to this end, are often deathly afraid of uncertainty. Whether critic or caretaker of religion, both often take care of a demand to be sure.[9] Storytelling offers a methodological way forward, turning to literary and artistic cultural devices and imagery, humanist resources, and, most importantly, stories colored by cultural affinity and mortality. Such a narrative focus, as if to characterize white religion as poetry and its alternative the unformed, unraveled edges of raw narrative, begins with a theory of poetry and what such a theory suggests about the anxiety of escaping the shame of stories yet to be told by their authors.[10]

"HELL IS – OTHER PEOPLE!"

Translated into English as *No Exit*, Jean-Paul Sartre's 1944 play tells the story of three people locked in a room for eternity, and in that room the character Garcin realizes that hell does not require fire, brimstone, or torture; it only requires the objectifying gaze of the other on one's self-image. With this recognition, Garcin famously concludes: "Hell is – other people!"[11]

The irony of the existential truism involves the other central aspect of the story, that the humanized and humanizing portraits leading to the conclusion that other people constitute hell come by way of a double recognition that all the characters are dead. That is, there's something of a relationship between death, and our status as dying perpetually as humans, and this objectifying gaze of the other. Hell becomes other people as we make objectifying use of others so we might not face fully our mortal end.

Sartre complained that his famous quote had been misunderstood, suggesting that "People thought that I meant by that, that our relations with the Other were always poisonous, that they were always forbidden relations. But I meant something quite different. I meant that if the relations with the Other are twisted, then the Other can only be hell… . The other is, fundamentally, what is most important in ourselves, in our own understanding of ourselves."[12] Perhaps, then, white devils who realize the other as their "hell" might be said to be guilty of a "twisted" relation to the other, a topic taking more focus in Chapter 5. Here, however,

Sartre's comments help to situate the contemporary moment wherein increasingly, white people are faced with impressions of themselves through the eyes of "the Other" – here referring to African American and other voices critical of the social system we have (all) inherited, and those who are championing the end of white world supremacy and dominance. Thanks to social media and the proliferation of technological communication, the gaze of the other has never been more readily available to white Americans. Furthermore, the parochialization of new outlets, the Foxification of news as some[13] have put it – that the stations we watch only regurgitate the assumptions we already hold – allows for yet more rejection and refutation of such gazes, meaning we remain lodged in hell by way of our own denial of the gazes, opinions, and commentaries arising from others.

But the situation is more existentially complicated than this. Sartre explains his point this way: "Other people are basically the most important means we have in ourselves for our own knowledge of ourselves. When we think about ourselves, when we try to know ourselves, basically we use the knowledge of us which other people already have."[14] It stands to reason, then, that in order to come to know ourselves within the contemporary period, by taking seriously the claims of many that white Americans are devils, to know ourselves might have to involve recognizing that not only do black images of white tell us that we are (all) "in hell," but that in the views of many, we've been the most devilish of the lot, treating our position in "hell" as a mandate to become the devil. Who else suggested that "Hell is – other people" than Garcin, the one who couldn't stand the criticism of others? Sartre leaves us with a paradox. A person is considered to be in bad faith (i.e., self-deceived) if they ignore the relation their self-image holds with the images from others, but that person will also be in bad faith if the perspectives of others are presumed to be more valid or authentic than one's own self-image. Hell is other people, in this case, because we are bound by them and yet bound to ourselves and our desire to be unbound by them. So how might we forge an escape? How might we learn to "number our days" in hell? Perhaps this "escape" will involve acceptance of paradox, discomfort, and the futility of escaping the shared situation of forcibly coming to know ourselves by holding in balance our vision of ourselves and the visions others hold of us.

A poetics of white religion

Modern poetry, as characterized by Harold Bloom, is born and dies through the anxiety of trying to be distinct from one's forebear only to reinforce the predecessor's value through attempts at uniqueness and distinction. Bloom's words beginning this chapter tell of the anxiety of trying to be the best by trying to be the first – offering insights into how to respond to white religion by foreclosing its "poetry," and the dangers of anxiety unresolved through story and cultural heritage. Bloom's theory of the anxiety of influence on the origins and end of Modern poetry offers a useful initial theoretical entry point for understanding how anxiety functions to reinforce a white religious outlook. Anxiety operates as source material in a limited religious outlook. In particular, I want to suggest that Bloom's focus on satan as exemplar of the "strong poet" suggests a need to think past "poetry," after having learned from poetry. That is, to learn about escaping the limits of escaping death.

Bloom's theory of poetry offers a poetics of social life and action. Social injustices like racism and homophobia arise out of an inability to embrace radical contingency, the jargon-laden term for human limitations framed around but extending beyond physical death. Who is thrust to the margins of society changes from one place and time to the next, but the fact of such margins remains relatively constant. Bloom offers insights into why these margins remain intact, even if taking new shape and face. Out of an anxiety attached to doing something different, those at the center of society are forced to reconstitute the margins through appeal to what has come before. Thinking of one's abilities as predicated on what has come before, causes things to remain more familiarly oppressive than new. The problem of changing society (for the better) involves the perceived strength offered by society to exact/enact adequate change.

In Bloom's theory, the young poet – anxious of his own identity – grows more anxious that the only tools at his disposal for poetic actualization require his predecessor. Modern poetry has this in common with white religion – indeed, one might argue that the modern poetic imagination is fueled by white religious sensibilities. God-idols come and go, their worship hinging on the anxiety of letting them go versus the anxiety of adhering to them so that one's sense of authority and ability (be it in the academy, finance, government, or any other field) is made possible. For example, the poet is forced to weigh the anxiety of distancing one's work from its predecessor against the anxiety of telling the world that he is better than his predecessor. Can he ever be great if he must rely on proving his greatness against the greatness of who has come before? Can the poet ever escape what has come before? Today, the white, theistic petit bourgeois social center is forced to weigh the anxiety of relinquishing racialized privilege against the anxiety of reinforcing it lest their authority not be obtained. Is it best to give up adherence to whiteness, or use it in ways advantageous to those victimized by it? More specifically, just how "black" are we in the white academy willing to turn our departments? One faculty member teaching and studying "black" things may make us feel "better" than our all-white faculty predecessors, but doesn't our fear of departments turning "too black" deconstruct any distance we think we've obtained from our predecessors? One black faculty member per department is considered needed and necessary, but white nerves often get frayed by talk of two or three. The same anxiety exists in many places with respect to gender equity, as well.[15] Such is the anxiety of influence in racialized, sociological terms, distilling a poetics of the Imago Superlata. Such a poetics functions autopoietically, much like god-idols, in that they inhibit escape from normative social arrangements. Overcoming this poetics – understood as an impossible escape from death – is actually and paradoxically only offered through its embrace.

Swerving into hell

Harold Bloom's *The Anxiety of Influence* (1973) argues that Modern poetry, from after Shakespeare up to the present, has been singularly guided by an Oedipally arranged anxiety complex. Bloom suggests that the need of the ephebe,[16] or young poet, to distinguish himself from his teacher or predecessor is the single most palpable feature of Modern poetry, giving birth to the very genre we understand today by this name.[17] For the poet, a tension exists between priority and authority, where being the greatest is taken to require being the first. Bloom offers six ratios of poetic misprision (i.e., techniques distinguishing ephebe from teacher)[18]; these ratios produce distinctiveness – a priority – but show a trace of one's reliance on a predecessor for greatness. Such reliance calls into question who is really great if reliance is necessary. For Bloom, this anxiety has been the touch mark of Modern poetry's brilliance, but also its downfall, as it stands to be "self-slain"[19] in the face of a lack of innovation *precisely because* it could not escape its anxiety of innovation long enough to actually innovate.

The first and "central working concept"[20] of these misprisions is that of the "swerve"[21] or "clinamen," a poetic device wherein the ephebe suggests that "the precursor poem went accurately up to a certain point, but then should have swerved, precisely in the direction that the new poem moves."[22] Bloom indicates that such "swerves" are misinterpretations, understood better as "simultaneously intentional and involuntary"[23] "acts of creative correction."[24] I want to suggest that in terms of race historically, such "swerves" have marked ongoing civil rights efforts, but come at a larger cost of reinforcing the supposed necessity of a white petit bourgeois social center and society. Emancipation, passage of Voting Rights Acts and Civil Rights Acts, and the contemporary fight for marriage equality offer instances of social "swerves," where social poets confuse priority with authority and think the social world more hospitable than before. Unchanged, however, these historic "swerves" have actually worked to reinforce white religion as normative, as they've seemingly confronted some of the god-idols created by it and yet have reproduced others in their stead.

Michelle Alexander's brilliant study of mass incarceration's contemporary assault on African American men, what she characterizes as *The New Jim Crow* (2010), provides a stark account of one white religious response to positive social changes like the Civil Rights Act.[25] That is, greater access to resources and protections of law allowing the voices of others to be heard has been met with a disciplinary dismissal of many of those voices through means such as increased policing, lack of economic possibilities, and, ultimately, mass incarceration and often felony convictions – convictions that in many cases take away the voting rights of those convicted. In other words, this new Jim Crow has sought to silence the voices that would give white Americans a vision of themselves that might remind us we exist in "hell" as "devils."

Who are the social poets instrumental to such social swerves? Gods? Men? Bloom sees little need to distinguish:

> The poet is our chosen man, and his consciousness of election comes as a curse; again, not 'I am a fallen man,' but 'I am Man, and I am falling' – or rather, 'I *was* God, I *was* Man (for to a poet they were the same), and I *am* falling, from myself.' When this consciousness of self is raised to an absolute pitch, *then* the poet hits the floor of Hell, or rather, comes to the bottom of the abyss, and by his impact there creates Hell.[26]

Thought of in social terms, Bloom's suggestion about the creation of hell foregrounds not suffering, but the establishment of the white man as a social "devil" as much as a social "god," a poetic validation of the Yakub myth of creation common to many American strands of Islam. For instance, Elijah Muhammad writes *in The Theology of Time* (1972) of Yakub's creation of "white devils," purportedly a race of blue-eyed "devils" that "does not have any nature of good in him and no mercy in his heart."[27] Important to note of this example is that I am not validating or exonerating such theological sentiments, but trying to demonstrate why such sentiments might have made their way into Nation of Islam discourse and what such ideas suggest sociologically about white men, in particular. Unlike the popular white response to these ideas that they are the sentiments of a crazy person, I would suggest they are instead a sociological analysis coming from someone who sees white American hatred of blacks as crazier still. To make clear how I am making use of these tropes of devil and satan, I return to Malcolm X's usage as he offers an important qualification:

> Unless we call one white man, by name, a 'devil,' we are not speaking of any *individual* white man. We are speaking of the *collective* white man's *historical* record. We are speaking of the collective white man's cruelties, and evils, and greeds, that have seen him *act* like a devil toward the nonwhite man.[28]

The Modern poet, like white American men historically, had been forced to choose, from the floor of hell, whether to become as strong as satan, or weak enough to worship "a god altogether other than the self, wholly external to the possible. This god is cultural history, the dead poets, the embarrassments of a tradition grown too wealthy to need anything more."[29] Notably, satan is not created until the "consciousness of self is raised to an absolute pitch,"[30] such that society comes to function as a god. And this poetic god is placed in tension with the "god of cultural history," of "dead poets."[31] So it goes that the poet is left to compete between the worship of a society having been created in the image of satan (precisely because it creates "satans"), or through an embrace of weakness in the face of dead poets.

Thanks to poetic influence, through such "swerves," white Americans have simultaneously understood ourselves to be progressing, while those victimized by white religion have had good reason to continue to regard white men as devils.

Even satan dies

Bloom arranges these misprisions through constant reference to strong or weak poets, arguing that "strong poets" do not distinguish between priority and authority, meaning that greatness is organized for them around being first. The moral exemplar of strong poetry, for Bloom, is satan from Milton's "Paradise Lost."[32] Strong poets refuse to sublimate, "condemned to the unwisdom"[33] of taking the first so as to arrive as the best. In fact, reviewer John Hollander suggests that because of its focus and Oedipal interests, Bloom's work offers an allegory helpful for understanding the anxiety America attaches to its "European father."[34] Bloom connects this anxiety to death, noting that ephebes begin "rebelling more strongly against the consciousness of death's necessity than all other men and women do"[35] leading, ironically, to the death of Modern poetry itself. For Modern poetry, perhaps for Modernity in general, the anxiety of escaping death both constitutes the central feature, and secures its death prematurely. Even autopoietic systems come to an end at some point.[36]

The connection Bloom makes between the anxiety of influence and its death-dealing effects for poetry looks schematically similar to the way god-idols such as whiteness hinge on manipulations of the proximity of a person or group to death, as already demonstrated in earlier chapters. For groups as for individuals, death is not escaped but is transposed onto other individuals and whole groups. A fear of death ultimately brings death about in even more severe terms, in that the anxiety of influence (as an anxiety associated with mortality and finitude) never escapes its object of influence. Indeed, a social death outweighs a physical death in this and many respects. Thinking of white religion through Bloom's theory helps to situate that death, however conceived or denied, cannot be escaped. Escape efforts only reinforce death's priority. Bloom notes:

> For Satan is a pure or absolute consciousness of self compelled to have admitted its intimate alliance with opacity. The state of Satan is therefore a constant consciousness of dualism, of being trapped in the finite, not just in space (in the body) but in clock-time as well. To be pure spirit, yet to know in oneself the limit of opacity; to assert that one goes back before the Creation-Fall, yet be forced to yield to number, weight, and measure; this is the situation of the strong poet, the capable imagination, when he confronts the universe of poetry, the words that were and will be, the terrible splendor of cultural heritage.[37]

The "terrible splendor of cultural heritage" is precisely the sort of hermeneutical frame left for adherents of white religion to reckon with, having long maintained an "intimate alliance with opacity" (though not an appreciation for it, necessarily) as a means of maintaining distance from uncertainty and limitation through dualistic registers. The time has come to embrace death or accept the permanence of hell, where white men function as satans, unable to embrace the "terrible splendor of [their own] cultural heritage" and reinforcing that terror in the process. Such an embrace of cultural heritage is "terrible" because it involves finally coming to terms with oneself and one's actions and limits as one dies. If, as suggested by philosopher Cornel West, "the paradox of Afro-American history is that Afro-Americans fully enter the modern world precisely when the postmodern period commences,"[38] then the paradox of Anglo-American history might be that its history is finally coming to an end and because of the shape of that history, Anglo-Americans have not cultivated the tools required to either overcome or endure such an impending death. Bloom's theory of poetic influence aids in making sense of such paradoxes. As concerning white religion and white men in particular, we are left to interpret ourselves as dying satans – and hope, in death, to be offered wisdom on how satans are formed. Such attention to the Yakub myth, in concert to Bloom's work, offers a way to explore and situate a historically well-known but little understood (by whites) idea about some black perceptions of whites. More than that, it offers a way to thematically and hermeneutically capture the contemporary moment for many of these white men, these "white devils." Perhaps, out of a greater ability to understand such judgments levied against them as sociological (instead of fundamental), it might be easier for us to realize where we find ourselves in light of previous attempts to address racism and the like:

> 'I seem to have stopped falling; now I *am fallen*, consequently, I lie here in Hell,' but he is thinking as he says this, 'As I fell, *I swerved*, consequently I lie here in a Hell improved by my own making.'[39]

Learning to "number our days" involves embracing that our days are already numbered, producing "hell" (per Bloom's characterization) out of which no escape is possible. How we respond to our time in this "hell" determines if we remain "satan." Will the weight of something like whiteness ever allow for something greater than a swerve? In the wake of the need to respond to white religion with a limited religious outlook, and the seeming relation between Bloom's strong poet and a dualist outlook part and parcel to the Imago Superlata, then a limited religious outlook will bring with it the specter and shadow of the weak poet, so that those beholden to white religion – especially straight, white American men with the privilege to deny we've been devils to many – might begin to fashion ourselves as weak. A limited religious outlook will follow the path of the weak poet, giving priority to "dead poets" and "cultural heritage." Hermeneutically speaking, white men might realize that relinquishing resources or certainty or abilities through a limited religious outlook is not a vulgar matter of ceasing to be "god" or "god-like," but is recognition that in the eyes of others, and because of one's own insecurities, we have been the embodiment of evil. A limited religious outlook might now begin to atone for having created hell in perpetuity even while swerving from the satans that have come before.

Escape from the "hell" created by white religion is not fully possible – that is, we can't easily escape religion or the god-idols created by religion, meaning that perhaps the easiest way to ensure an eternity in this "hell" is to think oneself able to escape it. As discussed below, this even involves the impossibility of fully escaping the god idea. Necessary, then, is finding a "new" means of engaging the god idea and religion. In the sections that follow, I offer a series of "swerves" in an effort to epistemologically shift gears, understanding such "swerves" as unable to provide full escape from the white, theistic petit bourgeois hell we have collectively written on social life. A growing awareness of such a history produces the sense of cultural twilight wherein many find themselves rulers of a hell they have created here on earth. Given this history, how might we number our days in hell?

UNCERTAIN HUMANISM

In this section, I begin by relaying a brief vignette from one of anthropologist Barbara Myerhoff's informants during her fieldwork engaging a dying population of Jews living in a retirement home in southern California in the mid-1970s. Though Myerhoff plays a central role later in this chapter, here her conversation with Shmuel is helpful for situating my first attempted "swerve."

Shmuel didn't know what to say, but he knew the topic was important. "'Tell me, Shmuel,' [Myerhoff] asked, "'didn't it confuse you, to love Judaism as you did, but see it condoning the sacrifice of an innocent victim for God's wishes?'"[40]

Shmuel replies, "Do you think that Judaism saves us from being men? Even as a boy, I saw Abraham's fault and knew it was his responsibility, not God's, to decide what was right."[41] Speaking to Barbara Myerhoff for the last time days before his death, Shmuel's theodicy is an anthropodicy, focused on human failings and complexity rather than divine responsibility. His ideas are thoroughly anthropocentric portraits of god, framed not around the utility of the god idea but the futility of the idea in the face of death.[42] Shmuel does not take up the slippery-slope fallacy so part and parcel of theodicy as an enterprise. Suffering is not causally related to "god" or free will one way or another. Shmuel's efforts don't appear to be getting god off of a theodical hook, so much as underscoring that god is of no consequence one way or another to a dying man. Instead, Shmuel focuses on Judaism's cultural and cosmic limitations, as if Myerhoff's question had been asked in bad faith. It had.

Shmuel, in defining culture, says this:

> It happens to be the Jewish way. I don't mean it is the best way, but it happens to be our way. That's all. It's planted in our gardens. Does that mean that other gardens should be destroyed? ... Culture is that garden. This

> is not a thing of nations. It is not about Goethe and Yeshivas. It is children playing. Culture is the simple grass through which the wind blows sweetly and each grass blade bends softly to the caress of the wind. It is like a mother who would pick up her child and kiss it, with her tenderness that she gave birth to it.[43]

Relegating god's worth below that of cultural heritage, Shmuel gracefully demonstrates that culture is an arbitrary human vestige with immense value. God, however conceived, comes from culture, akin to a flower or bush grown from the soil of the things people do and make and think. Shmuel's characterization of culture helps in understanding the moments when he does address the question of god directly:

> Do I believe in God, you asked me? What does any of this have to do with God? This I cannot say. Some people are afraid to be alone and face life without God. Hemingway killed himself because he was searching for something and couldn't find it. The wise man searches but not to find. He searches because even though there is nothing to find, it is necessary to search. About God, I would say I am an agnostic. If there is a God, he is playing marbles with us… . On this note about God, we finish now. You have all I can give you.[44]

Three days after these words were spoken, Shmuel died.

This brief vignette offers by analogy a way to understand the contemporary social moment for white people as it relates to possible continued reliance on the god idea. The concern for, over, or about "god" is as much directly relevant to contemporary racial dynamics where churches remain largely segregated, as it is another entry point for discussing fears over perceived or real losses of power by white Americans. Shmuel's agnosticism demonstrates the uncertainties of whether or not the social world is changing, whether or not whiteness or theism is losing functional ground. On the question of whether whites are losing real social power or not, Shmuel demonstrates that an actual answer is largely unnecessary, as the effects of feared loss of power run moot in the face of the overwhelming power afforded by recognizing that we all die. Here, Shmuel's theological commitments demonstrate a methodological uncertainty we might employ in the effort to attend to the social uncertainties around us. Shmuel begins to elucidate an interpretive adjustment that might offer wisdom as we move forward through twilight.

The uncertainty of escaping the hell of god

People die whether they believe in a god or not, even if what "death" means shifts according to time and space. In the end, this likely means there is credibility to the idea that death is actually humanity's one true god or functioning center, and culture offers a means to cope with and learn such things. What then does this mean, for escape attempts from "god" and the possibilities for carving out intellectual or social space where "god" is no longer operative? In this section, I address the question of escaping the idea of god through a discussion that puts in conversation Harold Bloom and Anthony Pinn, and from the back and forth produces a humanist perspective focused ultimately on uncertainty over the ability or utility of ever fully escaping the "hell" posed by the idea of god.

Shmuel's quick movement past the theodicy question, his turn to culture, and his ultimate final, uncertain, agnostic word on god, are of utmost importance in schematizing a limited religious outlook. His vignette offers an example of an *uncertain humanism*, and I want to explore this sense of humanism as a possible response to recognizing oneself residing – permanently – in a hell of one's own making. Uncertain humanism focuses on balanced human worth and ability, an intense agnosticism that includes but extends far beyond a doctrine of god, to also include an ethical posture that even if there is a god, that god might not be worth relying on. This uncertain humanism is also underscored by uncertainty about the social efficacy of such a reliance on humanism, as a life orientation or ethical posture more generally.

Uncertain humanism is initially defined through motivation. Humanists, as I understand them, are more concerned about human well-being and healthy, equitable interaction than anything else.[45] Uncertainty, as a modifier, is my contribution and qualifier, and is meant to promote the idea that agnosticism offers a helpful rejoinder to the certainty secured by any definitive statement about god-idols. It also emphasizes that humanism, however conceived, is of limited ability and worth[46] in responding to white religion. Indeed, many humanists remain very "religious" in their distinction-making preoccupation with gods and/or humans. An uncertain humanism remains agnostic on the question of divine – or human – (they're the same thing, keep in mind) being, ability, and value, so that preoccupation shifts away from the concept of god and towards the humanity of all; even, and perhaps especially, "believers."

To be sure, there is great peril to theism as I have defined it, as belief in the utility of belief. Here, I am not backtracking on that statement, but emphasizing that all "gods" are ideologically constructed (i.e., god-idols). Based on cultural options and contexts within the society, not all god-idols function with equal power, authority, or social effect. Theism is one such god-idol in need of intense censure. Other possibilities might not (necessarily) be so dangerous. Hermeneutically, "god" exists in the form of society and death. Not content with traditional theism or the functional atheism of Durkheim, a limited religious outlook follows an agnostic position, unsure of any ontological reality one way or another, but sure that functionally speaking, gods are very real and they are best held in check by understanding them as idols. Hence, "god-idol." A limited religious outlook does not worry one way or another about acute and/or cultural belief in the idea of god, but about whether or not such god ideas promote an exaggerated sense of certainty, human value, or ability. Such certainty can as easily come through a refutation of the god idea.

Bloom's anxiety of influence and his talk of strong and weak poets offers the possibility to "misinterpret" and "swerve" away from humanist theologian (and my graduate school advisor) Anthony Pinn. Early in his career (he an "ephebe" then; I, an "ephebe" now), Pinn sought to expose the compromise with suffering required by theodicy as it emerged or was ignored by black theology as an enterprise. Like Shmuel, Pinn only finds need to talk of such compromises as they force harm or misrecognition of the importance of specific communities.[47] On this refutation of theodicy, and on the preeminent focus on black culture and community, using Bloom I want to suggest that if thought about in light of the usefulness of Pinn's argument for the construction of what I am attempting here – a white response to white reliance on this Imago Superlata – Pinn "went accurately up to a certain point, but then should have swerved, precisely in the direction"[48] offered here.[49]

As a means of moving black theology forward, the young ephebe Pinn "swerves" against many of his predecessors[50] by arguing that the idea of god forces a compromise with human suffering that simply is untenable in light of the historical circumstances of African Americans.[51] In place of god, he offers to the black theological poets his position of strong humanism. In a passage meant to both clarify his position lest his interlocutors take his argument as something other than what it was and to rhetorically situate thinkers who have come before, Pinn writes:

> Weak humanism entails an increased sense of self and one's place in the human family. This position does not call God's existence into question. Anxiety arises, for weak humanists, when reflecting on the realm of god's activity in the world; not over the very existence of god … . The goal is to prevent the oppressed from underestimating their humanity and oppressors from overestimating their humanity.[52]
>
> For strong humanists, relatively sustained and oppressive world conditions bring into question the presence of any Being outside of the human realm … consequentially, humanity has no one to turn to for assistance … . Hence, strong humanism seeks to combat oppression through radical human commitment to life and corresponding activity.[53]

Of the problems of theodicy, Pinn, Shmuel, and I are in accord, both in terms of it forcing a compromise with suffering, and in terms of moving away from it as a direct intellectual interest. In what is admittedly a "swerve" of my own, I want to suggest that a limited religious outlook is not concerned with strong or weak varieties of humanist stances; it is more concerned that any chosen standpoint be shaky and uncertain. Semantic rejoinders that such a foundation in uncertainty offers a kind of certainty, in my estimation, run moot, as the point is not to be logically correct, but to elicit disruption of society functioning as god. The only foundation or *certainty* proffered here is the intuition of uncertainty posed by death, understanding that even in casting uncertain humanism as an option, I rely on a foundation provided by the bodies of others in setting the terms of what this perspective would look like. To embrace an uncertain humanism is to privilege a sense of uncertainty as a point of departure for humanist endeavors and interpretations of human social activity; white Americans are simply in no place to know, with certainty, anything definitively, as the costs of surety have been severe historically, and those costs have always deconstructed their ends.[54]

Pinn underscores the anxiety shaping the weak humanist. Presumably, as weak humanists are "not [anxious] over the very existence of god," he implies such anxiety *is* operative for the strong humanist. From my perspective, this "missing" statement about anxiety amongst the strong humanists is a concession, or a Derridean trace, indicating strong humanists are more indebted to "god's" influence than they want to admit. A "weak humanist" would exist with or without Pinn's suggestion that they hold no anxiety about the existence of god, but indeed, a strong humanist – per Pinn's own terms – is only created by that anxiety. Bloom offers what can be read as a homology to Pinn's work in *Why, Lord?*, when Bloom relays that Oscar Wilde's character Lord Henry Wotton tells Dorian Gray "that all influence is immoral,"[55] and later that disciples can be escaped[56] – meaning that one can seemingly overcome influence based purely on where one situates oneself in a discourse. And reliance on "discourse" indicates reliance on others, predecessors, be they poets or gods. Strength negates its strength through tacit or explicit suggestion that such strength comes from out of the blue. "Strength" comes from a concealed anxiety, hidden because its exposure would evince weakness.

In his more recent *The End of God-Talk* (2012), in a passage reminiscent of Wilde's suggestion that influence can be escaped, Pinn notes that "God is unnecessary, even for theologians."[57] And yet, noting its use as a symbol having run its course,[58] Pinn remains ironically indebted to the idea of god for the crafting of nontheistic humanism; god, as "non-theism," appears in a truly apophatic form, literally in the sense of negation (as in *not* theism) as opposed to the traditional interpretation of "apophatic" as knowing god through a logic of negation. Rather than saying what god is not,[59] Pinn sets about describing what the "not god" *is*. We see this in Pinn's turn to community as a centering idea, where he states that "African American nontheistic humanist theology seeks to be more than a theology of negation"; nontheistic humanism "must have a centering 'something,' a means by which to frame the nature and meaning of lived life."[60] My point is not to disagree with the logical need for such a centering concept, but to foreground the impossibility of escaping the demand for ideas I've sought to describe as "god-idols," where community serves in this capacity for African American nontheistic humanism. Admittedly, this arrangement is healthier than something like whiteness, but it still relies on stated need for a point of orientation and departure which, as my larger efforts attempt to demonstrate, always comes at a social cost. Where white religion is concerned, I am attempting to disrupt such appeals to normativity because the costs faced by non-whites given such arrangements historically have been excruciating. Escape from normative appeal is impossible, but might be mitigated whenever the problem arises. Such mitigation would be a constant deconstructive task.

A Christology or Ecclesiology could likely be written without reference to god, at all. In corresponding fashion, a truly "nontheistic humanist theology" might not utter the word "god," even as a rhetorical rejoinder. It would work vociferously to disrupt normative appeals and their subsequent demand for a sense of certainty or direction. To this extent, the word "god" simply wouldn't be necessary if the anxiety of influence were not also present. God's status as socially constructed or as merely a symbol does not make that symbol any less influential. To this end, though I agree that god as an idea is unnecessary as a meaning-making feature of human life, so too I argue that "nontheist" is not a descriptor of those who have escaped the hell of god, but those who remain indebted to the idea by virtue of the impossibility of full escape from the concept. Escape from god in this capacity would be an attempt to avoid the anxiety of influence by arguing that one is not a poet and so should not be judged against poetry. In the same way that an African American does not have to believe their worth or abilities to be below those of white Americans for that person to face the consequences of racism, functionally speaking, escaping the hell of god is an uncertainty at best.

In what can only be described as "poetic" synergy, Pinn's 2014 intellectual autobiography, *Writing God's Obituary: How a Good Methodist became a Better Atheist*, begins with an epigraph from Oscar Wilde:

> The true mystery of the world is the visible, not the invisible.[61]

Wilde and Pinn, poet and theologian, come together here as strong and yet weak, strong in their efforts to focus attention to the "visible" world, but weak in allowing "mystery" to make possible the shift away from an interest in things "invisible." This paradox elucidates the uncertain humanism I have in mind. In Wilde's case the "true mystery of the world," I would suggest, is not the visible, but the binary reliance of the visible on the invisible trace in perpetuity. Theologically speaking, the "true mystery" is not escaping or setting down the god idea through strong humanism or nontheistic varieties – the focus of Pinn's early and his more recent work,[62] respectively – but learning how to come to terms with living in a world where escape from the power of social and functional expressions of god is uncertain. And to connect my point to Milton, didn't such strong assumptions and efforts to escape god lead to the creation of satan and hell in the first place, by rebellion against god?

The strongest of poets and humanists end up reinforcing the necessity of their predecessors through the over-determined certainty that the hells we create for ourselves and for others can be escaped. Admittedly, I am relying more on this strong/weak distinction than does Pinn, himself – and I recognize that Pinn's later works often emphasize human limitation and the limited capacity we have as humans to think or do something better than what has come before. His notion of perpetual rebellion is just one (of many) moments where the humanist Pinn seems to recognize the impossibility of "escape."[63] But the parallels between Bloom's and Pinn's talk of strong and weak are *poetically* useful. That is, they offer instances of greater understanding of hermeneutics generally, and specifically with respect to different interests, motivations, and social locations. Through what Bloom refers to as misprisions, the young ephebe (Pinn, his students, or any poet wanting to stand out) overdetermines the predecessor's intentions or influence for the sake of taking priority, for being understood as "new." Reflexively and importantly (for understanding my argument) here I overdetermine Pinn's reliance on the god idea so that my work might be clarified as distinct from his, as I work to escape the hell of god, which for white Americans also involves attempts at escape from the racialized hell we have created. Surely, in my own way, I am guilty of the same crime – this is my point. To this end, the theopoetic axiom written at the gates of hell has something to say about learning how to "number our days." What is captured by Dante's "Abandon all hope, ye who enter here" if not an astute warning that escape from the hells we create is not possible when explicitly attempted? The strongest of poets are the most hopeful in an escape from hell. Understanding that the title of a book is a result of collaboration between authors, editors, and publishers, even still there is an irony attached to the title of Pinn's *Writing God's Obituary*. This irony, of course, is that "God" not "Pinn," ends up in the title. From the perspective of an uncertain humanist, any autobiography would inevitably involve writing one's *own* obituary. The strength of a humanism, or poetic license, rests not always on the arrogance of a young ephebe, but as much on the wisdom of a seasoned poet or thinker to admit to the paradox and irony and move forward without flinching – embracing death as an integral narrative arc writing the story of life. Hence, the strongest of poets or humanists land, in the end, back in hell, but a hell they've made from their own ingenuity. Does escaping "hell" involve a growing confidence and certainty of an escape route (as offered by the ephebe Pinn in his suggestion that an atheistic strong humanism, though not finite, is epistemologically and ethically better than its weak alternative), or is it made possible by giving up the certainty of an escape? An uncertain humanist looks for an escape, but does not expect one. It is humanist, in that it privileges a concern for humans, but it is beyond the scope of a limited religious outlook or an uncertain humanism to be concerned with the destruction of the god idea. It is certainly my position that theism as an idea is fraught with problems (Chapter 2 attests to that); however, my critique of theism is not about "god" as much as the functional and social reliance on belief. God, as an idea, is here to stay. Numbering our days in hell involves an end to escape attempts and an embrace of others in hell as a means to endure.

Gods, devils, and uncertain humans

A limited religious outlook seeks to limit the parameters of the god idea, but from a white normative context from which Bloom also writes, fighting against the god idea (with too much force or certainty) amounts to an equally "strong" *poetic* stance, marking such a concern an Oedipal complex and conceding the impossibility of escape from the hells of our own making. Functionally speaking, both atheism and theism are "real" to the extent that as ideas – as god-idols – they compete to shape identity and social options. Theism and atheism emerge together historically and both follow the parameters set in place by the Imago Superlata – meaning they are equally able to promote the sense of certainty I seek to trouble. Gods and devils arrive together in the form of a person. To this end, atheistic and nontheistic humanist varieties are of no greater use for a limited religious outlook if they begin with the certainty that god is not real. Agnosticism, unknowing or unknowability, is more helpful. Given Pinn's construal of humanism's options as a young theologian, and his more recent reliance on "god" as a symbol having lost its utility, and supposing "white" humanisms come in similar varieties, I want to suggest – as a white and humanist ephebe – that the best positionality towards humanism is through this prism of uncertainty, maintained by a privileging of humility, unknowability, the impossibility of fully escaping social issues like racism, but making a continued concerted effort to attempt precisely that. Thus, one treats all fights as "windmills"[64] but hopes that through ongoing dialogue and critical engagement such windmills might someday be written out[65] of the social world. An over-determined atheism is of no greater good than an over-determined theism for a community of white religious adherents who have made a practice of vacillating between positions of god-worship or self-deification as it suits social interest. In early 2015, it was an atheist, or more precisely "anti-theist" who was charged with the flagrant executions of three young Muslim college students in North Carolina.[66] Both options emerge as Modern means of over-determining one's own position, providing a façade of certainty in the face of limitation. Both must remain at our disposal for cultivating an uncertain, limited outlook on religion and the world more broadly. To so easily be construed as god or devil, the word on humans – white ones, in particular – is uncertain.

Aware of the perils of weak humanism, but with the recognition of the need to embrace a weak poetic stance within a limited religious domain, the outlook I wish to put forth is one of uncertainty. Responding to white religion is a humanist endeavor, given that social problems are firstly human problems. To disrupt such a thing requires thinking more of humans than their projections, the artists before the art, and the storytellers ahead of the stories. But humanism's usefulness is in no greater certainty than any other outlook, and marking humans as "most important" analytically or existentially is not the same thing as treating humans as supremely good or able. Doing the latter would cast uncertain humanism squarely within white religion, while my intent is to do otherwise. At best, humans are most important analytically because humans cause the most epistemological, ethical, and social problems and uncertainties. And humans are most important existentially because we are dying humans.

Not all hells are created equal: contextualizing uncertain humanism

In the analogy provided by both Bloom's talk of Milton, and the historic myth of the white man as devil/satan, something "new" means finding oneself outside of hell. But how does one escape "hell," or "windmills," however conceived? Escape ends up interpretively possible by setting down the anxiety associated with a "swerve" or other misprision and picking up a focus and reliance not on poetic creativity but on telling the stories of one's predecessors. Such stories are necessarily unique, finding priority because of parity, not in spite of it. In each chapter of Part II of *White Lies*, I try to tell such stories. Before that, I want to describe the work the telling of stories is meant to achieve, that of grounding social context as the point and rationale for interpretive variance amongst social actors as much as analysts.

Pinn and I come at our work having lived different lives, with a variety of geographic, generational, racial, and other factors marking our narratives as distinct. It may be poetic to read uncertain humanism as a "swerve" to distinguish me (the academic ephebe) from my intellectual forebear and closest influence. Yet, Bloom's theory of poetry does little to explore the significance of context, and indeed Bloom – in all his brilliant analysis – seems too mesmerized by Modern poetry to see the social implications of his analysis. My offering of uncertain humanism, then, might not only be a "swerve" in terms of the presentation of ideas, but a marker of the differing significance of an idea (god) based on one's context and the stories made by that context. Different narratives are of equal analytic importance, but are also composed of drastically different tones, textures, styles, and more. For instance, Pinn might respond to the above critique noting that he has never claimed to be the first African American humanist or nontheist, and that much of his work attests to that very point. More than "poet," Pinn has also narrated the perspectives of many who have come before him. One's own story or context is seemingly best exposed by telling the stories of others within a similar context. Attention to context provides a different valence to understanding how to escape the hells of our own making. Rather than Pinn's work simply reinforcing his inability to escape god, in narrating the stories of those prior to him, he makes such an escape (inasmuch as escape is possible at all). That is, in embracing those in "hell," he is able to escape by having set down the concern to escape. Indeed, in works such as *By These Hands: A Documentary History of African American Humanism* (2001), *Moral Evil and Redemptive Suffering: A History of Theodicy in African American Religious Thought* (2002), *Becoming America's Problem Child: An Outline of Pauli Murray's Religious Life and Theology* (2008), Pinn has been able to tell the stories of others, thereby coming to a greater ability to tell his own. A limited religious outlook works to contextualize similar efforts for scholars who find themselves near social centers. That is, a limited religious outlook can speak volumes on what a particular social location means for interpretation and analysis, but can say relatively little – very limited – in terms of how that context is escaped or how what is learned from it can be of much use to those outside of it. Indeed, transmitting and translating that which is learned in one context to another context is a very limited endeavor.

Important for interpreting the stories told within a white American context in a way that will allow for embrace of radical contingency is to correct for exaggerations of worth or ability by appealing to the staggering weight of the great counterfactual, death. Whites at social centers cannot simply tell stories – those stories must be told and framed in terms of their own death and the deaths such stories have historically caused for others. It is for a white limited religious outlook to limit its prescriptive comments to those with similar stories, and to glean its sources heavily from those similar stories, understanding that all stories, all gods and devils, submit – in the end – to death.

Given Pinn's context, it seems clear that god as a symbol is dangerous and in need of abandonment as it has been used as "a mechanism for protecting signs and symbols because of the ontological burden they bear."[67] Such claims are not only a result of the anxiety of influence but an anxiety attached to the social damage done by the idea, an anxiety rooted in life and fear of the consequences of a society organized around insider/outsider social arrangements.

In the case of an uncertain humanist outlook for white, theistic petit bourgeois Americans, the concern is not to exchange one prison of certainty (i.e., theism) for another hell of certainty in the form of atheism or nontheism. Uncertain humanism responds to the permanence of social hell by embracing those in "hell"[68] – all of us, gods and devils alike – more forcefully than most ideological postures cultivated as a response to this situation of social hell. In less caustic language, uncertain humanism explores each social context thoroughly through explorations of what others have done in those locations. It draws conclusions based on what others have done in and through social contexts and historical times and places. It follows Michel Foucault in understanding the Enlightenment project as an escape attempt from social responsibility and as a flight from social interaction.[69] Given the tenuous but genealogically significant relationship between the Enlightenment and humanism (broadly conceived), it is uncertain of humanism as well, and recognizes that this new iteration of it is as much connected to Enlightenment escape as it may, or may not be, a decisive break from such an arrangement. Along these lines, Foucault warns with nuance:

> From this [humanism's wide umbrella usage ranging from Marx to Christianity to National Socialism] we must not conclude that everything that has ever been linked with humanism is to be rejected, but that the humanistic thematic

> is in itself too supple, too diverse, too inconsistent to serve as an axis for reflection … . Humanism serves to color and to justify the conceptions of man to which it is, after all, obliged to take recourse … . I am inclined to see Enlightenment and humanism in a state of tension rather than identity.[70]

Understanding that "humanism" cannot serve as such an "axis for reflection," but in an effort to continuously "color" "conceptions of [humans]" by way of social context, identity, and material possibility, humanism remains useful albeit augmented with this *uncertain* modifier.

Uncertain humanism understands experience as not always shared across social context. And it remains uncertain of where to fully draw the lines between social contexts, but follows a process of starting with one's very specific context, and exploring the efforts and ideas of those seemingly closest to that initial starting point. For white Americans, through an uncertain humanism, work must be done to undo – an anxiety around *future* influence, not *past* influence – the social consequences of having created society as god in one's white, normative image, and not knowing how to die or live in the shadow of certainty. Such processes begin with the uncertain foundations of social context and location.

Readers might note two glaring omissions or inconsistencies to this point of the argument. The first is "why humanism at all?" and the second might be my overreliance on and overdetermination of Pinn as strawman and focus of my attention. I have organized the chapter this way precisely to demonstrate the *weaknesses* inherent in efforts to escape. Addressing this latter issue first, in my use of his work, Bloom might suggest that I *sound* as if I'm objecting to or challenging Pinn, but the ephebe's explicit engagement with a precursor is always a displacement of a more challenging, more fraught engagement with another, unnamed precursor, whose threat of influence is far greater. On this possible suggestion, I am guilty here of focusing too intently on the safer Pinn than on the actual object of my social inheritance – family, friends, colleagues, and white America. This charge might also extend to other portions of *White Lies* where readers might agree with my findings, but hope for more specific historical evidence supporting my claims. In one swift assessment, Bloom's analytic help focuses attention to the need and difficulty we whites often have at focusing on the other within us rather than our more frequent focus on the other outside of ourselves. To be sure, my anxious wrestling with Pinn speaks directly to the field of the academic study of religion, but such wrestling also serves as useful proxy for measuring the degree to which I, too, remain tied to white religion. Our need for self-reflexivity often swerves in directions we might more safely travel than in directions that would increase vulnerability. On this point, I simply hope this discussion of uncertain humanism is as instructive in its direct academic sense as it is in its exemplary, metonymic focus.

On the topic of why humanism at all, especially in light of my turn to Foucault, some might ask what is the good of humanism, given its baggage? Where "god" or certainty of perspective or field of vision is presumed, uncertain humanism "wants to believe," like the poster hung behind Fox Mulder's desk in *The X Files*, but it knows it cannot believe any longer. Ethical atheism meets with cosmological agnosticism and humility, offering guidance in the domains of religion and metaphysics, as much as politics, or education and scholarship. That is, white Americans who might follow an uncertain humanism choose not to *believe in* god because the social danger it causes is too great to justify such belief; not "believing" in humans, however, might preclude the white ability to recognize non-whites as human. Whether god in some otherworldly or transhistorical sense is actually real or not, remains an open question, as not knowing promotes the uncertainty embraced through this uncertain humanism. By my estimation, though the ecological focus of many post-humanist endeavors is instructive and helpful for broadening the scope of concern beyond traditional horizons, too few post-humanists focus enough on racial disparities. In fact, some have conjectured that there is more land set aside for wildlife in the United States than is owned by African Americans. Whether literally true or not, the point is significant: Life – all of it – is vitally important, but my focus on humanism is meant to refute any attempts that suggest or imply that all life matters but that do not specifically celebrate the more acute suggestion that black lives matter. On this ethical line, the ledger books of a limited religious outlook count post-humanist possibilities just as devilish as their humanist predecessors. Uncertain humanism stands at the gates between the "heaven" of post-humanist realization and the hell of its continued racialized denials reinforcing social hell for many in the United States. God-idols, for the uncertain humanist, are a guilty pleasure, and always come at the expense of another. Uncertain humanism echoes Fanon's cry for a new humanism,[71] in this a humanism for those who have attempted or are attempting to take off their "white masks."[72] Swerving away from their predecessors, only to find their faces as white as their masks, uncertain humanists are uncertain of this uncertain orientation's efficacy, but find solace in the discomfort of not knowing. God-idols serve partially as masks. To the extent that whiteness, as a god-idol, might be understood as a racialized expression of the inability to accept human limitations, uncertain humanism embraces blackness as the impossibility of fully accepting human limitations. Stated differently, whiteness turns its adherents into devils and the world into hell. Embracing blackness might involve learning to live in hell without turning into a devil.

Though it attempts to refute all god-idols offering a façade of certainty or orientation to those already at society's center, uncertain humanism is equally concerned to turn towards the stuff of culture (e.g., literature, music, dress, various rituals of artistic production, etc.) in an effort to move those from the center to the margins. The turn to culture also offers a consolation for such movement, and lastly, amounts to an effort to shift focus from the center of hell where devils dwell to the borders and margins creating hell.

MAKING UNCERTAINTY EXPLICIT

Uncertain humanism responds to the longstanding effort to make sense of the world, with correlations between cause and effect, by casting light on the consequences of these correlations. And to be sure, science and the field of psychology carry much historical and philosophical baggage when it comes to the perils of induction.[73] This notwithstanding, the contemporary interest in and emphasis on the field of implicit bias may offer some *limited* benefits for responding to such consequences. According to social psychologist Gordon Moskowitz, changes "to our surroundings [initiate] what the pragmatist philosopher John Dewey (1929) referred to as 'a quest for certainty.' The individual moves down a path to find an answer – to attain understanding and knowledge. And this path can either be smooth and easily traveled, or a rocky one fraught with effort."[74]

Religion, in its Imago Superlata expression, amounts to this quest for certainty. And I have been working to demonstrate the consequences of orienting oneself equitably along these rocky paths. Yet, in an admitted echo of rationalism's penchant for turning uncertainty into certainty, here I want to suggest that an uncertain humanism can make use of findings from the field of implicit bias so as to attempt to offset some of the negative effects of this demand for certainty. Here, I do not mean to buy into the rational claim that uncertainty transmutes into certainty, but simply to suggest that an always already uncertainty does not have to always lead to the subjugation or constitution or murder of those on social margins.

Social cognition brings with it biases. Period. Where contemporary race relations in America are concerned, white (and black) perceptions of white and black generally follow a path of black bodies tacitly, implicitly, regarded as fear-inducing, lacking the shared worth of white counterparts, etc. Such racial biases have even been shown in and with children.[75] In short, exaggerations of radical contingency are not always explicit. In fact, they are often implicit. Examples of this include everything from hiring and promotion practices on college campuses to the propensity of police to use disproportionate force against African Americans.[76] How then would an uncertain humanism, or a limited religious outlook, respond to these biases working under the surface of white social activity and ideation?

It would first accept that the perceptions we hold of others, in my terms these exaggerations, are "often what we believe we actually have seen in that person."[77] Yet, where behavior is concerned, and we might include ontological assumptions about identity generally (as identity is understood to be "operational acts of identification" anyway), implicit bias theory demonstrates that "perceivers" of persons are a "larger factor in determining how a behavior is interpreted than the actual behavior that is observed."[78] The perceptions we hold of others have much more to do with us than "them."

Uncertain humanism moves in the simple direction of uncertainty, unconcerned with assuaging or mitigating that discomfort, because it understands this uncertainty is pedagogical. Such a conscious focus on the embrace of uncertainty renders implicit biases explicit. The danger of collateral damage – that is, violence, etc. – is never fully overcome but as uncertain humanists choose uncertainty, the violence that would typically serve as a means of overcoming the uncertainty is mitigated because it would defeat the purpose or instruction made possible in the uncertain social moment.

To ground this discussion in the specific implications for white Americans, Moskowitz remains helpful in his discussion of Gaertner and Dovidio's 1986 study on white American perceptions of race. Moskowitz's summary is worth quoting in total:

> Many White Americans are conflicted and ambivalent about race. They value being fair and unbiased, as these are cherished components of the American creed. However, they also harbor resentful feelings about character flaws they see in stereotyped groups, and hold feelings of unease regarding being around such groups. These feelings lead to avoidance so as not to feel anxiety or discomfort. Guarding against an embarrassing transgression, such as saying something offensive or "politically incorrect," only heightens the anxiety. Yet the very same people, often unaware of their negative feelings, are consciously quite dedicated to the idea of egalitarianism. Their bias is subjugated and is not visible to themselves or others.[79]

The brief, but thorough assessment of white Americans on race offered here helps to demonstrate a couple of features important for this limited religious outlook. First, negative feelings or ideas (e.g., stereotypes, assumptions, exaggerations) are often subjugated, denied, hidden, concealed from view. The only glaring empirical problem with Moskowitz's characterization is that these hidden biases are not actually hidden from "others." Those who feel or face the effects of white American implicit biases know all too well that white Americans often carry resentment and anger directed explicitly or implicitly towards black Americans.

Second, and most significant, is that these negative biases as well as the egalitarian sensibilities seemingly keeping these biases in check, are rooted in anxiety, an inability to accept the uncertain dimensions of embodied limitation and uncertain social life lived with others. For many white Americans, *any* failure is always regarded as a moral failure. Following from a logic of distinction, this anxiety is assuaged through various manipulations of distinctions, of limits. Consequentially, implicit bias research helps to understand how prejudices and violence play out in the social world, as ideas find certain purchase in uncertain social soil. But even implicit bias discourse and research may fall victim to an inability to embrace uncertainty.

W.E.B. DuBois famously asked "How does it feel to be a problem?" as his measure of the black American experience.[80] An uncertain humanism poses a connected, but distinct question to white Americans: How does it feel to be a problem-maker? Unable to deal with feelings of uncertainty, white Americans have been very good at constructing "problems" to be "solved," as if an equation. Implicit bias discourse aids in some extremely practical and important ways, such as guarding ourselves against ourselves whether on juries, hiring committees, or as law enforcement – who literally hold human life or death in their (state-sanctioned) hands. However, a "problem" of problem-making is not solvable through reliance on specific strategies designed to save us from ourselves. Just as the attempt to escape hell reinforces our status as devils, so too do numerically or scientifically based efforts to put social bandages on existential bullet holes. If the analogy is unclear, implicit bias discourse does well to react to some of the collateral damage done by our flights from uncertainty, but offers little in the way of addressing the all-too-human fear of an all-too-human uncertainty. The problem of uncertainty is rendered affectively as "a problem" precisely because we have been problem-makers. Appreciative of what "on the ground" impact implicit bias research might have in offsetting race-based or racially charged murders and other crimes by the state and against African Americans and other marginalized groups, uncertain humanism is more concerned to sit with and within and as a problem. Uncertain humanism asks: How does it feel, white America, to not have a solution?

FOCUSING A LIMITED RELIGIOUS OUTLOOK

How ought such a culture, or such a religious orientation, be situated hermeneutically after having contextualized the hell of the Imago Superlata and our (limited) efforts to escape it? Here I offer another swerve, an analogy, that I hope is helpful in distinguishing a limited religious outlook from a white religious outlook. I suggest a means of focusing attention on those at the margins of "hell" and what those margins mean for those of us at the center learning how to "number our days." The condition of radical contingency is the basic human condition. I'm not interested in debating what, exactly, that *is*; radical contingency is merely the hermeneutical valence I attach to what it means to exist as a human in forced community. Hell, as described above, is not this basic condition, but an exaggeration of it by those who know not the social influence of their anxiety attached to death. Figure 4.1 shows my self-made bookshelf and books, seen from the standpoint of where I have written the bulk of this book, my basement. In this example, this image represents radical contingency. In what follows I am going to compare it to the raw materials of life presented to us.

"Religion," as a strategy for identity formation that relies on social and ideological distinctions and that responds to and out of radical contingency, can be thought of as a process of looking through a telescope. As a way to theoretically situate this usage of photographs, I turn to Susan Sontag, who suggests that photographs offer a way to flatten, transmit to many different contexts, the particular perils of one context. In her follow-up to 1977's *On Photography*, Sontag's final book before her death, *Regarding the Pain of Others* (2003), she explores the power of photography to connect various groups to situations of human suffering and pain. She notes that "in contrast to a written account – which, depending on its complexity of thought, reference, and vocabulary, is pitched at a larger or smaller readership – a photograph

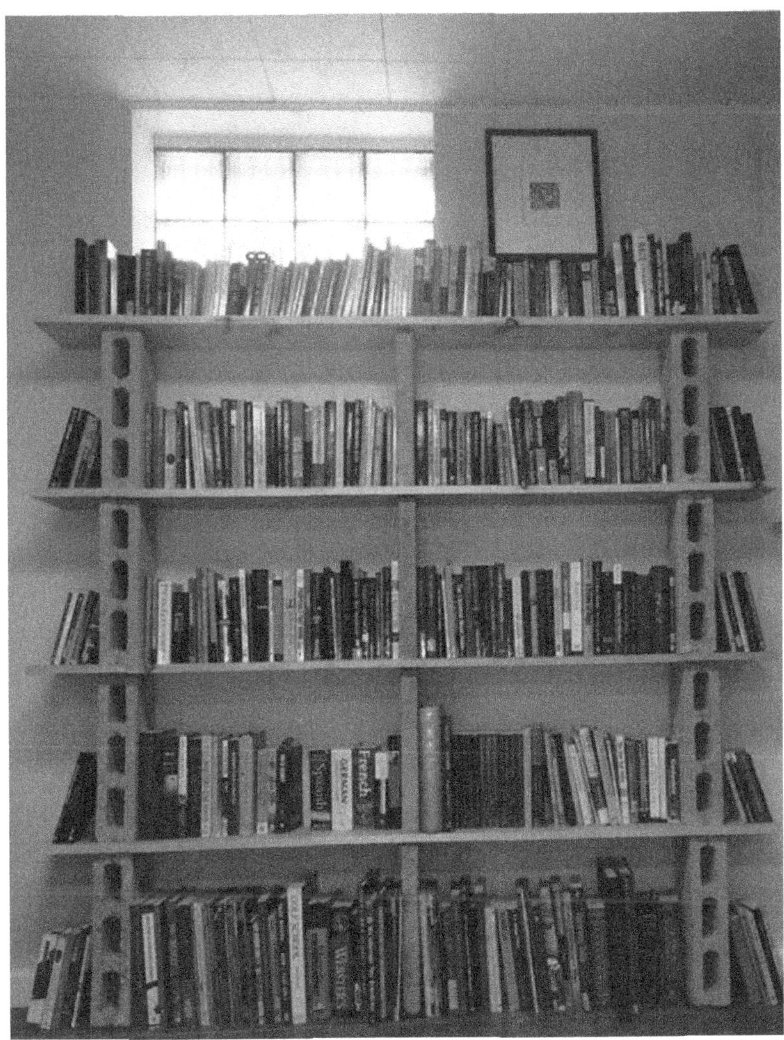

FIGURE 4.1 Personal photo representing radical contingency.

has only one language and is destined potentially for all."[81] Connecting Sontag's point to my above reference to "devils," I am interested to express to this particular context and to contexts of various sorts, what a limited religious outlook might "look like" seen from a white religious perspective. Also like Sontag's focus on the suffering of others, a limited religious outlook is meant to recast analytic focus towards the suffering of those at social margins and indeed, all those who suffer. If Figure 4.1 represents radical contingency, Figure 4.2 demonstrates the vantage point offered by white religious formation. This is the perspective of "devils" or "gods," depending on the moral valence we attach to those social actors.

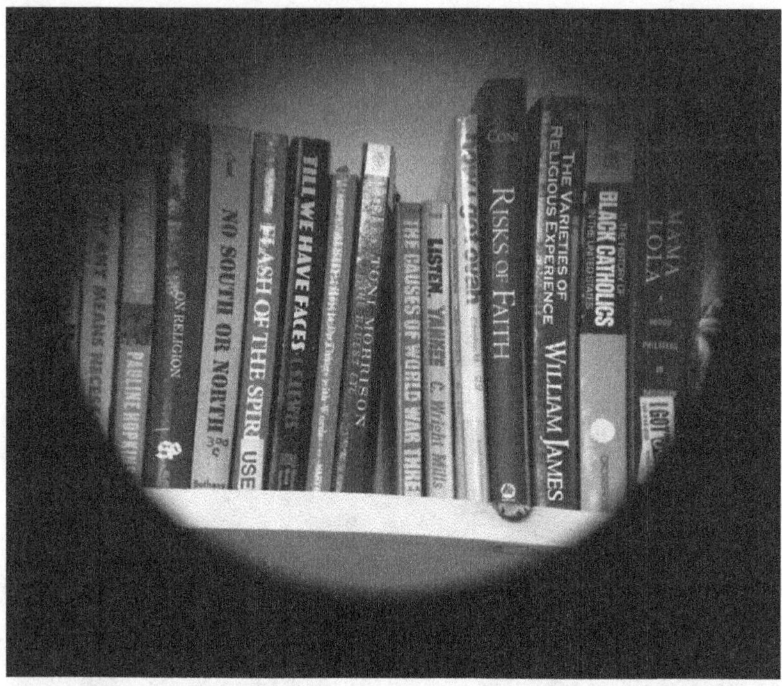

FIGURE 4.2 Personal photo representing an Imago Superlata outlook on radical contingency, an exaggeration of radical contingency.

Seen here focused on one of the shelves from the first image (right side, second shelf from top), like a telescope white religion offers a larger – exaggerated – view of someone or something. Looking through its small lens, shutting out the world and producing *black* margins through a focus on something specific, white religion magnifies and gives a sense of clarity to the viewer (i.e., the adherent). Adherents or "viewers" come to feel a sense of greater *certainty* about what is on the other side of the lens. A shelf of previously unidentifiable books has been transformed into a manageable number of books with specific titles, page lengths, cover images, topics, and the like. A vast array of radically contingent possibilities have been limited and the remaining possibilities appear as more necessary and useful than before. In short, white religion blocks out most data through a principal distinction (e.g., the black margin) and tertiary distinctions then come into view. Part I of *White Lies* has involved schematizing this process of identifying through distinction and bringing into focus the damage done by peering through a telescope of religion (i.e. identity) – indeed, damage done by simply using an arbitrary telescope in the manner in which it is organized. White religion, like a telescope viewed as it is designed, brings social-life into seemingly clear relief and focus at the expense of leaving out other possibilities and data.

What I have in mind here is similar in *scope* to philosopher V. Y. Mudimbe's characterization of Paul Ricoeur's hermeneutic as fundamentally wed to a particular western Christian tradition. Pay particular attention to the way Mudimbe moves back and forth between ideological and sociological concerns:

> It is the very foundation of this tradition, and particularly the posited singularity and specificity of Israel's history, that gives meaning to Ricoeur's hermeneutics and its ambition. We are really facing something like a firmly closed circle which expands by exaggerating its own significance from the internal logic of a dialogue between its own different levels of meaning. In effect, from the margins of Christianity or, more exactly, from the margins of a Western history that institutionalized Christianity, how can one not think that what is going on here is a simple exegesis of a well-localized and tautologized tradition that seems incapable of imagining the very possibility of its exteriority, namely, that, in its margins, other historical traditions can also be credible, meaningful, respectable, and sustained.[82]

Mudimbe forces us to recognize that, even in reflexive hermeneutical efforts, our *focus* seemingly requires not only the use of margins as optical parameters, but an exaggeration of the very logic making possible our field of vision. This religious process is bound by levels of exaggerations that "seem incapable of imagining the very possibility of its exteriority" wherein we find not only margins qua margins, but whole histories and historicities with social weight equal to our own – if only white religion, "this tradition," would allow us to recognize them as such. White religion ends up unable to correct its own blindness because its very vision relies on such blindness.

Admitting that trying to set down the "telescope" of religion amounts to an attempt to escape "hell," instead a limited religious outlook intentionally looks through the "wrong" end of the telescope. In doing so, the viewer grows more sensitive to the margins and borders created by white religion. Those margins are not so much exposed (they are apparent in Figure 4.2, also) as they are dilated while the focused image is constricted. To the extent that identity is the object of any religious focus, a limited religious outlook finds that one's presumed identity as distinct and clear grows more uncertain and is replaced by a new identity based on decay, senescence, or dying. The center is enveloped by the margins. Like Modern poetry or the human sciences, those whose identities have been predicated on their exaggerated proximity to death at the margins inform those at the center of an encroaching, ominous death.

A reversed telescopic view "focuses" attention in at least three places. First, towards a growing awareness of the apparatus that once provided clarity and now prevents even a balanced portrait of things as such. Second, at the level of the margins – here seen as the literal borders of the telescope, but representing those at social margins, growing and moving closer and closer towards the object of focus. The telescope (as religion) is made up of human social processes and ideas, is representative of social actors writ large. This outlook does not focus attention on those at the margins directly, but privileges the difficulty of such focused attention. Hence, there is not a shift in focus from one location to another, but an increasing uncertainty and blurry effect promoting recognition of the difficulty. In Figure 4.3, those margins are social while the margins of religion (as the actual device, the telescope) are privileged in their limitations, as well. Third, focus is obtained at the level of a growing unfamiliarity and uncertainty about the object of focus. Religion as an arbitrary, albeit intensely significant social technological "device" akin to a telescope, is made clear. What religion does, as a function, is privileged. It becomes easier to "see" religion as a structuring and structured "principle of division," ordering and classifying the "natural and social world" through "antagonistic classes."[83] Such classes correspond to identity, broadly understood. The sense of one's own identity is made possible by ignoring those at the margins after having outlined the very parameters of those margins. That is, white religion distinguishes so as to focus attention on the self or the community understood to rest at a social center. A limited religious outlook, then, seeks to foreground such processes while acknowledging that greater visual clarity is never actually afforded.

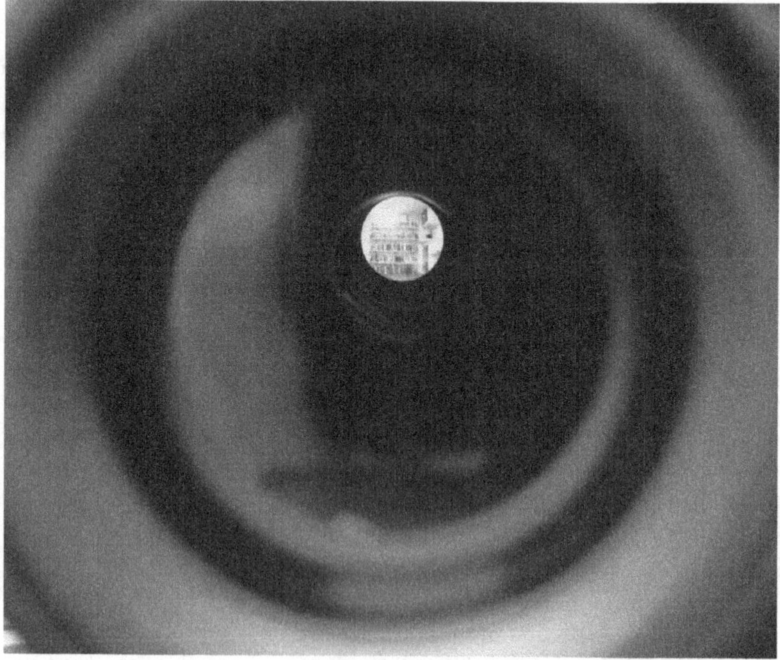

FIGURE 4.3 Personal photo representing a Limited Religious Outlook on radical contingency.

Moreover, a limited religious outlook "focuses" attention on the even more severe margins produced by the effects of a telescope. A photograph, as a snapshot of any place or activity, also serves in this capacity, with the function and formation of photos themselves aiding in producing the analogy of a limited religious outlook. As such, the actual images I use here can serve a function similar to that of the telescope photographed, as both the nature and function of "religion" are captured in the apparatuses of telescopes and photographs. As Sontag suggests, photos transmit the specific to the universal,[84] working *theologically* to technologically provide a semblance of certainty and clarity at the expense of bracketing out data that would emphasize insecurity.

Specifically, a limited religious outlook focuses on those forced to endure sacrifice and social suffering as a consequence of being on the social margins, furthest removed from a normative center, furthest removed from the god-idols reinforcing society as god. In the same way a backward telescope makes the viewer more acutely aware of the border of the telescope itself, a limited religious outlook foregrounds those social actors who make up the border framing god-idols – those who are sacrificed, and whose sacrifice focuses attention on the god-idol. The margins move so close to the center that, effectively, the limits of full social, or "religious," knowing are exposed by the immense variety of combinations of colors and shapes. Clarity is lost as what was once left out of sight bombards the center of the image. These border figures not only focus analytic attention on god-idols, but prevent the viewing of possibilities outside the telescope, outside of white religion. In other words, it becomes difficult to see white religion as anything other than the functional utility or justification of sacrifice.

The last level of recognition involves coming to terms with the loss of clarity and certainty provided by the reversed telescope. Here, the object photographed is pertinent to my argument. That is, I am talking again about a telescope specifically, turned in reverse. A limited religious outlook begins to chart how to move and think in a world that is blurry, uncertain, and surrounded by blackness. Such a shift would be a welcomed corrective to white religious blindness.

A social actor must decide through which end (of the telescope) to view the world: through an exaggeration of reality as clear and focused, or an exaggeration of the functional collateral damage done by such a telescopic positionality. White Americans are increasingly in a social position where they must decide which end of the telescope will provide their orientation. Exaggerations of radical contingency are telescopic snapshots, false representations of clarity and certainty. Transitioning towards an embrace of radical contingency, and offsetting its exaggerations, require the discomfort of walking through the world with shaky footing and uncertainty – perspectives become limited, one's placement in relation to the reversed telescope becomes uncertain – acknowledgement of the margins and borders becomes unavoidable; and also, those margins become difficult to ignore based on their growing numbers. A limited religious outlook prefers the focus on margins and uncertainty offered by a backward telescope. White Americans *choose* what to see, and what will be marginalized in the constitution of a field of vision. A limited religious outlook learns to see as if at a distance, in effort to make up for having lived with exaggerations – growing less concerned with the specifics of god-idols or adherence to them, and more interested in recognizing the panoply of options and possibilities that god-idols ignore.

Beginning to narrate a limited religious outlook

Reversing a telescope, figuratively of course, also focuses attention on the viewer – as in a mirror. A limited religious outlook, in learning more about what is not possible to say with certainty, finds that one's own story and its impact on the world come into fuzzy, but obvious relief. But what does a person do with such attention? A limited religious outlook frees adherents of white religion to turn the gaze on themselves without fear of reproach, interrogating their identity and finding that they can't quite see themselves in the same way as before. One comes to "see" that the visage of clarity offered by religion is determined by a series of self-imposed limitations and parameters. Reversing the telescopic vantage point of religiosity – of identity – where whites and those in places of privilege are concerned – transmutes social privilege into narrative permission.[85] The stage becomes set for the performance of one's own narrative without digression into solipsism and remaining open to expressing the fear of uncertainty.

Not all aspects of a story will be good, and the stories to be told by white religious adherents are pockmarked with the shame and dread noted by Bloom. But learning to "number our days" involves cultivating an understanding of the limits of religion and a subsequent decision to embrace those limits. This begins by telling the hard truths of white religious adherence translated into/as the stories of culture. But to force home the difficulty of a limited religious outlook: Think, for a moment, of the struggle of asking someone holding what they believe to be a "working" telescope, to grow comfortable with its use in reverse.[86] Such is the task now of convincing white Americans that their religion must be rejected. Functionally speaking, god-idols have worked to secure the feeling that one views the world through a telescope, focused and clarified – and that one is, as a result, super-human. The difficulty of convincing adherents that a backward telescope narrates a greater "focus" on equity and justice involves, then, narrating the story of the functional deaths of some of these god-idols, as well as narrating the functional *futility* of all god-idols in overcoming the most fundamental of human limits, physical mortality.

THE ORTHODOXY OF DEATH: STORYTELLING WITHOUT EXAGGERATING

Barbara Myerhoff (1935–1985) was a white, Jewish American anthropologist trained under anthropologist and cultural theorist Victor Turner. Her work would ultimately shape her life (and death). In tragic fashion, Myerhoff's work as an anthropologist actually became her life and death. She offers us a starting point for understanding that the hells we make are only ever "escaped" through embrace of those there with us. Cultural narratives, which demanded so much of Myerhoff's scholarly energy, might provide the vehicle for holding in balance cultural heritage, the finality and finitude of life, in ways that do not turn us into devils.

In the foreword to Myerhoff's *Number Our Days* (1979), Turner situates Myerhoff's insights through an idea popular at the time,[87] that of *homo narrans*, or "humankind as story-teller, implying that culture in general – specific cultures, and the fabric of meaning that constitutes any single human existence – is the 'story' we tell about ourselves."[88] A limited religious outlook takes narrative and storytelling as a powerful method, as means for coping with the uncertainty posed by a limited religious outlook and for describing what is seen of oneself in a mirror. In the previous chapter, I suggested that westerners have no culture. This may be true in the socio-ethical sense I suggested then, but it is not the whole truth from a historical standpoint. All people have a culture; whether it is celebrated, acknowledged, or hidden is a different story. This turn to culture leads further to story. And as I hope to demonstrate, our stories provide the means to reject our status as "devils" if we learn to embrace those with us in hell.

Sartre was wrong to cast his characters in *No Exit* as dead (even if he may have intended to make the point that because we will die, we act as if we are already dead); it is the dying that creates social hells. Coming to terms with our status as dying might allow us to more easily embrace those in hell with us, saving ourselves not from death, but through a shared concern that we die with others. In doing so, we might not escape hell, but we might no longer act like devils. Garcin rejected the social other because they expressed to him a version of himself cast by the other as if holding a mirror. Hell is other people only if we can't stand to embrace the devilish vision we hold of ourselves and that holds us from the possibility of escaping sameness so that we might see the difference that marks us as worth real value. After such a shift we will no longer be devils because we will have embraced finally what is worth embracing – our cultural roots that we have until now largely rejected for the sake of empty worship of god-idols.

What do stories responsive to white religion look like? Simply put, they would be stories that did not hinge on the construction of the other, but would mark intense wrestling with one's own cultural inheritance, those pieces we would want to celebrate and those we would want to reject. The work of Myerhoff helps in beginning to make sense of the meanings lodged within the stories we tell as white Americans. Being Jewish, she brings an acute and longstanding cultural heritage to her work and concomitantly offers a model that troubles uncritical renderings of who is or isn't white. Perhaps because of these nuances offered by her efforts, Myerhoff provides a distillation of what white religious reclamation of cultural heritage might look like. According to Myerhoff, "Always in these stories … the integrity of the person over time was their essential quest. In the process they created personal myths, not saying that it had all been worthwhile, neither that it had not."[89] Myerhoff's life and death imply that such a "quest" occurs through the narrative we craft of our own lives. Ontology, cultural meaning, and story come together in Myerhoff's *Number Our Days* as a triumph, of sorts, over binary rigid thinking that too often presupposes new to old, good to bad, orthodox to reformed, white to black, etc. To achieve this project Myerhoff looks in the direction of an elderly and dying community, only to later realize that this very work will provide her the eventual means to accept her own death.

Myerhoff, having been diagnosed with terminal cancer, came to embrace the beauty and structure of her cultural roots in a self-isolating, orthodox Jewish community. At one point, she is asked a question by a member of the community: "Could you be one of these [Orthodox] women?"[90] Myerhoff thinks carefully and notes that though she loves the rituals (as an ethnographer), they come with restrictions, and she couldn't follow those restrictions for more than an hour (as an adherent). Two weeks before her death, she recants on her earlier comments about restrictions. She notes that her earlier comments had not placed the restrictions in the context of a "god within." She'd thought of such restrictions in terms of something external, something she would have to bow to, such as "the priesthood or [an external] god giving her rules."[91]

Now frail and on the verge of death, she recognizes those religious and cultural restrictions as self-imposed and that self-imposition seems to give new life to their worth and value – more precisely, to the restrictions' ability to recalibrate human worth and ability in the face of death. Facing physical death had meant a new awareness and appreciation for limitations, those internally imbued, as honest assessments of physical and emotional human limits. These physical limits, framed in and with and against social and other sorts of limits, come to be seen as indicative of the need for human community. Myerhoff remains aware of the dangers posed by community, but comes to find importance and belonging in such a community having come to understand it as a constellation of other similarly limited humans. Speaking of her illness, she notes "suddenly here are restrictions. I can't walk the way I did. Eat. Breathe. The basic functions. Mother my children the way I did. Every day presents me with new [restrictions]. And every day, some days more than others, I have the choice as to whether I see those as restrictions or doorways to other possibilities."[92]

A limited religious outlook finds such self-imposed cultural and physical health restrictions as "doorways to other possibilities," in that through such restrictions, physical death is made conceivable. More pointedly, through limitations, hell is hermeneutically "escaped" in an ethical sense, because the view of hell itself is restricted by having recast that view towards those once on the margins of vision. A limited religious outlook is an outlook that seeks to reckon with human limitations and restrictions, and ultimately death, as an opening of new possibilities for human life flourishing. A limited religious outlook like this, with the help and support of culture, reverses the functional efficacy of the god idea. When one has relinquished god-idols in the face of death, the death-dealing god of society is transmuted into death as a god – not in the Heideggerian sense of a fetish, but as promoting humility and radical contingency. Death of god-idols comes in the form of submission to death and uncertainty: acceptance of that which cannot be avoided.

This is the central argument of Part II of *White Lies*: that a death-dealing and death-denying society would do well to begin dying with others in the sense of understanding death as a fundamental experience relatable by and to all – thus, an orthodoxy of death; flattening difference across different domains and social contexts such that the other in ourselves is made more palatable. Such a foundation will only be possible upon rejecting the manipulation of death enacted through white lies. The final two chapters of this book offer strategies for such dying. There is no triumph, no new birth in death; there is finality in a physical sense, even if there are "doorways to other possibilities." Such doorways, however, require a new understanding of what had once been restrictions masquerading as possibilities, and what are now possibilities arriving in the form of restrictions. For Myerhoff, death transformed her into an "Orthodox" woman – in a different, but equally "restricted" sense. She submitted to the orthodoxy of death, relying on her own community. But she did have the freedom, indeed the responsibility, to come to terms with what was happening in the final chapters of her life. She was learning that by limiting our expectations about religion's usefulness, we are freed to take full advantage of the limits at the heart of any religious imagination.[93]

An uncertain humanism, through adherence to the orthodoxy of mortality, comes to impose limits on self rather than fearing them coming from something external. For instance, Myerhoff, like many white women in the 1970s, had certain feminist sensibilities such that the patriarchal cultural framework of the Jewish communities she studied were at odds with many of her convictions. Hence, the question was not simply "could you be Orthodox?," but "could you be an Orthodox *woman*?" Remarkably, and as if to cast home the full import of her turn to narrative culture and its limits that might recalibrate senses of self and other in the face of death, she agrees in the final weeks leading up to her death to receive a Jewish get, the Jewish "divorce," similar to an annulment. Having been divorced previously, and in the constant audience of Orthodox Jewish men and women who want her to make good on Jewish custom before her death, she agrees. She is intentional about embracing this cultural ritual even though it flies in the face of many of the contemporary ideological perspectives that give her a sense of certainty and identity. In the face of the orthodoxy of death, Myerhoff ends up an Orthodox woman, after all.

NARRATING OUR DEATH *WITH* OTHERS

Myerhoff's acceptance of a "get" is an acute instance of embrace of one's radical contingency. In fact, it is also reclamation of radical contingency through an uncertain adoption of a cultural vestige working to exaggerate the radical contingency of yet others in other instances. A limited religious outlook is not concerned with the keeping or jettisoning of rituals necessarily, whether big or small, but with vantage point and hermeneutical outlook. There are ideas and practices that ought be jettisoned, the ritual of lynching and the belief in the soul being two examples among many, but a limited religious outlook is primarily concerned with the transformation of the means of exaggerating the radical contingency of others into the means through which one's radical contingency can be calibrated. Rituals and beliefs formerly exaggerating the radical contingency of others become narrative vehicles for telling the stories of our own radically contingent, limited, mortal, communal experiences. Myerhoff offers both methodological and existential clarity as to how stories told in the face of death offer a means of moving against a death-dealing social world.

Full embrace of one's own culture, the good and the bad, is important for a limited religious outlook, yet this outlook knows and guards against the continued embrace of the god-idols born from a specific culture. Functionally speaking, white religion offers adherents a sleight-of-hand diversion wherein radical contingency is responded to through the notion that society is god – a mechanism promising a temporary flight from death and limitation. Such is certainly one way to deal with death. Indeed, it is a popular option. Yet, in contradistinction to these white lies, and in an admittedly structurally framed nod to nature or disorder, etc., a limited religious outlook embraces radical contingency through culture. Working with the people of Fairfax while coming to terms with her own impending death, the wisdom of Myerhoff's work and life/death have coalesced into clarity:

> They presented me with an organic life. A life that was all of a piece. It had a totality, because of the way the people knew each other, because of the deep intertwining of their lives at every moment, on every level, on every relationship, and because of this envelope of belief that enfolds them all, so that there almost can't be a separate word for religion. It's not a separate category or activity; it's embedded in everything.[94]

Here, there is no binary distinction at work. Such a limited religious outlook situates a *real* – limited, creative, possible, dying – culture at the center of any orientation. Myerhoff follows Geertz; I want to simply focus attention on such a position as a response to the functional problem of god-idols constituting society as god. In shorthand form, having learned from Myerhoff, within a limited religious outlook death becomes the only sameness cutting across all our distinctions, and a focus on our many distinct cultures (i.e., Jewish, Irish, Italian, French, English, etc.) makes this perspectival shift both possible and more tolerable. Stated differently, the blurring of distinctions in the life/death of Myerhoff suggests that the final "swerve" against hell involves breaking down the distinction between life and death through a focus on narrative and cultural affinity. This turn to culture is not a flight away from death, but a flight towards activities and ideas and human connectedness that make the life of death tolerable. The embrace of radical contingency situates death as god, and culture the stuff we do as we wait on the impending theophany that cuts across all difference.

Myerhoff's work engages questions of narrative, identity, belonging, community, cultural affinity, death, and the elderly. Moreover, she clearly blurs lines between disciplinary boundaries and medium of presentation for her work. She was instrumental in bringing videography and documentary film-making into the anthropological norm, even winning an Academy Award for a documentary (*Number Our Days*, 1977) framed around her research at the Aliyah Senior Citizens Center in Southern California in the 1970s. The book by the same name arrived two years after the film. In the monograph treatment of her fieldwork at Aliyah Senior Citizens Center, she relays her anxiety about losing easy distinctions:

> I spent a great deal of time agonizing about how to label what I was doing – was it anthropology or a personal quest? I never fully resolved the question. I used many conventional anthropological methods and asked many typical questions, but when I had finished, I found my descriptions did not resemble most anthropological writings.[95]

In an embrace of radical contingency, an anxiety of awareness – not denial – starts the process. Myerhoff grows aware of the usefulness of self-imposed limits as she is forced to reckon with intensifying physical limits. Her individual body serves as a microcosm for understanding the workings of the larger community, and perhaps even society in general. Myerhoff's living death (and what she chose to do with it) offers white Americans a canvas for symbolization and cultural expression in the wake of the impending death of what has come before, or the imminent physical deaths all people face. Myerhoff dovetails with Mary Douglas in this regard.

Myerhoff knew early on that her work was not in keeping with "traditional" anthropology, and expressing herself in ways similar to Bloom's "swerve" and yet drastically different, she allows that anxiety to fuel her turn towards storytelling. Like Pinn's theological expression of African American humanists who have come before him, Myerhoff turns to the stories of Jews who have lived/died before her. She learns how to number her own days with this storytelling. Rather than seeking to blur priority and authority, Myerhoff literally turns to telling the stories of others who have come before. This first methodological point is important because the embrace of radical contingency involves the relinquishment of order, authority, and priority. Rather than blurring solipsistic lines of demarcation (priority and authority), she chooses to blur methodological lines in response to that very anxiety, crossing ethnography, folklore and myth, biography, cultural studies and more in the process. Myerhoff's "bad" ethnography, this methodological miscegenation, responded eloquently and powerfully to the demands of human beings towards death (in community). It involved letting go, understanding that it's okay and normal to ask such questions of order, but it is equally possible – and preferable – to accept the blurred lines of narrative because definite lines of demarcation produce god-idols that make death difficult to accept. Perhaps the first structural distinction out of which the sacred/profane emerges is that posed between physical life and death, transposed in/as social distinctions. If distinctions within a white religious perspective allow for focus on social centers at the expense of those on margins, then a blurring of distinctions might allow for stories told from social centers to take into greater account the concerns of those on the margins and to resist the storyteller's own desire for certainty.

These lines Myerhoff preferred to blur in her work and life took on a more pointed meaning when later in her life, while engaged in fieldwork in the Fairfax community of voluntarily isolated Jews in Southern California, she was diagnosed with terminal cancer. Her time with that community saw her turn towards cultural resources in the face of death, and this turn is important for understanding any limited religious outlook. But it is important to note that her realizations, in that final time of her "last fieldwork"[96] at Fairfax, were grounded in the wisdom born of the time she had spent, years before, in the Aliyah Seniors Center. Her time spent with the elderly and dying prepared Myerhoff well for her own death.

Another of the significant insights from Myerhoff's *Number Our Days* (1979) comes in the form of realizing that embrace of radical contingency does not mean embrace of the other, in the popular sense that racism will be erased through acceptance of diversity. Rather, the embrace of radical contingency is the embrace of one's heritage, the good and bad that it brings and has brought. In philosophical terms, it is not enough to see the face of the other cry out; responding to white religion demands seeing yourself as the other and understood anew. Where white Americans are concerned, this embrace of the hell of death involves taking responsibility for the worst of one's culture, such as the KKK, homophobes, etc. In hell, embrace of the other is embrace of devils. At best, a limited religious outlook uses the face of the other to see *oneself* as other – and this is an enterprise more demanding than engaging the other as such. For a brief grounded example, hiring an African American as a Chief Diversity Officer at a dominant institution is using the face of the other; hiring a Caucasian in the same capacity is the more difficult, but perhaps more necessary, decision. Myerhoff situates my point in its ethnographic expression.

> Working with one's own society, and more specifically, those of one's own ethnic and familial heritage, is perilous and much more difficult … . Identifying with the "Other," – Indians, Chicanos, if one is Anglo, blacks if one is white, males if one is female – is an act of imagination … . Identifying with what one is now and will be someday is quite a different process.[97]

Much has been made in area studies about turning to black sources and norms as a corrective to racism embedded in theology, anthropology, or any other discourse. But such a turn is not enough – it is important, but not enough – unless it is accompanied by a turn back towards one's own community. Myerhoff learned that the other is not nearly as dangerous or difficult to understand as the other in oneself. In Myerhoff's case, that community was a Jewish community. In the case of white Americans, what is required is a turn back towards white churches and ethnic communities of origin – the spaces and places where god-idols like whiteness have been produced – with the clarity of uncertainty offered by coming to terms with death, along with the confidence in knowing that those spaces have something to teach and learn about numbering our days. Such is required of a limited religious outlook. As if Myerhoff is describing white religion in practice, she contextualizes the anxiety that makes this learning to die for others so difficult:

> An insidious circularity has developed – ignorance, based in part on denial of our future, leading to fear and rejection of the elderly, engendering guilt that is often expressed as neglect or mistreatment, then more guilt, avoidance and ignorance; ageism is characterized by the same self-fulfilling processes that operate in racism. Our anxiety about the future is guaranteed by our own behavior, assuring that our worst unspoken, unspeakable fear will be realized: Our children will treat us as we treat our parents.[98]

Paraphrased through Bloom, we regenerate hell on earth with our fears about distinguishing ourselves from the places to which we owe our inheritance. Myerhoff situates the anxiety of influence in the stark clarity of a problem, a social problem. If Myerhoff is to be taken seriously, we are left to realize that more than a swerve is necessary if we are to respond adequately to the social problems we face. To press home the significance of Myerhoff, against the limited efficacy of Bloom, the "hells" in which so many find themselves, having only been strong enough to "swerve," can be escaped through the embrace of the ultimate source of the anxiety described by Bloom: death. To this end, poetry is "saved" if its self-immolation is embraced, allowing poetry to be born again, anew, outside the confines of the anxiety of influence guiding Modernity. In like manner, the white community, the topic of this book, might finally "escape" the hell of its own making, and consequentially escape its status as a society of white devils, if it embraces the uncertainty offered by the certainty of its death. Recognition of such death, ironically, involves no longer trying to escape the fundamental "hell" imposed on the human being by death.[99] Understanding that the anxiety of influence is ruptured not by appeals to the other, but by forcefully squaring with one's own heritage, history, and culture, Myerhoff's interest in the elderly is a fitting place to learn such wisdom. From the standpoint of a limited religious outlook, much of that anxiety stems from the anxiety of limitation and mortality. Anxiety is self-fulfilling; overcoming it requires first knowing it intimately and listening – as an ethnographer – to the stories it produces. Learning to tell one's own story, as Myerhoff learned and teaches now, is always to tell the story of one's death. It is to write one's own eulogy, with the tools of cultural heritage. Such narrating begins the process of responding to white religion. In telling our stories, the face of death is exposed as our face. White masks – all masks – deny death and thereby deny life.

Stories matter because people are simultaneously "too busy to stop and shape a tale with grace and art [as a trained novelist, anthropologist, or theologian], but too alive to imagination and verbal expression to be silent ... and its roots were in the heart and bones and genes."[100] In narrative, physical death and social death collide into possibilities for new life in old traditions. Such stories allow the formerly dead and dying – that is, the dying who become satans in their denial of death – to be transformed with new life, as suggested by one of Myerhoff's wisest informants:

> But finally, this group brought out such beautiful memories, not always so beautiful, but still, all the pictures came up. It touched the layers of the kind that it was on those dead people already. It was laying on them like layers, separate layers of earth, and all of a sudden in this class I feel it coming up like lava. It just melted away the earth from all those people. It melted away, and they became alive. And then to me it looked like they were never dead.[101]

If freed from the anxiety of having to escape that heritage, through culture, we appear in all our complexity and terrible beauty – looking as if we "were never dead."

NARRATING THE DEATH OF GOD-IDOLS

> And here it was. It was, in a way mine all along. It was what I belonged to without knowing it. And I suppose that's a treasure really, that they've given to me. If, if I can in my work, as an anthropologist, at the same time, make it clear to others who they are and what they feel and what they have ... if I can take what they've shown me and pass that through me and out into the world, then my work is done.
>
> *Barbara Myerhoff*[102]

Everyone dies. Physically, we all die at some point. Socially, too, communities are born, live, and die in accord with their specific quantities of members as well as the degree of power wielded by those communities. Everyone's days are numbered, as it were. But not everyone learns to number their days, and not all deaths are arrived at in the same way. A limited religious outlook encourages and cultivates an awareness and commitment to living/dying for and with others – that is, coming to final terms with one's own radical contingency. White Americans must begin to narrate our death with others; that is, relying on our community for our individual deaths (however conceived), and relying on that white community to remind us that we die together. That which collectively binds and has bound us together – a fear of death and uncertainty crossed and marked onto black bodies, historically – must be allowed to "die" so that we might learn to die together, within and extending beyond the white community. We must unite first through recognizing that our cultural inheritances denied for the sake of giving birth to god-idols are able to be recalibrated towards limiting our very reliance on those god-idols. On these efforts, we might unite first in this recalibration. We might then open ourselves (as white) to new aggregate[103] constellations of people, all of us, together, dying, narrating a new story of death with others.

As a scholar, my presentation of a limited religious outlook serves multiple ends. I am elucidating the "not always so beautiful" memories of a white community learning how to die, my own community of origin, and I see it as my responsibility as a scholar to "take what they've shown me and pass that through me and out into the world."[104] Only, my story must privilege the facet of our stories we have chosen to ignore: death and our death-dealing ways. Also, to ensure that white cultural resources are used as much and as often as possible to teach those at the center of a white religious orientation how to "number our days." Death, as a heuristic emerging from the only story shared by us all – that we all die – works to ensure that my telling of white heritage remains humble and uncertain. Failure to guard against certainty is the easiest path/past causing devils to remain in hell.

Myerhoff offers a model for learning to die with others because she comes to understand that our means of numbering our days occurs through embrace of one's cultural heritage, the stories about us told by us and by others like us, through a hermeneutic register of self-imposed restrictions and limitations. Her death arriving from cancer, and her identity as Jewish, do not negate her serving as a model for all white Americans to come to terms with the possibility of an impending social death. Such a social death will surely lead to more violence and white lies unless we are able to overcome our anxiety of death's influence through acceptance of that influence in shaping our social trajectory to this point. (Death is death; and death is always death-dealing unless embraced by the dying.) Whether for entire communities or individuals, Myerhoff offers a means of coping through a focus on cultural narratives. Though such narratives can cut in positive and negative ways, held in sight of radical contingency, they offer a resource to anyone interested in responding to white lies. In death, Myerhoff found her community and came to an awareness of her responsibility to that community, a community she says was "what she belonged to all along without knowing it."[105] By listening to that community, and relaying its stories as she heard and understood them, she offered herself and offers us now the narrative permission to tell the good and bad stories of our lives, our hatred of others and our love for others.

This chapter has told the story of how we – those devils remaining in hell – might be taught to "number our days." In what follows of *White Lies*, I seek to follow Myerhoff's hermeneutical example – not to cast her as a martyr to an unjust social system, but because in the face of physical death she found the courage to respond to cultural heritage – the good and the bad of it – in ways transformative for herself and for those around her. For "devils" like myself consigned by our own purported attempts to escape hell, to remain in hell, the hell of death requires the embrace of those within it. Through the stories that follow, those of the life and work of Carson McCullers and Lillian Smith, today's contemporary adherents to white religion might grow to understand the value of our cultural heritage, the importance of stories in the recalibration of human responsibility towards others, and the courage to begin living with uncertainty, limitation, and mortality in ways that are more life affirming than has been the norm to this point. Situating death as a kind of god requires telling and arriving at the passion narratives each person holds as a possibility for their death; that is, what is the risk or danger we are willing to expose ourselves to as we more equitably *focus* attention on the risks and dangers faced by those on social margins, historically? A limited religious outlook, in the hazy twilight of American religion, finds reason to believe that white Americans might hold within us the possibility for promoting a more equitable social arrangement. This, even though the possibility will likely involve letting go of something even more precious than life or certainty: eternal life.

Notes

1 Harold Bloom, *The Anxiety of Influence: A Theory of Poetry* (Oxford University Press, 1997), 26.
2 Original source unknown. Quoted in Barbara Myerhoff, *Number Our Days*, second printing edition (E. P. Dutton, 1979), xiv, 215.
3 Myerhoff, *Number Our Days*, 32.
4 Malcolm X, *The Autobiography of Malcolm X: As Told to Alex Haley* (Ballantine Books, 1992), 161.
5 Malcolm X, *Autobiography*, 183.
6 Malcolm X, "A Summing Up: Louis Lomax Interviews Malcolm X | Teaching American History," 1963, accessed December 15, 2014, http://teachingamericanhistory.org/library/document/a-summing-up-louis-lomax-interviews-malcolm-x/
7 I do not mean to suggest that this interpretive shift would fix all the world's problems, but that for the community of white Americans, focused attention to the inescapability of death is fairly novel. Talking *about* death, and learning how to die, to this extent, are very different things.
8 See, for instance, Stanley Hauerwas and L. Gregory Jones, *Why Narrative? Readings in Narrative Theology* (Wipf and Stock Publishers, 1997). Unlike narrative theology which seemingly seeks to expound upon classical and neo-orthodox theological endeavors, I am trying to trouble the efficacy of such efforts.
9 Russell T. McCutcheon, *Critics Not Caretakers: Redescribing the Public Study of Religion* (SUNY Press, 2001).
10 Many have told the story of white cultural inheritance, in terms of its social impact on others through the constitution of another *as* other. But most who have told such stories have not been white. This chapter attempts, in limited fashion, to address why this has been the case and how more white people – white Americans, in particular – might begin to tell their own stories more effectively and more fully.
11 Jean-Paul Sartre, *No Exit and Three Other Plays*, trans. Stuart Gilbert, reissue edition (Vintage, 1989), 45.
12 David Drake, *Sartre* (Haus Publishing, 2005), 60.
13 "The Foxification of News." *The Economist*, July 7, 2011, accessed December 16, 2014, http://www.economist.com/node/18904112

14 Jean-Paul Sartre, Preface to *No Exit!*, quoted in David Detmer, *Sartre Explained: From Bad Faith to Authenticity* (Open Court, 2011), 149.
15 For background on this point, I suggest two excellent volumes: Gabriella Gutiérrez y Muhs, Yolanda Flores Niemann, Carmen G. González, and Angela P. Harris, eds., *Presumed Incompetent: The Intersections of Race and Class for Women in Academia* (Utah State University Press, 2012); and Roderick A. Ferguson, *The Reorder of Things: The University and Its Pedagogies of Minority Difference* (University of Minnesota Press, 2012).
16 Bloom, *The Anxiety of Influence*, 10.
17 Ibid., 8–10.
18 Ibid.,14–16.
19 Ibid., 10.
20 Ibid., 42.
21 Ibid., 14.
22 Ibid.
23 Ibid., 45.
24 Ibid., 30.
25 Michelle Alexander, *The New Jim Crow: Mass Incarceration in the Age of Colorblindness* (The New Press, 2010).
26 Bloom, *The Anxiety of Influence*, 20–21.
27 Elijah Muhammad, "By Nature the Devil is Afraid of the Black Man," in *The Theology of Time*, Subject Indexed Abridged Version (Elijah Muhammad Books, 2004).
28 Malcolm X, *Autobiography*, 266, original emphasis.
29 Bloom, *The Anxiety of Influence*, 21.
30 Ibid.
31 Ibid.
32 Ibid., 19.
33 Ibid., 10.
34 John Hollander, The New York Times Book Review, Harold Bloom's *The Anxiety of Influence: A Theory of Poetry*, March 4, 1973, accessed March 10, 2015, http://www.nytimes.com/books/98/11/01/specials/bloom-influence.html
35 Bloom, *The Anxiety of Influence*, 10.
36 For further reading beyond *The Anxiety of Influence*, I would strongly suggest Harold Bloom, *The Art of Reading Poetry* (HarperCollins, 2005).
37 Bloom, *The Anxiety of Influence*, 32.
38 Cornel West, *Prophesy Deliverance!* (Westminster John Knox Press, 2002 [1982]), 44.
39 Bloom, *The Anxiety of Influence*, 45.
40 Myerhoff, *Number Our Days*, 54.
41 Ibid.
42 Here, the Jewish context is not meant to echo supersessionist ideas, but is focused on "context" in the abstract (although when time permits, I am eager to learn more of Jewish identity and its relationship to white identity). The Jewish context described here offers a portrait of human complexity rather than a locus for placing blame for that complexity.
43 Myerhoff, *Number Our Days*, 60.
44 Ibid., 74–5.
45 Important to note, I am intentionally not outlining Pinn's more established and systematic brand of humanism, such as developed in Anthony B. Pinn, *African American Humanist Principles: Living and Thinking Like the Children of Nimrod* (Palgrave Macmillan, 2004). I value this work, but for my interests here, the uncertainty of a newly developed humanist orientation – as offered in *Why, Lord?* –is more helpful. This organic and open-ended definition of humanism is adapted from a brief, albeit memorable, passage where Pinn as a young ephebe declares that "human liberation is more important than the maintenance of any religious symbol, sign, canon, or icon."

In the wake of a corpus of books clarifying his muted concern for "liberation" with a realist assessment of such possibilities, in keeping with an expansive, culturally mitigated understanding of religion and its signs, icons, and the like, Pinn's early words here provide foundation for uncertain humanism, because they distill the ontological and ethical core of humanism down to this concern for humans. In light of a variety of definitions and evolutions in the crafting of African American humanism as a religious option, Pinn's early description works better here than later robust definitions as it evokes ethical decision and uncertainty, two foci of this uncertain humanism. See Anthony B. Pinn, *Why, Lord? Suffering and Evil in Black Theology* (Continuum International Publishing Group, 1999), 11.

46 Worth and ability correspond to these two exaggerations operative as the foundation of the Imago Superlata, as explored throughout *White Lies* and outlined directly in Chapter 3.

47 Pinn, *Why, Lord?*, 10–11.

48 Bloom, *The Anxiety of Influence,* 14.

49 Here, I feel it is important to note that I am not critiquing Pinn through a kind of intellectual bad faith, in that it is obvious that *Why, Lord?* is not concerned with white contextual issues. Rather, as Pinn's concerns in much of *Why, Lord?* are parallel to my own here, I am using him as a rhetorical model and interlocutor. Where a white context is my concern, then I could not in good faith actually suggest that Pinn makes this swerve. I leave that up to those with contexts not my own. Here, however, I mean to weave in and out of criticism and celebration in a literary way, "writing" an interpretive vision that might be useful for white Americans and white scholars of religion to think through their relationships with colleagues, talking partners, and data coming from contexts not our own.

50 William R. Jones, author of *Is God a White Racist?* (1973), is an early thinker whom Pinn does not "swerve" away from so much as he takes Jones's philosophical argument and applies it to theology quite squarely and effectively.

51 Pinn, *Why, Lord?*, 10–11.

52 Ibid., 141.

53 Ibid.

54 If this argument runs as logically or ethically "weak" in the sense that it is paradoxical – or I seem to want to have my cake and eat it too – that is my goal: a weak strand of thought, as in the "weak" humanism outlined by Pinn that wants to retain belief in god while focusing concerns on the human. Though not concerned with "god," to be sure my argument is "weak" given Pinn's analysis offered in *Why, Lord?* "Strength" comes through denial and refusal to be denied.

55 Bloom, *The Anxiety of Influence*, 6.

56 Ibid., 6–7.

57 Anthony B. Pinn, *The End of God-Talk: An African American Humanist Theology* (Oxford University Press, 2012), 5.

58 Pinn, *The End of God-Talk*, 5.

59 Bernard Lonergan, *Method in Theology* (University of Toronto Press, 1990), 341.

60 Pinn, *The End of God-Talk*, 30, all of chapter two.

61 Oscar Wilde, *The Picture of Dorian Gray*, quoted in Anthony Pinn, *Writing God's Obituary: How a Good Methodist Became a Better Atheist* (Prometheus Books, 2014), 5.

62 See, for instance, Anthony B. Pinn's *The End of God-Talk*. Pinn's humanism has always been more focused on uncertainty than most options, but is still too certain that there is no god. The point is not whether god *is* or *is not*, but in using the uncertainty of the issue to produce particular results.

63 Pinn suggests that liberatory ethics are problematic because they are unrealistic. Using Camus and *The Myth of Sisyphus* as exemplifying the ethics of perpetual rebellion, Pinn calls for students of African American religion to start thinking of

ethical systems as disconnected from any institutional allegiance and begin to think of them in more realistic fashion, as the product of the religious impulse meeting up with historical circumstance and as always limited in achievement, where spaces of meaning making are created and then always break down. Perpetual rebellion becomes an ethical system based on constant jettisoning of the significations of oneself faced by others in history or today, and a constant resignification that recognizes that we will always be pushing a rock up a hill in terms of human existence and how we seek meaning in light of that existence. See Pinn, *Terror and Triumph*, 2003.

64 Miguel de Cervantes, *Don Quixote* (Wordsworth Editions, 1998).

65 Here, I mean to evoke the character Quixote's awareness of Cervantes, the author, and the tension throughout the novel wherein Quixote writes his own destiny against the destiny written by Cervantes – metaphoric of "god" here.

66 Tom Gjelten, "Some See Extreme 'Anti-Theism' as Motive in N.C. Killings," February 15, 2015, *NPR.org*, accessed February 15, 2015, http://www.npr.org/2015/02/15/386406810/some-see-extreme-anti-theism-as-motive-in-n-c-killings

67 Pinn, *The End of God-Talk*, 6.

68 Here, hell is the "heaven" of society; rejecting devil-status means recognizing that for many, society is hell, and responding to the dys-function of society by embracing those there with us.

69 Michel Foucault, "What is Enlightenment?" in Paul Rabinow, ed., *The Foucault Reader* (Pantheon, 1984), 32–50.

70 Foucault, in Rabinow, *The Foucault Reader*, 44.

71 Here, I recognize postmodern (e.g., Foucauldian) and transhumanist criticisms of humanism as ideology or political platform. Indeed, humanism can become as socially dangerous and vicious to humans, animals, and ecology as any other life orientation. I hope that the privileging of "uncertainty" has done enough to suggest that what I have in mind seeks to guard against these troubling dimensions of humanism, though I remain uncertain whether such danger is ever fully avoidable. Indeed, argument that such avoidance is possible, from my perspective, belies the very valorization of human ability and worth I have sought to characterize as socially dangerous.

72 Frantz Fanon, *Black Skin, White Masks*, revised edition (Grove Press, 2008).

73 For more on these perils, see Stephen Tomlinson, *Head Masters: Phrenology, Secular Education, and Nineteenth-Century Social Thought* (University of Alabama Press, 2013); and Edward J. Larson, *Sex, Race, and Science: Eugenics in the Deep South*, reprint edition (Johns Hopkins University Press, 1996).

74 Gordon B. Moskowitz, *Social Cognition: Understanding Self and Others* (The Guilford Press, 2004), 2.

75 Kenneth B. Clark and Stuart W. Cook, *Prejudice and Your Child*, 2nd revised edition (Wesleyan, 1988).

76 For more information, see Kirwan Institute for the Study of Race and Ethnicity, Cheryl Staats, *State of the Science: Implicit Bias Review 2014* (The Ohio State University), accessed February 22, 2015, http://kirwaninstitute.osu.edu/wp-content/uploads/2014/03/2014-implicit-bias.pdf; Christine Jolls and Cass R. Sunstein, "The Law of Implicit Bias," Faculty Scholarship Series Paper 1824 (2006), http://digitalcommons.law.yale.edu/fss_papers/1824; and Chris Mooney, "The Science of Why Cops Shoot Young Black Men," *Mother Jones*, accessed February 22, 2015, http://www.motherjones.com/politics/2014/11/science-of-racism-prejudice

77 Moskowitz, *Social Cognition*, 4.

78 Ibid., 4.

79 Ibid., 460.

80 W. E. B. DuBois, *The Souls of Black Folk*, unabridged (Dover Publications, 1994).

81 Susan Sontag, *Regarding the Pain of Others* (Farrar, Straus and Giroux, 2003), 18.
82 V. Y. Mudimbe, *The Idea of Africa* (Indiana University Press, 1994), 52.
83 Pierre Bourdieu, "Genesis and Structure of the Religious Field," in *Comparative Social Research 13*(1991) 3.
84 Sontag, *Regarding the Pain of Others*, 18.
85 This idea of "narrative permission" is inspired by a comment I once heard made by NPR's Michelle Norris. While discussing her social and artistic effort "The Race Card Project," she simply noted that asking someone to tell their own story serves as a kind of permission. See http://theracecardproject.com/
86 It also matters who "holds" such a telescope at all.
87 It would appear Turner had been reading Walter Fisher and Kenneth Burke at the time. Regardless, there is hardly a better way to capture Myerhoff's point of theoretic orientation than through Fisher's *homo narrans*. For more on this idea, see Walter R. Fisher, *Human Communication as Narration: Toward a Philosophy of Reason, Value and Action* (University of South Carolina Press, 1989); and Fisher's essay "Narration as a Human Communication Paradigm: The Case of Public Moral Argument," in *Communication Monographs* 51 (1984).
88 Victor Turner, quoted in Myerhoff, *Number Our Days*, xi.
89 Myerhoff, *Number Our Days*, 37.
90 Barbara Myerhoff, in Lynne Littman, *In Her Own Time*. Documentary, 1985.
91 Ibid.
92 Ibid.
93 For more information on the limits of religion, see David Tracy, *Blessed Rage for Order: The New Pluralism in Theology* (University of Chicago Press, 1996).
94 Myerhoff, *In Her Own Time*.
95 Myerhoff, *Number Our Days*.
96 Myerhoff, *In Her Own Time*.
97 Myerhoff, *Number Our Days*, 18.
98 Ibid., 19.
99 I mean to reference (though only loosely) Martin Heidegger's notion of being toward death. For more information, see Martin Heidegger, *Being and Time* (SUNY Press, 2010); and Magda King, *A Guide to Heidegger's Being and Time* (SUNY Press, 2001).
100 Myerhoff, *Number Our Days*, 37.
101 Rachel, an informant, quoted in Myerhoff, *Number Our Days*, 39.
102 Myerhoff, *In Her Own Time*.
103 I follow Bruno Latour's presentation of the "aggregate" within Actor-Network-Theory. See Bruno Latour, *Reassembling the Social: An Introduction to Actor-Network-Theory* (Oxford University Press, 2007).
104 Myerhoff, *In Her Own Time*.
105 Myerhoff, *In Her Own Time*.

REFERENCES

"The Foxification of News." 2011. *The Economist*, July 7, accessed December 16, 2014, http://www.economist.com/node/18904112

Alexander, Michelle. 2010. *The New Jim Crow: Mass Incarceration in the Age of Colorblindness*. 1st ed. The New Press.

Bloom, Harold. 1997. *The Anxiety of Influence: A Theory of Poetry*. Oxford University Press.

Bloom, Harold. 2005. *The Art of Reading Poetry*. HarperCollins.

Bourdieu, Pierre. 1991. "Genesis and Structure of the Religious Field." *Comparative Social Research* 13: 1–44.

Cervantes, Miguel de. 1998. *Don Quixote*. Wordsworth Editions.
Clark, Kenneth B. and Stuart W. Cook. 1988. *Prejudice and Your Child*. 2nd revised edition. Wesleyan.
Detmer, David. 2011. *Sartre Explained: From Bad Faith to Authenticity*. Open Court.
Drake, David. 2005. *Sartre*. 1st edition. Haus Publishing.
DuBois, W. E. B. 1994. *The Souls of Black Folk*. Unabridged. Dover Publications.
Fanon, Frantz. 2008. *Black Skin, White Masks*. Revised. Grove Press.
Ferguson, Roderick A. 2012. *The Reorder of Things: The University and Its Pedagogies of Minority Difference*. University of Minnesota Press.
Fisher, Walter R. 1984. "Narration as a Human Communication Paradigm: The Case of Public Moral Argument." *Communication Monographs* 51: 1–22.
Fisher, Walter R. 1989. *Human Communication as Narration: Toward a Philosophy of Reason, Value and Action*. University of South Carolina Press.
Foucault, Michel. 1984. *The Foucault Reader*. Edited by Paul Rabinow. Pantheon.
Gjelten, Tom. 2015. "Some See Extreme 'Anti-Theism' as Motive in N.C. Killings," February 15. *NPR.org*, accessed February 15, 2015, http://www.npr.org/2015/02/15/386406810/some-see-extreme-anti-theism-as-motive-in-n-c-killings
Gutiérrez y Muhs, Gabriella, Yolanda Flores Niemann, Carmen G. González, and Angela P. Harris, eds. 2012. *Presumed Incompetent: The Intersections of Race and Class for Women in Academia*. 1st edition. Utah State University Press.
Hauerwas, Stanley and L. Gregory Jones. 1997. *Why Narrative? Readings in Narrative Theology*. Wipf and Stock Publishers.
Heidegger, Martin. 2010. *Being and Time*. SUNY Press.
Hollander, John. 1973. "Harold Bloom's *The Anxiety of Influence: A Theory of Poetry*." *The New York Times Book Review*, March 4, accessed March 10, 2015, http://www.nytimes.com/books/98/11/01/specials/bloom-influence.html
Jolls, Christine and Cass R. Sunstein. 2006. "The Law of Implicit Bias," Faculty Scholarship Series Paper 1824, accessed February 22, 2015, http://digitalcommons.law.yale.edu/fss_papers/1824
Jones, William Ronald. 1997. *Is God a White Racist? A Preamble to Black Theology*. Beacon Press.
King, Magda. 2001. *A Guide to Heidegger's Being and Time*. SUNY Press.
Kirwan Institute for the Study of Race and Ethnicity, Cheryl Staats. 2014. *State of the Science: Implicit Bias Review 2014*. The Ohio State University, accessed February 22, 2015, http://kirwaninstitute.osu.edu/wp-content/uploads/2014/03/2014-implicit-bias.pdf
Larson, Edward J. 1996. *Sex, Race, and Science: Eugenics in the Deep South*. Reprint edition. Johns Hopkins University Press.
Latour, Bruno. 2007. *Reassembling the Social: An Introduction to Actor-Network-Theory*. Oxford University Press.
Littman, Lynne. 1985. *In Her Own Time*. Documentary.
Lonergan, Bernard. 1990. *Method in Theology*. University of Toronto Press.
Malcolm X. 1963. "A Summing Up: Louis Lomax Interviews Malcolm X | Teaching American History," accessed December 15, 2014, http://teachingamericanhistory.org/library/document/a-summing-up-louis-lomax-interviews-malcolm-x/
Malcolm X. 1965. (1992) *The Autobiography of Malcolm X: As Told to Alex Haley*. Ballantine Books.
McCutcheon, Russell T. 2001. *Critics Not Caretakers: Redescribing the Public Study of Religion*. SUNY Press.

Mooney, Chris. 2014. "The Science of Why Cops Shoot Young Black Men." December 1. *Mother Jones*, accessed February 22, 2015, http://www.motherjones.com/politics/2014/11/science-of-racism-prejudice

Moskowitz, Gordon B. 2004. *Social Cognition: Understanding Self and Others*. 1st edition. The Guilford Press.

Mudimbe, V. Y. 1994. *The Idea of Africa*. 1st edition. Indiana University Press.

Muhammad, Elijah. 2004. *The Theology of Time: Subject Indexed Abridged Version*. Elijah Muhammad Books.

Myerhoff, Barbara. 1979. *Number Our Days*. Second printing edition. E. P. Dutton.

Norris, Michelle. 2014. "The Race Card Project!," The Race Card Project, accessed June 24, 2014, http://theracecardproject.com/

Pinn, Anthony B. 1999. *Why, Lord? Suffering and Evil in Black Theology*. Continuum International Publishing Group.

Pinn, Anthony B. 2003. *Terror and Triumph : The Nature of Black Religion*. Fortress Press.

Pinn, Anthony B. 2004. *African American Humanist Principles: Living and Thinking Like the Children of Nimrod*. Palgrave Macmillan.

Pinn, Anthony B. 2012. *The End of God-Talk: An African American Humanist Theology*. Oxford University Press.

Pinn, Anthony B. 2014. *Writing God's Obituary: How a Good Methodist Became a Better Atheist*. Prometheus Books.

Sartre, Jean-Paul. 1989. *No Exit and Three Other Plays* trans. Stuart Gilbert. Reissue edition. Vintage.

Sontag, Susan. 2003. *Regarding the Pain of Others*. Farrar, Straus and Giroux.

Tomlinson, Stephen. 2013. *Head Masters: Phrenology, Secular Education, and Nineteenth-Century Social Thought*. 1st edition. University of Alabama Press.

Tracy, David. 1996. *Blessed Rage for Order: The New Pluralism in Theology*. University of Chicago Press.

West, Cornel. 2002 (1982). *Prophesy Deliverance!*. Westminster John Knox Press.

5

REJECTING THE "GIFT OF DEATH"

White social responsibility in twilight times

> The gift of death would be this marriage of responsibility and faith.
>
> *Jacques Derrida*[1]

> The concept of the soul, the spirit, finally even immortal soul, invented in order to despise the body, to make it sick, holy; to oppose with a ghastly levity everything that deserves to be taken seriously in life, the questions of nourishment, abode, spiritual diet, treatment of the sick, cleanliness, and weather.
>
> *Friedrich Nietzsche*[2]

What is the social responsibility of white Americans concerned that their religious beliefs or practices, those ideas and activities that structure and are structured by identity formation,[3] do not reinforce god-idols like whiteness or unduly reproduce the social consequences caused by adherence to those god-idols, to the extent that such a concern can be addressed at all? Is there a "right" way to do or be religious? In that religion is social, religious beliefs and practices will likely always produce positive and negative effects. But might there be tactics for cultivating certain religious beliefs and expressions that are less harmful, more socially responsible than popular options? This social responsibility would involve finding a way to celebrate social difference without ranking such differences in terms of capability or value; basically, such a religious outlook involves not positioning oneself above anyone else in importance or ability.

In the previous chapter, I began to articulate the sources, norms, and methods for a limited religious outlook. Here, I extend one expressive practice of this outlook by appealing to theological, philosophical, and literary sources as case study and resource to demonstrate that such social responsibility involves not only the surrender of theism (see Chapter 2), but also rejecting one of the principal effects of god-idol adherence, the belief in a personal conception of the soul and personal salvation. Stated bluntly, any beliefs held by white Americans that retain some version of personal salvation rely on the subjugation and ultimately, the sacrifice, of others, enabling social maladies like racism, homophobia, and the like to remain intact. Through what I want to characterize as a "pedagogic of death," where death grounds normative claims, I seek to argue that if white Americans want a litmus test, of sorts, for determining *if* they are remaining within a white religious register or are moving away from it, that test might be available through – and evidenced in – one's willingness to reject the concept of personal salvation for the sake of social responsibility, what I have thematically referred to as learning to die with others.[4]

TAKING SALVATION PERSONALLY

Philosophically speaking, this personal salvation I have in mind holds fast to the certainty of life, and life everlasting in the sense of "heaven" as a reward for fidelity and belief, found in the form of continuance of life, personality, and autonomy, or in the technological social ascendancy of achieving "heaven" on earth. This chapter discusses the relationship between this assured reward and its social costs. My argument does not seek to bolster a kind of white stewardship in the vein of the "white man's burden" nor does it transfigure believers into Christ figures. Rather, I am interested in disrupting the rationale behind such self-aggrandizing narratives, while accepting the limited capacity for such disruption. One avenue of address appears in this particular concept of personal salvation. Neither do I mean to suggest that all soteriologies are equally guilty of this personalized demand. Exceptions exist to every generalization, but on the whole, white American religious expression has been, and for many remains, solipsistically concerned with salvation.

A limited religious outlook refutes the belief in salvation as personal entry into the "kingdom of god," understanding such entry as homologous to a presumed triumph over death.[5] This includes traditional understandings of salvation framed in the future tense, as in "we await a Saviour, the Lord Jesus Christ, who will change our lowly body to be like his glorious body" (Phil. 3:20–21) and especially the past tense as in "by grace you have been saved" (1 Cor. 15:2).[6] It also includes both material-based expressions of this salvation (as promoted by many social gospellers and their contemporary heirs)[7] as well as otherworldly expressions found in Pentecostal and many other traditions. While there are admittedly as many differences amongst these positions as commonalities, my contention is that, whether understood as an individual salvation alone or an individual salvation within a group arrangement (i.e., the social gospel), both this-worldly and otherworldly arrangements for personal salvation inhibit white American (and especially Christian) social responsibility. Accordingly, this chapter also rejects the individualized expression of a "soul." I understand the "soul" as the thing "saved" by personal salvation, the name often given to individualized consciousness, the mind, the thing that talks to us in our head, that which seemingly escapes the boundaries of the material world. Personal conceptions of the soul serve as the perceptual chasm between the material world and the ideological world, preventing active concern for social actors across different social contexts.

This chapter speaks to and about white Americans, white Christians in particular, who employ this sense of soul and salvation. Examples are easy to find and include many Evangelical and prosperity-focused institutions, mainline Protestant denominations that recite the Nicene Creed,[8] and many others who have inherited the vestiges of such personalized beliefs but who might now identify as outside institutional religious communities. This arrangement could then include many "spiritual but not religious" types who still hold a *personalized* belief structure that includes an explicit or implicit desire for salvation. Indeed, I am refuting a major theological component of most Abrahamic religious traditions, but I limit my proscriptive comments to white Americans.[9] In the next section, I summarize why these personal ideas are problematic.

Personal salvation as the "gift of death"

White Americans concerned that their beliefs or practices not unduly reinforce white religion – e.g., that their beliefs or practices do more to refute racism, sexism, homophobia, and the like than to bolster such social injustices – would do well to *reject* what Jacques Derrida refers to as the "gift of death."[10] Accepting the "gift of death" requires the wedding of "responsibility and faith,"[11] which can be thought of as assuming or assenting to the proposition that what "ought" to be, will be, by virtue of its demand. Such a "gift" can be understood as the theological promise of personal salvation. I turn to Derrida as he provides focused attention to the topic of death and salvation, and because his efforts synthesize a number of philosophical perspectives space prevents me from fully exploring. For instance, philosophers Emmanuel Levinas[12] and Martin Heidegger[13] deeply inform Derrida's presentation of "the gift of death." By taking up Derrida, I am able to cover a number of philosophical thinkers and issues through proxy (Heidegger's being-toward-death, for instance)[14] without excurses[15] that would detract from my point. I hope to demonstrate that for a limited religious outlook social responsibility is arrived at through recognition that those on the social periphery have faced early and severe deaths disproportionately due to white denial of a basic existential truism: that we die with others.

Take for instance Derrida's example of the biblical figure Abraham's willingness to sacrifice Isaac on Mount Moriah. The well-known myth describes one salient expression of the denial of dying with others as the wedding of faith and responsibility. As the biblical narrative unfolds, we come to realize that Abraham's "faithfulness," his wedding of responsibility to faith (in this sense), is rewarded by god in the form of a substituted sacrifice so that Isaac might be saved. The death is *deferred*, thereby denying the relationship forged among all social actors where death is concerned. Effectively, it *promises* the end of sacrifice. But does not this story still require a sacrifice? Hence, there is something in such a wedding of faith to responsibility that requires death. More specifically, there is something in this "wedding" that demands the death of *another* so that the death of oneself or community might be avoided. The gift of death is the preservation of one's own life for another. In discussing Abraham's willingness, Derrida admits to his failure in this regard – that is, he too "receives" the gift of death – and thus Derrida offers a succinct diagnosis for understanding both how this gift functions and the social consequences of receiving personal salvation as this "gift of death."

Topically, it would at first glance appear that an "embrace" of the gift of death would be a kind of recognition of limits, boundaries, and finitude. But as it has played out, the "gift" has transcended the object of that gift, meaning that those who accept this "gift" are left – even if they consciously or unconsciously are motivated by recognition of limits – artificially escaping and rejecting finitude and human limitation. For those who "receive" this gift, the soul, salvation, and the afterlife (i.e., a certain sort of eschatological certainty) are made possible through a sacrificed wholly other god that is actually only a conceptual marker for sacrificed social others. By wholly other, I mean the utterly unknowable alterity of things, and follow Derrida as he outlines this gift as he sees it:

> The other in its infinite alterity, one who regards without being seen but also whose infinite goodness *gives* in an experience that amounts to a *gift of death* [*donner la mort*].[16]

This gift situates the social other as wholly other, giving the appearance that an economy of sacrifice has ended, that death has been overcome. But the gift actually only transposes that economy into a "transcendent" realm. This "realm," I argue, is little more than a conceptual marker for the space held socially and ideologically by illegible social actors on the periphery. "Heaven," it is worth noting, is filled with dead people, after all. Or such is suggested by many of the traditional American assumptions about this transcendent heaven. Here I mean to provide a different way of making social theoretical sense of such longstanding assumptions and ideas. Receiving this "gift of death" ensures that the economy of sacrifice continues in perpetuity for those deemed social others – the perpetual others of such sacrifice. Though it purports to reject the economy of sacrifice as it offers social insiders the promise of salvation, the "gift" actually keeps the economy intact. In this framework, sacrificial offerings move from social centers, are projected onto the idea of god, and projected yet again onto those who stand outside of social centers.

In an effort to address this framework, this chapter explores a question and warning posed by Paul Tillich when he underscores death as non-being[17]:

> Why do we care about the time after our death but not the time before it? The 'American way of life' is a blessing coming from the past, but it is also a curse, threatening the future.[18]

This "American way of life" is largely sustained by white Americans (and those who've bought into the false certainty of god-idols, consciously or unconsciously) as the perpetual recipients of "the gift of death," the gift of the rejection of finality made possible as "every one being [is] sacrificed to every one else."[19] Such sacrifices can never be justified[20] by those at social centers, and through the gift, "god" purports to take on the task of both justification and of ending the sacrifice. But "faith" in this divine justification falls flat, and sacrifices continue; necessary, then, are attempts to curb, slow down, this ongoing "curse" on the "American way of life."

To marry responsibility to faith, as Derrida suggests institutes the gift of death, is to abandon the limitations of human freedom posed by social responsibility and this marriage curtails the possibility for social equity, an experience of possibility within limitation. This social responsibility is the demand that freedom be expressed in relation to other social actors, cultivating the responsibility to no longer constitute social actors/agents as wholly others. Rejection of this gift – the eternal life promised from god's sacrifice – is thus required for those who do not want their beliefs or practices to reinforce differences in ability and value across social groups. Only after rejection of the personal soul, "invented in order to despise the body, to make it sick," disallowing its ability to "oppose everything that deserves to be taken seriously in life,"[21] it might be possible for white Americans to hermeneutically register those on social margins as social actors with full social access to resource and power, and equal in worth and ability to those at social centers. Indeed, this would entail a rupture of the logic constituting the center as qualitatively distinct from the periphery. Such a rupture might be cultivated through embrace of the multivalent pedagogical utility found in the idea of death, discussed next.

SKETCHING A PEDAGOGIC OF DEATH

Rejection of the "gift of death" is not a rejection of death, as such. Quite the contrary. Rejecting this gift concealing death within an exchange economy involves a kind of pedagogical embrace of the object of that gift, death. I define death as an idealized expression of the loss of physical, psychical, and social power – a constituent feature of life – indicative of a fundamental sameness that cuts across manufactured group difference. This is not to suggest death as a kind of embrace of meaninglessness or nihilism, but that the economy of death is a false economy to begin with. Rejecting the economy of death, to this end, is a rejection of the possibility of meaninglessness and nihilism, for it is the prospect and notion of some saved and others sacrificed that likely contributes to certain nihilistic social perspectives. That is, some are forced to endure a hell of meaninglessness on earth as they are prevented from access to euphemistic social heavens marked often by normativity. Further, rejecting this economy *means* no longer accepting a meaning made through the relegation of social others to positions of meaninglessness.

With this working definition of death, I offer a pedagogic of death. Here, I have in mind something different than Paul Ramsey's "Death's Pedagogic,"[22] in that Ramsey is focused principally on promoting a social openness to individual, physical death, such as euthanasia. My pedagogic taps into the anxiety and fear posed by the idea of individual, physical death, but with the aim directed not at the individual right (or ability) to physically die, but towards entire groups in a social sense. I also have in mind something a bit more socially focused than Kenneth Vaux's "Pedagogy of Death" used to teach pastoral bedside manner with the dying.[23] Rather, the pedagogic of death employed throughout this chapter is directed towards white American social responsibility, in terms of actual and perceived power and resource. Through such a pedagogic, the conceptual distance created by white religion between freedom (i.e., individual mind/ideas) and responsibility (i.e., material social reality) is brought together by localizing exaggerations of this freedom or responsibility in the counterfactual sameness provided by death. It achieves this by attacking personal salvation, transmuting that belief into an existential test for white Americans: continuing to "believe in" personal salvation suggests an ideological inability to accept real or perceived losses of power and marks us as willing to kill to prevent such losses. Accepting the finality of individual and group life opens the possibility of renewed (or maybe even "new") social responsibility. What does this finality, this death, look like?

With the blurring of physical, metaphoric, and social expressions of death, some readers might think I leave "real" deaths out of the story, erring on the side of philosophy and literary examples rather than concrete sociological data. I could juxtapose average lifespans between those at social centers with those at social margins. For instance, figures from 2009 indicate that African American men die, on average, five or six years before their white male counterparts.[24] But I am not interested in situating death as a means of social distinction (as these figures do), but in suggesting that physical death (as an idea) offers a pedagogical counter-narrative to the false promise that society somehow functions as a defense from death so long as distinctions remain intact. With this in mind, my concerns are precisely to address the abstracted ideological disparities – the ideas that allow a sense of differential value and ability – that often produce the very social conditions we find in such statistics. To this end, I follow Derrida's own motivations in writing *The Gift of Death*, examining the social consequences and function of philosophy and theology, but I reject his personal conclusions.

White Lies would not be necessary at all if an economy of sacrifice did not remain a constituent feature of social life in the west, a "permanent" feature for the "smooth functioning"[25] of many societies emerging out of the Abrahamic traditions – societies that alienate precisely through rigorous categorical and social distinctions, the original distinction perhaps posed between life and death. I discuss this relationship in the next section.

Life, death, and a twilight so long endured

Death is not the antithesis of life but is co-constitutive with life, and it is indicative of a loss of assumed power within life, broadly construed. This is the perspective of death seen through "twilight," the overarching hermeneutic holding the entire apparatus of *White Lies* together. Twilight attempts to keep in view both the life in death and the death in life (at a philosophical level) with an understanding of the social world as the contemporary space where social actors assume, seek, find, and lose power.

Life defines death and death defines life, much like theism and atheism are not so much opposing alternatives, as they emerge together as perspectival and lexical strategies for navigating the world. For instance, the claim that whiteness as a god-idol is dead is also a concession to recognition of the continued life of whiteness today. To speak of death as a kind of non-being, a *mere* counterfactual of being, reinforces the primacy of being, suggesting that whether conceived physically, metaphorically, or socially, death and life are co-constitutive. Like death, then, a dying whiteness is also a *living* whiteness. Clarity on this point is offered in the verb forms, dying or living, indicating that these positions are not only parallel perspectives of the same processes, but they emerge along a continuum.

Acknowledging this relationship between life and death, what can be made of Michel de Montaigne's famous suggestion, following Socrates and Cicero, that "to philosophize is to learn to die?"[26] Though Montaigne seems focused on the quality of individual life lived in the constant present awareness of physical death, how might his definition and position be further explicated in light of this approach? If Montaigne be taken literally, and if death amounts to a real or perceived loss of power, then philosophy would involve, at its best, teaching how to let go of power[27] and resource, coming to terms with "impotence in the face of death,"[28] and a growing awareness of possibilities afforded through embrace of death in/as life. Montaigne speaks to this pedagogical effect, noting that "he who should teach men to die would at the same time teach them to live."[29] Montaigne, however, was of the mind that this life would end and another begin, and so, on this point, his position is not completely my own. His efforts, however, foreground the usefulness of thinking on death's pedagogical significance.

Similarly demonstrating this utility, Ludwig Feuerbach poetically (and humorously) demanded in 1830 that "Death" be awarded the Doctor of Philosophy degree:

> Highly learned and esteemed gentlemen,
> May I hereby present before you Death
> In order that, in your lofty circle,

You may raise him to the doctorate ...
So then I implore you to receive
Death into the academy,
And, as soon as possible, to make
Him doctor of philosophy.[30]

Feuerbach seems to be suggesting that philosophy – the academy, more generally, too – wields too much power and not enough humility. The poem offers a double entendre, noting death's pedagogical use, but simultaneously pronouncing death as doctor *of the field of philosophy*, suggesting that philosophy might be healed of itself (its Hegelianism, to be specific) if it would just die. Learning to die with others, synonymous with the social responsibility I have in mind, follows Feuerbach and involves disrupting this assumption of power and finding ways to teach how real or perceived power might be let go, relinquished. This is achieved by turning death into a pedagogic, thematically and heuristically useful as means of reflexive pedagogical redress.

Death does not function to replace god-idols in an ontological sense, as in an "ultimate" god-idol, but is situated as an interpretive pedagogic, a modifier. Here is where I depart from many such as Montaigne, who finds in acceptance of death's uncertain certainty (i.e., the uncertainty of how and when we die, and the certainty that we die) an intensification and greater recognition of life's pleasures, and Heidegger's solipsistic fetishizing of death.[31] I am not "believing" that death is god, but I am suggesting that a community whose beliefs have been death-dealing for others ought to treat death as if it were their god, idol, or, better still, simply their teacher.

This pedagogical corrective takes place within a social environment of twilight, where death (of identity, of white religious efficacy) confronts us at seemingly every turn. Shifts in power require learning that one is dying, that one is living in the twilight of what they know, what philosopher Cornel West has referred to as a "Twilight Civilization," not in the sense that whiteness has yet died, but that beneficiaries (of a less and less functionally effective god-idol such as whiteness) are seeing "corrupt and top-heavy nation-states eclipsed by imperial corporations as public life deteriorates due to class polarization, racial balkanization and especially a predatory market culture," leading to "a pervasive cultural decay in American civilization."[32] Not only have those historically deemed social others never been afforded full access to the privileges extended to those at social centers, but those very centers are now eroding, lending fear to those at social centers and dismay, perhaps, to the marginal as the opportunity for greater access is rendered seemingly impossible. Recognizing that what once was a "white" America is on the decline does not equate to saying that things are better for those most victimized by white America. It simply means that whiteness and white America are witnessing the arthritic fingers, acrid feet, fettered face and hands, the shallow breaths of a civilization facing twilight, but without a historic or hermeneutic precedent for accepting this social decay. For instance, the gutting of the public school system; the shrinking of the middle-class; the loss of privacy; militarization of local and state police agencies. Adequate education, economic stability, privacy, relative safety, though never fully afforded (if at all) to African Americans, are on the decline for whites, as well. Casting white American social life as in decay – that is, American religion in twilight – and the current social arrangement as an expression of the realization of the nothingness it has feared, might lead to greater willingness (among white Americans) to finally address the conditions making such an arrangement possible.

Social responsibility begins when "my gaze, precisely as regards me [*ce qui me regarde*], is no longer the measure of all things,"[33] allowing exposure of the deaths that have been caused by this sort of solipsistic blindness while also exposing that the overall death-dealing system no longer functions effectively even for its former (and continued) beneficiaries. Unable to live because we have been unable to die, white Americans exist in perpetual twilight.

This pedagogic takes seriously (i.e., laughs and cries) the flippant passage offered by Molière's character Mascarille: *On ne meurt qu'une fois, et c'est pour si longtemps!*[34] [We die only once and for so long a time!] Mascarille notes the absurdity of life in death and death in life, an absurdity in that not only is life not fully lived because death is most often ignored, but that the paradox of this denial means "life" takes the shape of the thing feared, an eternal void of nothingness. Fear of nothingness, nonbeing or a loss of power thus produces its effects. "Death," as Montaigne helpfully reminds, "is less to be feared than nothing,"[35] and yet Montaigne, Heidegger, and as we will see, even Derrida, fear this nothingness to the point of defending an economy of sacrifice so that it remained at a perceptual and perpetual distance from life.

To live is not to one day die, it is to be currently dying. The pedagogic of death, situated within and foregrounding this twilight, demonstrates to those who have received the "gift of death" that we have not escaped the finality of death and, in fact, the gift has been a ruse. The assumption of power or resource safeguarded is only ever an assumption, per this philosophic reading. Learning to die with others in this twilight requires casting the comedian Molière in a "tragicomic" light – twilight – "recognition of the sheer absurdity of the human condition."[36] Failure to recognize such absurdity, this twilight, West suggests, "propels us toward suicide or madness unless we are buffered by ritual, cushioned by community or sustained by art."[37] The pedagogic of death is also meant to cultivate an awareness of this twilight for beginning to wrestle with what cultural resources remain for this community on the verge of "suicide or madness." To recognize twilight is to give voice to feelings of cultural decay, and to realize that nothing about this decay or decadence is new; it has been a constituent feature of the society and "civilization" we have called home. Indeed, to exist – in this arrangement – is to exist in this "nothingness." This pedagogic of death seeks to focus attention towards this "decay" as a kind of social "death,"[38] and the ubiquity of this "nothingness" an expression of the conditions making possible the very ability to see that it is about time to come to terms with the perceived loss of a power we've never actually held to begin with.[39]

SENESCENCE AND SOCIAL POWER

This teacher death (aimed at rejection of constructions of any social actors as *wholly other*) might help to promote a social responsibility facilitating a kind of social death, ultimately promoting a more equitable distribution of social power. That is, power (resources, influence, etc.) might move more cyclically through the hands of greater numbers of social actors, rather than disproportionately localize in insular (often racialized) social spaces. But how can my abstract argument find purchase on the ground, in churches, universities, white American homes as much as in department faculty meetings and police forces, etc.? Attempting as much, here I offer the idea of social senescence, an application of principles learned from attention to biological death, but directed towards the social world. In the biological sciences, senescence refers to a life process, a feature of life wherein life somehow "knows" to wrap things up, to die. The idea of senescence is easily captured by a falling leaf. How does the leaf know that its time is up? What tells the tree or the leaf that it ought to divert resources elsewhere so that the overall organism might remain alive? Senescence is this process by which living things know that death is required of life, as in the cyclical patterns of leaves falling from a tree in Autumn and returning in Spring.

The social responsibility I have in mind is captured by thinking of senescence in the very social world itself. Social senescence would involve the awareness of the need to relinquish certain social functions (i.e., god-idols, their effects in personal salvation, etc.) so that entire organisms might flourish. Responding to white lies requires an effort to inculcate a sense of social senescence amongst white Americans who find ourselves in need of coming to terms with material and/or imaginary losses of power, but who have rarely in fact come to terms with even that need.

Of the few prior uses of this term "senescence" I have found, most have been anecdotal rather than systematic. The earliest instance I found helps to define the idea, while it also foregrounds that a particular group of people, white American men, have been inclined to fear this social senescence. In a 1910 tome titled *American Men of Science: A Biographical Directory, Volume 2*, one essay mentions not only social senescence (as a warning of things to come), but even racial senescence, as the "scientific" study that was the subject of the essay sought to chart out the shrinking numbers of American (i.e., white) male doctors in the field. In an ominous passage, woeful in tone by my reading, it notes:

> *Racial senescence*, the lack of emotional stimuli and the accumulations of knowledge will probably set limits to the further advance of science … . Still a *highly specialized organism* is likely to become unplastic and extinct, and apart

> from physical exhaustion of the stock there is likely to be a *social senescence*. This is closely related to the lack of emotional stimuli. Great men and great achievements are likely to be associated with national excitement, with wars, revolutions, the rivalry or consolidation of states, the rise of democracy and the like. Such stirring events will probably disappear from the world civilization of the future, and it may be impossible to devise artificial stimuli adequate to arouse men from a safe and stupid existence. But exactly because within a century the great achievements of science may belong to the past, where the great creations in poetry, art and religion may perhaps now only be found, *it is our business to do the best we can to assure the race of an adequate endowment policy*.[40] (Emphasis added)

My appeal to death as a pedagogic is a means of producing "emotional stimuli" so that these "men," this "highly specialized organism" held sway by white religion, might not fear this social senescence, but rather, embrace it by coming to realize that only fear of it will produce the effects so many of us dread, and the consequences dreaded by all. Embracing social senescence might produce a more robust "endowment policy" (a future social stability guided not by sacrifice) by setting down a concern for "men" or an individual "race" alone. The promotion of social senescence as a benefit, framed in this chapter as the social responsibility to learn to die with others, might transmute the fear witnessed in this passage into a willingness to embrace the material and imagined shifting dimensions of social power.

My aims, then, involve the promotion of the need for social senescence amongst my particular data set and I rely on "death" as the principal pedagogical trope making this possible within this contemporary ideological and social moment of twilight, wherein people and groups who have not yet relinquished power are coming to either accept that need or feel that such losses are imminent.[41] I cannot be certain that this pedagogic will have the desired effects, but it is a start, a thought experiment, and cultural products – seen in this light posed by the twilight of life and death as one – offer resources that might aid in the rejection of an economy of sacrifice. I turn next to one of these resources.

WHITE HEARTS ARE LONELY HUNTERS

Here, I return to literature and narrative to present an allegory that might aid white Americans in coming to terms with the loss of a personal soul and salvation and how it relates to the loss of god-idols, giving pause and focus to what these losses suggest about the production of social responsibility. Throughout this book, I've blurred lines between god-idols, humans, material social realities, and fiction. The following allegory holds in tension these seemingly disparate ideas and localizes them in the person of John Singer.

Originally titled "The Mute"[42] and later published to much fanfare as *The Heart Is a Lonely Hunter* (1943),[43] white, female, bisexual, Marxist, Southern writer Carson McCullers's novel gives testament to racist, sexist, gendered, and economic distances posed between individuals and groups in the Southern U.S. in the early twentieth century. Its main character, "the Mute," John Singer, comes to be a storinghouse and springboard for the troubles faced by social actors across different social contexts. The mute simply wants to spend time with his mentally unstable friend, life-partner, and possible lover. Yet, other characters in the novel project their own and others' exaggerations of radical contingency onto him. Singer kills himself near the end of the novel, and an exploration of why, and how, this death takes place might provide insights about what social senescence would look like for white Americans.

The story, and Singer, offer four interrelated points. First, all of the characters foreground that social loneliness produced by god-idol adherence reinforces individual perceptions of different group values and abilities rather than flattening those presumed differences. Second, Singer serves as a god-idol for the other characters in the novel, offering a way of "seeing" how a god-idol functions. Third, Singer demonstrates the twilight of god-idols, offering a kind of embodied example of life in death and death in life of god-idols. Fourth, Singer's death presents an ethical paradox for white people, perhaps responded to if Singer's death is interpreted as a desire to kill the mechanism promoting qualitative group difference. These four points work together to promote social responsibility by providing an allegory for how to destroy the mechanisms that give god-idols power – mediated by a perception of power afforded these god-idols by social actors through belief.

The loneliness of god-idol adherence

McCullers's novel is a story about the loneliness reinforced when people elevate a person or an idea to the status of a deity. And all of the characters, including Singer, are guilty of this exaggerated religious expression. For a brief character summary, the novel tells the story of a variety of social actors, thrust together in a Southern town, and left to struggle with how to live, grow, love, and lose. There is Mick Kelly, a young white girl, whose father is out of work and forced to make ends meet by opening their home to guests. The Kellys rent a room to the mute John Singer. Mick Kelly's life choices are truncated by age, gender, and economics, and by an obligation to work for her family. Her desires to be a musician are put on hold indefinitely. She is also sexually ambiguous and presented as an early meditation on queer identity in the deep South. There is Biff Brannon, white owner of The New York Café, where Singer eats daily. This café serves as a kind of "chapel," where ideological projection, prayers, and the like are transmitted to Singer. There is Jake Blount, the white semi-vagrant carnival worker who seemingly has the world's problems figured out save for his inability to get anyone to take him seriously. There is Dr. Benedict Copeland, the African American doctor who also has the world's problems seemingly figured out, but whose anger about his own social position blinds him to those who might listen. Blount, blinded by drunkenness, and Copeland, blinded by anger at "the insolence of all the white race,"[44] are frustrated because their solutions to issues like racism go unheeded by those around them. And then there is Spiros Antonapoulos, Singer's best friend who once lived with him but now resides in an asylum after a mental episode. Antonapoulos serves as a kind of ultimate concern for Singer, their unity the only sense of love or security ever realized by Singer. Their disunity proves too much for Singer.

All of these characters are thoroughly "normal," almost unremarkable, but represent various identities and social contexts living in relative proximity to one another. They each come to befriend John Singer and make undue use of his inability to speak. He becomes a means for validating their own positions and frustrations, while his concerns remain largely unacknowledged and unresolved. Though Singer communicates through written notes and gestures, the other characters rely mostly on assumption, presumption, and belief in their communications with him. It might be said they wed their "responsibility" to faith at the altar of Singer's company.

Years after the publication of the novel, McCullers described John Singer this way: "His friends were able to impute to him all the qualities which they would wish for him to have" based on their "own desires … . In his eternal silence there is something compelling. Each one of these persons makes the mute the repository for his most personal feelings and ideas."[45] For instance, both Blount and Copeland relay to Singer – on different occasions – their perspectives on the usefulness of Marxism as a responsible strategy for correcting the world's ills. Interpreting Singer's nods and stares as validation, they end up only validating their own assumptions that they have the prescriptions for all the world's ills – if only they would take the medicine, themselves. These characters aren't meant to foreground hypocrisy so much as uncertainty, sadness, limitation, and the utter absurdity and seeming impossibility of different groups ever seeing themselves as more or less than different. Their social interactions, coming from a place of loneliness, reinforce the sense of solitude.

The irony, of course, is that their engagement with Singer is precisely motivated by the feeling of loneliness, isolation, and estrangement that his company merely reinforces. For his part, Singer is also guilty of this, as throughout the novel he longs for a return to his beloved Antonapoulos. On this first point, it appears that god-idols reinforce a loneliness which they are purported to address, but are likely responsible for themselves. The next section considers the prospects of Singer as such a god-idol.

John Singer as god-idol

John Singer functions in the capacity of a god-idol for each of the characters in the novel. In short, Singer holds in his person – his ontology, if you will – first- and second-order observation of the self and its god-idol projection. Each character brings their assumptions to Singer's ear, only for those assumptions to be justified and defended – rather than pushed or changed – based on the silence offered by Singer. Singer offers an analogy of the "one, true god" protected and defended by theists on different sides of the racial (and other) divides. The characters in McCullers's novel and American theists more generally all are doing different versions of the same thing – trying to make sense of their place in the world – but Singer's inability to communicate back ("god's" silence) sees to it that nothing bridges the artificial distances between different people – because reliance on that object creates the very distance it purports to overcome. In the person of Singer, these seemingly different people are brought into close proximity with each other; but functioning as a god-idol, Singer also prevents these characters from making use of this proximity to see themselves as more similar than different. In talking to Singer, their loneliness is seemingly assuaged only to be reinforced. They are never in conversation with difference in a way that would cause difference (i.e., the source of their loneliness) to be seen as a kind of sameness, able to flatten assumptions about ability and value. Stated in existential terms, each character's anxiety prevents their ability to see every other's anxiety influencing everyone's actions. Assumed social difference is reinforced, even as geographic and ideological differences are overcome. Jake Blount expresses this reification of differential ability through an epistemological judgment framed around traditional Christian themes:

> My first belief was Jesus … . My mind was on Jesus all day long … . Then one night I took a hammer and laid my hand on the table. I was angry and I drove the nail all the way through … . It was like being born a second time. Just us who know can understand what it means.
>
> Singer agreed with him.[46]

This self-aggrandizing, and at times redemptive suffering model of ideological comportment is reinforced through audience with god-idols. In "agreeing" with an us/them arrangement, Singer (i.e., god-idols) gets in the way of adherents knowing the "other" as anything but other. They stand in as wholly other – represented here by Singer's silence – but are made from the stuff of social others, social actors without voice.

The novel's narrator further underscores this connection between Singer and god-idols when describing Mick Kelly's thoughts on God:

> Everybody in the past few years knew there wasn't any real God. When she thought of what she used to imagine was God she could only see Mister Singer with a long, white sheet around him. God was silent … .[47]

Again, silence is the focus in this arrangement, and like the American religious expression under examination in *White Lies*, the color white provides a symbol for this silence. McCullers seemingly wants to privilege the relation between humans and these metaphysical categories as one of silence. Her efforts offer a model for white Americans to learn from, in that god-idols remain silent in their twilight. Characterizing her creation of Singer as "written in the simple style of a parable," her efforts were precisely to offer such a parable or allegory focused on how beliefs interact with or support social differences like race, sexuality, and poverty through this silence. Worth quoting at length is a passage from one of the book's early Prefaces:

> The broad principal theme of this book is … man's revolt against his own inner isolation and his urge to express himself as fully as possible. Surrounding this general idea there are several counter themes and some of these may be stated briefly as follows: (1) There is a deep need in man to express himself by creating some unifying principle or God. A personal God created by a man is a reflection of himself and in substance this God is most often inferior to his creator. (2) In a disorganized society these individual Gods or principles are likely to be chimerical and fantastic. (3) Each man must express himself in his own way – but this is often denied to him by a tasteful, short-sighted society. (4) Human beings are innately cooperative, but an unnatural social tradition makes them behave in ways that are not in accord with their deepest nature. (5) Some men are heroes by nature in that they will give all that is in them without regard to the effort or to the personal returns.[48]

Singer functions in the capacity of this "unifying principle or God," but the attempted unity is exposed as seemingly impossible. Singer's inability to speak, like the inability of any god-idol to respond to its adherents, is both the means of its power, and a "reflection of" the inability to overcome or fully respond to the paradox made visible within twilight. Singer does not speak back but is spoken to – by people who justify their own inconsistencies and limitations through the idea of god or in this case, Singer. He serves as a false bridge between different people who need to be building dialogical bridges, as well as economic, civic, and political bridges. For instance, the black doctor, Copeland, and the white drunk, Blount, hate each other. They will not and do not talk to each other, save in a few instances of coincidental action, and even in these moments their anger (at one another, the world, themselves) prevents equitable communication across lines of presumed difference. Throughout the novel, it is clear that if they would only talk to each other through genuine dialogue – instead of talking *at* Singer – they'd find themselves more alike than different, in a shared existential inability to make sense of this thing called life.

Note how McCullers's stated motivations point back to a critique of the society she deems "unnatural." McCullers focuses on society as a culprit in these proceedings, as being "disorganized" and "short-sighted." Such a society, according to McCullers, prevents humans from full creative expression. She even notes that an "unnatural social tradition" prevents them from cooperating as they would "innately." Lastly, McCullers may fall victim to that very "unnatural social tradition," as she implies some "men" are heroes. She seems to have in mind those who sacrifice themselves for some sort of greater good, a Christological heroism, a problematic redemptive suffering model of salvation through sacrifice, which is itself an expression of the gift of death. Singer, then, offers an allegory for understanding that god-idols ultimately reinforce group differences. But Singer *is* a *tragic* hero, forcing recognition of death and how death is understood in its relation to society. In the next section, I situate this connection between god-idols, their limitations, and society through the prism of twilight.

Twilight of a god-idol

Twilight is not a mollification of loneliness, but an exaggeration of it, meaning that such a hermeneutic is not to be embraced as a panacea, but is a warning, that loneliness and the social tragedies arising from god-idol adherence will likely worsen as these god-idols "die" as they remain silent. American religion, to the extent that it has been and remains "white" religion, is in no place to offset the past or contemporary social challenges it has helped to set in motion. Any adequate response will deconstruct the very constellation of assumptions and ideas shaping American religion, and that conceal the "white" sensibilities of this American religion. Singer's life and death help to make sense of this point.

Singer's life speaks in a way to recognition that whatever people or ideas are held most central have a bad habit of keeping people distinct and removed from their responsibility to each other, keeping them lonely. This includes belief in a personal soul. And initially, this feeling of loneliness intensifies. Foreshadowing Singer's death, Blount feels intense loneliness when he cannot find Singer: "Of all the places he had been this was the loneliest town of all. Or it would be without Singer. Only he and Singer understood the truth. He knew and could not get the don't knows to see."[49] Again, we see a relationship between silence and ingroup/outgroup dynamics. The ingroup is made possible by the silence that blocks dialogue with the ideologically constituted outgroup. Metaphorically speaking, one can only imagine the frustration a god-idol might feel in recognizing that its silence functions in this paradoxical fashion.

A letter written by Singer evokes McCullers's possible thoughts on what a god-idol might have to say of these practices:

> The others all have something they hate. And they all have something they love more than eating or sleeping or wine or friendly company. This is why they are always so busy.[50]

One implication of this passage seems to be that if only people could learn to love that which they hate, they would find themselves with time to enjoy life. To think back to Mascarille and Montaigne, learning to love what is hated might be another way of saying learning to truly live by learning to live in/as death. The issue of love emerges more fully below; worth noting now is simply the idea that a paucity of love (i.e., disconnectedness) contributes to a feeling of loneliness and isolation amongst those who ironically find themselves in close geographic and temporal proximity to each other, but feel themselves inaccessible and set apart.

For white Americans who might be thought of as these "lonely hunters," what can be learned from such an allegory, remembering that the weight of this silence was too much for Singer to bear? He kills himself. Learning of his best friend Antonapoulos's death in the asylum, and presumably exhausted from having been the silent voice *certifying* everyone else's sense of *certainty*, Singer "returned to his room with swollen eyes and an aching head. After resting he drank a glass of iced coffee and smoked a cigarette. Then when he had washed the ashtray and the glass he brought out a pistol from his pocket and put a bullet in his chest."[51] Singer's death suggests McCullers has in mind to express the absence of "god," promoting awareness that the social actors representing different social groups are alone (metaphysically speaking). Their god is dead. The story's narrator helps to situate the situation Blount and by analogy, white Americans, find ourselves in now – twilight – hearing of their god-idol's death: "The emptiness in him hurt. He wanted to look neither backward nor forward … . He had given Singer everything and then the man had killed himself. So he was left out on a limb. And now it was up to him to get out of it by himself and make a new start again."[52] Their god-idol was dead by its own hand. But Singer also represents an adherent to an economy of sacrifice, so his death might be understood as an expression of one person's decision to kill the mechanism reinforcing the inability of difference to see itself as sameness.

Could we see Singer as an example of a white hunter who finally decides to kill his soul so that others might live, or does his death mark an antiheroic willingness to die if selfish desires cannot be maintained? One of these desires is the personal soul, and he seems to have "died" due to a lack of meaningful connection, a lack made possible as god-idols stood in his way. Suppose god did once exist and the crucifixion signals the death of that god, just as Singer's death suggests the death of god-idols by their own "hands." Death of the personal soul, though intensifying loneliness initially, might allow for this twilight to offer the possibility of a "new start" for a community – an aggregate, really – in deep need of such an opportunity.

Responding to twilight

What does the person of Singer do with the god-idol of Singer?

> Singer was dead… . Now he could not be seen or touched or spoken to, and the room where they had spent so many hours had been rented to a girl who worked as a typist. He could go there no longer. He was alone.[53]

Singer leaves white Americans with a paradox, to be resolved only by us if at all, and based on how the story of Singer's death is interpreted. In twilight, death is unavoidable; the question involves whether this death will be meted out literally on a social plane or metaphysically. If admitting that in the figure of Singer, soul and god-idol collide, does Singer commit suicide or does he represent the theological possibility of killing one's personal soul, in a kind of metaphysical suicide? Asked differently, does Singer embrace or reject the gift of death? For now, I leave this as an open question.

Yet, I am interested in how the death of god – seen as the continuance of a story instead of the end of a story – is exemplified in Singer as the continuance of the economy of sacrifice in the social world, and it might have some allegorical benefit for those of us with a growing awareness that we ought no longer to rely on this economy. Indeed, the "gift of death," the god's preservation of one's own life for another, seemed to promise that such an economy had ended. Yet, Singer aids in understanding that the economy remains intact because as he represents a god-idol as a person, his death marks the death of social others at the moment when god-idols die. From such awareness, white Americans interested in disrupting white religion find ourselves now in a kind of forced protest atheist stance, if we do not mean for our gods to be racist, sexist, homophobic, etc.

In terms of possible moral censure, it is interesting to think that "god" kills godself out of frustration with god's own limited ability to bring people together. The social consequences of having not learned to die, not learned to live with others equitably, are such that "gods" would rather throw in the towel. In this assessment, the death of god-idols is self-imposed, prompted in this example by their own increasing social (dys)function; they find it time that their adherents become a kind of theological grownup.[54] As social needs and the makeup of such a society shift, then the god-idols and the mechanisms needed to produce and secure those god-idols come into greater competition with alternatives. Or, stated differently, there is an increasing lack of options for securing any modicum of certainty or proof in the qualitative distinction between those at social centers and those at the margins.

The death of John Singer – the entire novel, really – offers a sort of open-ended blueprint for coming to terms with the death of theism, whiteness, homophobia, and other god-idols, as well as their effects such as personal salvation. These deaths bring with them a loss of certainty but might also promote a kind of clarity that the certainty has come at the cost of projecting one's own desires and concerns onto a deaf mute. But they also provide a point of reference for more focused attention on how, and in what capacities, death is offered up as a "gift" to society and reinforced as an economy even when it is transposed onto a god-idol.

Connecting this point back to the example of John Singer, his death doesn't actually make the lives of the other characters "better" – perhaps better is impossible – it merely exposes (to the reader) the mechanism on which those characters had unduly relied, and his absence simply foregrounds the loneliness felt by the characters. The question of moving forward, of cultivating social responsibility, then, might involve where we situate the model offered by Singer in terms of more traditional allegories. Rather than read Singer as a Christ-figure, killing himself so that others might receive personal salvation packaged as the gift of death, perhaps white folks would do better to see him in the position of Abraham, albeit choosing a different ending than the one chosen by Abraham in Genesis. Through this shift in orientation, developed below, Singer might offer more resources for a group of white Americans who can no longer celebrate the "gift" of Jesus's death if they are to be concerned with promoting social responsibility within this twilight.

THE GIFT OF DEATH *AS* DEATH OF THE SOCIAL OTHER

Perhaps John Singer is better understood as Abraham than as Christ, in that his death can be interpreted as killing the sacrificial mechanism holding together the idea of society and preventing an equitable social arrangement where different social actors are afforded full privilege to that society. Abraham's son, Isaac, serves then as a means for capturing the personal soul as a functional mechanism. An alternative sacrifice is seemingly provided so that the "soul" can be maintained and kept intact. In Singer we find expressed Abraham, Isaac, and god. Perhaps white Americans would do well to recognize ourselves in the person of Singer, trying to determine the appropriate course of action, but also as "Isaac" – our personal soul and sense of salvation is tied to an altar and the god-idol who once promised an end to this economy is silent. Perhaps, society is a functional god demanding sacrifice today precisely because the god who broke into history has been hung on a cross.

Throughout these pages, my concept of the "god-idol" has meant to foreground the certain and uncertain effects of believed-in ideas. Of those beliefs inculcating a sense of certainty for the believer, "god" is an historical precedent as a sign or marker. "Idol," on the other hand, is equally a precedent in terms of casting light on the certain *uncertainty* posed by such appeals to god. God and idol collide in Genesis 22, the story of God's command to Abraham that he sacrifice his son Isaac. With total dedication, Abraham takes himself to the brink of such sacrifice, only for the "Angel of the Lord" to intervene:

> Do not lay your hand on the boy or do anything to him; for now I know that you fear God, since you have not withheld your son, your only son, from me.[55]

Wanting to define *White Lies* neither as (fully) constructive nor (fully) apophatic in its aim, it is forced to square with the complicated, *aporetic* ambitions of Jacques Derrida and his extended exploration of what this Abrahamic narrative suggests about why death has been treated as a gift for so long. Stated differently, neither deconstructive nor constructive theological enterprises have brought social suffering to an end – and perhaps, that is not their goal. Derrida's later writings seem to express such frustration, and offer uncertain clarity as to why it is so difficult for many of us to learn to die with others.

The wholly other as social other

What shape is taken by such a divinity arising from a limited religious outlook where god cannot be seen because god is dead? That shape of god *in absence* comes in the form of *nonbeing* framed around death. Death, in the most abstract sense, including both physical and social expressions, is the embrace of uncertainty forced through loss of power. As such, death can be treated functionally as a divine object. And yet, death has been registered as the antithesis of divinity through the "gift of death which is this marriage of responsibility and faith."[56] In order to better unpack this relationship, this "marriage" as Derrida refers to it, questions emerge: Does responsibility refer to the maintenance of faith, or to the jettisoning of faith? How do we answer this question, and proceed from it? Understanding how this "gift" functions to hide the object of death is central to developing the capacity for accepting social responsibility.

Cultivating social responsibility involves first recognizing the apophatic connection between social actors and the idea of god. In one dense chapter, Derrida argues that *Tout autre est tout autre* [Every other (one) is every (bit) other.][57] By this, Derrida renders Barth's *wholly other*[58] as a socially grounded tautology, meaning that for Derrida, "Every other (one) is God."[59] The social other serves in the capacity of a divine object of wholly other understanding, or in other words, alterity and unknowability as much as awe in the face of that otherness. Every social other is an expression of the wholly other; and the wholly other is expressed in the social other. But there is slippage between understanding the wholly other as death *qua* death; and because of the exaggerated proximity of the social other to death (alterity), the social other is taken for the wholly other. Derrida plays with this slippage but chooses to maintain the white lie that the gift is worthy of the giver.

Every being is an expression of nonbeing. John Singer's suicide exemplifies this at both first- and second-order observational levels; the person of Singer is a divinity precisely because the parable offered by McCullers holds in tension being and nonbeing. Derrida helps to unpack the philosophical significance of Singer:

> Every negative sentence would already be haunted by God or by the name of God, the distinction between God and God's name opening up the very space of this enigma. If there is a work of negativity in discourse and predication, it will produce divinity… . Not only would atheism not be the truth of negative theology; rather, God would be the truth of all negativity.[60]

Derrida here seems to be keeping intact the perseverance of the name god in the face of alterity and negativity, while at the same time tacitly suggesting that god appears in/as negativity. This negativity would find its locus or conceptual as well as embodied expression in death. Between god (as death) and "god's name" (as life), the gift of death is given and received in the "space of this enigma." Within this enigma the gift of death is exposed; blending responsibility with faith transposes death onto the wholly other alone, and humans are "introduced" to the concept of salvation from death through this process:

> For the game between these two unique "every other's" [humans and god], like the same "every other," opens the space or introduces the hope of salvation, the economy of "saving oneself."[61]

This "space" I have in earlier chapters sought to characterize as exaggerations of radical contingency, the distance posed between one community or individual (and death), and another community or individual (and death) through the projection of the god idea as anything *other than* an expression of social distance between those communities. That is, for salvation to be possible, the distance posed between god (i.e., death) and social others allows for "the hope of salvation." The Imago Superlata. The "marriage" of faith to responsibility is another example of this bridge spanning group social difference, built by the death of others through an economy of sacrifice undergirded by and allowing for "the hope of salvation." The body of others – substituting the wholly other for Isaac – comes to serve as the canvas on which this "space" or distance between freedom and responsibility is constituted and enacted for (and by) sacrifice. This is the same space as that in which, Mary Douglas tells us, bodies serve as the "canvas for symbolization"[62] – the space where meaning is made in/on/over bodies. False freedom is found through these nuptials between responsibility and faith. Thus, the gift of death provides the freedom to kill for the promise of eternal life, made possible by the distinction posed between those invited to this "wedding" and those left off the guest list.[63]

The gift of death is an economy of sacrifice

What is the relationship between responsibility, faith, and economy? Traditionally, responsibility has been registered in a Kantian sense,[64] as duty, an obligation fulfilled, expressed in Abraham's willingness to sacrifice Isaac. Abraham understood himself duty-bound to kill the very person most representative of the social hearth. God, as the story goes, intervenes, as Abraham's willingness was enough to appease god. But the willingness, out of a sense of duty conflated with responsibility, Derrida suggests "sets in train the search for salvation through sacrifice."[65] In short, framed in terms of physicality and embodied sacrifice, the Abrahamic duty seemingly promises the transformation of the economy of sacrifice into the sacrifice of such an economy.

Derrida suggests that out of Abraham's fulfillment of this "responsibility," god "reinscribes sacrifice within an economy" maintained by god/gods.[66] God, according to Derrida, "decides to *give back*, to give back life … once he is assured that a gift outside of any economy, the gift of death – and of the death of that which is priceless – has been accomplished without any hope of exchange, reward, circulation, or communication."[67] According to Derrida, such absolute responsibility is achieved through an "absolute renunciation" of all possible awards or rewards from god.[68] Responsibility is seemingly achieved by renouncing any need or demand for achievement. This suggests that if the social consequences of belief in god-idols are to be mitigated through a renewed focus on responsibility (social or otherwise), then that renewal will require an exploration of how salvation is enacted as an economy, and a coming to terms with that economy so that it might be offset. But Derrida doesn't seem to register the full social implications of this theological promise of an end to sacrifice. Stated differently, perhaps he errs on the side of logical rather than ethical un/certainty. I turn next to these consequences.

To receive the gift of death is to accept the death of social others

Derrida is of the mind that the story of Abraham offers a moment of clarity for reconstituting a sense of responsibility as only achieved upon relinquishing any demands for achievement. Responsibility, in its Judeo-Christian expression, is *to do and to do so blindly*, wedding faith and responsibility. Although Derrida does well to outline the problems associated with the gift of death, he does not give enough attention to the material consequences of the abstract theo-philosophical points he raises for those social actors left out of the narrative. My criticism here echoes Bourdieu's criticism of Derrida's critique of Kant's *Critique of Judgment*:

> It is an exemplary form of denegation – you tell (yourself) the truth but in such a way that you don't tell it – which defines the objective truth of the philosophical text in its social use… . Because he never withdraws from the philosophical game, whose conventions he respects … he can only philosophically tell the truth about the philosophical text and its philosophical reading, which (apart from the silence of orthodoxy) is the best way of not telling it [the truth].[69]

Following this line of criticism, in *The Gift of Death* Derrida remains far too wed to celebrating the philosophical and logical cohesion of the social arrangement called the gift of death; as a result, he remains indebted to the gift even as he works to establish many of the (social) perils of its (philosophical or theological) appeal. Capturing the significance of the Abrahamic tale with his paraphrased comment, Derrida notes that "you can count on the economy of heaven if you sacrifice the earthly economy." I agree that the function of theological projection and appeal is to ensure that those in social centers no longer have to look to those centers to find sacrificial offerings. The gift of death has been so long endured precisely because it functions relatively effectively at making those in social centers think they have been promised eternal life, that they have learned to die by learning to accept the promise of eternal life. But, as we know, this promise comes at the expense of social others. And Derrida's own failures at escaping the philosophical are instrumental for underscoring how particular brands of theology and theologizing have aided in simultaneously speaking to the problematic effects of the gift of death but remaining wed to it.

For instance, historian Edward Blum in his monumental *Reforging the White Republic* (2007) paints a portrait of the (white) American republic and the ways that a particular manipulation of concerns associated with the global *other* helped to solidify an exacting though nebulous racialized and religiously outlined "American" identity. During the latter half of the nineteenth century, anxieties connected to the fear that "the nation seemed to be falling apart"[70] were structuring and structured by an increase in American interest abroad. Blum compellingly demonstrates that domestic anxieties – that is, concerns over salvation (in the social sense I'm using the term here) – were assuaged "by exerting religious, economic, and political authority over foreign peoples."[71] The relationship between foreign and domestic issues was dialectical, whereby increasing interest abroad led to pathologizing statements about "peoples of Asia, South America, and Africa as ignorant children or subhuman demons" while the discourse made "the subjugation of African Americans" more palatable domestically, and worked to effectively *forge* an American (read: white American) identity and sensibility that "the United States was God's chosen nation."[72]

This functional theology of election, that the United States exists under the providence of god, ensures a socially grounded soteriology even in (and perhaps especially in) otherworldly expressions of salvation. Salvation, where white American religion is concerned, is conterminous with Manifest Destiny and its tertiary policies. Such a soteriological sensibility "tells" us, as Bourdieu would have it, "the truth but in such a way that we don't tell it."[73] This "truth" comes in the form of a reliance on the notions of salvation and god, and by its fruition, an economy of sacrifice. Missionary concerns abroad, as well as more explicit American policy interest abroad (whether in Africa or Asia, South America or Europe), work to ensure that a particular social other is crafted for the sake of exaggerating a distance from the "truth" about our (white) construction of the social other as a category.

An increasing concern for the global or economic other, that is, the "Isaacs" of the "white" world, had more to do with our identity as "Abraham." In a missionary zeal purportedly about saving others, those others come to be actually constituted as sacrificable, as marginal actors for whom our salvation relies on our concern over *their* salvation. Yet, this theological or eschatological and missiological concern was, rather, a concerted effort to forge a particular white identity as distinct from social sacrifices. Through this gift of death in social expression, sacrifices are externalized outward, exaggerated across oceans as much as time and skin color. We see these exaggerations imposed on those deemed social other as interpolations of the wholly otherness of an innocent, white American identity and nation. Indeed, the American identity grew "pure," "saved," as salvation obtained through the promise made possible by the gift of death, always and already made possible through a paternalistic and ideological assumption that relied on, yet skewed, the relationship between one person or group's "salvation" and that of the rest of the world. Whether at the turn of the twentieth century or the twenty-first, rhetorical concern to protect, defend, or fight for the "freedom" of other people and nations functions as protection for Americans from recognition that they (Americans) have undersigned a receipt for the gift of death. By this token, as American money reads, "in god we trust." That is, our stated effort to fight for the freedom of others creates the other so that we might retain the freedom to rely on those others as our sacrificial offerings. Are we white Americans like Derrida on this point, bound by our reliance on the sacrifices of others as he was bound to the "philosophical text?" Are we white Americans so wed to our theological conceptions of salvation that we simply cannot reject this "gift," now knowing the social sacrifices it requires? Or will we continue to justify these sacrifices by constituting the category of the other as a preoccupation with and proxy for killable or worthy of sacrifice?

Believing Derrida when – near the end of his life – he admits that he has not learned to live because he has never really learned to die,[74] I want to suggest that his failure was in not giving enough attention to those sacrificed within the Abrahamic story, those immediately connected to Abraham. Beautifully, though tragically too, Derrida gives honest assessment of his interpretive posture in an interview with *Le Monde* in 2004:

> So to answer your question, without further delay: no, I never learned-to-live. Absolutely not! Learning to live ought to mean learning to die – to acknowledge, to accept, an absolute mortality – without positive outcome, or resurrection, or redemption, for oneself or for anyone else. That has been the old philosophical injunction since Plato: to be a philosopher is to learn how to die. I believe in this truth without giving myself over to it. Less and less in fact. I have not learned to accept death. We are all survivors on deferral (and regarding deferral, from the geopolitical viewpoint in *Specters of Marx*, the emphasis is especially – in a world that is more inegalitarian than ever – on the billions of living beings – human and otherwise – who are denied not only basic "human rights," which go back two hundred years old and are continually being amplified, but are denied even the right to live a decent life). But I remain impervious to learning when it comes to knowing-how-to-die, I have yet to learn anything about this particular subject.[75]

Published less than two months before his death on October 8, 2004, this passage from the *Le Monde* interview juxtaposes learning to die with the stated concern for those denied "basic 'human rights,'" suggesting that he not only has genuine concern for these social others, but recognizes that something about his inability to learn to die prevents his ability to alter their (or his) social situation. "We are all survivors on deferral," he tells us as an ontological diagnostic, but witnessed rhetorically here is the enigmatic, paradoxical, aporetic "space" of exaggerations of radical contingency. Such a space is filled by these exaggerations, and one of the most severe of these is the exaggeration of the social other as wholly other making possible the gift of death, which offers the ability to see the relation between self and social other, but continuously fails to cross this social chasm.

In the pages of *The Gift of Death*, Derrida is keen to only register his social responsibility over and against himself, even as he acknowledges he – and Abraham/Isaac/God – are not completely alone. Stated differently, Derrida spends considerable time justifying the utility of secrecy – Abraham kept his attempted murder a secret – instead of exploring the full social impact *for social others* of this secret kept. I mean this literally, in terms of the text *The Gift of Death*, but also metaphorically, in terms of Derrida's own ideological commitments as his biological life came to a close. Truly learning to die with others, perhaps a better way of understanding what it might mean to learn to die at all, will involve not simply waxing on the men who made it to Mount Moriah or Golgotha, but those who are not present in the story, those on the margins. Though in a couple instances in *The Gift of Death* Derrida momentarily asks how Sarah, Hagar, and Ishmael might change the events of these sacrifices,[76] he never really overcomes his own assumptions about their wholly otherness to think through their concerns and include them as substantive contributors to his project. Here, if it is not clear, I am registering *The Gift of Death*, the theological text, as allegorical of its topic, a metonym for understanding the gift of death functioning to ensure that social others are only ever understood as wholly other – that is, inaccessible.

Derrida seems to inherit such a position from Heidegger, who suggests that "in the dying of the Other we can experience that remarkable phenomenon of Being which may be defined as the change-over of an entity from Dasein's kind of Being (or life) to no-longer-Dasein."[77] Heidegger (and by extension, Derrida) considers "the death of Others more impressive"[78] than one's own death, for what possibility such deaths hold as presenting a "beginning," a newness, a rupture of the logic of Dascin, of being. Thcy both rely on sacrifice for its possibility of rupturing an economy of sacrifice. Is such a logic not a motivating feature of genocide, historically? The gift of death ensures that genocide is justified alongside individual sacrifices, because the death of the other promises a greater possibility for something different. There is little wonder Heidegger was comfortable in Nazi Germany, and Derrida has so much trouble "learning how to die." They follow an assumption that promises salvation through this "ultimate" sacrifice of the other.

Rather than understand god as taking on the economy of sacrifice so that humans no longer have to sacrifice themselves, if we take seriously the suggestion that the social other and the wholly other have been conflated through the gift of death, then any theological suggestion of god bearing the sacrificial burden is more aptly understood as social others bearing that burden. Interpreting god's sacrifice as the continuous sacrifice of social others helps to rethink any suggestion that god's sacrifice disrupts the economy of sacrifice. Rather, the actual end to the economy of sacrifice is only obtained through the sacrifice of the mechanism making any of this possible, god-idols, and their effect and motivation, personal salvation and the soul.

Personal conceptions of the soul are akin to being "beyond the law," which Derrida suggests is the constituent feature of grace, and amounts to what, Derrida reminds us, Nietzsche called Christianity's "stroke of genius."[79] The stroke of genius, of Christianity, in this reading, is the externalization of sacrifice into the theological/metaphysical realm rather than sacrifice continuing as a material social practice. The economy of sacrifice is sustained at a social level precisely because it is purportedly no longer required by the new law. Its continued function is kept as a secret. The new is but the old, uninterrupted. Effectively, this kills "god," leaving god as wholly other, wholly other to the social arrangement. In other words, through the economy of sacrifice transmuted through ideological and mythical projection, the wholly other is properly constituted as social other. Given this arrangement, the social other is god because the social other is killed. Salvation is sought and promised through the sacrifice of "god" concealing the actual sacrifices of social actors. Abraham was willing to kill his own son so that the social fabric be mended. Christians, here speaking of U.S. white Christians though the analysis might be extended to certain other groups, follow the "new law" of sacrificing those outside the social center rather than those within it. The "new law" is not actually new, but is a theological manipulation of who is inside or outside of the law, with "inside the law" understood as the beneficiaries of the economy of sacrifice, "outside of the law" representative of those sacrificed, and "beyond the law" the position of executioners, i.e., Abraham, Darren Wilson, George Zimmerman, etc.

Derrida, proxy for many contemporary white Americans even if himself French, seems to have never learned to die because he never learned to live with others; to live without the law. Stated differently, he never stopped seeing a difference between himself and other social actors. He never came to know social others because the constitution of the wholly other, undergirded by a metaphysical claim about or sense of the soul, prevented the hermeneutical and social distance from closing between himself and those deemed social others. Derrida's focus on the "gift of death," as transposed from human to divine, doesn't actually accomplish the end of the economy. What it does is ensure that Abraham remain at the social center, while Isaac's mother and Abraham's "other" family are located in expanding concentric circles away from that social center, away from "Mount Moriah."

Derrida even situates Mount Moriah as a metaphor for society, which tradition has it "is the place where Solomon decided to build the House of the Lord in Jerusalem … also the place of the grand Mosque of Jerusalem, the place called the

Dome of the Rock … a holy place … and a disputed place … fought over by all the monotheisms."[80] This fighting, and the geophysical localization of this first gift of death, suggests that "this land of Moriah … is our habitat every second of every day."[81] This place and the story associated with it constitute the originary story of the gift of death as the economy of sacrifice, transposed outward to the "other" as god (of monotheisms) comes to be understood as wholly other, outside being, outside the social. Succeeding where Derrida failed might be made possible by exposing the "secret" of this economy, a secret exposed in (and as) the death of the personal soul. Yet, achieving this would mean nothing less than a shift away from a society of estrangement to something different – so different it would mean the death of this economy, promised by "god" but never delivered because we have remained ignorant that this end is ours to face with others.

This allegorical tale points to the place and time, the *axis mundi*, when totems were dislodged from material places and times, coming to be confused with the transcendent, when western history began as society became the functional "god." Therefore, this gift of death has everything to do with exaggerations of human value, differentially ranked, according to geographic and theological location, and to this extent, *history arises as a soteriology* as Abraham is "given" salvation having trusted in god. The closer to god, to "Mount Moriah," the closer to the *axis mundi*, the greater the perceived importance and ability. Abraham's willingness to kill Isaac, of course, represents the pinnacle of human possibility within this arrangement. Rejecting this gift of death, then, involves nothing less than a rejection of some of the most fundamentally held beliefs arising from this arrangement, beginning with the desire for salvation and the willingness to kill for it.

This initial theological sleight of hand – that is, the constitution of the wholly other as the social other – requires a theological tactic or response. This response comes in the form not of physical or social sacrifice, or even in the demand to sacrifice "god," but in hermeneutically treating death as god, and an embrace of love as the truth of social unity. For white Americans, such recognition requires a rejection of belief in an afterlife, personal salvation, and personal conception of the soul, used to determine who is inside, outside, above, or beyond the law.

Relinquishing any commitments to personal salvation or the soul might allow for the bridge between the social other and divine other to be partially severed, with other expressions of letting go (such as the death of god-idols) also working towards that end. This "bridge" to be severed has been ushered into history as an economy of sacrifice, witnessed tautologically through the stories of Abraham's sacrifice of Isaac and God's sacrifice of his own son, Christ, and too many other instances to name, including animal sacrifices and the sacrifice of the natural world as a whole if ecological exaggerations of radical contingency are taken into account. Salvation may be personal, and it may also invite responsibility, but through its reliance on an economy of sacrifice, responsibility is mutated into the duty to kill rather than a humanity that would recognize we die together. Someone, or something, pays the price for a "responsible" faith. In rejecting the gift of death, old and new "laws" are indistinguishable, and this secret of the "law" is understood as the economy of sacrifice. More must be said of how rejection of the apparatus of the law is made possible through the finality found in a god of death.

REJECTING THE "GIFT OF DEATH"

To conclude this chapter, and to provide a brief precedent for my rejection of the gift of death, I turn back to a lesser read book from a young Ludwig Feuerbach, in order to think through the possibility that a personal conception of the soul and of salvation are the fruits of the economy of sacrifice. To reject such "fruit" is no *actual* sacrifice, as personal salvations are effects to causes, but carry the weight of the *very* first cause, the flight from and denial of uncertainty. Rejecting the soul responds to the perils of sacrifice witnessed in the production, disciplining, and sacrifice of social others, but does not actually reproduce the economy of sacrifice. In a word, letting go of personal conceptions of the soul or salvation divorces faith from responsibility. It "kills" the *gift* of death by squaring with death at last. It also guards against the appropriation of death as redemptive. And it connects this rejection to its ultimate aim, a sense of social responsibility based on love as human unity. This is not a promise to end the reign of god-idols, but offers those wanting to reject such a religious orientation the means to know that they are no longer sustaining a theological position that justifies or requires an economy of sacrifice.

Feuerbach's lesser acknowledged *Thoughts on Death and Immortality* (1830) stands as a brash, unpolished polemic against the idea of personal immortality, arguing instead "for recognition of the inexhaustible quality of the only life we have."[82] As Feuerbach eloquently states his concern, "Those peculiar beings and strange subjects who think that they live only after life ... as they posit a future life, they negate the actual life."[83] Feuerbach's efforts are in refutation of an Hegelian and Christian "theoretical selfishness,"[84] out of which has come a skewed assessment of reality, as such. For Feuerbach, as for me, there is little difference between Hegelianism and Christianity's Modern development, given the synthesis of salvation and history. "For if there is life after death," Feuerbach suggests, "there cannot be life before death; one excludes the other; the present life cancels the future life, the future life cancels the present life."[85] This advocates that ideas such as personal immortality produce negative social effects. Similar in certain respects but still distinct from Montaigne's focus on the finality of life as a kind of personal experience intensifier – metaphorically, a kind of all-natural sweetener to the coffee cup of life – Feuerbach has in mind that personal salvation prevents the "present life" from being lived in an arrangement based on *love*, an understanding of unity premised on an embrace of the fundamental sameness of human personhood, as a quality not of distinction but of connectedness to all persons. His argument is simple: that a personal conception of the soul, guided by a Cartesian dualism wed to an Hegelian casting of god as history, makes it fundamentally impossible for Christians to do the one thing demanded of them above all else, to love unconditionally, to achieve unity amidst difference. This problem remains in place for white Americans, who either actively adhere to similar Christian doctrine today or who have inherited this ideological baggage in secular garb.

Feuerbach's rationale for such a position involves this concept of love, which he understands as "the unity of personhood and essence," meaning that distinctions, though bound up in any formula of love, are what must be properly contextualized as instruments for unity if the Christian demand to love is to be realized.[86] Consequentially, he offers a solution for responding to this selfishness and inability to love by foregrounding death as a way of refuting a personal conception of the soul, replacing it with a pantheistic cosmology.

Corresponding to Feuerbach in how both understand love as action-oriented, but in more grounded (non-cosmological) terms, social theorist bell hooks offers a similar justification for moving beyond the gift of death as she writes about love as a practice of freedom, not in an individual sense as offered by the Cogito, but a freedom to unify and work towards new social life options.[87] Written in response to what she refers to as an ideology and culture of domination, her words seem applicable to refuting the logic and economy behind the gift of death. She suggests that the world can be responded to in ways that do not reify the current structure of it through the cultivation of "a love ethic that can transform our lives by offering us a different set of values to live by."[88] hooks writes that fear

> is the primary force upholding structures of domination. It promotes the desire for separation, the desire not to be known. When we are taught that safety lies always with sameness, then difference, of any kind, will appear as a threat. When we choose to love we choose to move against fear – against alienation and separation. The choice to love is a choice to connect – to find ourselves in the other.[89]

I am not interested in Feuerbach's cosmological claims. My brief reference to hooks is meant to modify and correct for Feuerbach's cosmological shortsightedness. With hooks' insights in mind, I want to suggest that Feuerbach might be read as a social theorist. The idea that theology is anthropology cuts in both directions, as the uncertainty of full social knowing suggests that theology covers the ground of the unknown and unknowable social world. Indeed, I inherit this position from Feuerbach: "This world is the world of the Gods."[90]

Feuerbach is useful as a social theorist here because he distinguishes between gods and humans based on limitation; gods are unlimited, humans limited,[91] but he always reminds us that these gods are but human projections. His writings, then, offer extended materials for exploring the effects of how, and to what degree, limitations are acknowledged by white social actors. Personal salvation, promising a triumph over death, suggests then that those who hold such a position feel themselves to be gods, unlimited ultimately and supposedly proven so through a believed-in triumph over death. That god-status seems to be an effect of receiving the gift of death. This rejection of personal immortality offers a strategy for exorcizing the independent, subjective personhood and sense of the soul from the scope of white religious possibility. Doing so ensures – albeit with an existential force more akin to an axe than a scalpel – that whatever the ultimate concerns held by white Christians and white Americans more generally, they might no longer support an economy of sacrifice or the god-idols that rely on such sacrifices. Noting that death is both the "ultimate act of communication"[92] and the ultimate manifestation of limitation,[93] Feuerbach underscores the rationale for a pedagogic of death:

> For death can be conquered only before death. But this can be accomplished only by the total and complete surrender of the self, only by the acknowledgment of universal will, the will of God, only by the appropriation of his will and the knowledge and perception of the essential truth of death that must be connected to this appropriation.[94]

Unlike Derrida's gift of death, which retains the will of the self through the sacrifice of godself, here Feuerbach offers an alternative to the economy of sacrifice suggesting that by relinquishing a sense of self, the will of god – unity – can be achieved. When white Americans proffer a "complete surrender of the self," then the will of god (i.e., the will of the social other) might be done. Unity would mean inclusion at the social center, an end to social otherness as wholly otherness.

While the gift of death, as Derrida suggests, allows Abraham to fulfill a kind of duty, it is an irresponsible social duty, relying not only on the constitution and maintenance of the social other as wholly other, but on the sacrifices of those social others. In *not* sacrificing Isaac, Abraham sacrificed humanity through the false promise that humanity would be "saved." Yet, in not sacrificing "god" in this arrangement, Abraham turned this myth into history. Personal salvation achieves no responsibility at all, because it addresses such responsibility by killing those at social margins who bring this responsibility [uncomfortably] to the minds of those at social centers. In terms of continental philosophy, Emmanuel Levinas may be right in suggesting that the face of the other *tells* those at social centers "Do not kill me,"[95] but this telling alone does not ensure that the affective disposition of those at a social center guided by an economy of sacrifice will be able to do anything *other than kill* the other. Wedding this faith to responsibility is to selfishly escape the responsibility to not kill by acting as though killing is the highest duty and responsibility of "faith."

John Singer, as a model for white Americans, can be read in two ways: killer of Isaac or killer of the soul. Responsibility would involve choosing to kill neither social others nor those at social centers, instead choosing to "kill" the mechanism holding them as distinct. The death of personal immortality is not simply a litmus test or an ersatz good substituting for the physical deaths of white Americans; it is the actual means of refuting the economy of sacrifice, killing it – an idea – instead of people.

In my estimation, Feuerbach's refutation of personal immortality helps to set in place social conditions that might promote the responsibility demanded by the face of the other, but it remains paradoxical, in that achieving this responsibility requires the dissolution of the "other" as wholly other. For instance, it pushes against any language that seeks to distinguish between heaven and earth, forcing recognition of the hells and heavens experienced on earth daily by those within or outside of social centers. Refuting personal salvation offers a means of embracing social responsibility as this paradox, but choosing to die with, if not for, those social others formerly registered as wholly other. Killing the soul – not the social other – is what might ultimately kill the idea of the wholly other as social other. Violence, killing, is paradoxically required, just as Derrida makes clear, but choosing to embrace death as a pedagogic opens white Americans to the possibility of putting to death something other than those socially othered. In "killing" the soul, we finally respond to this gift by choosing *not* to kill actual people. This rupture of the sacrificial economy begins with exposure of death as an object that unites us all.

EXPOSING THE "OBJECT" OF DEATH

Derrida concludes *The Gift of Death* by quoting an incredibly dense passage from Charles Baudelaire's *The Pagan School* (1852). Baudelaire notes "the danger is so great that I excuse the suppression of the object."[96] Following Baudelaire, Derrida seems to suggest that both science and philosophy have (to that point in history) been left wanting, unable to balance the concerns of each other, leading to "homicidal and suicidal literature."[97] Fear of such "literature" might have been what piqued Derrida's interest in death and theology in the latter years of his life, as well as his deconstructive task throughout his corpus. Baudelaire's critique is reminiscent of Nietzsche's aims in *The Gay Science* of correcting for the stultifying certainties falsely promised by romanticism and positivism.[98] But for Baudelaire, this "danger" seems to involve the homicidal and suicidal tendencies of religious hypocrites. But what is the object whose suppression is forgiven?

Derrida, in a passage forgiving the suppression of this object, and one of the rare instances he stops deconstructing and starts constructing, suggests that in order to prevent the "negation or destruction" of the gift of death – by this, he means that it be exposed as theological trickery – then another suppression is necessary: "the gift suppresses the object (of the gift) … keeping in the gift only the giving, the act of giving, and intention to give, not the given [death], which in the end doesn't count."[99] For Derrida, the exchange matters, and the exchange must continue. The object suppressed is death. Death, as the object of the gift, is lost to the exchange of sacrifice; the object is suppressed and social others are taken for the wholly other. For example, if we think of this arrangement as a literal exchange of a gift – a wrapped present given to an/other – Derrida is suggesting that the giving of the gift is more important than what is inside the box. The asymmetry between the gift giver and receiver is unable to be balanced – that is, assumed differences in the ability and value of each are taken for granted – because the object of the gift is left inside the box, unable to flatten this arrangement through mutual concern, or through adoration, respect, or otherwise concern for the object of the gift.

Feuerbach, speaking also of death as an object, offers an alternative focus. Feuerbach is interested in the present, the actual gift inside the box, not the social exchange. Focused on the death of the personal self, he indicates that any sort of dismissal, disavowal, or "suppression" (to recall of Baudelaire's language) of this object is harmful. Indeed, suppression of this object and privileging the "gift" may say something about the longstanding desire to learn to die, the focus of so many philosophers and theologians for so long. "But the nothingness," writes Feuerbach, "the death of the self at the moment of isolation, at the moment when it wishes to exist without the object [in other words, when it wishes to 'suppress' the object], is the revelation of love, is the revelation that you can exist only with and in the object."[100] Where love is concerned – or for my purposes, social responsibility – there can be no suppression of the object of death. The gift of death pivots on the giving, but in accepting this gift, the recipient is left without access to the very object needing to be faced, death. Feuerbach pulls no punches:

> Only when the human once again recognizes that there exists not merely an *appearance of death*, but an actual and real death, a death that completely terminates the life of the individual, only when he returns to the awareness of his finitude will he gain the courage to begin a new life … .[101]

Here, Feuerbach gives principal attention to the "actual and real death" always faced in and as life. Death, this "actual and real" death, Feuerbach suggests, aids in the formation of attention. And where is that attention to be directed? According to a "logic of limitation"[102] wherein an infinite creator subjects itself to space and time, an intrinsic, pantheistic, or even monist suggestion indicates that god is expressed in the finite capacity of organic, mortal bodies.

Effectively, Feuerbach's refutation of a personal sense of the soul can be imagined as Abraham having realized that the only thing needing to be sacrificed is the mechanism of theological projection supporting any notion of an afterlife and guiding the inability to see different social groups as equal in value and ability. That is, Feuerbach is seeking to "sacrifice" the economy of sacrifice so that actual sacrifices might end; his efforts expose the economy as the veneer of salvation masking a "gift" of death distributed – given – to those socially othered. God's salvation of Isaac privileges exchange, as death is "suppressed." The "gift" stays wrapped. This is precisely why John Singer offers a kind of Abrahamic narrative, albeit with a different ending. Singer "opens" the gift, revealing its secret, through his own death because his absence (a metaphor not for physical or social death, but the "death" of the personal soul) shifts attention away from the gift economy to the object of death, finitude, and limitation. The other characters in McCullers's novel remain lonely and uncertain white (and black) Americans, but their ability to appeal to valuative and agential differences amongst social groups is diminished. In counterpoising Abraham with Christ with Singer, or in offering alternative imaginings of their actions and choices, I don't mean to place judgment on any particular tradition, but to privilege the possibility that such imagined alternatives might aid in the refutation of the economy of sacrifice, an economy which constitutes social actors as either gods or sacrificial offerings to those gods. This is not necessarily the only solution, but perhaps it does offer a socially and ethically focused suggestion that might ensure that the system of sacrificial exchange undergirded by a certain conception of the afterlife and the soul is ended.

SALVATION IN TWILIGHT TIMES

In a section of *The Gift of Death* left underdeveloped in terms of the (possible) impact of the topic on his overall argument, Derrida relates the Abrahamic tale to the heart, suggesting the narrative is "a meditation or sermon on the heart, on what the heart is and more precisely what it *should be* should it return to its correct place ... in its correct *site* [emplacement], that is the very thing that gives us food for thought concerning economy."[103] White American "hearts" have been lonely hunters because we have sought to find our "correct place" through a lonely practice, that of being "hunters" – killing those who would give life and color to the world, or those who would change our vision of that world as intrinsically salvific. Even in seeking an alternative to our loneliness, most of us remain killers now, told to kill the mechanism making possible this murderous loneliness: personal salvation.

For these reasons, McCullers's character John Singer offers a contemporary tale that might augment the Abrahamic and Christological economies of sacrifice, as it provides a cultural narrative that might help us "lonely hunters" at social centers come to terms with the death of any conception of the soul or an afterlife, a death that would mean learning how to live without hunting other humans. "Culture," some scholars of death suggest, "is the primary vehicle through which ... the pangs of death are lessened,"[104] but it is also the place where "fear of life's end is learned from and perpetuated."[105] My continued turn to cultural resources, such as McCullers and next Lillian Smith, attempts to provide an unraveling of this fear, dread, anxiety, and absurdity of life in death and death in life. But no promises can be made that a new path will be possible that does not, at some level, reinforce the logic of sacrifice producing and sustaining god-idols. So how does this actually play out for white Americans?

Where McCullers's own life is concerned, Singer's death is a sort of mandate that she expects more of herself and more from those around her and likely, more from all of us. Yet, she was under no assumption that the cultivation of such social responsibility would be contagious or that it would not be negated by yet other unexamined ideas and practices. In the final chapter, I engage the life of one of McCullers's contemporaries, Lillian Smith, and the tragic occasion of one of their interactions. Both of them largely rejected the constitution of social others as wholly other – as unknowable save for their alterity. So do I.

White Americans seem to be in the position that we cannot be sure our traditional religious beliefs or practices do not reinforce white religion's casting of social others as wholly other. Because of this, we might do well to renegotiate the terms of some of our most cherished ideals, the personal conception of the soul being one of these. Whether this requires abandoning an entire tradition remains to be seen, but perhaps the process might begin by choosing one Sunday morning to stay in bed, find a copy of McCullers's book (or another), and begin to "worship" something different,[106] cultivating social responsibility through reflexive engagement with cultural resources that might call into question, critique, or cast new light on the limits of contemporary white American identity and its ongoing reliance on and celebration of an economy of sacrifice. Isn't this what the characters in McCullers's novel failed to do? Resources for this responsibility are countlessly available, and finding them might just offer a more socially responsible way to spend the limited, finite time we have together. Having killed the idea of a personal salvation, and embraced a growing social responsibility, white killers might begin to "hunt" not people but concrete resources, tactics, and dialogues for equitable, limited existence in an increasingly diverse, exceedingly radically contingent, social world. Then it might be said that we white Americans have begun to live because we have begun to learn to die with others.

Notes

1 Jacques Derrida, *The Gift of Death ; & Literature in Secret* (University of Chicago Press, 2008), 8.
2 Friedrich Nietzsche, *On the Genealogy of Morals and Ecce Homo, Edited with Commentary by Walter Kaufmann*, trans. Walter Kaufmann (Vintage Books, 1969), 335.
3 Pierre Bourdieu, "Genesis and Structure of the Religious Field," 1–3.
4 My suggestion should not be read as a covert appeal to "collective salvation" either. By social responsibility, I mean to suggest a program for interaction no longer based on the demand for salvation, or the presumption that salvation is possible.
5 I intentionally conflate the basic idea of life after death with the question (some) might have in terms of a reward or punishment. Salvation is the continuance of life, not the reward for a life lived faithfully.
6 See the discussion of salvation found in Alan Richardson and John Bowden, *The Westminster Dictionary of Christian Theology* (Westminster John Knox Press, 1983), 519–21.
7 See, for instance, Walter Rauschenbusch, Anthony Campolo, and Paul Rauschenbusch, *Christianity and the Social Crisis in the 21st Century: The Classic That Woke up the Church* (HarperSanFrancisco Publishers Group UK [distributor], 2008). Though Rauschenbusch is remembered for his attention to social salvation, I understand even

such utopian visions as guided principally by an inability to wrestle with social difference, and understand such projects as rooted in personal attempts to escape both death and its effects. Indeed, as Gary Dorrien has made clear, this movement was filled with leaders whose vision of the Kingdom on Earth left truncated options for African Americans. See also Gary Dorrien, *The Making of American Liberal Theology: Idealism, Realism, and Modernity, 1900–1950* (Westminster John Knox Press, 2003).

8 Though the statement of belief does not, in many or even most instances, correspond to daily lifestyle or commitment, I am here only noting the connection between the Nicene Creed and the style and arrangement of salvation under scrutiny here.

9 To those who would suggest I am here setting up a strawman, I encourage them to try and demonstrate that the stated arrangement is not one of the major strands of white American Christian thought in the United States.

10 Derrida, *The Gift of Death*, 5.

11 Ibid., 8.

12 Of my position on Levinas, I agree with his claim that the face of the other reveals the call to responsibility. But I do not find Levinas helpful for addressing this asymmetrical arrangement. Asymmetry is an expression of the "chasm" between the material and ideological "worlds." For more on Levinas, see Emmanuel Levinas and Richard A. Cohen, *Ethics and Infinity: Conversations with Philippe Nemo* (Duquesne University Press, 1985).

13 Heidegger's eventual embrace of National Socialism hangs as a warning, a shadow, over *White Lies*, in that too much sympathy for those at social centers will always reinforce the construction and subjugation of the margins. Heidegger's intense individualism plays out through the justification of group atrocities. He is, in a sense, emblematic of the danger of taking the "medicine" I offer, but not following the directions. Those "directions" involve understanding *White Lies* as hermeneutical and not metaphysical, ontotheological, or ontological.

14 See, for instance, Martin Heidegger, *Being and Time* (SUNY Press, 2010), 260–67.

15 I look forward to future work that might spell out a fuller philosophical genealogy of my argument.

16 Derrida, *The Gift of Death*, 5, original emphasis.

17 While I define death in terms of the loss of power, and Tillich defines it in terms of non-being, his definition fits within mine, and thus his framing of this question remains useful both thematically and as a sociological snapshot of the fear of lost power shaping theological assumptions and presumptions about possible alternatives.

18 Paul Tillich, "The Eternal Now," quoted in Herman Feifel, *The Meaning of Death* (Blakiston Division, McGraw-Hill, 1959), 33–34.

19 Derrida, *The Gift of Death*, 70.

20 Ibid., 71.

21 Friedrich Nietzsche, *On the Genealogy of Morals and Ecce Homo*, 335.

22 Vigen Guroian, *Life's Living Toward Dying: A Theological and Medical-Ethical Study* (Wm. B. Eerdmans Publishing, 1996).

23 Kenneth L. Vaux, "The Pedagogy of Death," *Religious Education* 85, no. 4 (September 1, 1990): 509–87.

24 U.S. Department of Health and Human Services, "United States Life Tables, 2009," January 6, 2014, accessed March 10, 2015, http://www.cdc.gov/nchs/data/nvsr/nvsr62/nvsr62_07.pdf

25 Derrida, *The Gift of Death*, 86.

26 Michel Eyquem de Montaigne, "That to Study Philosophy Is to Learn to Die," in *The Complete Essays of Montaigne* (Stanford University Press, 1958), 56.

27 I would also suggest that this "letting go" of power has as much to do with coming to realize that power is never actually "held," but is a mirage or dream, insulated from and insulating human recognition and misrecognition of radical contingency.

28 Clifton D. Bryant, *Handbook of Death and Dying* (SAGE, 2003), 9.
29 Montaigne, "That to Study Philosophy Is to Learn to Die."
30 Ludwig Feuerbach, *Thoughts on Death and Immortality* (University of California Press, 1981), iii.
31 J. E. Malpas and Robert C. Solomon, *Death and Philosophy* (Routledge, 2002), 145.
32 Cornel West, *The Cornel West Reader* (Basic Books, 1999), 115.
33 Derrida, *The Gift of Death*, 28.
34 Molière, Leman, Leloir, and Montaiglon, *Le dépit amoureux* (J. Lemonnyer, 1888), 130.
35 Montaigne, "That to Study Philosophy Is to Learn to Die," 56–64.
36 West. *The Cornel West Reader*, 89–90
37 Ibid.
38 My application of this term is informed by Orlando Patterson, albeit not identical to his usage. Patterson suggests death involves the cessation of social, psychological influence and cultural authority – again, matters of power and resource. Of social death, Patterson goes on to describe intrusive and extrusive versions: being deemed a permanent outsider and an insider who has ceased to belong, respectively. I am indebted to his ideas, but I want to trouble the finality of "death" in a way Patterson does not. Orlando Patterson, *Slavery and Social Death: A Comparative Study* (Harvard University Press, 1985), 1–5, 38–39.
39 Of Heidegger on decadence, see Frank Schalow, *The Renewal of the Heidegger Kant Dialogue: Action, Thought, and Responsibility* (SUNY Press, 1992), 12.
40 *American Men of Science: A Biographical Directory* (Bowker, 1910), 577.
41 For more information on those who feel this loss as occurring already, see Michael Kimmel, *Angry White Men: American Masculinity and the End of an Era* (Nation Books, 2013).
42 Carson McCullers, *Illumination and Night Glare: The Unfinished Autobiography of Carson McCullers* (University of Wisconsin Press, 2002), xii.
43 Carson McCullers, *The Heart Is a Lonely Hunter*, 1st Mariner Books edition (Mariner, 2004a).
44 McCullers, *The Heart Is a Lonely Hunter*, 85.
45 McCullers, *Illumination*, 4.
46 McCullers, *The Heart Is a Lonely Hunter*, 151.
47 Ibid., 119–20.
48 McCullers, *Illumination*, 4.
49 McCullers, *The Heart Is a Lonely Hunter*, 285.
50 Ibid., 215.
51 Ibid., 326.
52 Ibid., 345.
53 Ibid., 341–2.
54 Dietrich Bonhoeffer, qtd. in Thomas J. J. Altizer and William Hamilton, *Radical Theology and the Death of God*, softcover edition (Bobbs-Merrill Company, 1966), 115.
55 Genesis 22:12. Bible. New Revised Standard Version.
56 Derrida, *The Gift of Death*, 8.
57 Ibid., 82.
58 Karl Barth, *The Humanity of God* (Westminster John Knox Press, 1960), 37.
59 Derrida, *The Gift of Death*, 87.
60 Jacques Derrida, "How to Avoid Speaking: Denials," in Harold G. Coward, Toby Foshay, and Jacques Derrida, *Derrida and Negative Theology* (State University of New York Press, 1992), 76.
61 Derrida, *The Gift of Death*, 87.
62 Mary Douglas, *Natural Symbols: Explorations in Cosmology*, 3rd ed. (Routledge, 2003), xxxvii.

63 Indeed, such themes of insider and outsider are constantly engaged by Carson McCullers. See, for instance, Carson McCullers, *The Ballad of the Sad Café: And Other Stories* (Mariner Books, 2005 [1951]); and Carson McCullers, *The Member of the Wedding* (Mariner Books, 2004 [1946]).
64 Derrida, *The Gift of Death*, 114.
65 Ibid., 93.
66 Ibid., 95.
67 Ibid., 95–6, original emphasis.
68 Ibid., 96.
69 Pierre Bourdieu, *Distinction: A Social Critique of the Judgement of Taste* (Harvard University Press, 1984), 495.
70 Edward J. Blum, *Reforging the White Republic: Race, Religion, and American Nationalism, 1865–1898* (LSU Press, 2007), 211.
71 Ibid., 211–212.
72 Ibid., 212.
73 Bourdieu, *Distinction*, 495.
74 Jacques Derrida, "I Am at War with Myself," *Le Monde* interview, August 19, 2004, accessed January 15, 2015, http://www.egs.edu/faculty/jacques-derrida/articles/i-am-at-war-with-myself/
75 Derrida, "I Am At War with Myself."
76 Derrida, *The Gift of Death*, 110.
77 Heidegger, *Being and Time*, ss 238.
78 Ibid.
79 Ibid., 82.
80 Derrida, *The Gift of Death*, 70.
81 Ibid., 70.
82 Ludwig Feuerbach, *Thoughts on Death and Immortality* (University of California Press, 1981), ix.
83 Ibid., 133
84 Ibid., xxii.
85 Ibid., 133.
86 Ibid., 29.
87 bell hooks, *Outlaw Culture: Resisting Representations* (Routledge, 2006), 243–50.
88 bell hooks, *All About Love: New Visions* (William Morrow, 2001), 88.
89 Ibid., 93.
90 Ludwig Feuerbach, *The Essence of Religion* (Prometheus Books, 2004), 61.
91 Ibid., 63.
92 Feuerbach, *Thoughts on Death*, 121.
93 Ibid., 162.
94 Ibid., 126.
95 Gary Gutting, *Thinking the Impossible: French Philosophy Since 1960* (Oxford University Press, 2011), 123. See also, Emmanuel Levinas and Alphonso Lingis, *Totality and Infinity: An Essay on Exteriority* (Duquesne University Press, 1969).
96 Charles Baudelaire, "The Pagan School," quoted in Derrida, *The Gift of Death*, 112.
97 Ibid., 112.
98 Friedrich Nietzsche, *The Gay Science: With a Prelude in Rhymes and an Appendix of Songs* (Vintage Books, 1974).
99 Derrida, *The Gift of Death*, 113.
100 Ibid., 126.
101 Ibid., 17.
102 Ibid., xxvii.
103 Derrida, *The Gift of Death*, 97, original emphasis.
104 Clifton D. Bryant, *Handbook of Death and Dying* (SAGE, 2003), 12.

105 Bryant, 118.
106 This idea could as easily be characterized as learning to not "worship" anything, learning to live without the perceived need or demand to/for worship.

REFERENCES

Altizer, Thomas J. J. and William Hamilton. 1966. *Radical Theology and the Death of God.* Softcover edition. Bobbs-Merrill Company.

American Men of Science: A Biographical Directory. 1910. Bowker.

Barth, Karl. 1960. *The Humanity of God.* Westminster John Knox Press.

Bible. New Revised Standard Version.

Blum, Edward J. 2007. *Reforging the White Republic: Race, Religion, and American Nationalism, 1865–1898.* LSU Press.

Bourdieu, Pierre. 1984. *Distinction: A Social Critique of the Judgement of Taste.* Harvard University Press.

Bourdieu, Pierre. 1991. "Genesis and Structure of the Religious Field." *Comparative Social Research* 13: 1–44.

Bryant, Clifton D. 2003. *Handbook of Death and Dying*. 1st ed. SAGE Publications.

Coward, Harold G., Toby Foshay, and Jacques Derrida. 1992. *Derrida and Negative Theology*. State University of New York Press.

Derrida, Jacques. 2004. "I Am At War with Myself." *Le Monde*, August 19, accessed January 15, 2015, http://www.egs.edu/faculty/jacques-derrida/articles/i-am-at-war-with-myself/

Derrida, Jacques. 2008. *The Gift of Death ; &, Literature in Secret.* University of Chicago Press.

Dorrien, Gary J. 2003. *The Making of American Liberal Theology: Idealism, Realism, and Modernity, 1900–1950.* 1st ed. Westminster John Knox Press.

Douglas, Mary. 2003. *Natural Symbols: Explorations in Cosmology*. 3rd ed. Routledge.

Feifel, Herman. 1959. *The Meaning of Death.* Blakiston Division, McGraw-Hill.

Feuerbach, Ludwig. 2004. *The Essence of Religion*. Prometheus Books.

Feuerbach, Ludwig. 1981. *Thoughts on Death and Immortality: From the Papers of a Thinker, along with an Appendix of Theological Satirical Epigrams, Edited by One of His Friends.* University of California Press.

Guroian, Vigen. 1996. *Life's Living Toward Dying: A Theological and Medical-Ethical Study.* Wm. B. Eerdmans Publishing.

Gutting, Gary. 2011. *Thinking the Impossible: French Philosophy Since 1960.* Oxford University Press.

Heidegger, Martin. 2010. *Being and Time.* SUNY Press.

hooks, bell. 2001. *All about Love: New Visions*. HarperCollins.

hooks, bell. 2006. *Outlaw Culture: Resisting Representations.* 1st ed. Routledge.

Kimmel, Michael. 2013. *Angry White Men American Masculinity and the End of an Era.* Nation Books.

Levinas, Emmanuel and Richard A. Cohen. 1985. *Ethics and Infinity: Conversations with Philippe Nemo.* 1st edition. Duquesne University Press.

Levinas, Emmanuel and Alphonso Lingis. 1969. *Totality and Infinity: An Essay on Exteriority.* Duquesne University Press.

Malpas, J. E. and Robert C. Solomon. 2002. *Death and Philosophy*. Routledge.

McCullers, Carson. 2002. *Illumination and Night Glare: The Unfinished Autobiography of Carson McCullers*. University of Wisconsin Press.

McCullers, Carson. 2004a. *The Heart Is a Lonely Hunter*. 1st Mariner Books edition. Mariner.

McCullers, Carson. 2004b. *The Member of the Wedding*. Mariner Books.

McCullers, Carson. 2005. *The Ballad of the Sad Café: And Other Stories*. Mariner Books.

Molière, Leman, Leloir, and Montaiglon. 1888. *Le dépit amoureux*. J. Lemonnyer.

Montaigne, Michel Eyquem de. 1958. *The Complete Essays of Montaigne*. Stanford University Press.

Nietzsche, Friedrich. 1969. *On the Genealogy of Morals and Ecce Homo Edited with Commentary by Walter Kaufmann*, trans. Walter Kaufmann. Vintage Books.

Nietzsche, Friedrich. 1974. *The Gay Science: With a Prelude in Rhymes and an Appendix of Songs*. Vintage Books.

Patterson, Orlando. 1985. *Slavery and Social Death: A Comparative Study*. Harvard University Press.

Rauschenbusch, Walter, Anthony Campolo, and Paul Rauschenbusch. 2008. *Christianity and the Social Crisis in the 21st Century: The Classic That Woke up the Church*. Harper San Francisco Publishers Group UK [distributor].

Richardson, Alan and John Bowden. 1983. *The Westminster Dictionary of Christian Theology*. Westminster John Knox Press.

Schalow, Frank. 1992. *The Renewal of the Heidegger Kant Dialogue: Action, Thought, and Responsibility*. SUNY Press.

U.S. Department of Health and Human Services. 2014. "United States Life Tables, 2009," January 6, accessed March 10, 2015, http://www.cdc.gov/nchs/data/nvsr/nvsr62/nvsr62_07.pdf

Vaux, Kenneth L. 1990. "The Pedagogy of Death." *Religious Education* 85(4): 509–587.

West, Cornel. 1999. *The Cornel West Reader*. Basic Books.

6

REQUIEM FOR WHITENESS

Mourning, freedom in uncertainty, and the final embrace of twilight

> The world is white no longer, and it will never be white again.
>
> *James Baldwin*[1]

> We are the strange fruit of that way of life. We who are white.
>
> *Lillian Smith*[2]

In 1955, James Baldwin, one of the greatest American writers of the twentieth century, wrote in his *Notes of a Native Son* that "the world is white no longer, and it will never be white again."[3] Writing while in residence in a small town in Switzerland, his words were meant for an American audience. Baldwin was under no illusion that such a statement corresponded to an empirical political reality[4]; he meant to convey that tides had shifted, the massive ship of western expansion and colonialism and American racism had seemingly run aground. He told us that the world is white no longer, not because such a world was (or is) already palpable, but rather because he seemingly understood the complexity involved in the co-constitutive nature of the production and maintenance of whiteness and its reliance on blackness, globally. With the U.S. context in mind, Baldwin seems to have been suggesting that white Americans could no longer call Baldwin a "stranger,"[5] they were no longer able to "make an abstraction of the Negro."[6] On this point, he writes,

> The time has come to realize that the interracial drama acted out on the American continent has not only created a new black man, it has created a new white man, too. No road whatever will lead Americans back to the simplicity of this European village where white men still have the luxury of looking on me as a stranger. I am not, really, a stranger any longer for any American alive.[7]

For Baldwin, talk of "strangers" and the end of the white world spoke to "the historical perception that the world was on the point of a momentous transformation and that the end of the old racial order, if not present, was at least in sight."[8] Pressing this further, whites could (and likely might) remain fearful of Baldwin or those who look or act like Baldwin, but we can no longer escape that fear, precisely because our chosen path to address this fear historically has unraveled. In so many words, whiteness has "othered" itself. For my purposes here, in light of the above passage, perhaps one could argue that white Americans here arrive at our own alterity in and through such recognition – when and where the recognition of the stranger causes some dissonance within the imagination of white subjects, who now must come to grips with our own "strangeness" in relation to the other. Thought of, too, in light of a presumed success from the previous chapter – that white Americans might relinquish claims to salvation – then this final chapter addresses the idea of whiteness more generally.[9] There is never a moment that white Christian American inheritance does not influence options, but here, my data are not any particular sociological group, but a focused assessment of whiteness looking back at its beneficiaries, as if into a mirror, wherein we the beneficiaries see ourselves for the first time (in a sense) – as other.

This final chapter offers one hermeneutical strategy for coming to terms with this white otherness (not to be confused with racialized marginality, but rather, "otherness" as in the precarity of finding oneself in a newish strange predicament, where perceived unity and coherence is both realized and threatened) through the suggestion that whiteness (in terms of its assumption of singularity and homogeneity) has died. As such, now, we whites sit at its funeral, confronted with the uncertainty faced as we come to terms with how to live without whiteness, without this flawed innocence and the certainty it has traditionally afforded and provided such a demographic. Who will we be moving forward? By what criteria will a white American identity be crafted or judged?

Following Baldwin's words and the social situations to which they point, I want to suggest that white people may sit now at the requiem for whiteness. Specifically, I argue that by hermeneutically treating whiteness as if it has died, our reliance on it (as whites) becomes and will become over time more apparent. Situating whiteness as "dead" in its ability to guard against personal and social uncertainty marks a moment when whites might learn to live with a growing degree of uncertainty. Just as Baldwin notes, a "new white man" has been created as white men no longer are able to register black others as "stranger[s]." Here, I reverse the typical gaze of stranger and other, by suggesting a thought-experiment of conceiving of whiteness as dead, so that whites are forced to recognize ourselves as the stranger, for we are just now, as "new white men,"[10] learning to live within the social arrangements and historical circumstances we created, without the same explicit or implicit means of social othering at our disposal. Ostensibly, we have othered ourselves from our very means of othering. Whiteness has died.

I do not mean that whiteness as an idea has died – for ideas can never *fully* "die." Rather, I mean that the functional utility of whiteness can no longer work effectively enough to produce a modicum or sense of innocence or certainty. My argument here is not that the "old racial order" is no more, but that bringing about such an end might more adequately be achieved (if at all) by having white people come to terms with a loss that is already feared by many whites. By treating the central concept of that "old racial order," whiteness, as if it has died, then Baldwin's prophetic voice might find greater social purchase. Ironically perhaps, thinking whiteness dead has implications for the white ability to *see* whiteness in practice. The death of whiteness arises, hermeneutically, from the idea's existential unraveling, its waning ability to construct and sustain racialized difference, even if such a death remains on sociological or historical horizons.

NOTICE OF DEATH

Traditionally, a requiem is a mass held for the recently deceased, that their souls be remembered in their passage from this life to the next. We white Americans find ourselves now at a requiem for a god-idol – a funeral, of sorts, for our whiteness that has died. By this "death," I mean the end of the ability to fight, ignore, or otherwise deny experiences of human limitation and uncertainty through racialized means, producing an uncertainty of thought, action, and social possibility. Such a death forces recognition of necessary human interdependence beyond the ideological boundaries of those who did (or do) adhere to whiteness. Thought of as a funeral "to come" at some point in the future, this requiem pronounces whiteness – as *interpreted* amongst many whites – as dead, lost, missing, inaccessible, increasingly functionally inept, and offers final words of guidance to better enable those who might struggle to accept the pending death of whiteness. By rhetorically inciting this requiem, I hope to offer strategies useful to people still needing to learn to live without it.

Where white Americans stand now in the face of an uncertain world, where whiteness might no longer promise a façade of certainty, these beneficiaries have reason to mourn this loss. By "loss," I mean the recognition of being deprived or denied something of particular individual and/or collective value. Privileges procured by whiteness, though unwarranted and often unacknowledged, are no less loved or valued even if they are unjustified. Where whites, beneficiaries and adherents of whiteness, are concerned, the death of whiteness requires mourning. This does not mean celebrating whiteness, but lamenting its loss just the same. This death charges us with lamentation and confrontation with a new (old) vision of ourselves. To those whites and all who benefit from the effects of whiteness, those who might find themselves "at" this "requiem," we might understand ourselves through white lesbian novelist Lillian Smith's reappropriation of the concept of "strange fruit"[11] – where whites hang, within the twilight of the old and new, onto a dead or dying "way of life" made possible by a whiteness increasingly witnessed (by its beneficiaries) precisely because the loss of it (whether real or imaginary) is registered with greater clarity.[12] White Americans, by and large, don't know what to make of whiteness. For how can we when it has remained largely invisible, unsited, uncited, and therefore, unsighted. That is, the normativity of whiteness has allowed it to not be named; we know it is no longer appropriate to appeal to it, but also know that it remains there to be used in times of duress. Only by constantly calling into question the efficacy of such use will we learn to live with this uncertainty.

Strange white fruit refers to the affective sensibilities of white people, rather than suggesting that "strange white fruit" be used as a proxy in the same manner as (black) "strange fruit." So for instance, when talking about visibility and invisibility, or death or life of whiteness, I am not citing an empirical domain. This is not a sociological statement or analysis. Rather, I use this term "strange white fruit" to offer a final interpretive strategy for whites to wrestle with uncertainties enacted as our old and new *white* identities collide. This chapter has been written with a dizzying fluidity meant to represent this uncertainty – again, as if at a funeral, not wanting to believe in the death so strongly that there is denial, moments of recognition of loss, confusion, and tacit fear. It is for this reason that this book ends with the short poem indicating that white Americans really don't know what to do now that whiteness has died/is dying/might die as a consequence of the stranger within ourselves. Awareness of the death of whiteness is not the death of the idea, or the end to the pain experienced by non-whites because of this idea. It is, for whites at least, recognition of the paradox we find ourselves in – and feel ourselves in – today. I have been one of these believers, this strange white fruit, and the tone and prescriptive comments of this chapter note how I, as much as other whites, am just now beginning to see ourselves as uncertain, confused, strange. The myth of white innocence is seemingly lost; admitting to uncertainty appears the order of the day. We have lost a principal ideological mechanism providing our certainty, a loss of something we didn't all even realize was so seemingly valuable.

To begin responding to this loss, rather than relying on black voices alone to do the work of a critical whiteness response, I discursively rely on white thinkers across genres such as fiction and academic sources, methodologically doing what most projects about whiteness do *not* – that is, doing the work for ourselves (as much as possible) without a problematic asymmetry that mimics and reinforces how much of this work is done *in* culture and society – relying on the racialized other to do the work of calling whiteness out, to task, and into sight. This work is for the many white Americans who have not "seen" whiteness, even if they have seen the effects of whiteness; I see this work as trying to give an account of whiteness without ultimately relying upon the backs of black bodies to do that heavy lifting for me/us (white people). This chapter, to this extent, is a kind of reflexive rewriting of the first chapter, but here the strange fruit are finally – if inchoately and caustically – understood to be the perpetrators of such violence historically, the white Americans who are just now seeing whiteness come into view. I am revisiting in some ways the inability of whiteness to do that work for ourselves/themselves while also calling for an ethic of responsibility to do this work without relying on the "other." For us/them (whites), whiteness has not been and will not be "visible" until it dies. So here I imagine that it has died so that it might.

OBITUARY

Whiteness, the racialized expression of a fundamental inability to accept limitation and uncertainty, has died.

Though the actual time and place of birth of Mr. Whiteness is unknown, it has been said that his "social" birth took place in the Southern part of the United States in the decades following the Civil War and word of his birth soon spread across the country. Conceived during the nuptials of Enslavement and Colonialism, Mr. Whiteness would go on to lead a storied life only dreamt of by his parents.

He was autodidact by education, but celebrated his influence on all areas of intellectual inquiry, including and especially the ivory towers of academia. He worked in a variety of fields including education, politics, engineering, law and law enforcement, business, religion, art and entertainment, and sports. He had a flare for individualism and worked to ensure that individuality served as a dominant motif for groups throughout the United States.

Throughout his life, he fought tooth and nail against death and dying, treating death as a form of taxation without representation. He contributed substantially to scientific and technological developments to overcome death, but in the end, Mr. Whiteness found his efforts limited. As adept with the pen as much as the rifle, Mr. Whiteness exerted an impact in all spaces he dared to travel, and he traveled globally and extensively. He fought the scourge of communism and collectivist thinking for decades through secrecy, ever-increased funding for military expenditures, and attempted extermination of collective thinking in Southeast Asia, the Middle East, Central and South America, and many parts of Africa.

He was known for extending opportunities to his most cherished friends and family. For his loved ones, he would help to ensure laws and economic regulations provided them with advantage and relative safety. Those dealing with this loss remember his magnanimity. He leaves behind a host of colleagues, family, and friends, most notably, he forged a long-standing love affair with his ideal woman, named Victoria, whose thinness, frivolity, and general silence he revered for its manageability. His most cherished associates include patriarchy, heteronormativity, elitism, greed, and theism.

Despite such an illustrious career, he sought to live in relative obscurity and out of the spotlight. Only in death, and the pain felt by this loss, is his full impact on those around him being realized.

What does it mean to have believed in invisible things that become visible just as they seemingly die? Of course, black Americans have "seen" whiteness as visible for quite a long time. The viciousness of lynching discussed in Chapter 1 exposed (to many African Americans) an ideology of adherence to whiteness maintained by white perpetrators. But methodologically, how do we whites, strange *white* fruit, handle "invisible things?" I bring *White Lies* to a close with a methodological reminder that the death of a god-idol is not about the *literal* end of god-idols, but the reconstitution of god-idols in a new way. I cannot call it into death without calling it into life so that it might be seen, made legible. Legibility here means exposing that which has hidden for too long under the material veneer of its constituent other – blackness.

What I have attempted is to call that which has been invisible into materiality, so that it can die, and so that a new social arrangement or arrangements be made possible, to the extent they are possible at all. This new arrangement involves acceptance of intense uncertainty, a freedom enacted through social responsibility as opposed to a freedom *from* social responsibility – made possible not through an imposition of *uncertainty* and limits on others, but by facing squarely the limits and uncertainty of oneself and one's own community in a way that attempts to not scale and rank bodies.

As with any funeral, time is spent here reflecting on what might have been, what conversations and words could have been spoken, and what might occur now upon acceptance of this loss. Specifically, though running the risk (an always already risk) of reifying new and more dangerous and pernicious god-idols in the wake of those no longer functioning, I hope that acceptance of the loss of whiteness opens the possibilities for a freedom in limitation to unfold through three principal areas of discussion. First, these possibilities require adequately and equitably mourning the loss of any conceivable means of affective or social certainty. Second, new social possibilities require coming to terms with the uncertain relationships between this loss of whiteness and other god-idols. This would involve a continued attempt to find analytic and interpretive means for living within the discomfort of social and epistemological uncertainty. And third, new social arrangements require facing the many dimensions of uncertainty that await finally letting go of a god-idol. Letting go brings with it the freedom to mourn the loss of god-idols, the freedom to acknowledge the relationship between different god-idols as increasingly complex, and the freedom to begin to live as social actors in an uncertain, radically contingent world.

Thus, *White Lies* concludes with a series of snapshots of uncertainty, as in the letting go of or unraveling of a rope (as in a lynch rope), ending by beginning to sight some of the unanswered/unanswerable questions that trouble even my own (or a reader's) certainty in the argument presented in (and as) this book. Lastly, in an effort to thematically capture this requiem, I have broken the chapter into four sections, as in the program of a funeral: invocation, eulogy, homily, and benediction. In some instances, such as the "eulogy" section, attention is focused not on literally eulogizing whiteness but rather on understanding its continued life (even as functionally dead) as it relates to other possible god-idols. Just as a eulogy might describe certain important relationships held by the decedent, then this eulogy for whiteness focuses on the relationships between whiteness and other god-idols like patriarchy, theism, heteronormativity, and others. These final pages, then, are for those who are sitting at a requiem for a loved one but who have yet to come to full terms with the implications of that loss, and for those who have accepted the loss but are not sure what to do now.

INVOCATION

How are those whites who find themselves at this requiem to interpret themselves or the task that *lies* before them now? We whites might understand ourselves as "strange [white] fruit" in that we have ignored, denied, or fought against our full humanity as radically contingent. We have been white liars, believing "fictive truths"[13] about exaggerated identities. Accepting the death of whiteness will therefore require taking stock of the lies we have told and continue to tell about ourselves and others. We have ostensibly alienated ourselves from reality because we haven't been able or willing to accept reality. We have always already been the strangest fruit of all.

This invocation begins by situating ourselves as the constituent building blocks providing our own ability to see "whiteness" in social practice and custom. Specifically, this ability hinges on registering this god-idol as functionally dead, opening us to possibilities for mourning this loss in a way that does not celebrate the life of whiteness but learns from its tragic, complicated history.

Strange white fruit hanging from dead, uncertain branches

White Lies ends as it began, with strange fruit. The exploration of whiteness began by hermeneutically situating its "birth" in the practice of lynching, sighting whiteness by relying on those very bodies dehumanized by the idea in practice. The motivations for lynchings have far more to do with the perpetrators of vigilantism than they do with their victims, and that extends to discussion of those events. Lynching was (and is) the result of a community so scared of uncertainty they kill to protect themselves against its recognition. Here, that uncertain reality is confronted by retaining the image of strange fruit (for its historical reminder and existential imagery) but with the work of Smith in mind, focusing attention towards white bodies, strange *white* fruit. White religion, the system of distinction-making made possible by violence-inducing ideological exaggerations of human worth and ability, is sustained by an ironic solipsism guiding adherents and beneficiaries, ironic because it safeguards itself by acting as if it is concerned with others. To turn this solipsism against itself, I suggest that lynching created its "strangest" fruit in its white beneficiaries, producing a community so scared of the uncertainty of human existence that they chose to dehumanize themselves through the dehumanization of others.[14]

Whiteness has long been a constituent feature of white American religion. White American religion (as we understand it today as a field of investigation for history, cultural studies, religious studies, the social sciences, etc.), for its part, has been shaped by the solipsistic sleights-of-hand purporting concern for others and by the constant fear of having to face the strangeness within ourselves. As this requiem is an experiment in imagination, a few words might be mentioned to remind us of what, precisely, has "died." This historical reminder can be situated in two ways: First, in terms of historical anecdotes grounding the "stuff" of American religion in a concern for salvation through purity. Second, regarding the claims made by some scholars about what American religion is or has been; "American religion," as a critical category, might no longer be useful. The death of whiteness would have an impact on both concrete social interaction and on analytic and rhetorical rendering of such social interaction.

Where American religious history is concerned, developments in the United States followed a model of economic liberation *tied to* economic anxieties. As noted in Chapter 2, Max Weber, though his efforts can be deconstructed in many nuanced ways,[15] leaves a lasting impression on us that fear and anxiety rooted in salvation shaped much of American religious life.[16] Anxieties connected to economic freedom influenced the shape of popular American theological discourse, while anxieties arising from demands for justification of having been metaphysically saved through works shaped the economic and social landscape of the United States. In Bourdieusian language, the "fields"[17] of economics and religion have always overlapped and mutually shaped American religious life. In effort to assuage anxieties associated with both, distinctions between insider (i.e. saved) from outsider (i.e. damned) mark American religion since the Puritan establishment in the seventeenth century but extend far beyond it. Exemplified as much by enslavement, Jim and Jane Crow, and the contemporary police state as by the Salem witch trials, the nineteenth century liberal theological debate over "true religion,"[18] and the white social gospel movement whose leaders often championed either assimilation or outright separation of the races,[19] American religion has been *white*. All of these well-known instances of what might be called "American religion" rely on distinctions imposed so as to procure an identity marked by distance from uncertainty. The single thread binding together much of what we call American religion and cutting across these well-known examples to include ordinary, secular, and typically referred to as "profane" forms of identity orientation has been this social distinction making practice serving to assuage existential fires, fears and anxieties that we have been told can be quenched with white lies. By this token, though exceptions and outliers are numerous, the overwhelming majority of American religious expression historically is rooted in our Puritan heritage in both historical terms and ontological ones – the effort to be pure, unblemished, "white." American religion in practice and in its academic expression has therefore been one extended white lie, as if an effort at purity could be obtained by limited, uncertain humans who by their very ontology are anything but "pure."

As scholars of religion, it may prove that until we admit to this unifying feature of American religion – that is, that it has actually been *white* religion – we run the risk of reinforcing these lies. Fearing the loss of analytic precision that such a shift might produce finds us remaining in bondage to whiteness precisely because its function relies on that very fear, and until such a shift takes place, our efforts to see whiteness – much less kill it – will never come to fruition. For instance, sociologist Robert Bellah describes American religion as pluralistic in content though held together by a tenacious American individualism grounded in personal experience, in particular the experience of salvation. He reminds that very early on, such an individual experience "was a prerequisite for acceptance as a church member."[20] Scholars could interpret this insistence on the individual (on its own terms) as the quintessential feature of American religion, but if keeping sight of whiteness, the concern for individualism deconstructs itself in the form of it serving as an entry into group belonging and membership, giving credibility to Weber's long-standing thesis. If the U.S. is a nation of individuals, then doesn't that preoccupation with individualism connect us as a group? Whiteness has been simultaneously the feature holding such a group "together," but notably its life has ensured that this concern for normative group belonging be framed in exactly the opposite terms, as individuality. Blind to the impact of whiteness, many assessments of what American religion is have simply reinforced the story American religion tells itself and others. Academic or methodological distinctions do not offset the social distinctions shaping our fields of vision. The story of our personal distinction-making practices structuring or structured by American religion is in fact a story demonstrating the specific distinctions that have historically shaped group distinctions between us/them, insider/outsider, white/black.

Celebrated historian of American religion Martin Marty comes closer to this recognition of the impact of whiteness in his *A Nation of Behavers* (1976). In this book, Marty offers a new map for charting the shifting cartographical landscape of American religious history – that is, that history changes and so too then must the tools we use to make sense of that history. His suggested map places a premium on identity and the activities of group adherence that shape identity; Marty refers to his work and focus on identity as a means of mapping "other coherences" connecting the many expressions of American religious pluralism.[21] Defending his shifted interpretive posture, he notes that "If the relation of beliefs and social behavior has come to the fore, this is in no small measure the result of a manifest expression of quests for group identity and social location."[22] American religion, historically and especially at the time of his writing, was cutting across traditional institutional and ideological boundaries, and so greater attention to social behavior was necessitated because simple group affiliation had seemingly broken down by the 1960s.

Working to make sense of the changing American religious landscape post 1960s, Marty's work (perhaps knowingly or not) is wrestling with the anxieties associated with the growing uncertainties of "American" identity in the wake of social protests, and I would add that these protests were calling into question the authority and power of whiteness. Such social shifts make an impact on American religion and as a consequence, he is seeking to find an intellectually honest way to make sense of the changes. There is also a tacit political dimension or concern attached to his efforts, evidenced in his summary of the ideological current of American religion: "In old-fashioned language, this means that 'at the hour of death' (when group belonging is not too important) in the midst of ontological shock, they commit their destinies to the God or gods in whom they have believed."[23] In other words, in the face of both acute uncertainties (as arises in a natural or social disaster) and general, slow growing uncertainties associated with the rupture of power and authority attached to normative dominance, American religious expression gives new birth to old gods. One example of this refocus on normativity is demonstrated by Marty when he writes that "Mainline religion had meant simply white Protestant until well into the twentieth century. At mid-century, however, the pace of change in Catholicism and Judaism had been so rapid that they joined Protestantism as being part of the normative faith in pluralist America."[24] Marty's insights ought be a warning about the possible death of whiteness, even as white particularity is only anecdotally acknowledged by him.

Marty spends considerable time exploring the rise of "ethnoreligion" (e.g. black or Latino/a religious affiliation and theology) as a frame for understanding American religious history during the mid to latter part of the twentieth century. He suggests of this period that "the old American majority, 'white Protestants,' most of them of Anglo-Saxon descent, were finally seen to be a racial or ethnic expression, much as they had regarded the classic 'minorities' to have been."[25] Marty's assessment is helpful for underscoring the American religious preoccupation with identity, but he seemingly ignores the genealogical impact of the ascendance of "ethno-religion" against the growing racial awareness of mainline groups in tandem with the inclusion of Catholics and Jews within the ranks of the "normative faith in pluralist America." Ostensibly, one might suggest that the twentieth century expansion of normative faith in America is influenced by growing racial recognition (non-white Catholics and Jews, excepted) such that they organize as normative along their racial lines in the wake of threats to the authority associated with white normativity. That is, American religion gives new birth to old gods, or god-idols, as it were. The new twentieth century mainline establishment, consequentially, looks very different (theologically) but very similar (racially). I would argue that the preoccupation with identity marking American religion (at the time of Marty's writing as suggested by his argument) has largely always been the case, and that the growing expression of black, brown, female, queer, etc., agency in the public sphere saw a subsequent shift towards greater reliance on racial identity serving as a proxy for "religious" identity. American religious trends, as much as history, are then ostensibly "white" as dominant groups have remained preoccupied with retaining a sense of their own identity and insulating themselves from the growing recognition of marginal identities. That is to say, so long as mainline (read: white) American religious belief or practice continuously frame marginal groups *as marginal*, as a "problem" to be solved, then their beliefs and practices amount to "operational acts of identification"[26] meant to prevent recognition of them (us/whites) as a problem, as strange fruit.

Concluding his efforts, Marty suggests that "If there has indeed been an 'identity incident' [in American religion]" then surely there will be "other kinds of events and preoccupations" requiring yet other maps for comprehension.[27] Appreciative of the work of both Bellah and Marty, and the discourses they have helped to shape, here I offer the start of one possible new "map." If American religion is preoccupied with identity today (as Marty suggests) or throughout its life (as I am suggesting), and if identity is always formed over and against others all engaged in a "battle for identity"[28] using the tactics and strategies of distinction-making, then imagining the death of whiteness so as to give fuller analytic treatment to it is worth investigating further. Perhaps, working to more adequately account for the "white" in American religion will give scholars a more complete, albeit *uncertain*, portrait of what we study and provide wisdom for proactively shaping social possibilities within the twilight of American religion. Such an accounting, both paradoxically as much as poetically, seemingly requires our attendance to a funeral.

Here, we sit at the funeral (i.e. recognition/moment of legibility) of a god-idol for whom we have murdered others, one of the first times we are able to see this dead god-idol and our reliance on it, feeling a small sense of the loss this god-idol has imposed on others for so long. In face of death, our white lies grow silent. The loss of whiteness, then, opens the possibility for becoming fully human – that is, not attempting to transcend limitation and uncertainty, but embrace it as the new particular foundation for human social interaction. This does not mean that other more dangerous god-idols might not emerge. Perhaps they will. This dangerous possibility is precisely the impetus for my argument – that, due to the real and perceived threat of the loss of these god-idols, white Americans would do well to accept their loss by learning to die for others, what we might now come to understand as dying *with* others.

Lillian Smith spent much of her career exposing the oppressive and repressive dehumanizing forces shaping social life within a segregated U.S. South, and a racist and sexist nation more generally. Her words and writings are often in the style of a lament, a sadness evocative of the frustration of having learned "that the human relations I valued most were held cheap by the world I lived in."[29] To this extent, Smith was not simply an anti-racist, anti-sexist activist, but a writer who wrote about such things for the audience of perpetrators and beneficiaries, with the somber affective disposition of someone wrestling with their continued love for a community unaware of "the consequences of this stubborn refusal to give up" a way of life that "is dead"[30] and in such refusal, remains death-dealing. More than simply "held cheap," white human social relations historically have relied on dastardly means of refuting the uncertainty posed in the wake of certain physical death and forced reliance on others in light of that death.

Smith's first novel *Strange Fruit* (1944) hinged on the premise that the typical notion of strange fruit, made famous by Billie Holiday, "black bodies hanging in the summer breeze,"[31] was sustained and made possible/probable because of a dearth of white cultural awareness and acumen; that is, the result of intense oppression at a social level and repression at a psychical level. Murder often sustained these forces. For Smith, these extreme lengths of defending the sense of certainty suggested that white people were the actual "'strange fruit' of that way of life,"[32] due to the relative interpretive normalcy of lynching (meaning the practice wasn't regarded as "strange" by most whites), while also due to the incredible strangeness of white reflexivity – its inability to "see" itself. The strangest of fruit is the fruit that refuses to understand itself as "fruit," using "fruit" here as a euphemism for the human situation of radical contingency. We whites are this strange fruit.

God-idols, then, as already gestured towards, function in the capacity of the "ropes" from which such "fruit" hangs, exaggerations of human ability and value the twisted strands of these "ropes," keeping our existential fears and anxieties seemingly "off the ground," our feet dangling above the social world and our ability to interpret our proper value and ability within that world. In other words, god-idols presuppose and give possibility to the assumption of a distance between individual, personal existential concerns and social realities. By this arrangement, we – this strange white fruit – hang, unable to embrace radically contingent freedom because we have yet to let go of dead god-idols.

Importantly, I do not mean to suggest a shared experience between black and white where lynching is concerned historically, or to "poach" from the storehouse of black suffering for the sake of white existential concern. Rather, this strange white fruit's inability to let go of the god-idols to which we cling is one of the central impetuses for the historical practice of lynching – meaning, that until we, the perpetrators, are able to see ourselves in this capacity – as strange fruit – then the murderous literal lynchings of non-whites will only continue in the various forms demonstrated over these pages (Trayvon Martin, Jordan Davis, Michael Brown, Islan Nettles, etc., etc., etc.).

This strange fruit heuristic offers an example of what social senescence – that is, the awareness and process of knowing when to die, the awareness of when to "let go of god-idols" – looks like in practice, in that "letting go" involves an awareness that one is "fruit" – that one is radically contingent – and then acceptance that it is time to fall from the tree, to die, a kind of death of self and recognition of this "new white man" noted by Baldwin, and whose strangeness is made visible by Lillian Smith. God-idols are only as powerful as the number and vocality of their adherents, and as such, as adherents learn to die (i.e., learn to embrace a self-aware practice of uncertainty and limitation), then the god-idols themselves "die." Hence, there is a connection between James Baldwin's trust that he never will be registered as a "stranger" again (i.e., his alterity will never ensure white ignorance of their own alterity) and the idea that the white world is ending, or in my words, that whiteness is dead or dying.

Lillian Smith was aware most of her life of the interrelatedness of human social actors, exemplified in the example of Baldwin, as well as the extended examples

Smith provides. Further, she spent great energy attempting to teach white culture how to let go, how to accept the need for its death. And she did this under what biographer Rose Gladney has referred to as a death sentence, as Smith battled cancer from 1953 until her death on September 28, 1966. Writing from within this "death sentence," Smith would use "her past to speak and write about the future – the future of the South, of the world, of humanity itself."[33] This chapter pays homage to these efforts by Smith, looking to her as a moral exemplar of the freedom of letting go, emphasizing the limits involved with the practice of letting go in this capacity, and playing with the concepts of life and death and past and future in order to offer this requiem for whiteness. There is no way of determining if Smith's cancer added a layer of complexity or awareness to her ability to write about and "see" whiteness in practice. It at least offers a sobering reminder that white people ultimately face a similar physical fate of death, and that in the face of that death, it is still possible (and perhaps even probable) that insights are afforded about learning to live as fruit fallen/having let go of appeals to false idols like whiteness. Loss of anything so valuable as a god-idol, change of any stripe, is uncertain. Like any death of a loved one or the death of a benefactor, the loss of a god-idol or its material resources must be mourned and accepted in the fear cast by an uncertain life in and around death. This process of mourning begins here, in recognition and lament that we see ourselves finally as strange white fruit.

In what follows, I privilege the uncertain dimensions of accepting this loss. Specifically, I turn next to the uncertain possibilities for mourning a god-idol that seemingly has no virtues to be mourned, but that has been loved without being seen, hidden behind the very visible consequences of its operation (i.e., privileges), and must be lamented in its loss.

Uncertain mourning: who are we, without you?

Mourning is dangerous, especially for a community that has historically sought to assuage the uncertainty and sadness of loss through various, often violent, forms of denial. Often – and especially in totemic[34] arrangements as is the case of whiteness – loss seemingly demands atonement. Lynching is one example of the extremes to which communities will go in response to perceptions of loss. Contemporary vigilante murders like Zimmerman's execution of Martin are another example of these extremes. Such atrocities are part of a confluence of activities that seek to assuage existential uncertainty by creating social certainty. But these murders never achieved their aim, as the post-acquittal life of Zimmerman is proof to his own (and our collective) uncertainty experienced in the aftermath of Martin's murder.

The quest for certainty has never done anything more than deny or conceal uncertainty. To this extent, whiteness was never "alive" because it never *fully* achieved its functional mandate. Though today, the uncertainty it never really concealed is seemingly revealed in greater and greater detail. Recognizing this uncertainty suggests that it might also be necessary to mourn whiteness, in that the grief of its loss is psychologically and socially real insofar as it is felt and has a bearing on social options, and to the extent that the practice of mourning, if understood as a collective exercise, holds the possibility of acknowledging together that this thing called whiteness has died, that we no longer have access to it. Zimmerman (and all those like him and those he represents) belongs to white America, he is our creation. And responding to him requires as much moral censure of his actions, as the more difficult work of taking even his existential feelings of loss into account. Failure to do so would be to ignore and leave intact an aspect of social life (and our *white* response to it) creating the conditions for Zimmermans to walk around, "carrying a gun and stalking young black men."[35]

Even atrocities, catastrophes of history, must be mourned by those that have benefitted from them; the mourning of the contemporary loss of white innocence, then, also requires the mourning of a history's worth of denials. Failure to mourn leaves unresolved tensions and an inability to fully accept the death. These dangers might be avoided if an uncertain mourning is cultivated based on the recognition that we are this strange fruit. Uncertain mourning offers a program for mourning that does not cause such intense guilt (for mourning this loss) that the issue is repressed, the loss denied, and the whiteness is reborn in a new form. An uncertain mourning – the uncertainty of having guilt even about the practice of mourning something like whiteness – is what prevents the mourning from centering the mourner as a moral cause in a normative sense. This issue of mourning is not simply a means of increasing the receptiveness of white Americans to my argument; the practice of mourning, of bereavement, is part and parcel to learning to die with others, in that it promotes greater existential closeness to the topics of death, loss, uncertainty, and insecurity, what Judith Butler has referred to as *The Precarious Life*. We mourn together because we lose others and die together. At these existential limits, we are all of us precarious. Though white Americans are not often regarded as existing in a precarious situation, Butler offers guidance as applicable to whites (mourning whiteness) as to anyone else:

> When we lose certain people, or when we are dispossessed from a place, or a community, we may simply feel that we are undergoing something temporary, that mourning will be over and some restoration of prior order will be achieved. But maybe when we undergo what we do, something about who we are is revealed, something that delineates the ties we have to others, that shows us these ties constitute what we are, ties or bonds that compose us. It is not as if an 'I' exists independently over here and then simply loses a 'you' over there, especially if the attachment to 'you' is part of what composes who 'I' am. If I lose you, under these conditions, then I not only mourn the loss, but I become inscrutable to myself. Who 'am' I, without you?[36]

Moving past the relationship between the co-constitution of white identity and racialized others (a co-constitutivity that has often resulted in violence), Butler is helpful for underscoring the reliance of an "I" on a "You," but white people must come to see that the "strangeness" of the other (procured through violence), the "you," is and has been in ourselves all along. Who is *the other* in ourselves, between ontological possibility and historical peril that constitutes the white "I" by often killing the racialized "You?" Who are whites without you, whiteness, without perceived innocence or certainty? Butler notes the connection between mourning and acceptance of finality as well as the connection of that finality to the sense of self experienced by the mourner. Do (or will) white Americans not need to ask "who 'am' I, without you?" to whiteness, to the idea undergirding the sense of security and certainty – even often anonymously – in the wake of its perceived death? Failure to do this difficult work would further create distance between those selves who have so often employed this god-idol, and recognition of our own radical contingency, our recognition that who we "are" has always been actually answered without the ontological aid of whiteness (it is an "idol," after all). Now, the "death" of whiteness marks a moment to see oneself in one's full uncertainty and limitation. Only through the practice of mourning will even those who have outlined precarity for others for so long come to recognize our own precarious life.

For these reasons, this requiem for whiteness necessarily involves mourning and works to simultaneously wrestle with such affective responses while forcefully infusing them with an awareness of radical contingency – that is, the social world reminding us that existential loss is never faced alone. In other words, even funerals rely on a variety of social actors. It is important that legitimation of a death occurs in the constitution of a crowd. This means that not only is mourning possible and necessary, but it is important that a means of mourning be provided so as to increase the numbers of those who will attend the requiem for whiteness. What this mourning looks like, the shape it takes, will determine if loss is truly embraced, or if the letting go of certainty and security becomes yet a new means for the securing of such certainty. Next, I explore the criteria and "look" of such mourning.

Earlier in this book, I sought to describe whiteness (and other god-idols) as operating according to a totemic social system, a system wherein insider and outsider group allegiance is determined through the arbitrary ascription of objects with meaning, and the further arbitrary ascription of those objects as corresponding to specific group identities. I suggested that contemporary race relations in the U.S., as understood and responded to by many anti-racist activist whites, often follows a piacular logic guided by an assumption that death or loss has come as a result of the white community and consequentially, an atonement of sorts is required of that community that might make right what has been made wrong. Such logic suggests that racism can be responded to if racists punish themselves. In fact, I argued that this entire volume might follow this expiatory logic. The practice of mourning, following Durkheim, I suggested as one example of these rites, wherein forced silence, immolation, and the like are imposed (by the larger society, or its representative leaders) on either insider or outsider group members.[37] Such practices have, as their aim, the reconstitution of group cohesiveness in the wake of social ruptures caused by things like death. Piacular mourning seems to be what Butler discusses in noting that temporary mourning might provide "restoration of prior [social] order."[38]

Initially, piacular rites seem to offer a means of mourning that is not celebratory in the positive moral sense; rather, these are "sad" occasions where "everything that inspires sentiments of sorrow or fear"[39] is marked in order to cultivate some sort of response or reaction to it. They offer the means of commemorating whiteness's death and visibility without celebrating it as an object. These rites remain problematic because of their demand for atonement. Thus, piacular rites can be understood as rituals of mourning wherein objects are noted as having met a "calamity" or are treated as deplorable.[40] Given the long history of negative impact on the social environment from the concept of whiteness, it might seem as though such a piaculum is in order. However, although piacular rites are not celebratory, as a means for mourning whiteness, they remain problematic.

Piacular atonement has as its goal the healing of a community, efforts to bring a sense of social certainty back into view. The problem of this piacular arrangement of mourning is that it follows the logic of atonement wherein "death demands the shedding of blood,"[41] most often the shedding of outsider blood. But as my effort here is to embrace the feeling of social uncertainty, and as I do not wish to reinforce a sacrificial logic, piacular mourning is dangerous.

Piacular rites end up not a means of an impossible atonement, but do more to simply recreate and reify the "moral state of the group."[42] That is to say, were *White Lies* to follow a piacular logic, it would undoubtedly respond to the deaths caused by insider/outsider arrangements by reinforcing those at the social center as dominant. Piacular mourning, following philosopher Eric Schliesser's work, amounts to a continued casting and interpretation of those who mourn as a "moral cause,"[43] a position that gives too much credit to white religious adherents. Perhaps, this tendency is avoided by remembering that it remains an open question as to whether whiteness is in fact "dead," while it also is worth noting that whiteness is not a "person" as is the typical cause of piacular mourning. Put another way, political sociologist Mark Worrell, in an article demonstrating the strategic, self-loathing sensibilities of political Buchananism, quotes an important passage from Durkheim on this point: Piacular rites situate mourning as "a matter of duty … because those collective demonstrations … restore to the group the energy that the events threaten to take away."[44] If following a piacular logic, mourning would reinforce the centrality and energy (i.e., power) held and seemingly lost by the group. Consequentially, letting go, embracing limitation, must guard against such a restoration. If whiteness were mourned through a piacular logic, then whiteness would be reborn anew as a continued inability to accept limitation and uncertainty.

White Lies attempts to rupture this piacular logic rather than reinforce it. Letting go, embracing limitation and uncertainty, is not retributive punishment, but acceptance that there is no atonement possible. There is no justice for the dead, only a new hope for justice for the living dead, those who have yet to understand that life and death are only illusorily correlated in a binary arrangement.[45] There is, then, a danger inherent in mourning whiteness, a danger I have sought to mitigate firstly by casting us, those who mourn, as strange white fruit, left only with the prospects of uncertain mourning – that is, the mourning of certainty itself. In the next section, I attempt to outline what this uncertain mourning might look like in practice.

Uncertain mourning and the "sadness that has no name"

Uncertain mourning, from the context of strange white fruit, offers the means to accept the loss of whiteness in a way that does not rescue certainty by seeking atonement, but relies on fragile, uncertain memories to mourn, arriving at a "sadness that has no name," an uncertain silence born from the sadness of realizing that the thing lost, missed, grieved, offers only broken, half-thought memories. Recognizing that many of us learn to hate from the same people who teach us how to love is unnameable sadness. Uncertain mourning taps into the existential feelings of loss so that acceptance of uncertainty is made more possible with respect to the loss of the loved one, and with respect to outlooks on future possibilities. By existential feelings of loss, I mean the affective responses seemingly dislodged from the social and felt through interpersonal emotional registers, but grounded in embodied loss, often of a loved one.

On November 17, 1953, novelist Carson McCullers went to visit Lillian Smith in Clayton, Georgia.[46] The two were both white Southern writers, both established literary figures who sought to expose – in various ways – the negative, repressive impact of ideas on social life. The November visit was cut short by a phone call informing McCullers that her husband, Reeves McCullers, had killed himself the day before in Paris, France.[47] Though Smith and McCullers were never able to build the relationship they seemed to desire, they had an interest in each other and provided support at various stages in each other's career. The death of Reeves McCullers was one opportunity for support.

In January of 1954, while writing within the shadow of her own cancer diagnosis, Smith sent a letter to McCullers, the contents of which help to demonstrate uncertain mourning. Smith's letter to McCullers, only portions of which are discussed here, provides a map for mourning that laments the loss without attempting to resituate its effect of casting the mourner as a moral cause. The following letter, through metaphor, remains uncertain and tragic, sure of the pain of loss, but seemingly cognizant that blithe sentimental expressions of celebration of life are not in order. The letter evokes feelings of confusion, uncertainty, and sadness. The letter casts mourning as the loss of power, and memory the storehouse for (recognition of) such power. In particular, Smith's roadmap for lament relies on two central concepts, that of memory and unnameable sadness. Smith first writes of:

> The kind of day when my tongue says "beautiful" and my heart mourns. Always those winds blow harder on my memory than on the mountain and I

> am driven back to an empty house and empty rooms that greedily spread over my whole life, sometimes; refusing to budge. Just taking over as if they have a right to stay. What happened on windy days long ago, I have no faint idea; but when such a day comes, I have to go back, like a ghost, to my childhood and wander it. Without map; without destination.[48]

Smith here notes the overwhelming power of memory, a power seemingly afforded in large part because memories are so fleeting, memories of "houses" and "rooms" left "empty" from "days long ago." If a piacular form of mourning looks forward in time and sees/seeks blood, an uncertain model of mourning looks backward, realizing that individual recollections might say something about the time or "way of life" as it was experienced by the mourners.

I look to Smith's letter with theorist Maurice Halbwachs's suggestions that memories are incomplete, that individual "minds reconstruct memories under the weight of a society," and that such a society "obligates people … to give [memories] a prestige that reality did not possess."[49] Smith's words seem to refute such atoning social obligations. In the letter, memories connect to the weight of a past social world and individual memories offer a proxy for understanding collective or communal experience. But Smith's presentation of these particular memories seems to fight against the demand for cohesiveness and "prestige." For Halbwachs, memories aren't part of an effort at certainty[50]; however, they can be caught up in such an effort. Here, I'm seeking to ensure memories of whiteness do not promote certainty, and Smith, "without map; without destination," offers ironic, paradoxical, and euphemistic "guidance." We are not following her, but simply, dying with her and her wisdom. Furthermore, if Halbwachs's suggestion that a child dislodged from her original society and transplanted into another would have an increasing paucity of memories (from home) in the wake of that rupture,[51] then perhaps Smith's reference to childhood evokes a recognition of different social options (e.g. segregation vs. integration) and the damage done to a person's memories as a result of such dehumanizing social practices. There are no tidy answers here, no certain recollections, only vague ghost-like spectral wanderings that do more to trouble certainty than to provide it, at the time it is desired most severely.[52]

Smith's ruminations on memory suggest a tenuous, but pervasive connection to heritage, family, and community, as much as a recognition of various, uncertain social options enacted (or not) in time, more akin to "wind" than the strength of a "rope" that might be provided by appeals to god-idols. If piacular atonement could be said to hold onto god-idols in that it reinforces a sacrificial offering and logic of sacrifice where blood must be shed, uncertain mourning lets go, hoping "winds" will carry social actors in new, uncertain directions. Memories, whether cultural memories or interpersonal (as such lines are blurry) are uncertain, often unavailable, and yet vital – of most importance, but impossible to trust fully. Our memories here are as uncertain as our social contexts, and the impact of those contexts on our ideas.

Smith continues her letter:

> So, I write you from Clayton but really from a lonely corner somewhere in the past, to say hello and thank you and wish you well. It would be nice to talk. I have never talked to you. Always we begin and there are – interruptions. Small ones, most of them; and the one big one which I pray you have somehow made your peace with. A hard six weeks you have had. I know this. I know there have been terrors and regrets, and sudden revelations, and grief, and a sadness that has no name. Always, if we could name the sadness, if we could find the word, we feel the sadness would lift. It is like stumbling across an old grave stone with no name and no date. Sorrow is like that. One cannot name it. If one only could … name it and find a little date in time for it. Then we could drop a small flower, a tear, and compose our life around it.[53]

Reeves's death was for McCullers a material expression of loss. The loss of a lover, a soul mate, is one of the most difficult moments in life,[54] producing for many what Smith notes as an inexpressible sadness, a "sadness that has no name."[55] This loss and its sadness offers a metaphor for the loss of god-idols and the false sense of security and certainty that they offer. Will white people weep when we hear "madmen" crying out that whiteness is dead?[56] And would silence or apathy at that suggestion imply that whites fail to realize that whiteness is dead, or realize its death but find no reason to weep? Though Reeves is not a god-idol in the same sense I discuss in Chapter 5 in relation to the character John Singer from McCullers's *The Heart Is A Lonely Hunter*, the loss of Reeves to suicide was devastating for McCullers, and it required mourning, just as a kind of mourning is necessitated for whiteness so that the grief it has imposed on others might be recognized by those who feel its loss now. The connection between Singer and Reeves on the point of suicide is also representative of the tenuous constitution of god-idols themselves. Notably, Smith's letter to McCullers suggests an embrace of the destabilizing effects of loss, a loss eerily nearly prophetically enacted years earlier in the form of McCullers's character Singer, who also committed suicide. Given such weighty circumstances, much can be learned from Smith's letter. It encourages sadness, not finding ways to name (and overcome) this loss, but to endure it through the profundity it poses.

Some might suggest, for instance, that my framing this within a funeral-like setting might help the social actors involved make more out of less, to celebrate something instead of register it as troublesome. Often, funerals bring out the "best" in those who are mourned, as Halbwachs reminds collective memories often do. Smith's somber account of memory forces recognition of the complexity of a life. Reeves and Carson McCullers's relationship was – as many public romances – famously tumultuous; divorced and yet remaining connected, they seemingly gave to one another the best and worst each had to offer. Smith's noting of "terrors, regrets and sudden revelations" seems to imply her own awareness of just how complicated Reeves and Carson's relationship had been. Loss ruptures, causes uncertainty, doubt, and the forced recognition that often, those who are mourned did as much to teach how to hate as how to love.

With this complication in mind, Smith's suggestions for McCullers's bereavement offer possible insights into what the mourning of god-idols will look like, what "empty rooms" of memories of whiteness might *feel* like, recognizing both the sadness of the loss of the relationship as well as the sadness of recognizing the costs once attached to preserving the relationship in life. Following Smith's suggestion in *Killers of the Dream* that "personal memoir" is in another sense "every Southerner's memoir,"[57] I offer myself as one auto-ethnographic example of this recognition in terms of both whiteness and theism. I have been afforded intense privileges from reliance on whiteness, too numerous to name, and more often than not I have remained silent in moments when I recognized that those privileges came at the expense of others. The death of whiteness marks a sadness that such privileges might no longer be afforded and a moment to recognize my complicity in allowing the costs of that relationship to play out in harmful ways for others. In like manner, the educational opportunities making possible my Ph.D. and research began through mainline white Christian church-based relationships and scholarships, such that were it not for theism's social import and impact, I would not have had the possibility to pursue advanced degrees. Quite literally, were it not for the importance many white Americans place on the belief in the idea of god and the power of whiteness to determine who has privileged access to social possibilities, my educational opportunities might not have been possible. A peculiar sort of wisdom is gleaned from recognizing that those who teach us to love are also those who teach us to hate. Though the language of love and hate is intentionally melodramatic, it also cuts to the quick of white life for so many of us in the United States, especially those of us concerned to respond to the privileges attached to our social inheritance.

White Lies began by telling a story about a debate that took place at a university between scholars appreciative of the turn to context and hermeneutical variance, and those exemplified by Modern European History, who felt the loss of his authority and worth in the wake of the contemporary focus on context. Taking white context seriously requires admitting that my racialized and ideologically-based privileges are so fundamental to social possibilities that they helped to make possible even my ability to deconstruct and refute the arguments offered by Modern European History – bringing to light that even in death (or the fear of death and loss), privilege is not so easily relinquished. Mourning the deaths of these god-idols involves recognizing the possible loss of such privileges (e.g., higher education scholarships, and other social options made possible in reward for adherence to god-idols) as much as it also requires facing squarely the costs of such privileges.

Sorrow can come at the realization that many of the people and ideas most beloved are the very places where learning to exaggerate the radical contingency of ourselves and others takes place. Smith recalls in *Killers of the Dream* that "the mother who taught me what I know of tenderness and love and compassion taught me also the bleak rituals of keeping Negroes in their 'place.' The father who rebuked me for an air of superiority toward schoolmates from the mill and rounded out his rebuke by gravely reminding me that 'all men are brothers,' trained me in the steel-rigid decorums I must demand of every colored male."[58] In my case, as one of countless examples, the grandfather I loved and whose heart gave out too soon joked that "if I'd only receive a heart transplant, then I'd be okay … even if I woke up with a hankering for watermelon because my new heart came from a nigger," the implication being that the heart might come from an African American who had died violently and prematurely.

The sorrow of learning to love and hate in the same place seems impossible to name, perhaps out of shame at having been the beneficiary of such tragic social arrangements. And Smith does not offer suggestions for naming, but a reminder to McCullers that she understands and grieves with her. Loss exposes the conditions that have provided a sense of certainty and social solipsism, forcing recognition of the uncertainty that has been hidden through both love and hate. As Smith's letter demonstrates, all that can be done (while grieving) is to expose the loss as an awareness of namelessness, and fill in the holes of memory with grief.

Where white existential responses to the loss of whiteness are concerned – there is no atonement. There is sadness, grief, lament, and sorrow. Learning to die with others does not involve some sort of piacular balancing of the ledger books marking who lives and dies. A balanced awareness of radical contingency is not found through the totemic "demand for blood."[59] Learning to die with others means learning that even sacrificial death for self or others will not correct for past and current social injustices. Rather, it involves living with the legacy and memory of loss in the contemporary uncertain moment – posed by continued reliance on (and love for) those who may or may not have accepted the death of whiteness. For the deaths of god-idols as much as for physical, material people, this sorrow that cannot be named takes shape through the forced reliance on others (i.e., radical contingency), as in the case of Smith's letter to McCullers, or the example of my grandfather's reliance on another person's donated heart (even as he continued to *other* that person during such an embodied, serious form of reliance), or as symbolically modeled when family friends or church members bring over platters of food to the families of the recently deceased. Uncertain mourning involves learning to live with an open wound, and within the awkwardness of living and acting with other wounded people, embracing the sorrow of loss that has no name.

With this description of uncertain mourning in place, and the letter from Smith serving as the central feature orienting this invocation at the requiem for whiteness, I turn now to a kind of social eulogy for whiteness, describing its life lived in relation to other god-idols, and how we might approach that life in the wake of its death.

EULOGY

Due to this forced reliance on others who might not yet have heard of the death of whiteness but who might fear the danger of such a loss, and out of the panoply of god-idols born through social actors and interaction (those god-idols not yet visible but alive), uncertain mourning does not ensure that god-idols stay "dead," or that other god-idols are not waiting to take up the task of concealing uncertainty. Indeed, mourning is but one expression of a freedom in uncertainty. Fighting against and understanding the reliance of one god-idol on others is an integral component promoting the freedom to let go. So as this requiem moves forward, I present a rendering of the relation of one dead god-idol to another as part of a confluence of assemblages, indicating that this funeral is not a time to celebrate an easy victory over whiteness, but requires ongoing analytic efforts to stay vigilant in the face of an easy slippage back into a false sense of certainty.

Some assemblage required

In Chapter 3, I sought to characterize god-idols as bound up within a battle for identity that takes place on the bodies of social actors. Jean-François Bayart helped to demonstrate that god-idols interact with "operational acts of identification"[60] that come together to constitute the things referred to as "identities." Mary Douglas aided in my effort to show that such concepts find purchase and impact on the social world as they are projected onto real, material bodies.[61] What I did not discuss fully there – wanting to privilege the embodied impact of god-idols on identity formation – was the relationship between different god-idols working together in certain instances as assemblages.

While many intersectional theorists have noted double and triple jeopardy faced in terms of actual social identities posed, here I'm focused on offering an apparatus for holding in tension the sameness and differences of god-idols, not identities. Again, I might note the hermeneutical underpinnings of my efforts. Where whites are concerned, scholars have much available material to read about, say, the triple jeopardy faced by the "identities" of black poor women working in tandem (that is, "blackness," "poverty," and "gender").[62] Indeed, identity remains an incredibly popular topic of discussion amongst scholars across fields. But following James Faubion's suggestion that such a focus on identity "did not fully take off and it remains to be seen what will happen with it,"[63] I am working to focus attention on the inverse: the ideological arrangements bearing down on certain social actors to produce such double, triple, or quadruple identity-based jeopardy.

In seeking to trouble intersectional models of identity as relying on a presumption of subjectivity as well as an insular assessment of each identity-marker working with, but remaining distinct from, the others, Jasbir Puar's notion of assemblage is helpful in that it "is more attuned to interwoven forces that merge and dissipate time, space and body against linearity, coherency and permanency."[64] In a sense, assemblage theory dislodges "identity" from the bodies of subjects to more readily expose the impact of affective movements on those bodies. Intersectionality arguments tend to imply stasis within a matrix of identities – surety – where assemblage privileges fluidity, movement, uncertainty of identity, and gives attention to the full weight of impact from objects/symbols as they interact with bodies. God-idol reliance is intensely complex and co-constitutive. Arrangements of god-idols shape material outcomes for bodies in space and time, in that the privileging of affective fluidity (instead of cohesive identities) helps to trouble god-idols' function of manipulating and reifying artificial distinctions so as to procure senses of certainty. Puar describes the brown body and turban (of a Sikh) as an example of an assemblage, wherein body and object work co-constitutively to present and project meanings seemingly referencing identities.

Here, I want to suggest that god-idol(s) + adherent = assemblage. Whiteness never functions in isolation from other god-idols or as removed from the embodied realities of adherents as well as non-adherent outsiders. Together, in a myriad of possibilities, they constitute an assemblage in any given social setting localized on the bodies of social actors.[65]

In simpler terms, and as example, a god-idol of whiteness is as likely to be sexualized and gendered (as is witnessed in the sexualization of lynching) as much as heteronormativity influences the posterity and shape of whiteness eulogized here. People and groups are held in the grip of a pantheon of god-idols, of which whiteness and theism are but two. And such god-idols are not alone, nor do they work in isolation. Again for instance, sexism may be rampant in one community where racism is not, but such effects of god-idols are never fully distinct and neither are the god-idols themselves. Understanding these god-idols in accordance to an assemblage will offer greater abilities, down the road, to chart where different god-idols carry different weight, so that the impact and interaction of different god-idols in any given social setting might be more adequately ascertained. Accordingly, homophobia might be deployed in different geographies for competing interests, as Puar's work suggests is the relationship between homonationalism and the constitution of the "terrorist."[66] Such a perspective seems sensitive to Puar's suggestion that "there is no entity, no identity, no queer subject or subject to queer, rather queerness coming forth at us from all directions, screaming its defiance, suggesting a move from intersectionality to assemblage, an affective conglomeration that recognizes other contingencies of belonging (melding, fusing, viscosity, bouncing) that might not fall so easily into what is sometimes denoted as reactive community formations – identity politics."[67] While I am trying to remain sensitive to the embodied rationales behind such "identity politics," but to begin thinking beyond the analytic confines of rigid presentations of "identity" as fixed, secure, even if admitted to be multivalent, I turn to Lillian Smith, who is an early example of someone who exposed shared relationships between race, sexuality, and religion without necessarily reifying thin inherited interpretations of identities. In fact, she seems to have understood that it was precisely because of the complexities of any "identity" that interrogation of raced and sexed and gendered identities was (and is) necessary.

Smith's work *Killers of the Dream* is an early instance of taking seriously the co-constitutive forces (i.e., god-idol assemblages) shaping social options and identities as if a cosmic cookie cutter. For instance, Smith argues in the 1940s that repressive personal forces translate into equally confusing, overlapping oppressive forces in both the practice of lynching and beyond it. She suggests that "basic lessons [about identity] were woven" of "such dissonant strands as these; sometimes the threads tangled into a terrifying mess," noting that some of these strands "have to do with what we call color and race ... and politics ... and money and how it is made ... and religion ... and sex and the body image ... and love ... and dreams of the Good and the killers of dreams."[68] Smith's words demonstrate an early awareness of the co-constitutivity of these issues – these god-idols as I've called them – her analysis not conflating identity with the ideologies shaping identity, understanding them as myriad constellations of assemblaged forces. Smith notes that

> Sex and hate, cohabitating in the darkness of minds too long, pour out their progeny of cruelty on anything [i.e., physical bodies] that can serve as a symbol of an unnamed relationship that in his heart each man wants to befoul. That, sometimes, the lynchers do cut off genitals of the lynched and divide them into bits to be distributed to participants as souvenirs is no more than a coda to this composition of hate and guilt and sex and fear, created by our way of life.[69]

Smith discusses these material realities in terms specific not only to the murdering of black bodies, but the sexualized dismemberment of the black body. The simple psychoanalysis and loose talk of "heart" offers a salient early instance of a white writer interested to demonstrate to white Americans the assemblage of ideas shaping material realities at an affective level, similar to the contemporary sophisticated (erudite) argument offered by Puar. Smith made sure to frame these issues around life and death, the proximity of life to death and death to life, and the impact of the anxiety of death on the shape of social life, even noting the paradox of the "dominant free" whites who were "so bound by anxiety that it could not be released [artistically, culturally, etc.]."[70] Instead, this anxiety played out on bodies, most often violently. As a result of these unreleased anxieties, this "*sacred way of life* [emphasis hers] put us on our knees in idol worship."[71]

White Lies has not been an iconoclastic, heretical effort to be merely provocative by simultaneously conflating traditional notions of race, god, and belief, but a demonstration that co-constitutive ideological assemblages have already been present for many whites as exemplified by practices such as lynching, homophobia, and more, undergirded by theistic sensibilities, making our (at times) "well-intentioned" beliefs and practices idolatry to begin with. White scholars of religion, and white Americans more generally, cannot continue to "mask evils" like racism, sexism, homophobia and the like as theologically or socially justified (as overt or as collateral) or continue to suggest that the solution to these issues is some version of "go to church on Sunday," as Smith reminds us is a popular rejoinder offered for how to face these issues. To date, most efforts within the academic study of religion to respond to whiteness or white privilege have followed this model of theological corrective.[72] Yet, such efforts are akin to trying to respond to one component of an assemblage by firmly embracing another component within the same assemblage. Unfortunately, these idolatrous assemblages were and are the "killers of the dream" of an equitable society, cheapening even (and perhaps especially) the "human relations [we] valued most."[73] I have sought to "kill" these killers' ideological weaponry – the god-idols – by an extended treatise involving learning to die with others. We now sit, therefore, at the requiem for one of these god-idols. I have here sought to underscore how this god-idol interacts with other god-idols producing the "sacred way of life" that has left us white Americans as strange white fruit.

Much more work will be necessary to dismantle such things more fully, to the extent that dismantling is possible at all, but the task begins in understanding that these ideological weapons are never isolated, but work together in ever increasingly complex ways. In the next section, I offer a way to approach such complexity, such uncertainty of interpretive possibilities and security.

Looking backwards to measure the future danger of whiteness

God-idols come together with bodies as an assemblage, shaping social options and identities while externalizing options and assumptions about identity onto the social world. I have discussed many god-idols while analytically focusing on some above others, notably the two that have (seemingly) most strongly shaped my own social context to this point. Whiteness and theism have taken the focus in lieu of other god-idols like heteronormitivity, greed, patriarchy, and the like. Admittedly, this skewed analytic treatment has occurred partly because I have to manage space and time. But it has also been the consequence of examining my own social location and determining that these two god-idols seemingly hold a particular form of danger as a consequence of the degree to which they are imbued with power from their adherents. Where sexism is concerned, I look forward to future work exploring how the social options and contexts made possible by certain god-idols dictate the degree to which I am even able to make a generalized claim about "white people." Ought I, simply, to limit my comments to white men? This seems the obvious answer, but to be fair to my experiences and data, I have learned much about how to worship whiteness and theism from white women, leaving me uncertain as to the efficacy of a further qualification in all instances.

There is analytic utility in treating each god-idol as an individual "component" – that is, a piece of an assemblage – while never losing sight of, say, the relationship between homophobia and racism, or classism and sexism, etc. As occurs in assemblage theory, multiplicity and uncertainty mark actual assemblages as much as this uncertainty also shapes efforts to understand these assemblages. Willing to risk a bit of analytic uncertainty on how other god-idols function, I have privileged whiteness principally. Now, remembering these sections are part of a "eulogy," it may be asked why, if all god-idols are part of assemblages, whiteness is eulogized in isolation? Why mark it as "dead" without similar suggestions about the other god-idols going into an assemblage?

Whiteness, dead or alive, continues to exert a particular perniciousness as a component of any assemblage, as such assemblages are employed by whites who continue to benefit from the weight of the idea. Indeed, Puar also suggests that assemblages work in and through a securing of the "ascendancy of whiteness" ideologically, opening up the possible adherents to whiteness to extend beyond race or ethnicity.[74] This suggests whiteness still requires "measurement" in a kind of analytic isolation, knowing full well that measurement is heuristic and uncertain.

Such a "measurement" is possible by turning to an uncertain literary memory of one of the earliest examples of critical whiteness discourse, Herman Melville's *Moby Dick* (1851). Literary theorist and novelist Toni Morrison suggests that the "truth" Melville sought to convey "was his recognition of the moment in America when whiteness became ideology."[75] As to the impact of this birth of whiteness, Morrison imbricates that Ahab – representative here of (white) American social actors – "has lost to [whiteness] personal dismemberment and family and society and his own place as a human in the world."[76] The following passages are unequaled (in my opinion) in balancing the severity of the dangers the concept imposes on others, the co-constitutive ideological operation of whiteness with other god-idols, and the actual close proximity of whiteness to death:

> This elusive quality it is, which causes the thought of whiteness, when divorced from more kindly associations, and coupled with any object terrible in itself, to heighten that terror to the furthest bounds. Witness the white bear of the poles, and the white shark of the tropics; what but their smooth, flaky whiteness makes them the transcendent horrors they are? That ghastly whiteness it is which imparts such an abhorrent mildness, even more loathsome than terrific, to the dumb gloating of their aspect. So that not the fierce-fanged tiger in his heraldic coat can so stagger courage as the white-shrouded bear or shark.[77]

Is not this still a brilliant way to capture the particular perniciousness of whiteness as it coalesces with other god-idols, each "masking" the other in "abhorrent mildness," a racialized sexism or a homophobic whiteness being two examples of this "mildness" in practice, but it is precisely the whiteness that so "staggers courage." Appealing to naturalistic taxonomies of polar bears and great white sharks as metaphoric of social issues at the time, here Melville does not reinforce a simple inverted form of colorism,[78] but offers one of the first instances of an assemblage theory where whiteness is measured within its assemblage for its particular perniciousness in tandem to its relation to other god-idols left abstract within the metaphor. Melville even situates the metaphysical, floating qualities of the idea of whiteness in his suggestion "Bethink thee of the albatross, whence come those clouds of spiritual wonderment and pale dread, in which that white phantom sails in all imaginations?"[79] The particular perniciousness of whiteness is its expansive impact on the "imaginations" of "all," the influence of its augmenting of social life and perceptions of it in the form of manipulations of fear and dread.

Melville, who Cornel West suggests is one of very few white American writers to "grasp crucial aspects of the black condition" within a twilight civilization,[80] is wont to point out the particularity of whiteness (as normative) marking its increased social perniciousness and danger. He is not accidentally describing whiteness as a sociological concept, but the whale was (even at the time of his writing) an allegory for coming to terms with ideas such as whiteness, the question of enslavement, and the topic of race relations in the United States. Though admittedly the mid-nineteenth century is contextually distinct from today, in terms of the perniciousness of the idea of whiteness – alive or dead – the context remains cohesive and Melville's words continue to ring true. In a note of clarification about whiteness's relation to other of what I refer to as god-idols, he elaborates these interstices, retaining the specificity of each component so that the dangers of one are exposed:

> With reference to the Polar bear, it may possibly be urged by him who would fain go still deeper into this matter, that it is not the whiteness, separately regarded, which heightens the intolerable hideousness of that brute; for, analysed, that heightened hideousness, it might be said, only arises from the circumstance, that the irresponsible ferociousness of the creature stands invested in the fleece of the celestial innocence and love; and hence, by bringing together two such opposite emotions in our minds, the Polar bear frightens us with so unnatural a contrast. But even assuming all this to be true; yet, were it not for the whiteness, you would not have that intensified terror.[81]

Whiteness, even in the midst of assemblaged theories of difference and identity, still retains its unique terror precisely because it is that which for so long has remained innocuously masked as a paragon of virtue, grace, civility, and beauty.[82] And yet, such maskings have concealed the true character of whiteness as the racialized expression of a fundamental inability to accept limitation and uncertainty. To bring the discussion back to James Baldwin's suggestion about the end of the white world, he writes that "when, beneath the [white] mask, a human being begins to make himself felt one cannot escape a certain awful wonder as to what kind of human being it is."[83] Again, who will we whites be now as whiteness seemingly loses its life – drowned/drowning in a sea of uncertainty posed by social difference ever encroaching on it, requiring us to pull back this mask. What will we find? Melville offers a clue. Indeed, Melville even notes of the great white shark that the French call this shark "Requin," taken from "'*requiem eternam*' (eternal rest)" as an "allusion to the white, silent stillness of death"[84] this *white* shark imposes – a stillness it has seemingly, and finally, imposed on itself: death.

White identity is not more important or significant than another, whether framed as morally valuable or reprobate, and likely, whiteness as a god-idol is not in every instance more vicious or powerful than any other god-idol. Again, I am not talking here about identities, but about an assemblage of god-idols that shape options for identity. Assemblage theory aids in outlining the parameters of social options made possible by adherence to these god-idols by other social actors, as well as the options assumed possible thanks to one person or group's own adherence. To look at god-idols for their different affective effects is not to rank identities, but to provide space for determining the degree to which different god-idols (working as an assemblage) impact and shape possible arrangements of identities. Whiteness takes precedence for Melville precisely because it is the mechanism that often most severely allows me – and many other white Americans – to treat our identities as more important in value and ability than another. This is not an effort to suggest that different identities, differentially oppressed, are scalable in terms of the severity of oppression faced, but to suggest that different god-idols do different amounts of work for different groups in terms of both oppression and privilege. As such, I have principally been interested in the work done by the god-idol of whiteness within the overall apparatus offered in this book. In other words, here as elsewhere, I am privileging god-idols that differentially work to presume an asymmetrical distance between and across assumed identities. For many, if not most white Americans, this requires continued attention to whiteness, specifically, understanding full well that it cannot be fully dislodged from heteronormativity, patriarchy, theism, or any of the god-idols that serve as the scissors cutting out "operational acts of identification" that are then arranged as "identities."[85]

Next, I turn back to Smith and her work at the Laurel Falls camp for girls, as a means of offering a homily, looking forward to possibilities of white acceptance of uncertainty, a process likely to begin within the very spaces providing and provided by privilege.

HOMILY

What are whites to do, how are we to act, in this time of twilight, when sitting at the funeral of a god-idol whose danger remains alive in its particularity? Actions, moving forward, might involve learning to live in the uncertainty posed by dead god-idols, "living dangerously" to quote Nietzsche in his *Gay Science*,[86] but rather than, as Nietzsche suggests, a danger born from abandoning a concern for others, here living in the danger of uncertainty would involve recognition of radical social connectedness, radical contingency. The death of whiteness offers a freedom found through embrace of limitation and uncertainty, as well as a social maturity in recognizing that innocence sought will never be found because the former means of having sought it now – forever – precludes that possibility. Accepting this death of whiteness, then, offers the possibility for learning to live anew within this freedom offered by radical contingency.

Freedom within the limits of exaggerated privilege

Lillian Smith's life and work at the Laurel Falls camp for girls offers a model for learning to live in the twilight that disrupts the efficacy of exaggerations. Stated differently, one might begin to euphemistically "live dangerously" by offering a model for embracing oneself as "strange fruit" in the sense Smith described of white people and by learning to let go of the ideological ropes from which we hang.

Such an embrace of uncertainty, ironically, might first rely on some of the very structures set in place by these exaggerations, using the "master's tools" in this first instance. More specifically, whites might begin to use the spaces made possible by affluence and privilege – here, I have literal church buildings and other properties owned by ecclesial bodies in mind as well as university settings and other civic and social spaces, along with family homes – as the locations where we might learn to live without exaggerations and fight against a heritage of exaggerations. And perhaps, as Smith's comments about cultural roots and heritage will demonstrate, these might be the ideal locations for such work to begin.

Laurel Falls was a high-end [white] girls' summer camp in Clayton, Georgia. Given the age of the campers, the setting would prove an occasion to deconstruct many of the assumptions these young girls had learned at home, and reconstruct positions on the world that were more life affirming and cognizant of the perniciousness of segregation, racism, sexism, and more.

"Miss Lil" (as she was known by many at the camp) Smith was originally from Jasper, Florida, daughter to a successful white business owner who lost his fortune in 1915. In an effort to make a new start, Lillian's father moved the family to Clayton, Georgia. Lil's parents opened Laurel Falls camp in 1920, catering to wealthy white girls. Herself the product of a similar affluence, Smith grew up globally well-traveled for a white Southern woman of the age, with siblings traveling the globe and she herself with the means to travel, and study. Taking up a teaching position for a time in China, she began to see the oppressive circumstances of colonialism, and soon that awareness would offer critical insights about the United States. Lil's travels to China and elsewhere helped to open her up to the interdependent asymmetries of social life in the Southern U.S. She recounted: "I began to understand the warped, distorted frame we had put around every Negro child from birth is around every white child, also."[87] This "distorted frame" would inform her suggestion that white people were "strange fruit." Smith's worldliness brought to bear a social attention to the identities connected through these "distorted frames." These distorted frames I have cast as exaggerations of radical contingency, efforts to skew human relations away from death and limitation. At an early age, and long before a critical mass of whites were noting the relationships between such exaggerations, Smith realized that such exaggerations stunted the moral, epistemological, and aesthetic growth of whites as well. Given the opportunity in 1925 to return to Laurel Falls to take over the camp, Smith packed her bags to return home to the strangest of fruit. She transformed this personal opportunity into the catalyst for "on the ground" work in disrupting these exaggerations.

Campers participated in typical summer camp activities like tennis, swimming, horseback riding, and the like, but to quote one former camper, "we had these *other* deep adventures of thinking and feeling"[88] that sought to engage campers with the wider world beyond the camp, the South, and affluence. Of these "deep adventures," another camper muses that she "often wondered how many of the parents really knew a lot of the intellectual activity that was happening at camp."[89] In both small groups and larger campwide lectures and discussions, Miss Lil would often remind campers that the topics of these conversations would likely "not be popular to say among your friends [back at home]."[90] These conversations often included frank discussion about sex and sexuality, race, segregation, lynching, gender dynamics, and a host of other topics unpopular given the cultural climate of the South at the time.[91]

The camp also served as a vehicle for solitude and inspiration for Smith's literary efforts. *Strange Fruit* (1944), her novel about an interracial love affair between a black woman and white man in the South,[92] was written at Laurel Falls. Selling over three million copies, this novel was turned into a Broadway show and put Smith on the literary map. *Strange Fruit* transmuted the traditional usage of that phrase as marking the lynching of African Americans into exposure of the repressed sexualized tensions undergirding and interwoven with race relations. Repressed whites were cast as the strange fruit of segregation, an early effort to situate the problems of lynching and white fear of miscegenation as "white" problems, caused by whites (instead of blacks) and to be solved by whites (instead of blacks). Smith recalls: "To me the phrase 'strange fruit' had nothing to do with lynching. I had used it before in an essay, in which I had talked about what segregation had done to white culture. And I had said: we are the strange fruit of that way of life. We who are white."[93] Taking the popular usage as a critique of whiteness, it became a foundation for working against the ideological assumptions guiding the embodied social practice of lynching.

Though the actual impact of the camp on these young girls and the relationships they would form in their lives is as uncertain to measure as any other variable, what does seem to have happened at Laurel Falls was a growing *awareness* that a white social context did, in fact, exist, and that it was made possible by social and economic privileges secured through repression and violence. Given the ethical and moral codes espoused by those within this context, almost exclusively white and Christian, over and against the intense repression and violence, Laurel Falls became a space for white young women to understand themselves as "strange fruit," the strangest of all fruit in that they hung from ideological constructs that prevented them from knowing themselves in their uncertainty, or as Smith put it, "Being armored in arrogance he finds it hard to genuflect to an unproved God, and impossible to relate to Him. How Strange! For we all cling to meanings we cannot prove ... ."[94] The costs of this repression had been extraordinary, and Smith wanted nothing more than to begin to respond to it through the channels available to her. Interestingly, working to make this "strange fruit" visible relied on further repression where other god-idols weighed as heavily as whiteness, in shaping social possibilities. In what follows, I explore the continued flights from uncertainty that occurred even in Smith's fight to expose racialized uncertainty.

The twilight of Laurel Falls

Throughout *White Lies*, twilight has referred to the impossibility of ever fully eradicating the Imago Superlata, even in moments of direct refutation of it. Overcoming these exaggerations of radical contingency is uncertain. Given this uncertain outcome, the benefits of whites fighting to kill whiteness and accept its functional ineffectiveness are practical: the concept dehumanizes its beneficiaries as much as its victims (everyone is victimized by it, though to varying degrees) and the god-idol is no longer a guarantee of feeling secure or certain. Thus the question of "why bother" involves both simple practical dimensions and a general ethical concern that, when given the choice, it is morally appropriate for white Americans to live life in a fashion more equitable than previous arrangements.

To suggest eradication is fully possible would, of course, amount to an exaggeration of ability, an agential exaggeration. A few examples from Laurel Falls help to demonstrate the paradoxes of fighting against such a system, and help to underscore that the embrace of uncertainty is not a social panacea, or a clever way of finding social certainty by calling it another name. Rather, it is a constant recognition of human limitations continuously exaggerated even when we seek to mitigate those exaggerations.

In 2006, thanks to support from The Documentary Institute at the University of Florida, Suzanne Niedland and Anberin Pasha produced and directed a short film about Smith's work and life at Laurel Falls, titled *Miss Lil's Camp*. The documentary brings together four women, three white former campers, and one African American former worker at the camp, to reminisce and celebrate the camp setting and the impact "Miss Lil" had on those around her. A story unfolds about a fight against repression made possible by reinforcing repression in other instances.

In terms of interpersonal relationality, the camp had as large an impact on Smith as she had on it and its campers. Lil met another counselor, Paula Snelling, who had worked at the camp when Lil's father ran it, and the two became lifelong lovers and partners, also eventually serving as co-directors of the camp. Given their location in the U.S. South and the risks to the camp at the prospect of being exposed as lesbians, the two were forced to remain silent and closeted regarding the most powerful and personal aspects of their relationship.[95]

One camper remembers that "Lillian Smith was about freedom and choice." And yet, she had to "be totally discreet about what her own choices had been. She never shared those with campers."[96] Paula and Lil lived closeted, not able and willing to fight openly against homophobia, seemingly more willing to channel that energy in the direction of topics and issues where their white privilege would afford greater impact, such as with the issue of racial discrimination. Fighting repression on one front seemingly reinforced repression in other areas.

Both Paula and Lil "were interested in ideas, in literature, and in psychology"[97] according to Smith biographer Rose Gladney, and their activism was meted out through these intellectual interests. They served together in an editorial capacity for the journals *Pseudopodia, North Georgia Review*, and *South Today*. These journals, and their larger efforts, were shaped largely by a conscious effort to publish both black and white writers. They often hosted parties with highly integrated (and often prominent) guest lists. Smith counted as friends Mary McLeod Bethune, Paul Robeson, Martin Luther King, Jr., Eleanor Roosevelt and many others.[98] She is also remembered as a personal literary mentor to writer and activist Pauli Murray.[99] Many of her relationships with prominent African Americans were forged intentionally at these gatherings, devoted mostly to bringing women of various backgrounds together. In one invitation sent to Murray, Smith stated of her intent: "I want you as friends to come together and begin personal relationships that may give us all deep pleasure... . There are many white women who should know you."[100] Willing to risk awkwardness for the sake of earnestness, such invitations and gatherings were commonplace, and Smith grew to count a number of prominent African Americans as friends through such measures. Many of these friends and public figures would be discussed in the camp setting, causing campers "to look up to" these artistic and social visionaries – and all the while, homosexuality remained hidden while racism and sexism were attacked.

In the literary arena, *Strange Fruit* (1944) would offer Smith a way to address both racism and sexism within the truncated options of twilight.[101] *Strange Fruit*'s attack on the sexualization of race and the racialization of sex, and the cultural depravity of whites based on these ideological miscegenations was met with derision as much as fanfare.[102] The book was banned in many places, including Boston, MA, and even the U.S. Postal Service refused to ship the book for a time.[103] *Strange Fruit*, Smith recounts, "was the bomb that shattered a conspiracy of silence ... we were under what I had always called a bale of cotton. The cotton had been stuffed into our mouths so that we couldn't talk and so that we couldn't hear others. That began to lift, and once the conspiracy of silence is broken, then we began to ask questions."[104] Here, worth noting, as with the strange fruit inversion, Smith reappropriates traditional associations of cotton with blacks – working within (and with) the social context she found herself a part of – to demonstrate the white responsibility for those associations. *Strange Fruit*'s publication brought with it hate mail, and an unsolved fire was even set at Laurel Falls. The grassroots-styled energy begun at Laurel Falls erupted into a growing awareness that no longer could whites conceal their own existential, social, and political interests in segregation. The curtain had been drawn back on repressive exaggerations of radical contingency. Not resolved, but exposed! Resolution, rehabilitation would take place more slowly and always at the expense of other compromises. Laurel Falls' campers and programming provided that opportunity, so long as conversations about sexuality remained vague, and the practical interests in such discussions remained concealed.

Smith made a point to have frank discussions about race, religion, and white social life, and some of these discussions had consequences beyond the borders of the camp. One former camper recounts that Smith was once asked pointedly about lynching, and her response was simply to make it clear that "lynchings did happen, and that they were wrong because it was wrong to treat another human being as an inferior."[105]Another camper recalls that Laurel Falls is where she learned that "you have to see the way things are [in the world] and see the ramifications of the way things are."[106] In many "Sunday services," others remember that Miss Lil would teach the campers to begin to "make a conscious effort not only to reach out, but to pull the curtain away from those things that we were denying,"[107] such as segregation and lynching. Still another former camper recounts that on one occasion, something learned at Laurel Falls caused tension in her household. Coming home to scold her father on his treatment of African Americans, she was not allowed to go back to Laurel Falls. Another camper remembers her father suggesting that "Now, what Miss Lil says at camp is fine for camp, but that's not the way we act around here."[108] As Smith tried to demonstrate to the campers, silence was more deadly than confrontation and exposure of social injustices. But even such efforts also reinforced problematic social arrangements at the camp itself.

Willie Mae Sanford, African American and former staff member at Laurel Falls, remembers the camp was taking place in a "sad time," when "white people didn't have nothing to do with us [African Americans]."[109] She even remembers that white children would call her (an adult at the time) a nigger. "Lil was different," Sanford remembers, noting that "Lil would treat everyone the same." And yet, Sanford was never treated as a white staff member, much less a camper, even if she was treated humanely by Smith. The camp, even as it worked against segregation, reinforced the practice by relying on black servers and only allowing white campers. This segregated arrangement is pronounced even in the reunion witnessed in the documentary. In one scene where the white women begin singing the song of Laurel Falls, the black woman smiles in silence, her silence giving voice to the segregated arrangement at the time that prevented her full inclusion in the activities. In other words, Sanford was never allowed or did not want to learn the words to the song. An answer to which of these possibilities occurred is not provided in the film. Interestingly, the legacy of these conditions bleeds into the contemporary moment, as the African American woman is once again othered as the white ladies recite the refrain sung nightly at the council fire of Laurel Falls:

> In the stillness of the twilight,
> in our mountainous abode,
> let us pledge our allegiance to her Laurel Falls code.[110]

Does twilight have a coding? Or is it the rationale behind social codes? I do not mean to conclude this section by implying a shared assumption that the lyrics here suggest Smith or the campers were working with the same definition of twilight I've made use of so extensively in these pages. However, the term, showing up here in the lyrics to the camp's nightly refrain – at a camp that transformed privilege into a moment to expose exaggerations of radical contingency and cultivate alternative ways of living more equitably while reinforcing other continued exaggerations in the process – may simply be an uncanny coincidence. But it works as a descriptive reminder of twilight, as well, where we strange white fruit remain uncertain of even whether or not this embrace of uncertainty will adequately address social realities like racism. Twilight is not a historiographic marker, but a heuristic white Americans might use to come to greater awareness of the ontological dimensions of social life in light of contemporary, confusing social conditions. In such conditions, uncertainty of thought and action brings with it the fear of extolling great harm to others (as evidenced by whiteness born as an outgrowth of fear associated with uncertainty). But if we embrace this twilight, such uncertainty also offers the moment to profess "allegiance" to a freedom lived (finally) within limitation, within the twilight of god-idols like whiteness.

Recognition of twilight, for the campers as much as for Smith, began in the social locations provided by the very privileges that recognition of twilight seeks to disrupt. Indeed, white privilege, if it is anything, is the privilege to deny this twilight. And such recognition is not without problems in terms of reinforcing certain social injustices as it fights others. But it does offer a start. In the next section, I conclude this homily by noting where twilight takes strange white fruit.

The transformative power of embracing twilight

The question of where twilight will take strange white fruit is answered by asking what does twilight sound like? What does it look or feel like? In a word, heritage. White cultural inheritance had such an impact – albeit painful – on Smith that she chose to live within it, within the pain, most of her life. Like twilight, maybe even because of it, heritage and social inheritance cannot be fully escaped. Perhaps such an escape attempt would be problematic however one set about it. Where the death of whiteness is concerned, wouldn't escape amount to a flight from uncertainty rather than an embrace of it? Isn't the most dangerous unknown that which we find within ourselves and our communities, perhaps finding it even here, now, at this requiem for whiteness? Asking no longer "who am I without whiteness" but "who will I choose to be" as I leave this funeral carrying the legacy of whiteness, regardless. Baldwin again serves as racialized foil and wise sage framing Smith's utility here. Elsewhere in *Notes of a Native Son*, Baldwin suggests that "a *what*" – as in "what am I?" – "can get by with skill but a *who* demands resources."[111] Understanding the "what" of "what are we as white?" to have something to do with this twilight, the "who" will be answered in terms of where we find resources. Smith's efforts at the cultivation of such resources can be understood through the Deleuzian notion of "minor literature," an effort to "use the polylingualism of your own tongue, to make a minor or extensive use of it, set the oppressed character of this tongue against its oppressive character."[112] Smith is one such resource where whites now might begin to answer the question of who we are (or want to be) by looking backwards towards who we have been.

The summer of 1948 was the last for the camp, in part because of Lillian Smith's poor health and desire to focus more attention on her writing. But despite the closing of the camp, Smith remained based in Georgia. Unlike other Southern writers such as her friend Carson McCullers, Smith chose to stay in the South for her continued writing. She notes, "Many times, I felt that if I went to New York to live or Paris to live, that all of it would begin to fade. And it hurt, but I wanted it to hurt. Because I think a writer stops writing when the wound heals."[113] Rather than follow the paths of, say, James Baldwin, Richard Wright, or her white contemporary McCullers (Wright and McCullers were friends, McCullers even staying in Wright's Paris home),[114] Smith wanted to *feel* the pain of segregation and continued repression, as it seemingly connected her literary efforts more closely to the authenticity of her argument. It also might have been understood by Smith that black and white flight from the U.S. to Paris involved different motivations and different social conditions fled and found in the U.S. and abroad, respectively.

Smith's geographic stasis might also be read as a kind of embrace of the letting go of privilege, the conscious decision to embrace *existential* uncertainty precisely by critically examining the most familiar, most intimately known social relations and realities. Smith stated that Georgia "is where my roots are. I want my mind to cover the whole earth. But I want my *mythic* roots to stay there, the roots in the imagination to be on home ground."[115] Rather than read her choice to stay at home as a fear of difference and otherness preventing a desire to travel, Smith makes clear that her choice was in the direction of embracing the otherness of a white identity, of this strange white fruit cast finally in its alterity and strangeness. Baldwin and other blacks fled to Europe to escape American whiteness, American religion; for us whites, the only real "escape" from whiteness is found in its death made possible through full recognition of the legacy the god-idol leaves behind. For us, there is no escape; until it is faced, we carry it with us to the ends of the earth.

Smith's writings had so impacted the literary world that she certainly had the means to leave, to live in a place where blacks and lesbians were treated more equitably by whites, but to do so seemed to Smith to risk the ability of her words and efforts to find continued diagnostic purchase with the audiences and issues she worked so hard to speak to and to expose. She here serves not so much as a literal geographic model whites must follow, but through heritage, Smith demonstrates the impossibility of escaping twilight. Smith offers a literal geographic example, yes, but also serves as a metaphor for ideological movement, in that whiteness (as this inability to accept limitation) can only be killed, if its beneficiaries do not run from this deathly thing, but learn to live with its legacy, live without appealing to it as a god-idol by keeping it close in memory. Whites do not, to this end, need so much to learn to embrace the uncertain face of those we have deemed social others, but to embrace the uncertain recognition that whites *are* other, even and especially to ourselves – strange white fruit.

Smith ended up paying a price for staying in the South. As her public image waned, her literary efforts were met with being remembered well as a "race" writer, but never regarded as a writer whose greatness transcended parochial, topical issues. And yet, so much of her writings suggest that these critiques are to misunderstand her point: that the personal or parochial is what connects us all to the grandiose and transcendent. The personal would remain "paramount" for Smith, serving as the means of "breaking down the barriers of ignorance and suspicion that had divided the races for centuries."[116] Remembered in the literary world as this topical figure, for many others who knew her – the girls at Laurel Falls and the many who perceived her brilliance in exposing social denials as courageous and ahead of her time – "she is someone who lives in the memories so powerfully."[117] Buried at Laurel Falls, Smith's epitaph reads:

> Death can kill a man: that is all it can do to him;
> It cannot end his life. Because of memory... .[118]

The epitaph, as it blurs life and death with memory, offers wisdom for understanding whiteness in twilight times. The death of whiteness will not necessarily "end [its] life." Indeed, "because of memory," whiteness might live on in weakened functional power, or it might finally give reason for whites – those "at" this "requiem" – to begin to help recast social arrangements in new, more equitable ways. What we do with memory, how we face death, will mark the life or death of whiteness and determine just how ominously the shadow of twilight will hang in the twenty-first century over uncertain social possibilities. Uncertain of the future of whiteness, this uncertainty looms as my final word on this discussion, the attempt to "kill" these white lies, this funeral. How uncertainty is faced, embraced, fled, or obtained will shape the future impact of past memories of strange fruit, realizing now that we are hanging from the ropes of dead god-idols.

BENEDICTION

As a way of drawing my argument to a reflexive end, I offer here a benediction in the form of a blessing of uncertainty – framed in terms of a series of critical rejoinders to the more "certain" dimensions and claims made and employed in *White Lies*. Benediction, in this instance, is not an otherworldly appeal, but a final public admittance that human limitation marks the horizon of any field of vision, particularly with respect to the constitution of this particular intellectual project, and more generally, as we live life as strange white fruit learning just now how to let go of god-idols. Treating each of the following vignettes as metaphoric of the ideological ropes from which we whites continue to hang, I let go of these ropes and begin to embrace instead the freedom of uncertainty and my radically contingent reliance on others.

Letting go of universal applicability

Who holds this limited religious outlook on the freedom of uncertainty found in the death of whiteness? Though I hope that this book will be of use to many, a limited religious outlook is certain of the importance and impact of social context on what can be known or judged. I am certain that a focus on social context, understood as the myriad resources, ideas, artifacts, and motivations, structured by and structuring group allegiance and affinity, has a *certain* impact on an awareness of fundamental uncertainty. I am seemingly certain of this uncertainty exposed by group difference and have worked to limit all of my prescriptive judgments to the white theistic petit bourgeois community serving as my data, not as a simple strawman, but precisely to force confrontation with such a context for those who occupy it. Inasmuch as the overall apparatus I have spelled out is registered by some as universally applicable, I remind that I am offering white Americans, in particular white American scholars of religion, insights about how to make sense of ourselves and our work, nothing more.

I have tried to limit appeals to the universal or situate them in terms of the universality of physical death. Although some readers might suggest that I, like Lévi-Strauss suggests of Sartre, "exchange one prison [of universality] for another,"[119] I hope that my prison, constructed not with a disregard for human suffering but in response to it, is at least a bit less harmful to all social actors than the prisons of white religion whose bars and cell blocks are made of white lies (whiteness, theism, etc.). If "the savage mind totalizes,"[120] then I remain "savage" in that I have sought to manipulate such totalizing tendencies in ways less socially destructive than positions based on assumptions about human possibility and the power of distinctions.[121]

On this note, Smith offers one more example for this requiem for how *not* to respond to the social problems of particularity through universal appeals. Her final novel, *One Hour*, published in 1959, tells the story of a little girl who accuses a church-goer of attempted molestation. The accusation is false in the scheme of things, but the accusation is enough to send a church community and a marriage into a tailspin. As most critics have suggested, the novel is derivative, its characters do not give much reason to pull the reader into their concerns, and the attempted profundity of the novel simply never finds purchase.[122]

Frustrated that she was largely celebrated as a "race" novelist, Smith's aims in *One Hour* were to prove her literary merit beyond the particularities of the South, or race or gender discrimination. She herself even wrote: "I think *One Hour* may be the first American novel that has dealt directly and on so many levels with the problem of the human being caught in his many traps" such as "science, art, God, freedom," etc.[123] Though the racialized and gendered contexts of the characters color the backdrop of the plot, the focus is on universal applicability – the many shared "traps" humans face.

Perhaps, the critical failure of this work (that is, its lukewarm public reception, it being ignored by many of her contemporary writers) might be thought of as the result of Smith's assumption that the "traps" she faced, or that white Americans faced, were somehow the same "traps" faced by everyone, such that almost no attention to contextual variance is provided in the novel. Details and scenes in the novel go underdeveloped, the "deep" portions of the novel remain flat precisely because this novel about the costs of human existence fails to privilege social asymmetries and intense contextual variety within this shared existence.

With an eye towards Smith's seeming failure to realize that the only universally applicable premise she could offer is the intense particularity of social context rooted in cultural responses to death (erring on the side of the bulk of white artists, philosophers, theologians and the like who too often take the part for the whole), Smith's last work is a reminder that even the most committed to rejecting whiteness can momentarily succumb to its ghost of certainty. I am fairly certain that there are very few instances of human existence that can be taken as certain or as universal. Physical death, experienced eventually by all social actors, is one of these. I am certain that physical death is a human experience shared by all, albeit exaggerated in severity for some by their constitution as "other." To paraphrase Michel de Montaigne one final moment: "Long life and short life [and the social contexts leading to different life spans and qualities of life] are made all one by death. For there is no long or short for things that are no more."[124] Though the ways people die are as varied as the length and quality of any life lived, the experience of physical death (that it happens to everyone) connects us all. Black, white, rich, poor, etc., are held together, shown as same instead of different through death as it has historically been treated in much of philosophy. And I have made use of death throughout the book for this reason. But even death – especially the death of god-idols – remains a proposition fraught with uncertainty.

Through a privileging of uncertainties posed by social context, and recognition of a certain sort of relation to all social contexts based on death, white freedom in uncertainty will then involve balancing a white social context in similar proximity to the distance between death and all other social contexts. Again, I have set out to answer the question of why white American Christianity and racism have worked so well together, why so much of "American religion" has been "white religion," and then offer an answer for how to trouble this socially and epistemologically problematic euphemism, this white lie. The answer is this embrace of uncertainty, and this embrace begins by sighting and questioning the efficacy and ability of continued use of these god-idols.

Letting go of certainty in the death of whiteness

It would be fair of readers to ask of whiteness: Has the tomb of whiteness really been filled, or does it remain empty? Or a more dangerous proposition still, did the metaphoric tomb (of the white American Christian Jesus) once receive this lifeless whiteness and has that whiteness been resurrected? In other words, does my rhetorical strategy (borrowed from James Baldwin) of speaking whiteness into death really promote the uncertainty required to "kill" whiteness once and for all? These questions are heuristic as posed here, but are embodied and visceral for those who face exaggerations of radical contingency with a severity and frequency I do not. *White Lies* has attempted to demonstrate the death-dealing effects of a death-denying white community to that community, so as to call into question the ability to deny death any longer, so that it might be accepted rather than denied. That is, I have worked to establish that learning to die with others means learning that one is dying already. But just as Baldwin's pronouncement that the white world has come to an end[125] was clearly ahead of (or outside of) historical circumstance, what will come of my similar pronouncements taking place at the requiem for whiteness? Baldwin's words did not produce an end to racism or a "white world," and I am under no illusion that my words will have even a semblance of the impact of Baldwin's. But my effort amounts to a rhetorical strategy for seeing an eventual and literal end to the ability of whiteness to shape social life. Ideas cannot be destroyed. But the power we invest in them can be ruptured or altered. Where whiteness is concerned, its power can also remain intact through new instances of an old racism.

Ongoing events like the rise of extremist groups in the United States[126] call into question the *actual* sociological death of the impact of whiteness and other god-idols on the social cartography of the contemporary world. Moreover, brilliant studies such as Eduardo Bonilla-Silva's *Racism Without Racists* (2009) make it clear that commemorative totemic rituals are constantly enacted helping to keep whiteness alive. Bonilla-Silva suggests that adherents to an ideology telegraph their adherence as if "wearing a piece of clothing," "presenting yourself to the world" through a "certain style."[127] Two examples of these rites include rhetorical statements like "I am not racist, but ..."[128] and the increasing popularity of terms like "thug" which stand in for the more traditional "nigger."[129] These seemingly simple instances, though all too common, amount to a style telegraphing the worship of the god-idol of whiteness, dead or alive. Countless rituals like these, in addition to other arguments (I could include to demonstrate) that racism is alive and well even if in new forms,[130] over and against vigilantism and continued racialized, gendered, and economic disparities in the United States make me *certain* that whiteness, for many, remains alive and well. Many white Americans remain "strange fruit" to the extent that they consciously or unconsciously hold fast to these god-idols, telegraphed by the "style" they cultivate amongst adherents, even as social tides may shift that call into question the life of these god-idols. I am uncertain if the freedom found in uncertainty will cause the remaining strange fruit to let go, but I am certain that efforts must continue that will constantly call into question the functional power of this god-idol. These efforts must include attention to rhetorical and philosophical dismantlings of power, such as Baldwin and Smith both employed throughout their writings, that do very real damage to the ability of whiteness to exaggerate the radical contingency of social actors with the same power it wielded historically.

Letting go of the certainty of an argument

The concepts of certainty and uncertainty shape all of these pages, so much so that readers might find I collapse into a kind of certainty provided by the very notion of uncertainty. Stated in terms of the god-idols engaged, readers might find I reinforce and recast whiteness in "certain" terms, which would mean I am repeating aspects of the functional process I seek to trouble. Indeed, the blurring of so many distinctions, as well as my constitution of white petit bourgeois theistic Americans, are, of course, their own brand of distinction making.

On this logical point I may be found guilty and Part I addresses this conundrum, the frustration of never fully overcoming the twilight of the god-idols. I am uncertain as to whether or not certainty is ever fully afforded in any intellectual or social field. I am certain that all claims to certainty require a kind of faith, an assent to a proposition of one kind or another; that is, we cross induction chasms through appeals to the many god-idols *White Lies* has sought to expose. For instance, even famed philosopher David Hume's critique of induction[131] – that is, his critique of the fallacy of assuming a relation between cause and effect – was made partially possible (in my estimation) by a social context where different people were ranked as worthy and able enough to be included within or outside of that context. Hume's racism[132] indicates that he too assented to the faith-based proposition of his context's superiority over other contexts. Aware of the dangers of this sort of faith as well as the seeming inescapability of our reliance on it, the preceding sections on Smith's Laurel Falls err on the side of story-telling, leaving the multitude of possible implications for my argument open-ended, because given the uncertain dimensions and compromises with white religion necessitated by argument and analysis, I am left with story, heritage, "memories" of "empty rooms"[133] that remain "empty" as only now dead god-idols can – and did – and do – fill them.

The efforts of Part II have focused more so on offering actual suggestions (e.g., a limited religious outlook, the relinquishing of personal conceptions of the soul, the embrace of uncertainty) that might be useful for white Americans in this "fight," that we might come to know ourselves and the social impact of these "selves" in a way that might offset some of the more pernicious aspects of a white American religious experience and social context shaping and shaped by god-idols. Doing so seems to involve an embrace of the uncertainty posed by death, threats to power, and social group difference. This embrace is perhaps made possible through the privileging of limitation, within the uncertainty posed by social context, and may help to produce a socially responsible freedom in limitation made possible through letting go of assumptions, presumptions about certainty, and a limited outlook on human social possibilities. To the extent that *White Lies* argues for the embrace of uncertainty and limitation as a response to the dangers of assumptions about human possibility, value and certainty in such claims, it will have accomplished its uncertain task.

For a final instance, the back and forth about whiteness as dead (or not), and the back and forth between physical and metaphoric definitions of death, is not a matter of intellectual laziness or sloppiness on my part, but is instrumental for developing the uncertainty I am discussing. To end with certainty (as if whiteness can die, will die, must die, and will never resurrect again) would rely on unchecked privilege guided by a Christian logic of resurrection or liberation – to foreclose and seriously deny the active and ongoing process that allowing privilege and domination to die, requires. The dialectical tension between certainty and uncertainty that I end with here is as much a reflexive awareness of the constant work we, white people, must do to guard against arriving at a position of a certitude of white liberative arrival, as it is recognition that, in effect, and as I have tried to show throughout (sometimes consciously, other times, not so much), certainty enacted by whites, has, for too long, been certain death for others and to the other.

Thus, the approach put forth in *White Lies* is philosophically aporetic, a paradox. Have I been talking *about* white lies and how to respond to them, or have I simply added my name to the long list of white liars? In response to this paradox, the concept of death cutting across various domains and intellectual fields – death of people, death of ideas, death of theological possibilities – is where I localize all of my "certain" claims, holding in tension the arbitrary constitution of my data and ideas about them with the fundamental human situation of mortality. In other words, I have sought to reach a terminally ill audience with the most pressing means of formation of attention available: the certainty of physical death and the limits and uncertainties exposed by flights away from these ends. My talk of uncertainty is not inductive, rationalized certainty in a new form, or what might be *mis*understood as a kind of post-racial claim or appeal. Rather, it holds in front of us what is the single most fundamental constitutive feature of my data set, the large-scale inability to accept the finality of physical and social white life and the social and existential uncertainties posed by this certain claim – that we, "the strange [white] fruit of that way of life,"[134] and the god-idols we worship – will one day die.

Baldwin, whose wisdom regarding the life and death of whiteness sets the first words of *White Lies* in motion with the epigraph beginning this book, offers one of the last words, as well.

> The really terrible thing, old buddy, is that *you* must accept *them*. And I mean that very seriously. You must accept them and accept them with love. For these innocent people have no other hope. They are, in effect, still trapped in a history which they do not understand; and until they understand it, they cannot be released from it. They have had to believe for many years, and for innumerable reasons, that black men are inferior to white men. Many of them, indeed, know better, but, as you will discover, people find it very difficult to act on what they know. To act is to be committed, and to be committed is to be in danger. In this case, the danger, in the minds of most white Americans, is the loss of their identity.[135]

Indeed, as Baldwin notes, "the world is white no longer"[136] but how white Americans will answer the question of who we will be now, how we will respond to this loss of identity, remains to be narrated. Courageously responding to this loss offers the possibility to free us from a history of denial that we might learn to live dangerously for the sake of the other inside of ourselves as much as outside. Between the space of our fear of courage, or courage in face of fear, beginning to respond to white lies will require finally learning to accept and love ourselves – uncertain, limited, failing, losing white bodies. The loss of our identity is the gaining of the opportunity to learn, at long last, how to die with others, and we learn through this process, how to die at all. What this loss, this death, means for the strange white fruit of that way of life will be answered as either a story of freedom in uncertainty and limitation or renewed social, ideological, and physical forms of bondage. We stand now at the requiem for whiteness, preparing to leave, uncertain of all but the end of innocence, unsure if or how this end will mark a new beginning.

ELEGY FOR WHITENESS

> SOMEWHERE – in desolate wind-swept space –
> In Twilight-land – in No-man's-land –
> Two hurrying Shapes met face to face,
> And bade each other stand.
> "And who are you?" cried one a-gape,
> Shuddering in the gloaming light.
> "I know not," said the second Shape,
> "I only died last night!"

Thomas Bailey Aldrich, "Identity" (1900)[137]

Notes

1 Bill Schwarz and Cora Kaplan, *James Baldwin: America and Beyond* (University of Michigan Press, 2011), 11–12.
2 Lillian Smith, in Suzanne Niedland and Anberin Pasha, *Miss Lil's Camp* (BusEye Films, 2008).
3 Schwarz and Kaplan, *James Baldwin*, 11–12.
4 Ibid.
5 James Baldwin, *Notes of a Native Son*, reissue edition (Beacon Press, 1984), 159–75.
6 Ibid.
7 Ibid., 173–75.
8 Schwarz and Kaplan, *James Baldwin*, 12.
9 For background on how I define these white people, along with their relationship to theism or whiteness more generally, see Chapters 1 and 2. Here, "white people" continues to mean a white petit bourgeois ideal, radiating outwardly as "most Americans."
10 Baldwin, *Notes of a Native Son*.
11 As noted later in this chapter, this proposed alternative hermeneutical rendering of white Americans as "strange fruit" is not to suggest or compete with the historical reality of black bodies as "strange fruit," but is meant to cast whiteness as "other" by way of the very "othering" devices it has made use of historically.
12 I have in mind a kind of contemporary expression of Plato's Allegory of the Cave. Think, instead, of a community that has lived its entire life with air conditioning, but without the recognition that air conditioning is an artificial construction of social and material reality. Only when air conditioning stops working, stops functioning, does it begin to become apparent that life has been lived (to this point) with an unknown advantage.
13 Charles H. Long, *Significations: Signs, Symbols, and Images in the Interpretation of Religion*. 2nd ed. (The Davies Group Publishers, 1999), 184.
14 My argument does not intend to "other" those whites victimized by lynching historically, or to shortchange such stories for the sake of easily packaging these ideas. Though exceptions are certainly a fixture of any argument, hanging above or buried beneath its claims, I contend that white people were the principal beneficiaries of the historical practice of lynching, in terms of both who was literally killed and what functional work those lynchings sought to do in the social world.
15 Especially worthy of deconstructing are Weber's reliance on teleology and the function of charisma.
16 See, for instance, both Max Weber, Hans Heinrich Gerth, and C. Wright Mills, *From Max Weber: Essays in Sociology* (Oxford University Press, Galaxy, 1958); and Max Weber and Anthony Giddens, *The Protestant Ethic and the Spirit of Capitalism*, trans. Talcott Parsons. 2nd ed. (Routledge, 2001).
17 Pierre Bourdieu, "Genesis and Structure of the Religious Field." *Comparative Social Research* 13 (1991): 1–44.
18 Gary Dorrien, *The Making of American Liberal Theology: Imagining Progressive Religion, 1805–1900*. 1st ed. (Westminster John Knox Press, 2001).
19 Ralph E. Luker, *The Social Gospel in Black and White: American Racial Reform, 1885–1912* (University of North Carolina Press, 1998).
20 Robert Bellah, *Habits of the Heart* (Perennial, 1985), 232–3.
21 Martin E. Marty, *A Nation of Behavers* (University of Chicago Press, 1976), 12.
22 Ibid., 8.
23 Ibid., 13.
24 Ibid., 53–4.
25 Ibid., 159.

26 Jean-François Bayart, *The Illusion of Cultural Identity* (University of Chicago Press, 2005), 92–3.
27 Marty, *A Nation of Behavers*, 204.
28 Bayart, *The Illusion of Cultural Identity*, 252.
29 Lillian Smith, *Killers of the Dream* (W. W. Norton & Company, 1994), 29.
30 Smith, *Killers*, 233–4.
31 Billie Holiday, *Strange Fruit*, n.d.
32 Lillian Smith, in Niedland and Pasha,*Miss Lil's Camp*.
33 Rose Gladney, "A Letter from Lillian Smith," in *Southern Changes: Southern Regional Council* 10, no. 4 (July–August 1988), from the original held at the Carson McCullers Collection, Harry Ransom Humanities Research Center, The University of Texas at Austin, accessed March 11, 2015, http://beck.library.emory.edu/southernchanges/article.php?id=sc10-4_009
34 See Émile Durkheim, *The Elementary Forms of the Religious Life* (Dover Publications, 2008).
35 Anthea Butler, "The Zimmerman Acquittal: America's Racist God," *Religion Dispatches*, July 14, 2013, accessed August 24, 2013, www.religiondispatches.org/dispatches/antheabutler/7195/the_zimmerman_acquittal_america_s_racist_god/
36 Judith Butler, *Precarious Life: The Powers of Mourning and Violence* (Verso, 2006), 22.
37 Durkheim, *Elementary Forms*, 390.
38 Butler, *Precarious Life*, 22.
39 Durkheim, *Elementary Forms*, 389.
40 Ibid., 389.
41 Ibid., 394.
42 Ibid., 403.
43 Eric Schliesser, "The Piacular, or on Seeing Oneself as a Moral Cause in Adam Smith," in Martin Lenz and Anik Waldow, eds.,*Contemporary Perspectives on Early Modern Philosophy* (Netherlands, Springer, 2013), 159–77, accessed March 11, 2015, http://link.springer.com/chapter/10.1007/978-94-007-6241-1_10
44 Émile Durkheim, quoted in Mark Worrell, "The Veil of Piacular Subjectivity: Buchananism and the New World Order," *Electronic Journal of Sociology* (1999), accessed March 13, 2015, http://www.sociology.org/content/vol004.003/buchanan.html
45 Jacques Derrida, *Specters of Marx: The State of the Debt, the Work of Mourning, and the New International* (Routledge, 2006), xviii.
46 Carson McCullers, *Illumination and Night Glare: The Unfinished Autobiography of Carson McCullers* (University of Wisconsin Press, 2002), 202.
47 Gladney, "A Letter from Lillian Smith."
48 Ibid.
49 Maurice Halbwachs, *On Collective Memory*, trans. Lewis A. Coser (University of Chicago Press, 1992), 49–51.
50 Ibid., 51.
51 Ibid., 37–8.
52 Darlene O'Dell, *Sites of Southern Memory: The Autobiographies of Katharine Du Pre Lumpkin, Lillian Smith, and Pauli Murray* (University of Virginia Press, 2001), 80.
53 Smith, quoted in Gladney, "A Letter from Lillian Smith."
54 On the Holmes-Rahe Stress Inventory, Death of a Spouse, Divorce, Marital Separation, and Death of a Loved One rank as four of the top five most stressful life events. McCullers experienced all four with Reeves. Accessed March 13, 2015, see http://www.stress.org/holmes-rahe-stress-inventory/ for more on this scale.
55 Smith, quoted in Gladney, "A Letter from Lillian Smith."
56 Here, I use an allusion to Nietzsche's proclamation that "god is dead." See Friedrich Nietzsche, *The Gay Science: With a Prelude in Rhymes and an Appendix of Songs* (Vintage Books, 1974).

57 Smith, *Killers of the Dream*, 21.
58 Ibid., 27.
59 Durkheim, *Elementary Forms*, 394.
60 Jean-François Bayart, *The Illusion of Cultural Identity* (University of Chicago Press, 2005), 92.
61 Mary Douglas, *Natural Symbols: Explorations in Cosmology*, 3rd ed. (Routledge, 2003), xxix.
62 Deborah King, "Multiple Jeopardy, Multiple Consciousness: The Context of a Black Feminist Ideology," *Signs* 14, no. 1 (1988): 42–72.
63 Paul Rabinow, George E. Marcus, James Faubion, and Tobias Rees, *Designs for an Anthropology of the Contemporary* (Duke University Press Books, 2008), 34.
64 Jasbir K. Puar, *Terrorist Assemblages: Homonationalism in Queer Times* (Duke University Press, 2007), 212.
65 In technical language, and following Gilles Deleuze and Felix Guattari, progenitors of the assemblage theory espoused by Puar, "latitude and longitude are the two elements of a cartography" (Deleuze and Guattari 260–1) wherein assemblages are mapped given the multiplicity of arrangements. God-idols serve as the "latitudinal" (i.e., affective, ideological) component of an assemblage, including as many or as few god-idols as are held by any given adherent, while the actual body – here, still following Mary Douglas's suggestion that the body is the canvas for symbolization (Douglas, *Natural Symbols*, xxxvii), serves as the longitudinal component. Wedding Douglas to Deleuze and Puar's notion of assemblage is not a moment of theoretical miscegenation so much as an effort to take seriously Douglas's contention that a proportional relationship exists between bodily control and social control, while acknowledging that such a suggestion must be dislodged from the binary rigidity of the grid/group, in terms of its tacit suggestion that identity is rigid even if falling along a continuum. In other words, I am not attempting to have my theoretical cake and eat it, too, but attempting to find a way to demonstrate that more than a personal or positional continuum exists within the panoply of "operational acts of identification" (Bayart, *The Illusion of Cultural Identity*, 92) that shape god-idol construction. Perhaps my argument is in the direction of Douglas's call for a three-dimensional rehashing of the grid/group (Douglas, *Natural Symbols*, xxix), such an added dimension made possible by a turn to assemblage theory at the cost of the precision that is part and parcel of Douglas's effectiveness. See Gilles Deleuze and Felix Guattari, *A Thousand Plateaus: Capitalism and Schizophrenia*, trans. Brian Massumi (Minneapolis: University of Minnesota Press, 1987), 260–1.
66 Puar, *Terrorist Assemblages*, xxvii.
67 Ibid., 211.
68 Smith, *Killers of the Dream*, 27.
69 Ibid., 162–3.
70 Ibid., 212.
71 Ibid., 220–1.
72 For examples of the sorts of work I have in mind, see: Elaine A. Robinson, *Race and Theology* (Abingdon Press, 2012); J. Kameron Carter, *Race: A Theological Account* (Oxford University Press, 2008).
73 Ibid., 29.
74 Puar, *Terrorist Assemblages*, 24–32.
75 Toni Morrison, "Unspeakable Things Unspoken," in Sterling M. McMurrin and Grethe B. Peterson, eds., *Tanner Lectures on Human Values, XI [11]* (University of Utah Press, 1990), 123–163, 141.
76 Ibid.
77 Herman Melville, *Moby Dick* (New American Library, 1892 [1851]), 180.
78 For a brief definition of colorism, see Fabricio Balcazar, Yolanda Suarez-Balcazar, and Tina Taylor-Ritzler, *Race, Culture and Disability: Rehabilitation Science and Practice* (Jones & Bartlett Learning, 2010).

79 Melville, 180.
80 Cornel West, *The Cornel West Reader* (Basic Books, 1999), 100.
81 Melville, 180.
82 Valerie Melissa Babb, *Whiteness Visible: The Meaning of Whiteness in American Literature and Culture* (NYU Press, 1998), 87.
83 Baldwin, "Stranger in the Village," in *Notes.*
84 Melville, *Moby Dick*, 180.
85 Bayart, *The Illusion of Cultural Identity*, 92.
86 Friedrich Nietzsche, *The Gay Science: With a Prelude in Rhymes and an Appendix of Songs* (Vintage Books, 1974), 228.
87 Niedland and Pasha, *Miss Lil's Camp.*
88 Ibid.
89 Ibid.
90 Ibid.
91 Darlene O'Dell, *Sites of Southern Memory: The Autobiographies of Katharine Du Bre Lumpkin, Lillian Smith, and Pauli Murray* (University of Virginia Press, 2001), 83–4.
92 Lillian Smith, *Strange Fruit: A Novel of Interracial Love* (Reynal & Hitchcock Publ., 1944).
93 Niedland and Pasha, *Miss Lil's Camp.*
94 Smith, *Killers of the Dream*, 236.
95 Niedland and Pasha, *Miss Lil's Camp.*
96 Ibid.
97 Ibid.
98 Ibid.
99 Lynne Olson, *Freedom's Daughters: The Unsung Heroines of the Civil Rights Movement from 1830 to 1970* (Simon & Schuster, 2001).
100 Smith, quoted. in Olson, *Freedom's Daughters*, 65–7.
101 Smith, *Strange Fruit.*
102 Judith E. Smith, *Visions of Belonging: Family Stories, Popular Culture, and Postwar Democracy, 1940–1960* (Columbia University Press, 2004), 116–17.
103 Margaret Rose Gladney, quoted in Lillian Smith, *One Hour* (The University of North Carolina Press, 1994), viii.
104 Niedland and Pasha, *Miss Lil's Camp.*
105 Ibid.
106 Ibid.
107 Ibid.
108 Ibid.
109 Ibid.
110 Ibid.
111 Baldwin, "Equal in Paris," *Notes of a Native Son.*
112 Giles Deleuze, Félix Guattari, and Robert Brinkley, "What Is a Minor Literature?" *Mississippi Review* 11, no. 3 (January 1, 1983): 13–33, 27.
113 Niedland and Pasha, *Miss Lil's Camp.*
114 Carson McCullers and C. L. Barney Dews, *Illumination*, 62–3.
115 Niedland and Pasha, *Miss Lil's Camp.*
116 Olson, *Freedom's Daughters*, 66.
117 Niedland and Pasha, *Miss Lil's Camp.*
118 Ibid.
119 Claude Lévi-Strauss, *The Savage Mind* (University of Chicago Press, 1968), 249.
120 Ibid., 245.
121 I make no claims that I (or anyone) is ever able to fully assess when, and how, one social setting is "less-harmful" than another, or in determining for whom such lessening occurs. I can remain confident in suggesting that the contemporary arrangement of

social life in the United States can be improved upon, for all social actors. I hope *White Lies* will be a small step or arrow cast in a direction that might help to bring about such an improvement.

122 Dennis W. Petrie, "Lillian Smith: A Southerner Confronting the South: A Biography (review)," *MFS Modern Fiction Studies* 3, no. 4 (1987): 684–85, doi:10.1353/mfs.0.1326.

123 Smith, *One Hour*, xi.

124 Michel Eyquem de Montaigne, "That to Study Philosophy Is to Learn to Die," in *The Complete Essays of Montaigne* (Stanford University Press, 1958), 56–67, 64.

125 Schwarz and Kaplan, *James Baldwin*, 11–12.

126 See the Southern Poverty Law Center website for more information about the rise of hate groups in the United States, accessed March 11, 2015. http://www.splcenter.org/what-we-do/hate-and-extremism

127 Eduardo Bonilla-Silva, *Racism without Racists: Color-Blind Racism and the Persistence of Racial Inequality in America*, 3rd ed. (Rowman & Littlefield Publishers, 2009), 53.

128 Ibid., 53.

129 "Richard Sherman: Thug Is Now 'The Accepted Way of Calling Somebody the N-Word,'" January 25, 2014, *Huffington Post*, accessed March 13, 2015, http://www.huffingtonpost.com/2014/01/22/richard-sherman-thug-n-word-press-conference_n_4646871.html

130 Another academic treatment of contemporary racism that calls into question the "death" of whiteness is Imani Perry's argument about "post-intentional" racism, marking contemporary racism as no longer about recognition and awareness of racism in a moralistic sense. See Imani Perry, *More Beautiful and More Terrible: The Embrace and Transcendence of Racial Inequality in the United States* (NYU Press, 2011).

131 Jeremy J. White, *A Humean Critique of David Hume's Theory of Knowledge* (University Press of America, 1998), 86.

132 Cornel West, *Prophesy Deliverance!* anv. edition (Westminster John Knox Press, 2002), 62–3.

133 McCullers, reprinted in Gladney, "A Letter from Lillian Smith."

134 Lillian Smith, in Niedland and Pasha, *Miss Lil's Camp*.

135 James Baldwin, *The Fire Next Time* (Vintage Books, 1963), 8–9, original emphasis.

136 Schwarz and Kaplan, *James Baldwin*, 11–12.

137 Thomas Bailey Aldrich, "688. Identity," in Edmund Clarence Stedman, *An American Anthology, 1787–1900; Selections Illustrating the Editor's Critical Review of American Poetry in the Nineteenth Century* (Houghton Mifflin, 1900).

REFERENCES

"Richard Sherman: Thug Is Now 'The Accepted Way of Calling Somebody the N-Word'." 2014. *Huffington Post*, January 25, accessed March 13, 2015, http://www.huffingtonpost.com/2014/01/22/richard-sherman-thug-n-word-press-conference_n_4646871.html

Babb, Valerie Melissa. 1998. *Whiteness Visible: The Meaning of Whiteness in American Literature and Culture*. NYU Press.

Balcazar, Fabricio, Yolanda Suarez-Balcazar, and Tina Taylor-Ritzler. 2010. *Race, Culture and Disability: Rehabilitation Science and Practice*. Jones & Bartlett Learning.

Baldwin, James. 1963. *The Fire Next Time*. Vintage Books.

Baldwin, James. 1984. *Notes of a Native Son*. Reissue edition. Beacon Press.

Bayart, Jean-François. 2005. *The Illusion of Cultural Identity*. University of Chicago Press.

Bellah, Robert. 1985. *Habits of the Heart*. 1st ed. Perennial.

Bonilla-Silva, Eduardo. 2009. *Racism without Racists: Color-Blind Racism and the Persistence of Racial Inequality in America.* 3rd ed. Rowman & Littlefield Publishers.

Bourdieu, Pierre. 1991. "Genesis and Structure of the Religious Field." *Comparative Social Research* 13: 1–44.

Butler, Anthea. 2013. "The Zimmerman Aquittal: America's Racist God," July 14. *Religion Dispatches,* accessed August 24, 2013, religiondispatches.org/dispatches/antheabutler/7195/

Butler, Judith. 2006. *Precarious Life: The Powers of Mourning and Violence.* Verso.

Carter, J. Kameron. 2008. *Race: A Theological Account.* Oxford University Press.

Deleuze, Gilles and Félix Guattari. 1987. *A Thousand Plateaus: Capitalism and Schizophrenia,* trans. Brian Massumi. 1st edition. University of Minnesota Press.

Deleuze, Gilles, Félix Guattari, and Robert Brinkley. 1983. "What Is a Minor Literature?" *Mississippi Review* 11(3): 13–33.

Derrida, Jacques. 2006. *Specters of Marx: The State of the Debt, the Work of Mourning, and the New International.* Routledge.

Dorrien, Gary. 2001. *The Making of American Liberal Theology: Imagining Progressive Religion, 1805–1900.* 1st ed. Westminster John Knox Press.

Douglas, Mary. 2003. *Natural Symbols: Explorations in Cosmology.* 3rd ed. Routledge.

Durkheim, Emile. 2008. *The Elementary Forms of the Religious Life.* Dover Publications.

Gladney, Rose. 1988. "A Letter from Lillian Smith." Text. *Southern Changes: Southern Regional Council* 10(4), July–August, accessed March 11, 2015, http://beck.library.emory.edu/southernchanges/article.php?id=sc10-4_009

Halbwachs, Maurice. 1992. *On Collective Memory,* trans. Lewis A. Coser. 1st ed. University of Chicago Press.

Holiday, Billie. n.d. *Strange Fruit.*

Holmes-Rahe Stress Inventory. American Institute of Stress, accessed March 13, 2015, http://www.stress.org/holmes-rahe-stress-inventory/

King, Deborah. 1988. "Multiple Jeopardy, Multiple Consciousness: The Context of a Black Feminist Ideology." *Signs* 14(1): 42–72.

Lévi-Strauss, Claude. 1968. *The Savage Mind.* University of Chicago Press.

Long, Charles H. 1999. *Significations: Signs, Symbols, and Images in the Interpretation of Religion.* 2nd ed. The Davies Group Publishers.

Luker, Ralph E. 1998. *The Social Gospel in Black and White: American Racial Reform, 1885–1912.* University of North Carolina Press.

Marty, Martin E. 1976. *A Nation of Behavers.* University of Chicago Press.

Melville, Herman. 1892 (1851). *Moby Dick.* New American Library.

Montaigne, Michel Eyquem de. 1958. *The Complete Essays of Montaigne.* Stanford University Press.

Morrison, Toni. 1990. "Unspeakable Things Unspoken," in Sterling M. McMurrin and Grethe B. Peterson (eds.), *Tanner Lectures on Human Values, XI [11].* University of Utah Press, 123–163.

Niedland, Suzanne and Anberin Pasha. 2008. *Miss Lil's Camp.* BusEye Films.

Nietzsche, Friedrich. 1974. *The Gay Science: With a Prelude in Rhymes and an Appendix of Songs.* Vintage Books.

O'Dell, Darlene. 2001. *Sites of Southern Memory: The Autobiographies of Katharine Du Pre Lumpkin, Lillian Smith, and Pauli Murray.* University of Virginia Press.

Olson, Lynne. 2001. *Freedom's Daughters: The Unsung Heroines of the Civil Rights Movement from 1830 to 1970.* Simon & Schuster.

Perry, Imani. 2011. *More Beautiful and More Terrible: The Embrace and Transcendence of Racial Inequality in the United States*. NYU Press.

Petrie, Dennis W. 1987. "Lillian Smith: A Southerner Confronting the South: A Biography (review)." *MFS Modern Fiction Studies* 3(4): 684–685. doi:10.1353/mfs.0.1326.

Puar, Jasbir K. 2007. *Terrorist Assemblages: Homonationalism in Queer Times*. Duke University Press.

Rabinow, Paul, George E. Marcus, James Faubion, and Tobias Rees. 2008. *Designs for an Anthropology of the Contemporary*. Duke University Press Books.

Robinson, Elaine A. 2012. *Race and Theology*. Abingdon Press.

Schliesser, Eric. 2013. "The Piacular, or on Seeing Oneself as a Moral Cause in Adam Smith," in Martin Lenz and Anik Waldow (eds.), *Contemporary Perspectives on Early Modern Philosophy*, 159–177. Studies in History and Philosophy of Science 29. Springer Netherlands, accessed March 11, 2015, http://link.springer.com/chapter/10.1007/978-94-007-6241-1_10

Schwarz, Bill and Cora Kaplan. 2011. *James Baldwin: America and Beyond*. University of Michigan Press.

Smith, Judith E. 2004. *Visions of Belonging: Family Stories, Popular Culture, and Postwar Democracy, 1940–1960*. Columbia University Press.

Smith, Lillian. 1944. *Strange Fruit A Novel of Interracial Love*. Reynal & Hitchcock Publishers.

Smith, Lillian. 1994. *Killers of the Dream*. W. W. Norton & Company.

Smith, Lillian. 1994. *One Hour*. The University of North Carolina Press.

Southern Poverty Law Center. n.d. "What We Do-Southern Poverty Law Center," Southern Poverty Law Center website, accessed March 11, 2015, http://www.splcenter.org/what-we-do/hate-and-extremism

Stedman, Edmund Clarence. 1900. *An American Anthology, 1787–1900; Selections Illustrating the Editor's Critical Review of American Poetry in the Nineteenth Century*. Houghton Mifflin.

Weber, Max, Hans Heinrich Gerth, and C. Wright Mills. 1958. *From Max Weber: Essays in Sociology*. Oxford University Press, Galaxy.

Weber, Max and Anthony Giddens. 2001. *The Protestant Ethic and the Spirit of Capitalism*, trans. Talcott Parsons. 2nd ed. Routledge.

West, Cornel. 1999. *The Cornel West Reader*. Basic Books.

West, Cornel. 2002 (1982). *Prophesy Deliverance!*. Westminster John Knox Press.

White, Jeremy J. 1998. *A Humean Critique of David Hume's Theory of Knowledge*. University Press of America.

Worrell, Mark. 1999. "The Veil of Piacular Subjectivity: Buchananism and the New World Order." *Electronic Journal of Sociology*, accessed March 13, 2015, http://www.sociology.org/content/vol004.003/buchanan.html

POSTMORTEM

A warning

When religious expressions fail to address the existential needs of adherents, and when the gods created die rather than teach how to die, then embrace of uncertainty offers the moment for creative response. Learning to die with others is learning to live amongst the dead, living with a loss that if embraced fully, should be mourned and grieved (as any physical death might be treated). The final chapter speaks to this need. But this treatise on the death of whiteness and the twilight of white American religion must end with a warning. Assuming that the death of whiteness opens new possibilities, some of those possibilities could cause untold harm and destruction. Death, as an event or heuristic, is not a panacea, neither is uncertainty anything other than what it literally means: we do not know. We do not know what our particular white American community will do, the steps we will take, as we hear of whiteness's death and as we wrestle with others and ourselves in this twilight. If history is any indicator, we should not celebrate, but be fearful. Those who know not of their own deaths know less still of humanely engaging others.

Friedrich Nietzsche's "Madman" once ran to the marketplace and announced: "Do we hear nothing as yet of the noise of the gravediggers who are burying God? Do we smell nothing as yet of the divine decomposition? Gods, too, decompose. God is dead. God remains dead. And we have killed him."[1] The Madman from Nietzsche's famous story will go (on to) say that he has come too early, as "his time is not yet" to inform men[2] simultaneously of the death of god and the possibility such a death offers for men to achieve the "greatest deed of history," becoming gods themselves.[3]

For many white Americans, whiteness was once this god and its death offers time to theorize the life and death of the god-idols created in the United States, bringing new clarity to the Madman's words. But *White Lies* is as much a concession that the Madman's diagnostic was correct and that the time has come to tell his story, as it is a warning against the *Ubermensch* response and will to power Nietzsche's Zarathustra would later offer as replacement. I have attempted, in part, to proffer an explanation of why Nietzsche was led down such an individualized, exaggerated path.[4] The Madman's challenge remains incumbent upon us, but the greatest deed is not to become gods unchecked and unencumbered by social, cultural, and intellectual inheritance, but to realize the consequences of having attempted to be gods – now deceased – and to learn how to live in the permanent twilight of white American identity.

Notes

1 Friedrich Nietzsche, *The Gay Science: With a Prelude in Rhymes and an Appendix of Songs* (Vintage Books, 1974), 181–2.
2 Here, I purposefully keep the non-inclusive language used by Nietzsche's Madman, as a way of pointing out the androcentric, masculine intent of Nietzsche's project, and consequentially, his influence on my project.
3 Nietzsche, *The Gay Science*, 181.
4 Friedrich Nietzsche, *The Will to Power* (Vintage, 1968).

REFERENCES

Nietzsche, Friedrich. 1968. *The Will to Power*. Vintage Books.
Nietzsche, Friedrich. 1974. *The Gay Science: With a Prelude in Rhymes and an Appendix of Songs*. Vintage Books.

INDEX

Abraham (Biblical Figure) 109 n90, 180, 219–22, 235–243, 246, 248–9
agnosticism 181–3, 187, 191
Aldrich, Thomas Bailey 298
Alexander, Michelle 53–4, 176–7
Alighieri, Dante 186
Aliyah Senior Citizens Center 205–6
Altizer, Thomas J.J. 123, 133–6, 154, 161 n72
American Exceptionalism 84, 89
Anderson, Benedict *see* imagined communities
Anderson, Victor 27
Angell, Stephen 128
anomie 119
anthropology 2, 122–32, 142–3; field of 15–16, 18, 127; as method 127–9, 205–6; preoccupation with identity 136; as scholar's data 127, 156; subjectivist turn in 92, 129; as theology 92, 113 n162, 122–3, 136–7 245
Anthropology of Ethics 125, 132
Anti-Semite and Jew 140
anti-Semitism 139–41, 151, 154
anxiety: of death 50–1, 57 n14, 80–85, 94, 99, 110 n107, 205, 207, 222, 280; economic 16, 134, 140; of identity loss 171, 205; of influence 173–8, 183–5, 188–91, 193–4, 205–9; of meaninglessness/nihilism 71, 230, 249; of salvation 264
atheism 69, 189, 236; as Christian Atheism 69; co-constitutivity with theism 86–7, 101, 109 n89, 187, 223; as ethical posture 79, 181; as methodology 182; as a social problem 75
atonement 43, 83, 269–75, 277

bad faith 112 n161, 136, 146, 174, 180, 212 n49
Baldwin, James 15, 27, 257–9, 268, 283, 291, 295–6, 298
Barth, Karl 131, 236
battle for identity 16, 117, 121–2, 124, 136, 156–9, 278; inevitability of 142, 267; in institutions 153, 175
Baudelaire, Charles 247–8
Bayart, Jean-François 14, 16, 117, 120–6, 132, 136, 139, 142, 278, 301 n65
Becker, Ernest 30, 100
Being and Nothingness 19 n16 and n20, 124, 140
Bellah, Robert 265–7
belonging 76, 80, 84, 127, 208–9; individualism as belonging 265–6; race as emblem of 36, 66; relationship to exaggeration 150, 279; relationship to sacred/profane binary 142, 146, 202; and social death 252 n38
Bethune, Mary McLeod 288
Big White Lies *see* god-idol
black theology 59 n55, 183

blackness 19 n9, 38, 41, 78, 145, 199, 278; definition of 26, 104, 191; as ontological blackness 27, 37, 59 n55; preoccupation with 122; relationship to whiteness 29, 35, 39, 47, 191, 257–9, 262; as salvation 155
Bloom, Harold 15, 169, 173–9, 182–4, 186–88, 190, 200, 205, 207
Blum, Edward 96, 239
bodies (enfleshed) 4–11, 26–41, 99, 156, 248, 267–8; as canvas for symbolization 2, 40, 144–50, 205, 237, 262, 278, 301; and identity 122–6, 141–3
Bonilla-Silva, Eduardo 295–6
Bourdieu, Pierre 13–14, 20 n28, 31, 33–5, 38, 58 n38, 75, 77, 79, 83, 108 n71, 125–6; legitimation/objectification of religious identity 127–8, 138, 142, 238–9; as Marxist-structuralist 93, 155; on religious capital 151, 264; structured and structuring distinctions 133, 141
Boy Scouts of America 96
Brown, Michael 2, 11, 36, 42, 68, 79, 96–7, 268
Bush, George W. 121, 130, 136, 154
Butler, Anthea 1–4, 10, 65, 68–70, 82, 93–5, 98, 128, 138
Butler, Judith 270–2
Byrd, Jr., James 46, 60 n95

Camus, Albert 100, 160 n26, 162 n100, 212–13 n63
Cannon, Katie 27
Captain Cook 129–30
Carlier 117–22, 130–1, 136–40, 154, 159
Carter, J. Kameron 57 n14, 68–70, 78
certainty of uncertainty 296–8
church burnings 29, 42–3
Church Dogmatics 131
Civil Religion 75
Civil Rights Act 176
Civil Rights movement 53, 176
classism 141, 282
Clayton, Georgia 273, 275, 285
clinamen (poetry) 176
colonialism 118–21, 139, 257, 261, 285
colorblindness/postracialism 46, 53, 297
Cone, James 27, 29, 37, 59 n55, 70, 137–8
Conrad, Joseph 117–21, 125, 130, 132, 135–6, 139–40, 151
Coy, Edward 40
culture 5, 83, 91–2, 120, 130–142, 170–1, 180–3, 191–4, 200–8, 224, 245–9, 260–9, 286

dark energy 155
Davis, Jordan 67, 93, 97, 112 n147, 268
death: as co-constitutive feature of life 99–100, 223–6; as hermeneutic 5–7, 109 n95, 134; as idol 99–100, 107 n50, 112 n154; Jesus' death 101–3; as killing 2, 8, 11, 66; as non-being 221–3, 251 n17; as 'numbering our days' 169; as object 247–8; orthodoxy of 8, 200–203; as pedagogic 70, 218, 221–6, 246; as physical 15, 26–55, 99, 152, 171, 208; as social 143, 152, 171, 208–9, 226–7
Deleuze, Gilles 291, 301 n65
Derrida, Jacques 1, 3, 7, 14–15, 18, 100, 217, 219–22, 225, 235–43, 246–49
Descartes, René 92, 94, 244
Dilthey, Wilhelm 153
Donald, Michael 45–7, 60 n95
Dorrien, Gary 83, 250–1 n7
Douglas, Mary 14, 40–1, 123, 138–9, 144–6, 153, 155–7, 205, 237, 278, 301 n65
dualism 104, 155, 178, 244
DuBois, W.E.B. 1–2, 7, 13–14, 27, 193
DuRocher, Kristina 29, 41
Dunn, Michael 67–8, 97
Durkheim, Emile 14, 18, 19 n19, 35–41, 58 n43, n44 and n50, 71, 87, 105 n14, 109 n90 and n99, 111 n128, 138, 141–2, 144, 162–3 n110, 182, 271–2

Ellender, Allen J. 38
emancipation 35, 79, 176
End of God-Talk 184
Enlightenment 189
Enscausa sui 148
enslavement 27, 35, 72, 119, 137, 261, 264, 283
ephebe 176, 183, 186, 188; as strong poet 178–9, 190, 211 n45; as weak poet 179, 187
ethic of noblesse oblige 84
ethic of perpetual rebellion 186, 212–13 n63
ethical domain 123–8, 132, 136–7, 144, 148, 151, 155–6
ethnography 80, 126, 131, 138, 147, 205, 276
eulogy 208, 262, 277–85

exaggerated radical contingency 10–11, 19 n16, 30, 33, 38, 70, 90, 110 n107, 132, 237; bodies as cosmic screen 143–6, 156–7, 295; existential function 30–1, 241; producing god-idols 73, 89; producing identity 120, 132; and sacred/profane distinction 121, 128, 141; schematic for analysis 146–50; social function 31–2, 196; as white lies 143, 251 n27, 285–6
existential/existentialism 2–3, 5, 7–11, 14–16, 19 n16, n19 and n20, 38, 91, 93, 96, 105 n14, 123, 160 n26, 289, 307; exaggerations *see* exaggerated radical contingency; function/dysfunction of whiteness 30–34, 44, 48, 50–5; as hermeneutic 2–3, 7, 70, 172–3, 204, 263; and idolatry 56, 99–100, 141; and meaning 110 n104, 273; paradox 99, 128, 141, 148, 230; relationship to belief 82, 89, 104, 110 n107; relationship to ethics 132, 144, 158, 219, 222; relationship to ritual 36, 47; as uncertainty 5, 268–70, 291, 297; as white ethnographic data 140, 277
Exterminate All the Brutes 118

Fanon, Frantz 27, 155, 162 n100, 191
Fabian, Johannes 103, 112 n162
Faubion, James D. 14, 74, 97–9, 125–6, 132, 278
Ferguson, Missouri 67, 79
Feuerbach, Ludwig 80, 86–7, 90, 109 n89, 129, 145; anti-Hegelianism 224, 244–5, 248; thoughts on death 223–4, 244–8
Fields, Karen 36
Flood Christian Church 42
Ford, Ezell 2
Foucault, Michel 132, 189–90
Foxification (of news) 174
functionalism: function of soul 235; as method 2, 15, 25, 35, 105 n14, 182; principal function 133, 141, 158; theism as functional 66–90, 92–104; whiteness as functional 12–17, 27–53, 60 n105

Gaiman, Neil 25
Garcin 173–4, 201
Garner, Eric 2, 67, 96–7
Gawker Media Group 157–9
Gay Science 247, 284
Geertz, Clifford 131, 204
Genesis 22 235
genocide 241
Gingrich, Newt 82–3
Gladney, Rose 269, 288
god 12; as society 71, 81–2, 138–41, 157, 204; as ultimate concern 26, 70–5, 80–86, 229, 246 as wholly other 17, 220–1, 226, 230, 236–7, 241–50
god-idol: absence of 236–7; analysis as religious tradition 156–7; as assemblage 278–84, 301 n65; definition of 12–13, 20 n26, 31, 44,141; dysfunction of 44–56, 157–9; exaggerations of identity 120–41, 146–50; as floating signifier 2, 10, 55, 84, 93; function of 30–5, 99–100, 141–3, 152, 200, 268; as *habitus* 20 n28; humanism as 180–3, 191; limits of 96, 145–6, 208–10, 231; and loneliness 228–35; marking the paradox of distinction 91, 104, 109–12 n103, 153, 178; silence of 230–1; as subsystem 88–90; suicide of 234; theism as 70–76, 84; whiteness as 56
Goffman, Erving 148
Golgotha 100, 104, 241

Hagar (Biblical Figure) 241
Halbwachs, Maurice 274–5
Hartigan, John 50–2
Harvey, Paul 96
hate/hatred 68, 140, 231–3, 273–7, 280, 289; hate crime legislation 45–6; hate groups 48–50
Hauerwas, Stanley 171–2
Hays, Henry 45
Heart Is a Lonely Hunter, 17, 43, 227, 275
Heidegger, Martin 203, 214 n99, 219, 224–5, 241, 251 n13
hermeneutics: contextual variance 91, 136, 188, 194, 197, 225; as/of death 7, 39, 243, 258; Imago Superlata outlook *see* Imago Superlata; of a limited religious outlook 172, 204, 209, 221, 299 n11; as method 25, 48, 57 n14, 156, 251 n13, 278; as opacity 27, 146, 178; of reversal 141; of twilight *see* twilight
heritage 85, 123, 127, 170–1, 174, 178–81, 201–10, 264, 274, 285, 290–92, 296
heteronormativity 144, 147, 171, 261–2, 279, 284
Holiday, Billie 267
Hollander, John 178
homo narrans 201, 214 n87
homophobia 140–1, 147, 156, 170, 175, 218–19, 234, 279–82, 288

hooks, bell 15, 103, 139, 245
Hopkins, Dwight 27
Houma, Louisiana 38
humanism 17, 155, 162 n100, 180–94, 203, 211–12 n45, 212 n54 and n62; post-humanist and trans-humanist critique 189, 191, 213 n71
Hume, David *see* induction (fallacy)
Hurston, Zora Neale 27

identity 58 n43, 99, 120, 239; academic identity (as critic or caretaker) 131, 153–4, 173, 209–10; loss of 175, 190, 197–208, 224, 258, 298, 308; as 'operational acts of identification' 132, 192; relationship to god-idols 6–12, 25–37, 46–7, 51, 69, 119–59, 239, 278–84, 301 n65; religion as 3–4, 77–84, 140–1, 194, 264–7; theology and anthropology preoccupation with 133–9
ideology of domination 245–6, 297
ideological alchemy 128, 130–1, 138
idolatry 9–10, 13, 20 n25, 31, 67, 99, 128, 228–9; as ethical response 104; inevitability of 56, 149, 280–1
Ignatiev, Noel 82
imagined communities 144, 151
Imago Dei 90, 123
Imago Superlata 12, 33, 49, 72, 121, 123, 146, 159; as dualist 155, 179; escape from 194–210; as essentially 'theological' 104; as expansive god-idol reliance 84, 121–24, 171; exposed by ethical domain 124–6; producing the last 'other' 139–41; relationship to sacrifice 122, 237; schematic of 149–50
individualism 251 n13, 261, 265
induction (fallacy) 192, 296
implicit bias theory 192–4
Interpretation of Cultures 131
intersectionality 149, 156, 278–9
Isaac (Biblical Figure) 219, 235, 237, 239, 241–3, 246, 248
Ishmael (Biblical Figure) 241

Jackson, Jr., John L. 131–2, 153–6
Jasper, Texas 46, 60 n95
Jennings, Willie James 68–70, 78
Jesus/Christ (Biblical Figure) 96, 100–3, 218, 230, 295; crucifixion of 233, 235
Jim and Jane Crow Laws 27, 37–39, 72, 170, 264
John 3:16 100–1
Jones, Serene 101
Jones, William R. 69, 212 n50
Judaism 102, 169, 180, 200–4, 207, 209, 211 n42, 266

Kant, Immanuel 91, 94, 110 n119; and social responsibility 237–8
Kaufman, Gordon D. 92, 111 n124
Kayerts 117–23, 130–1, 136–40, 154, 159
Kelsey, George 20 n25, 42
Killers of the Dream 43, 276–7, 280–1
King, Jr., Martin Luther 76, 288
Ku Klux Klan 45

Last Poets 15–16, 65, 67, 71–2, 74, 78, 102
Laurel Falls 284–90
learning to die 1, 13–15, 81, 100, 152, 23–166
learning to die *with* others 1, 13–15, 159, 209, 218, 224–5, 241, 270, 277, 281, 295, 307
Levinas, Emmanuel 219, 246, 251 n12
Lévi-Strauss, Claude 55, 132, 139–41, 152, 154–5, 293
liberation 133, 157, 211–12 n45, 264, 297
Limited Religious Outlook 16, 169–75, 179–210, 218–19, 236, 293, 297
Lincoln, Bruce 28, 125
Lindqvist, Sven 118
Little White Lies *see* exaggerated radical contingency
Living the Death of God – A Theological Memoir 134
Lomax, Louis 170
Long, Charles 27, 56, 89, 94, 110 n107, 134–6, 163 n136
loneliness 121, 228–34, 249, 275
Lono (Polynesian god) 129
love 71, 85, 96, 100, 180, 202, 209, 228–33, 243–6, 248, 259–77, 280–7, 298, 300 n54
Luhmann, Niklas 14, 18, 19 n19, 66, 70, 87–94, 97–100, 103, 105 n21, 109 n94, n95 and n96, 110 n104 and n109, 111 n135, 112 n149, 162 n110
Lynch, Pat 96–7
lynching 10–11, 15–16, 26, 57 n19, 60 n95, 95, 170, 289; othering of beneficiaries/strange 'white' fruit 263–9, 299 n14; as ritual 27–55, 101–2, 111 n134, 145, 155, 204; sexualization of 27, 279–80, 286

MacIntyre, Alasdair 86–7, 92–3, 101, 109 n89 and n90
Madman (Nietzsche) 17–18, 307–8, 308 n2
Makola 118–19
Malcolm X 120, 158, 170–1, 177
Malcomson, Scott 38
Manifest Destiny 239
Martin, Trayvon 1–2, 6–11, 52, 60 n95, 66–8, 90, 93–97, 112 n147, 137, 268–9
Marty, Martin 265–7
Marxism 107 n56, 189, 227, 229
Maturana, Humberto R. 94, 96–7
McBride, Renisha 11
McCullers, Carson 15, 17, 43, 210, 228–36, 249–50, 273–7, 291, 300 n54
McCullers, Reeves 273–6, 300 n54
McNaughton, Jon 80–1, 108 n70
Melville, Herman 282–4
memory 43, 53, 145, 152, 273–7, 282, 292
metaphysics 33–4, 72, 108 n76, 109 n95, 129, 140–1, 191, 231, 251 n13; effects of distances/differences 102, 135, 155, 230, 234, 242; ontologization process 38, 86, 264, 283
Mill, John Stuart 84–7
Milton, John 178, 185, 188
miscegenation laws 37–9, 42, 286
Miss Lil's Camp 287
Mobile, Alabama 45
Moby Dick see Melville, Herman
Modernity 5, 57 n14, 178, 207
Modern European History 4–6, 276
Modern Poetry 173–8, 188, 197
Molière 225
le Monde 240
de Montaigne, Michel 14, 223–5, 233, 244, 294
Morrison, Toni 282
Moskowitz, Gordon 192–3
Mount Moriah 219, 241–3
mourning 17, 43–4, 259, 263, 269–78
Mudimbe, V.Y. 197
Muhammad, Elijah 177
Murray, Pauli 188, 288
Myerhoff, Barbara 15–16, 169, 180, 200–210, 214 n87

Nation of Behavers 265–7
Nation of Islam 177
Natural Symbols see Douglas, Mary
Nettles, Islan 268
New Jim Crow see Alexander, Michelle
New Testament 100
Nicene Creed 219, 251 n8
Niedland, Suzanne 287
Nietzsche, Friedrich 17–18, 25–6, 55–6, 133, 135, 217, 242, 247, 284, 300 n56, 307–8, 308 n2
No Exit 173, 201
North Georgia Review 288
Notes of a Native Son 257, 291
Number Our Days see Barbara Myerhoff

Obama, Barack 42, 80–2, 96
Obeyesekere, Gananath 129–31
obituary 185–6; for whiteness 261
Oedipal Complex 176, 178, 187
One Hour 293–4
Outpost of Progress 117–20, 130

pantheism 154, 245, 248
Paradise Lost see Milton, John
Pascal's wager 83, 86, 92, 108 n76
Pasha, Anberin 287
patriarchy 12, 106 n27, 149, 261–2, 281, 284
Perkinson, James 7–8, 19 n18, 30–31, 70
personal salvation/soteriology 17, 218, 234–5, 249–50; as 'gift of death' 219–226, 244–7; relationship to history 243; relationship to the law 242
piaculum of whiteness 43–4, 271–4
Pinn, Anthony B.: and humanism 157, 182–90, 205, 211–12 n45, 212 n49, n50, n54 and n62 and n63; religion/ritual 15, 27–9, 34, 37, 39, 110 n104 and n109
positivism 153, 247
poverty 65, 73–75, 93, 231, 278
prayer 2, 8, 40, 76, 82, 84, 98, 228
Precarious Life see Butler, Judith
prison industrial complex 15, 26, 54, 72, 74
Pseudopodia 288
Puar, Jasbir 278–80, 282, 301 n65
Puwar, Nirmal 97, 145

queer theory 4, 143, 278–9

race 1–13, 27, 30–6, 109 n89, 177, 231, 288–9, 292, 294; as curse 135; and implicit bias 192–4; intersectionality 140, 231, 279–84, 286–9; as orientation 89, 227; relations across race 271–2
racism 2–20, 20 n25, 45, 50–4, 65–9, 75, 122, 140, 154–7, 162 n102, 170–9,

185–7, 206–7, 218–19, 229, 257, 271, 279, 281–96, 303 n130
radical contingency 7–9, 19 n16, 30–5, 44, 51, 72, 90–1, 194; denial/misrecognition of 70, 136, 143, 192, 251 n27; embrace of 175, 189, 199, 203–10, 271, 284; as paradox 143–9, 158
Ramsey, Paul 222
Rank, Otto 30
rap music/hip hop 50, 67, 78, 97
rationalism/rationality 91–2, 99, 129–31, 192, 244–5
Reforging the White Republic 239
religion: academic study of 123–38, 154–9, 172–3, 190–1, 212 n49 and n63, 280–1, 293–5; American religion as white religion 66–81, 225, 232–9 263–9, 307–8; definition of 3, 33, 85, 110 n109, 126, 192; as form of capital 151; as identity-formation 194, 196; as misrecognition of limits 33, 58 n38, 108 n72, 200; relationship to death 1, 5, 7, 250, 263, 291–2; as social field 31, 71, 218; as a system 88–92, 110 n104; as white 1–4, 7–13, 58 n43, 121, 149–52, 199, 204
Religion Dispatches 68
Rice University 92
Ricoeur, Paul 86, 100, 109 n90, 153, 197
ritual/s: function of 25–6, 35–6, 45, 54, 156; as limiting 204; of mourning 272; of reference 11, 27–47, 58 n41, 101; relationship to violence 145; of whiteness 16, 37–44, 295–6
Robertson, Pat 147
Robeson, Paul 288
Roosevelt, Eleanor 288
Ruston, Louisiana 26, 34, 40, 56 n4

sacred/profane binary 8, 38; blurring of distinction 15, 128–40, 155–7, 163 n136; creation of 33–7, 140–50, 206; as social/existential binary 16, 120–3, 141
sacrifice 2–4, 28, 39–47; bodily offerings 65–72, 88, 93–104, 112 n147; economy of 144, 220–7, 233–50, 272–4; of information 88; location of 111 n134, 219–21; producing margins/distance 145–7, 218; self-sacrifice 104–5, 117, 150–5, 199
Sahlins, Marshall 123, 129–30, 134–5, 142
Sanford, Willie Mae 289–90
Sarah (Biblical Figure) 241
Sartre, Jean-Paul: as ethnographic data 19 n17 and n19, 123, 140, 143, 293; as theorist 8–10, 17, 19 n16 and n20, 30, 124, 132–3, 139–41, 148–54, 160 n26, 162 n110, 173–4, 201
savage mind 293
Schliesser, Eric 272
secrecy/silence 177, 229–33, 238, 241–44, 248 261, 271, 273, 275, 288–9
segregation 15, 37–9, 43–4, 50, 54, 78, 145, 274, 285–6, 289, 291
sexism 12, 75, 141, 156, 219, 279, 281–2, 285, 288
sexuality 9, 33, 35, 42, 231, 279, 286, 288–9
Shakespeare, William 176
Shakur, Tupac 152
Shmuel *see* Myerhoff, Barbara
Significations 135
Singer, John 17, 227–36, 246–9, 275
Smith, Lillian 15, 17, 30, 42–3, 210, 249–50, 257, 259, 263, 267–9, 273–81, 284–94, 296
Snelling, Paula 287–8
social/society 31–2, 44, 71; as 'hell' 171–4; Lockean theory of 71; social body 144; social divine 70–1, 220–37; as a system 90, 109 n99
social other 17, 103–4, 154–5, 173–4; as wholly other 220, 236–7
social power 3–17, 31–4, 44, 49, 51, 56, 58 n39, 66–87, 96, 104, 111, 121–9, 133–59, 170, 181, 208, 221–36, 251 n17 and n27, 252 n38, 265–76, 281, 290–7
social senescence 197, 226–8, 268
Sontag, Susan 194–5, 199
Solomon (Biblical Figure) 242
soul 147, 204, 217–21, 227, 232–5, 242–50, 259, 297
Souls of Black Folk, 27
South Today 288
Southern Poverty Law Center 42, 48
stand your ground law 96
Stormfront 84–7
Strange Fruit 286–8
strange fruit/strange white fruit 17, 257–70, 285–92, 296, 299 n11
structuralism 132, 154–5
suicide 152, 225, 233, 275; metaphysical 234, 236
swerve (poetry) 176–80, 183, 188, 190, 194, 204–5, 207, 212 n49 and n50
systems theory 66, 87–100, 102–3, 110 n104